Becky Renee McLaughlin
Hysteria, Perversion, and Paranoia in *The Canterbury Tales*

Research in Medieval
and Early Modern Culture XXV

Studies in Medieval
and Early Modern Culture LXXI

Becky Renee McLaughlin

Hysteria, Perversion, and Paranoia in *The Canterbury Tales*

———

"Wild" Analysis and the Symptomatic Storyteller

DE GRUYTER

MEDIEVAL
INSTITUTE PUBLICATIONS

ISBN 978-1-5015-2726-5
e-ISBN (PDF) 978-1-5015-1410-4
e-ISBN (EPUB) 978-1-5015-1406-7

Library of Congress Control Number: 2020933815

Bibliographic information published by the Deutsche Nationalbibliothek
The Deutsche Nationalbibliothek lists this publication in the Deutsche Nationalbibliografie;
detailed bibliographic data are available on the Internet at http://dnb.dnb.de.

This volume is text- and page-identical with the hardback published in 2020.
Cover image: "TV City" © Barbara Agreste
Printing and binding: CPI books GmbH, Leck

www.degruyter.com

Contents

Acknowledgments

With a book that has been in the works for such a long time, it is hard to remember all of the people who deserve my gratitude. But I shall start by thanking Joan Copjec, the inimitable professor who first turned me on to Jacques Lacan and under whose direction I wrote my dissertation, *Pilgrimage Gone Awry: The "Theatricks" of the Chaucerian Unconscious*. She has been, and will always be, a model professor and scholar, the one I would most like to resemble. Begun as a dissertation completed in 1996, this book has been a long time in the making. There were times when I nearly abandoned it, but, fortunately, there were people along the way who encouraged me to continue: Peter Travis was the first to respond with real enthusiasm to my use of Lacanian psychoanalysis in conjunction with Chaucer, and Sarah Stanbury was the second. Both invited me to deliver papers on panels they had organized for the MLA, and to both I am deeply grateful, especially for their encouraging words regarding the book that I was then attempting to write and that you now hold in your hands. Janet Thormann was the third medievalist to respond positively to my work, publishing a shorter version of my essay on the Reeve in *ANaMORPHOSIS* in 2002. I wish she were still alive to see that this book has now been published. I would also like to thank Peter and his co-editor, Frank Grady, for including my essay "Chaucer's Cut" in the second edition of *Approaches to Teaching Chaucer's Canterbury Tales*. Getting to see my essay nestled in amongst those of so many fantastic medievalists was a real shot in the arm at a time when I most needed it. Another shot in the arm came when I shared the idea of "shadow" and "central" chapters with my friend Frye Gaillard, who encouraged me to write a book proposal and send it out before I allowed doubt to set in yet again. Within a few months of following his well-timed advice, I had a contract with MIP. It was then that I got some much-needed support from my old graduate-school chum Carolina Randolph Steup. With one foot in early modern literature and the other in psychoanalysis, she was the perfect reader of my manuscript, and I owe her a huge debt of gratitude for her unflinching honesty, careful mapping of each chapter, and thoughtful suggestions for revision. To my former professor Bill Quinn, the first to make Chaucer come astonishingly alive for me in the classroom, I also owe a huge debt of gratitude, for he was willing to read the manuscript and supply feedback despite the fact that he was in the midst of travels abroad at the time. On the home front, I wish to thank my friend and colleague John Halbrooks, who brought me on board as co-organizer of *Chaucer: Sound and Vision*, a delightful conference held at the University of South Alabama, where we both teach. This conference gave me an opportunity to try out some

https://doi.org/10.1515/9781501514104-001

of my book ideas on a receptive audience. He, too, was one of my readers, giving me particularly useful remarks on the two chapters covering perversion. My partner and colleague, early Americanist Pat Cesarini, was not just an astute reader of my manuscript but an important sounding board for my "wild" ideas. Being able to talk through an argument with someone so keenly intelligent, insightful, and responsive as he was like having my own household deity and muse. Every writer should be so lucky! They should also be so lucky as to have had the wonderful editors I have had to work with at MIP—Shannon Cunningham and Marjorie Harrington—and at De Gruyter—Christine Henschel. Many thanks to all, including my fantastic copy editor Laura Kopp! Finally, I would like to thank my parents and son, all three of whom have given me something vastly important, something that I could not have written this book without. My father gave me his love of literature and history. My mother gave me her love of psychology and self-help. And my son gave me, quite simply, his love.

Introduction, or A Long Preamble to a Tale

> I am a pilgrim and a stranger
> Traveling through this wearisome land ...
> —Folksong, origin unknown

Oscillations

Writing as damnation: what I call the "primal pedagogical scene" occurred in 1966 when I was in the second grade. My family was living in the Belgian Congo, where my father was a bush pilot and I was attending a school for "mish kids."[1] Those were the days when the frustration that attends sounding out words was beginning to abate. Those were the days when I was falling in love with the voluptuous curves of my newly learned cursive hand. And then my English teacher—a woman who wore severe, black glasses, pursed lips, and a tweed suit in spite of the hot climate—assigned a book report. I read the book, wrote the report, and made what turned out to be a costly mistake. Looking at the words and sentences on the pages of lined paper, I imagined them as live creatures imprisoned behind fences of barbed wire, and it occurred to me that I could free them by cutting out each of the sentences with a pair of scissors. I carefully cut around the upward and downward loops of letters such as "h" or "y," thoughtfully considering how to approach the dot of the "i." When I had finished cutting out all of the sentences in my book report, I stacked them in the proper order and tied a ribbon around them. This tidy packet was what I handed in to my teacher, whose name was Mrs. Gorham but which I shall always hear in my mind's ear as "Mrs. Gore-'em," for her response to this *découpage*-style essay was immediate and brutal: "You ought to be ashamed of yourself! Go stand in the corner." For the rest of the period, I stood with my eyes traveling up and down the seam where two walls came together. Did I feel ashamed, as I had been told that I should? Yes, for I connected shame with sexual misconduct, and thus this reprimand served to link pedagogical transgression with sexual.

---

1 For readers who are disturbed by the colonial implications of the missionary-kid-in-Africa scenario, I would like to make it clear that while our family occasionally rubbed shoulders with missionaries who were in the Congo to proselytize, my parents had agreed to go to Africa not to "spread the gospel" but to function as something akin to Peace Corps workers. Nevertheless, we must have looked to the Congolese very much like their former Belgian colonizers with our white faces, stucco house, and VW Kombi.

https://doi.org/10.1515/9781501514104-002

Like the primal scene, the primal pedagogical scene played a fundamental role in the constitution of my episteme and life in general, and the way I reacted to it determined my relations to teachers, my pedagogical preferences, and my capacity for epistemological satisfaction. Perhaps not surprisingly, what followed in its wake was a struggle with two warring impulses: to please and to provoke. Initiated by standing in the corner, itself a liminal space, I began in later years to shuttle back and forth between two responses to authority, one of which was to gratify it and the other of which was to rebel against it. In order to please or provoke the subject-supposed-to-know according to my whim, I vowed never again to neglect to ask the question of "Che Vuoi?" or "What does the Other desire?" Although the receipt of Mrs. Gorham's angry reproach was painful, it became one of the anchoring points of my identity, a dyspeptic blend of the dutiful and disruptive, for I was in some respects shapeless and ill-defined until Mrs. Gorham "cut" into me with her words. For better or worse, puncture led to punctuation: I became an English teacher.

Reading as salvation: during one of my oscillations toward the deferential and dutiful, I found myself attending a Christian coffeehouse whose Friday night meetings involved musical entertainment by rock groups such as God's Power and Light Company followed by a sermon with a big emotional wind-up, the grand finale of which was an altar call. At the close of one such meeting, I was moved to raise my hand in response to the preacher's inevitable question, "Do ya wanna be saved?" Oh, yes, I thought, for I was sure that my twelve-year-old soul was as black as the hell I envisioned every night as I tried desperately and generally unsuccessfully to escape into sleep. And so as timid as I was, I found myself making the trek to the altar and joining hands with the proselytizer. After we had "prayed together" (which really amounted to his praying and my listening in a kind of cloyed awe), I was asked to commit to reading the Bible every day. I kept my promise to the proselytizer for the next several years, dutifully beginning on page one and proceeding through the text without skipping a word. But I must confess that, at some point, what I called "reading" degenerated into merely allowing my eyes to pass over the black marks on the page, and the number of black marks grew fewer and fewer as the years passed. At this point, I found myself in a dilemma. Although I had begun to doubt that reading the Bible in this mechanical way was the key to salvation, I was afraid that breaking my promise to the proselytizer would only make slimmer my already slim chances of avoiding hell. And thus I was bound to the book, a most pathetic of readers, clinging to the letter of the law.[2]

---

2 Because these two scenes function as what I call "primal pedagogical scenes," I have written

It was during this time, when I was concerned with my salvation and the part writing and reading played in it, that I had on the shelf above my bed two books that sat cheek by jowl with the Bible. One was *The Autobiography of Maxim Gorky*, and the other was *The Canterbury Tales*, both of which had been given to me by my father. (In fact, I still recall with pleasure hearing laughter erupt from his study and being called in to listen to him read a passage of Chaucer.) Because I had made no promise to read either book, and because neither was offered as a means of salvation, I treated them with less seriousness, certainly with less discipline, than the Bible. Nevertheless, I did wish to please my father, and so I read enough of *Maxim Gorky* to know that Gorky received some rather rough treatment as a child, once being hurled against the stove during one of his grandfather's drunken rages. Fortunately, neither my grandfather nor my father was given to drunkenness or to violent rages, but, like many a child reared in the "Bible Belt" and saturated with its Calvinist concepts of total depravity and limited atonement, I believed that I was in the hands of an angry god who held me over "a wide and bottomless pit, full of the fire of wrath"[3] and that in due time my foot would slide and the slender thread from which I dangled would be severed.

Was it simply by dint of sitting in close proximity to the Bible and an autobiography that *The Canterbury Tales* became for me a personal text of bliss, one that arises out of my history "like a scandal (an irregularity)" or "the trace of a cut"?[4] And what of it did I read in those days? Not much. Just enough, in fact, to be able to say that, technically speaking, I was reading it. Like a good little fetishist, I allowed two tales to stand in for the whole, a phenomenon that frequently occurs in the American classroom and that is made to sound respectable through the nomenclature of the "excerpt." Perhaps it has something to do with notions of the American spirit that the two most regularly assigned tales are those told by the brash Miller and the equally brash Wife of Bath. While the Miller is a kind of medieval Rambo, a man who takes things by force and who wins by a show of manly strength, the Wife of Bath speaks to the entrepreneurial spirit so revered in the U.S., acting the part of the good businesswoman by exchanging sex for money and/or moments of personal freedom. By the time I actually encountered these tales in a formal classroom setting, I had already discovered that men act like battering rams, knocking doors off their hinges, and that women get their ears boxed unless they learn how to subtly manipulate

---

about them in slightly different contexts in other publications. See "Sex Cuts," 65–90. See also "Literature, Theory, and the Beatific Effects of Reading," 159–74.

3 Jonathan Edwards, "Sinners in the Hands of an Angry God," 504.

4 Roland Barthes, *The Pleasure of the Text*, 20.

the men who hold them in thrall. The lesson to be learned, if you were a girl, was to appear dutiful but to be disruptive on the sly. This was, I suppose, the same lesson I learned as a reader: appear interested in so-called "high art" but get your real kicks from something else, namely that incipient (and insipid) pornography so many young girls of my generation glutted themselves on, the Harlequin romance. The fact that all of these books were located in the bedroom and initially read in bed (not only the "locus of irresponsibility," as Roland Barthes refers to the bed,[5] but also the locus of sexual fantasy, and, later in life, the locus of carnal activity) is certainly not without significance. In fact, I have often thought that if my students understood the practice of reading as Barthes does—that is, as an erotic activity—they would seek out a much closer relationship with books.

Although I had determined early in life never to marry, a determination I failed to follow through upon, the Wife of Bath appears to have remained a model for me well into college, arising like a ghostly specter on the oddest of occasions. For example, while I was an undergraduate, I was taking a modern novel course that had as its central text *Man and His Fictions: An Introduction to Fiction-Making, Its Forms and Uses*. The book is still on my shelf, having, like a precious relic or memento, escaped a number of garage sales, and although I have searched the contents and index for mention of Chaucer, there is none. And so it is with some bemusement that I recall an argument that arose, during the course of this class, on the Wife of Bath. My memory tells me that I said the gap-toothed, spurred Wife of Bath was correct in her answer to the question that lies at the heart of psychoanalysis, *Was will das Weib?* "Yes," I asserted, "women *do* want mastery. Better women than men." To which a more politically correct female classmate of mine retorted, "No, they want equality." (It is interesting that we both spoke of women in the third person as if we were not speaking of ourselves.) The drama or "theatricks" of the discussion that followed can easily be imagined, for it continues to play itself out in every bedroom and classroom across the country.

My next encounter with Chaucer came at the end of my college career when, with B.A. in hand and no clear notion of what to do with it, I made a pilgrimage across the Atlantic. Like the Kerouacian beat generation who did not know where they were going but wanted to get there fast, I believed that if I traveled far enough and long enough, I would figure out where I was supposed to go. And so in the fall of 1981, I was standing on the outskirts of London, knapsack on my back, hoping to hitchhike to Canterbury but feeling dismayed to find myself wait-

---

5 Roland Barthes, "An Almost Obsessive Relation to Writing Instruments," 181.

ing in the company of a pack of Druids on their way back from Stonehenge. "Who's going to pick up such a motley crew of pilgrims?" I wondered. But, soon enough, a young fellow driving a ramshackle white van stopped for us. He was either on speed or in a race with the devil, for almost before the back doors had swung closed and we had arranged ourselves on the van's seatless floor, we were hurtling down the highway at a truly ungodly velocity. I do not know what the Druids were saying to themselves, but I was remarking to God that I would from this moment forward try to be a better Christian if he would let me make it to Canterbury alive. Maybe God, or Thomas à Becket, or Chaucer himself heard my prayer because, before long, the van came to an abrupt halt, and we were dumped back onto the safety of our feet just a few miles away from the city limits. A van, with its four wheels, may be more akin to a horse than I am, but for obvious reasons, I thought it appropriate to walk into Canterbury, heavy laden, as if I were a fourteenth-century peasant on her way to the site of an important martyrdom. As Hélène Cixous says in *Three Steps on the Ladder of Writing*, "The true poet is a traveler. Poetry is about traveling on foot and all its substitutes, all forms of transportation."[6] Was *The Canterbury Tales* being (re)written on my body, tattooed onto the soles of my feet as I trudged, still bristling and trembling—nay, *horripilating*—into Canterbury?

When I met up with Chaucer again, I was far from Canterbury, living the sedentary life of a graduate student working toward an M.A. If I had been sidling up to Chaucer all those years, approaching him from aslant, now I was taking him frontally. Or so it seemed. The course was a Chaucer course, and the text to which I became cathected was *Troilus and Criseyde*. I was a diligent student, dutifully reading the assignments, not mechanically but with concentrated attention, and enthusiastically participating in classroom discussions. When it came time to write the final paper, however, I found myself doing the Jekyll-and-Hyde dance again, under the sway of that old oscillation. Against my professor's better judgment, I wrote a paper on obsession, giving Chaucer's *Troilus and Criseyde* and Proust's *Swann's Way* equal play. "Proust?" my professor asked with raised eyebrows and furrowed brow. "What's Proust doing in a Chaucer class?" He may have been right to discourage me because, in some respects, I was still avoiding direct treatment of Chaucer, still not owning up to the magnificent pull he had on me.

Although my professor later admitted that the paper was better than he thought it would be and that I had successfully avoided a number of pitfalls into which he had anticipated my falling, he did not give me the grade for

---

6 Hélène Cixous, *Three Steps on the Ladder of Writing*, 64.

which I had been hoping. This was, perhaps, another puncturing moment that led to punctuation, for rather than leaving Chaucer's medieval world behind, I enrolled in a class on the "Scottish Chaucerians," taught by the same professor who had just knocked me out of the saddle with his lance-like pen of red ink. In this class, I fixed on Robert Henryson's *Orpheus and Eurydice* perhaps because, like Orpheus, I find it impossible not to look back. (In fact, when we read Chaucer, are we not always looking back?) There was in Henryson's treatment of the myth an odd contradiction or curious disjunction between the narrative and its accompanying *moralitas*. And so in the hope of explaining this curiosity, I traveled to Scotland to do research on Henryson's old stomping grounds. After many months of immersion in medieval philosophy, theology, and philology, I produced an M.A. thesis that surely must have made me a contender for the title of most-knowledgeable-about-a-slightly-obscure-medieval-Scottish-poet's-least-admired-work. If all this sounds rather academic, there was something else—another project upon which I was hard at work—that was less so. I had gotten married just a few short months before making plans to put an entire ocean between my new spouse and me. While one aim was certainly scholarly (can I be true to Henryson's text?), the other was purely personal (can I be true to my husband?). The trip to Scotland, then, was a test: could I come home with completed thesis in hand and marital fidelity intact? Because of Mrs. Gore-'em, the textual and the sexual are never far apart. Indeed, they are hopelessly enmeshed, coupled, wedded. Sometimes blissfully, sometimes not.

My dalliance with Chaucer finally came to a head when after four years of doctoral work on subjects decidedly modern, I fell headlong into the medieval by auditing a course on *The Canterbury Tales*. The audit itself suggests a kind of surplus or return of the repressed, for there was nothing to be gained, officially speaking, by taking the class. I had already completed my course work and passed the comprehensive exams, and so this audit stands as a moment of excess that is hard to account for but in which I (re)found Chaucer. This time, however, there was no ducking or dodging. I had to look what is called Chaucer's masterpiece in the eye. Was I running away from something or hurrying toward it when I decided—against all advice otherwise—to write my dissertation on this very text? "You're not a medievalist; you can't write on Chaucer," said one. "It's academic suicide," said another. "You'll never be marketable." All I could offer in defense of what must have looked like insanity was something akin to "Me and Mr. Chaucer / we got a thing going on." Admittedly, our relationship was a scandal, which is to say, I had fallen in love with the wrong text, but there was no helping it. Or, if I were to attempt to shirk the blame, I might argue as Barthes does that it was Chaucer's fault, not mine: "The text chooses me, by a whole disposition of invisible screens, selective baffles: vocabulary, references, readability, etc.; and, lost in the midst of a text (not *behind* it, like a *deus ex machina*) there is always the other, the author."[7] Did Chaucer seek me out ("cruise" me) without knowing where or who I am? As I sit here writing, I want to answer, yes, that he came looking for me, that I was both his "whit wal" and his Canterbury Cathedral, the beginning and the end of his pilgrim-age—and he mine. But whoever fell in love with whom does not really matter, for the bottom line is this: the very thing that had been under my nose all of those years, the thing that I had not really bothered to look closely at, was sud-denly the most important, the thing most worth looking at. *The Canterbury Tales* had been just "a prattling text" that was going nowhere "until desire, until neu-rosis form[ed] in it."[8] But why, one might ask, did desire come to settle itself so securely in this particular text, and how did the neurosis form? I do not know how to answer these questions explicitly, but perhaps in telling stories, exposing my symptoms, answers will emerge. Like Montaigne, "Could my mind find a firm footing, I should not be making essays, but coming to conclusions; it is, however, always in its apprenticeship and on trial."[9]

It could be argued—and maybe I would want to make the argument myself—that choosing to write about *The Canterbury Tales* was just another swing of the pendulum, another moment in which oscillation had taken me to the outer reaches of the disruptive, to a confrontation with the law, to the self-destructive. (It could even be argued that this oscillation is precisely what brings the subject itself into view, for the subject is nothing more than a pulsation, something that appears and fades, appears and fades.) If so, perhaps that is as it should be, for Chaucer himself betrays a similar oscillation when he begins *The Canterbury Tales* with the "dutiful"—a tale told in poetic lines by a devout knight, loyal to church and monarch—and ends it with the "disruptive"—a sermon in prose, de-livered by a parson who smells like a Lollard. While it may be open to debate whether Chaucer was fully sympathetic to the Lollard movement, which had been set in motion by anti-clerical feeling and by John Wyclif's theory of domin-ion, we do know that Chaucer's good friend and patron, John of Gaunt, support-ed Wyclif until he attacked the doctrine of transubstantiation and that he re-tained in his household men who were known to favor Lollardy despite Richard II's suppression of a Lollard petition. Less debatable, however, is the fact that Chaucer was writing during a time when a series of upheavals—demo-graphic, economic, natural, and political—was bringing an end to the medieval

---

7 Barthes, *The Pleasure of the Text*, 27.
8 Barthes, *The Pleasure of the Text*, 5.
9 Michel de Montaigne, *Essays*, 235.

ecclesiastical system. In 1348, for example, came the arrival of the bubonic pla-gue. In 1378, the Great Schism created two rival popes. And in 1381, the Peasant's Revolt erupted, a mob uprising during which, among other atrocities, John of Gaunt's palace was burned and the Archbishop of Canterbury beheaded. This was, then, a time in which old masks were falling and new ones had not yet been made, a time in which gaps and puckers were beginning to appear in the fabric of medieval society. The time was ripe for critique but still too early for reformation.

The father (pope and king alike) may have been dying, his mask slipping, but he had not yet drawn his last breath, and maybe this is why we find Chaucer telling tales at the end of his life. "If there is no longer a father, why tell stories?" asks Barthes, answering his question with yet another: "Isn't story-telling always a way of searching for one's origin, speaking one's conflicts with the Law, enter-ing into the dialectic of tenderness and hatred?"[10] If, as Barthes seems to sug-gest, storytelling is a way of speaking our ambivalence toward a father who holds us over the bottomless pit of hell, then each of Chaucer's pilgrims is, to one degree or another, an outlaw, risking his or her relation to or position in the symbolic order. The pilgrims are playing for very high stakes, not just a free supper upon return to the Tabard Inn. And thus *The Canterbury Tales* makes manifest the "deep play" of an often fierce struggle with the father in all of his many guises, and clearly Chaucer, along with a number of his pilgrims, believes as Barthes does that the "text is (should be) that uninhibited person who shows his behind to the Political Father."[11]

Chimney-Sweeping

Many metaphors have been used to suggest the kind of work entailed by psycho-analysis, the theatrical and the surgical two of the most prominent. But the one I find most appealing because of its humorous and humble metaphorical value is "chimney-sweeping," Anna O.'s word for the storytelling she engaged in during her treatment by Joseph Breuer. As Rachel Bowlby points out in her introduction to *Studies in Hysteria*, the analogy of chimney-sweeping "associates the talking

---

10 Barthes, *The Pleasure of the Text*, 47.

11 Barthes, *The Pleasure of the Text*, 53. Unfortunately, neurotics are rarely uninhibited unless inebriated, and thus when they show their behinds to the father, political or otherwise, they are unwittingly doing little other than paying obeisance to the Other's desire. Because neurotics have failed to thoroughly detach themselves from their parents, they are always in thrall to the Other—even when they spend all of their waking hours considering how to rebel against it.

cure with routine, daily life, necessary household work. Like all domestic tasks, chimney-sweeping is never finally done."[12] What Bowlby's comment implies is that the work of analysis, whether clinical or pedagogical, is never finally done, nor does the need for storytelling—again, whether on the couch or in the classroom—disappear, never to return. And thus it is with the metaphor of psychoanalysis as ongoing housework and/or homework that this book constructs Chaucer's fictional pilgrimage to Canterbury as a journey into the symptom and, further, into the unconscious itself. Beginning with the spectacle of hysteria, traveling through the perversions of fetishism, masochism, and sadism, and pulling into the terminus with paranoia and psychosis, the chapters that follow explore the ways in which conflicts with the (Oedipal) law play themselves out on the body and in language.[13] For Chaucer's *Canterbury Tales* is rife with issues of mastery and control that emerge as conflicts not only between authority and experience but also between power and knowledge, the word and the flesh, rule books and reason, man and woman, same and other—conflicts that erupt in a macabre sprawl of broken bones, dismembered bodies, cut throats, and decapitations. Although contracts are generally supposed to forestall violence, in any contract violence is both an origin and an outcome as Derrida has noted, and thus when the pilgrims assembled at the Tabard Inn agree to participate in the storytelling contest, which Harry Bailly articulates in terms of contract, violence is destined to break out.[14]

The reader hostile to psychoanalysis might argue that my analysis of Chaucer's storytelling pilgrims is "wild," and perhaps it is, not because of ignorance or omnipotence but because of the sort of contradiction with which Barthes introduces *The Pleasure of the Text*:

> Imagine someone [...] who abolishes within himself all barriers, all classes, all exclusions, not by syncretism but by simple discard of that old specter: *logical contradiction*; who mixes every language, even those said to be incompatible [...]. Such a man would be the mockery of our society: court, school, asylum, polite conversation would cast him out: who endures contradiction without shame?[15]

It may be the case that, like Hesiod's two Strife-broods, there is good contradiction, which makes us human rather than mere automatons, and bad. Barthes invites us to imagine someone who discards the fear of logical contradiction. Imag-

---

12 Rachel Bowlby, Introduction, xxxi.
13 In my discussion of how I teach *The Canterbury Tales* in *Approaches to Teaching Chaucer's Canterbury Tales*, I say much the same thing. See "Chaucer's Cut," 158.
14 Jacques Derrida, "Force of Law," 47.
15 Barthes, *The Pleasure of the Text*, 3.

ine, then, the hysteric with her "incompatible syntheses,"[16] her multiple identifications, her conversion symptoms, her self-repudiating discourse, and, in the case of Anna O., her mixing of English, French, and Italian. Imagine *moi*.[17] Attempting to endure this contradiction while keeping shame at bay, I function as the anti-hero of whom Barthes speaks, for in taking my pleasure with *The Canterbury Tales*, I bring together a number of what are sometimes thought to be incompatible modes of thinking and writing: the autobiographical, the clinical, the pedagogical, and the scholarly. At times, I take up the "proper" distance from the reader by adopting a traditional scholarly approach to *The Canterbury Tales*, while at other times, I draw uncomfortably close through autobiographical "shadow" chapters that deal specifically with self-analysis and its potential pedagogical uses. This is my attempt to recreate, in some tangible form, the subject as split between the ego and the unconscious. If I appear to privilege one type of chapter over another by referring to one as "central" and the other as "shadow," that is merely because we tend to privilege conscious thought over unconscious. But, in fact, conscious or ego discourse is associated with the false self, while unconscious "discourse" is associated with the (psyche's) truth. Because the unconscious is a reservoir of noxious desires, beliefs, and prejudices, however, the truth of the psyche is not always pretty. In fact, it sometimes stinks to high heaven as you will soon see.

Although I believe this book will add new insight to the existing scholarship on Chaucer, I also believe that simply to add more is not enough. One must add differently. Thus, what I am attempting is an exploration and exposition of the underbelly or "secret history" of academic activity, which call attention to the fact that scholarship and pedagogy are always ruled by the same ambivalences, misprisions, misrecognitions, and prejudices that govern subjectivity. As Rebecca Bullard argues in her introduction to *The Secret History in Literature, 1660–1820*, the genre of the secret history requires a "transverse" reading practice that directs us "to read *across* boundaries: between texts, literary traditions, cultures, and geographical territories."[18] My approach, like that of the secret history, embraces the "both/and" of generic representation rather than the "either/or," and thus the shadow chapters speak to or against the central chapters, creating

---

16 This phrase comes from Catherine Clément, in Hélène Cixous and Catherine Clément, *The Newly Born Woman*, 8.

17 Because the *moi* is another name for the ego in Lacanian terminology, the *moi* is closely associated with the imaginary and the fictional nature of images. The *je*, on the other hand, is associated with the symbolic and the realm of language. The *moi* becomes a *je* when the subject is able to name herself.

18 Rebecca Bullard, Introduction, 7.

both a dialogue and an interruption not unlike that between conscious and unconscious chains of discourse, not unlike that between one Canterbury pilgrim and another.[19]

One of the benefits of this approach, as suggested by its form, is that it works on a number of levels more or less simultaneously, addressing concerns that fall under the various rubrics of the pedagogical, the political, and the theoretical. For I attempt not only to make new inroads into the treatment of Chaucer's most contradictory and symptomatic pilgrims—the Prioress, the Pardoner, and the Physician, for example—but also to render less obscure psychoanalytic concepts that students often find difficult to grasp. (If Lacan is the instrument of Chaucer, so, too, is Chaucer the instrument of Lacan. By this, I mean that if I engage in psychoanalyzing Chaucer's pilgrims, as some may describe what I do, I do so not merely to shed new light on Chaucer's fictional characters but to illustrate and illuminate psychoanalytic concepts. And so, like any good analysis, it has an educational aim.) To achieve these ends, I circulate around and through three pedagogical questions: 1) How are we to teach a medieval text to students of the twenty-first century? 2) How are we to teach theoretical discourses such as feminism(s), psychoanalysis, and queer theory when each is radically opposed to the existing power structures so often implied by the intersection of teacher and student? And 3) what role should autobiography and/or personal anecdote play in the classroom? Clearly, these pedagogical questions point to political questions, one of which is who is authorized to speak about Chaucer and how. In juxtaposing the scholarly (an impersonal discourse) with the autobiographical (a personal discourse), my hope is that the shadow chapters will act as moments of disruption, unsettling or, at least, jostling the authority of the scholarly voice that makes itself heard in the central chapters. Put slightly differently, the shifts between central and shadow chapters might be said to represent the shifts between pseudo-analyst and pseudo-analysand. Rather than suppressing one voice or the other, both will be allowed to speak.

This multi-vocality is, in some respects, an attempt to resist closure and thus to mirror the principle embodied by *The Canterbury Tales*, for as Rosemarie McGerr argues in *Chaucer's Open Books*, "[w]hat *The Canterbury Tales* does is to illustrate, in the debates among the pilgrims and in the juxtaposition of the tales [...], the limitations on any single, mortal, temporal point of view or monologic discourse. At any point in the process of the poem, our temptation to come

---

19 The form this book takes, with its oscillations between central and shadow chapters, is also meant to suggest (or even mimic) the disconnection that often exists between scholarship and pedagogy, a disconnection that I dislike and wish to repair.

to a final decision about any issue discussed is undercut by the introduction of another voice."[20] As I have read article after article on Chaucer and his poetry, I have come to realize that the scene of the critical debate is a repetition or mimicry of the *mise-en-scène* dramatized in *The Canterbury Tales*. Chaucer's poem itself has become the scholar's Canterbury, and everyone who writes about *The Canterbury Tales* is a pilgrim of sorts—some on better mounts than others, some with spurs, some with false relics but each one jockeying for position, each one with a "tale" to tell, each one hoping to win the storytelling contest by asserting the final authority. What I am attempting to work against, then, is the aggressive, defensive, protective voice that many scholars adopt when confronted with an object of criticism. What I am also attempting to work against is, as Michael Warner identified it in 2004, "a widely felt disenchantment with the idea of literature, which students in a technologically changing climate increasingly encounter as archaic."[21] Sixteen years later, the disenchantment of which Warner speaks has only become more obvious—or so it seems to me— hence the need for a pedagogy that will make the study of literature seem less archaic to our technologically savvy, texting students.

One way to create this kind of pedagogy is to give students a psychoanalytic vocabulary big enough to grapple with both the fictional world of literature and the factual world of its readers and the socio-historical culture they inhabit. Many of the students I teach are in the process of discovering who they are as sexual beings, and thus they respond positively to a discourse such as psychoanalysis, which does not shy away from matters of sexuality and which has the capacity to question orthodoxies concerning sexual identity rather than simply reproducing them. It was, in fact, my sexual hang-ups that led me to psychoanalysis, which may be only one framework among many, but, given the particular set of questions and problems that I was confronted with when I first became acquainted with it, it, like *The Canterbury Tales*, ceased to be a prattling discourse and became the one in which desire formed.

Another and interrelated way to create this kind of pedagogy is to introduce into the classroom what I call "auto-theory" and/or what Jane Gallop refers to as "anecdotal theory." Arguing along the same lines that I am attempting to, Gallop states that anecdote and theory "carry diametrically opposed connotations: humorous vs. serious, short vs. grand, trivial vs. overarching, specific vs. general. Anecdotal theory would cut through these oppositions in order to produce theory with a better sense of humor, theorizing which honors the uncanny detail of

---

20 Rosemarie McGerr, *Chaucer's Open Books*, 152.
21 Michael Warner, "Uncritical Reading," 16–17.

lived experience."[22] Although Gallop admits that the personal remains a vexed question despite feminist pedagogy's embracing of it, she also argues that it was feminist epistemology that taught her the value of revealing the personal experience behind the professional product. It has done the same for me, as has Richard Miller's concept of "institutional autobiography."[23] In *Writing at the End of the World*, Miller argues that only by acknowledging the personal dimension and recognizing the role it plays in our scholarly work will academic writing remain meaningful. Although I could not agree more, I would go further and argue that writing institutional autobiography is important not only for our scholarly but also for our pedagogical work. If we are to "address the student as a whole person" as Michael Roth and countless others including John Dewey have encouraged us to do, we have to *be* whole persons.[24] And introducing the personal into an institutional venue such as the classroom or a literary monograph allows us to be teachers, scholars, and *persons* all rolled into one.[25] Scholars in the humanities are not alone in having recognized the value of the personal, however. Having arisen among the ranks of the social sciences, "evocative autoethnography" trains its gaze "inward" onto the "self" while at the same time training its gaze outward onto the larger social context in which the self is embedded.[26] Using their personal experiences as primary data, autoethnographers "research themselves in relation to others."[27] In fact, the autoethnographic methodology as described by Carolyn Ellis closely resembles the psychoanalytic methodology as described by Lacan, for both acknowledge and accommodate "subjectivity, emotionality, and the researcher's influence on research, rather than hiding from these matters or assuming they don't exist."[28]

Arguing that it is not only fruitful but necessary to address emotions in the classroom, Megan Boler voices the hope in *Feeling Power: Emotions and Education* that teachers will begin to become aware of how their pedagogy is dictated by their emotions and of how "curricula that neglect emotion (for example, teaching students never to use the word 'I' in writing as it is 'too personal'—a

---

22 Jane Gallop, *Anecdotal Theory*, 2.

23 Richard Miller, *Writing at the End of the World*, 138.

24 Michael S. Roth, *Beyond the University*, xv.

25 I have made a similar plea for the personal in "The Wounded Student and the Crisis of Desire in the Contemporary Classroom," 8–9.

26 While "evocative autoethnography" is Carolyn Ellis's coinage, the description comes from Norman Denzin, *Interpretive Ethnography*, 227. Although I understand why Denzin uses words such as "inward" and "self," I enclose them in quotation marks because I take issue with the idea of an inner self that only I have knowledge of.

27 Robin Boylorn and Mark Orbe, *Critical Autoethnography*, 17.

28 Carolyn Ellis et al., "Autoethnography," Art. 10.

phobia in part reflecting the fear of emotion in higher education) deny students possibilities of passionate engagement."[29] It is interesting to ponder how my book report might have been received if Mrs. Gorham had been aware that her unjust pedagogical act was informed by her own emotions (and psychological baggage). Did she ever consider the impact that the unstated subtext of her emotions would or did have on me? It seems unlikely given that affective response has traditionally been downplayed in the classroom and that emotions are notoriously difficult to define—disgust, for example. Although many confuse disgust with a purely physical sensation such as nausea, William Ian Miller convincingly argues that it is an emotion and that, like all emotions, it "is a feeling *about* something and in response to something, not just raw unattached feeling."[30] While emotions may be discounted in the classroom, however, they are not discounted but acknowledged and talked about in psychoanalysis, and this, along with its storytelling and interpretive practices, is one of the reasons that I am drawn to psychoanalysis as a unique pedagogical tool.

Cutting Up

This book could go by many names: *Postmodernizing Chaucer*, or *Tracing Chaucer's Cuts with Jacques the Knife*, or even *I Read Him My Way*, but whether a more appropriate title might have been chosen can be decided later, when all is said and done. We can, in the fashion of Wallace Stevens, "[l]et be be finale of seem." Given the subject matter of this book, how we cut and are cut by acts of signification, perhaps it is not shameful to admit that other titles are possible and that, like Rodrigo S. M., the narrator of Clarice Lispector's *The Hour of the Star*, I am afraid of starting. Writing is not easy, he says: "It is as hard as breaking rocks. Sparks and splinters fly like shattered steel."[31] Not only does the act of writing require a tremendous amount of exertion, but also it is a dangerous act, producing sparks that might jump into flame and burn us or flying splinters that pierce like arrows, bury themselves in our flesh, and fester. Our very bodies are at stake when we write, especially when we are writing what might be called the "secret history" of the anecdote.[32] And that is why this book, at its most fundamental level, is about bodies and the stories their symptoms tell. If Chaucer

---

29 Megan Boler, *Feeling Power*, xvii.

30 William Ian Miller, *The Anatomy of Disgust*, 8, his emphasis.

31 Clarice Lispector, *The Hour of the Star*, 19.

32 See Joel Fineman, "The History of the Anecdote: Fiction and Fiction," 49–76, and April London, "Secret History and Anecdote," 174–87.

and his storytellers are symptomatic, so, too, am I—hence my reference to myself as the *moi*. But if writing is such a frightening prospect—hard work that puts us and those around us in danger—why do it? Jean-Paul Sartre has already provided us with one good answer: we write in order to bring the world and human relations into existence, for as storytellers we are one of the avenues by which things are made manifest. Relations multiply because of our presence in the world. And just as we create a connection between one object and another (the Wife of Bath and the horse upon which she rides, for example), we also set in motion a dialectic between writer and reader: "the operation of writing," Sartre argues, "implies that of reading as its dialectical correlative and these two connected acts necessitate two distinct agents. It is the conjoint effort of author and reader which brings upon the scene that concrete and imaginary object which is the work of the mind. There is no art except for and by others."[33] Writing creates relations, and so, too, does reading.

Writing is hard work, but reading is equally so as Lacan points out when he says to those who have been attending his seminar on *Antigone*,

> It may have seemed demanding to some of you. [...] I might almost say that on this occasion I have put you to the test of eating raw rabbits. It is on account of this procedure I have adopted—and it's no doubt quite a demanding one obviously, quite a tough one—of requiring you to accompany me in breaking the stones along the road of the text [so] that it will enter your body.[34]

If writing puts the body at stake, so, too, does reading. Both acts require a body and, of necessity, both acts transform the body. In fact, as Anthony Bale points out in *Feeling Persecuted*, "[m]edieval people did not see books and pictures as something separate from themselves—either from their minds or bodies—but as recreational objects which could touch, impress, hurt or wound the reader or viewer."[35] Because of the book's performative quality, medieval people described books as "quicke bookis," that is, as "living books—the word made flesh."[36] Even more so than ours does, the medieval world saw a physical engagement between body and book. When Chaucer wrote, then, he was stretching his hand out into the centuries ahead like a lover groping for his beloved in the dark of some unknown and unknowable future. In writing, he was disclosing his world and offering it, as Sartre would say, "as a task to the generosity of the reader."[37] If

---

33 Jean-Paul Sartre, *What Is Literature?*, 37.
34 Jacques Lacan, *The Seminar of Jacques Lacan, Book VII*, 284.
35 Anthony Bale, *Feeling Persecuted*, 19.
36 Bale, *Feeling Persecuted*, 20.
37 Sartre, *What Is Literature?*, 54.

we are to be generous, we must take his hand and allow ourselves to be pulled backward into his world but also pull him forward into ours. We must, as Lacan urges, break the stones along the road of the text that will allow *The Canterbury Tales* to enter our bodies.

But why take Lacan's hand and pull him along for the ride? For me, there are personal reasons that will be revealed in the shadow chapters, and for this I make no apology since I think it absolutely crucial to have a personal stake in what we say, write, and tell stories about, especially in the classroom. For now, however, let me go on record as stating that, unlike some feminists, I do not believe that psychoanalysis as practiced by Lacanians is either an inherently essentializing or patriarchal discourse, but it certainly has the ability to ruffle feathers, for at its heart lies the concept of the unconscious and the phenomenon of transference. Despite accusations to the contrary, one of the most laudable characteristics of Lacanian psychoanalysis is its resistance to moralizing and normalizing treatment of the analysand, for as Lacan states in "The Direction of the Treatment," while the analyst directs the treatment, she does not direct the patient, nor does she, like many an American therapist, give the analysand advice, telling him what he should or should not do: "The first principle of this treatment, the one that is spelt out to [her] before all else [...], is that [she] must not direct the patient. The direction of conscience, in the sense of the moral guidance that a Catholic might find in it, is radically excluded here."[38]

Lacan's principles of treatment are not the only reason to take him along for the ride, however. A second and more important reason is that it makes good pedagogical sense because of his quest for a radical new pedagogy that would allow the one called "master" to adopt and speak from the position of "other," which necessarily entails the non-mastery suggested by the unconscious.[39] A pedagogy based on otherness and that assumes a position of non-mastery would, it seems to me, stand a good chance of upsetting what Paulo Freire refers to as the "banking" concept of education whereby the teacher deposits information into the students' empty educational accounts.[40] When Lacan advocates a style of teaching that would "break with the mirror game of 'the subject presumed to know,' as well as with that false, narcissistic understanding inherent in all dual relationships,"[41] he, too, is challenging the "banking" concept of education by undermining the teacher's absolute authority and breaking with a dual relationship that pits teacher against student in a hostile

---

38 Jacques Lacan, *Écrits: A Selection*, 227.
39 Shoshana Felman, *Writing and Madness*, 130.
40 Paulo Freire, *Pedagogy of the Oppressed*, 58.
41 Felman, *Writing and Madness*, 130.

and oppositional dance. Lacan's radical pedagogy finds its counterpart in Chaucer's fictional pilgrimage, for it is a game of *fort/da* gone awry. The pilgrims leave the Tabard Inn—the cotton reel gets tossed away and the word "fort" uttered—but the pilgrims never return, and thus the "da" dies in the throat. Mastery of anxiety is not achieved, nor is control of the situation. Departing from the security and comfort of mastery and control is a frightening but also an exciting prospect because it means letting go of the reins, allowing the horse to lead us to a place where mastery does not exist, a place where the "mirror game" of the subject-supposed-to-know shatters into a million whispering shards.

"How are we to teach what psychoanalysis teaches us?" asks Lacan, to which he answers that we are to put obstacles rather than transparency to use: "[to] teach *about* and *through* misprision, about and through interpretive stumbling blocks and textual distortions."[42] When Lacan advocates obstacles rather than transparency, he does not mean assimilation, or locating one complex of signifiers within another, but the establishment of a new order or permutation in the signifying chain. As Bruce Fink says of Lacan, he is

> [...] adamant about refusing to understand, about striving to defer understanding, because in the process of understanding, everything is brought back to the level of the status quo, to the level of what is already known. Lacan's writing itself overflows with extravagant, preposterous, and mixed metaphors, precisely to jolt one out of the easy reductionism inherent in the very process of understanding.[43]

If we believe as Lacan does that deferring understanding eliminates reductionism and promotes *frayage*, which is a breach in or break from the usual path, then we can certainly argue that one of the most useful aspects of Chaucer's *Canterbury Tales* is that it is written in Middle English, the language itself representing the margin between what is familiar to most contemporary speakers of English (Modern English) and what is utterly unfamiliar (Old English). Although no language is transparent, we often make the mistake of thinking that our own language is or our own words are, that somehow there is a simple and complete correspondence between what we say (the words that we speak) and what we mean (the intended message sent to the listener). Reading a text in Middle English, however, mobilizes the obstacles inherent in language. In fact, part of the reason that Chaucer and Lacan are such compelling bedfellows, or fellow pilgrims, is precisely *because* of language. What better place than in *The Canterbury Tales* to recognize Chaucer's Middle English as a pedagogical touchstone for the "oth-

---

42 Felman, *Writing and Madness*, 131.
43 Bruce Fink, *The Lacanian Subject*, 71.

erness" of language, or language as the big Other? Because Chaucer's Middle English is the uncanny double of Modern English, it seems at once *heimlich* and *unheimlich* to students of the twenty-first century. Many Middle English words look like and even mean the same thing as words we use today, while others appear to belong to the vocabulary of a foreign language. What is useful in this description of Middle English as an example of the uncanny is the potential pedagogical gain: while a certain amount of familiarity with an object of study such as a language or a text can put us at ease, a concomitant lack of familiarity can eliminate or undermine the faulty assumptions and hasty conclusions that often accompany the familiar. In fact, Wendell Berry convincingly argues in *Standing by Words* that "one of the great practical uses of literary disciplines, of course, is to resist glibness—to slow language down and make it thoughtful."[44] As he says in prose that seems akin to poetry, "[V]erse checks the merely impulsive flow of speech, subjects it to another pulse, to measure, to extra-linguistic considerations; by inducing the hesitations of difficulty, it admits into language the influence of the Muse and of musing."[45] In other words, we resist the glib and the impulsive in order, first, to be able to thoughtfully grapple with what we read and, second, to be able to stand by what we say in response to it.

And thus one answer to Lacan's question is to teach about and through the interpretive stumbling blocks and textual distortions of an uncanny text such as *The Canterbury Tales*. Part of my pedagogical strategy involves an oscillation between Lacan's question and mine, "How are we to teach what psychoanalysis teaches us?" and "How are we to teach *The Canterbury Tales?*" The purpose of this back-and-forth movement is to create a stage upon which to work out the "play"—or, perhaps more accurately, to play out the "work"—between the medieval and the postmodern, literature and theory, the scholarly and the autobiographical. On this stage, however, we occupy the gap, a marginal space from which we can look in two directions but never comfortably situate ourselves in either. Like the split subject, who must acknowledge its castration (its asymptotic relation to and/or its non-coincidence with its mirror image), Chaucer's text is split: there is a temporal gap between Chaucer and his twenty-first-century readers. Psychoanalysis views this split or gap as the unavoidable condition of the subject—or, in this case, the text—for it was precisely the incompatible syntheses of the hysteric that allowed Freud to found psychoanalysis and thus completely alter our way of viewing the world.[46] Because the hysteric made strange the nor-

---

44 Wendell Berry, *Standing by Words*, 28.
45 Berry, *Standing by Words*, 28.
46 I say something similar in "Chaucer's Cut," 158.

mative concept of what a woman should be, or want, Freud was led to recognize that the very nature of sexuality is aberrant. Like sexuality, textuality, too, is aberrant. Any normative concept of what a text and thus a pedagogy should be, or do, occludes the possibility of breaking new ground.

It has been our tendency, at least since the Enlightenment, to divide the world of experience into knowable pieces, categories, and periods, but psychoanalysis has challenged the way we organize this world. It has played a central role in undermining the confidence we have placed in these "knowables," thereby helping redefine what it means to "know." Because Freud proposed that neurosis had its roots in repressed memories, the subject could no longer be thought to be the master of its domain. Following in Freud's footsteps, Lacan rejected the agency and authority of the empirical "I," which believes in the transpicuity and objectivity of its own perceptions as well as in the cohesiveness of consciousness and reality. Instead of trusting in reason and empirical testing, Lacan surmised that we are characterized by implicit subjectivity, ambivalence, and misrecognition. What psychoanalysis calls into question, then, is the confidence Western thought places in the "cogito" as the origin of all knowledge. It is not surprising, therefore, to find someone such as Cixous, who puts a feminist twist on psychoanalysis, arguing that the repression of the unconscious is the foundation of Western ideology and that a thoroughly political female text would be one that is informed by an unconscious freed of certain cultural strictures. Sounding very much like the Wife of Bath, who announces that her "joly body schal a tale telle,"[47] Cixous argues in *The Newly Born Woman* that "[w]oman must write her body,"[48] but this kind of writing is, as she says, "not done without danger, without pain, without loss—of moments of self, of consciousness, of persons one has been, goes beyond, leaves."[49] Upon reading my autobiographical shadow chapters, perhaps the reader will admit that what Cixous says is true, for I have been forced to wade hip deep into my psyche's quagmire in order to write my body's *anekdota*,[50] and this has entailed the danger of betrayal, the pain of confronting

---

47 Geoffrey Chaucer, *The Canterbury Tales*, II, 1184–85. Although I realize that the Man of Law's epilogue is a problematic link, considered by many scholars to be a canceled or "cut" passage, I find it useful to think of the epilogue as a return of the repressed. And thus in this one instance, I follow John H. Fisher, who assigns these lines to the Wife of Bath. Given the Wife of Bath's interest in and many references to the body, it seems more convincing to me that she would refer to her "joly body" than would the Squire, the Summoner, or the Shipman. See *The Complete Poetry and Prose of Geoffrey Chaucer*, ed. John H. Fisher.

48 Cixous and Clément, *The Newly Born Woman*, 94–95.

49 Cixous and Clément, *The Newly Born Woman*, 86.

50 The sixth-century *Anekdota* was Procopius's scandalous revision of his earlier *History of the Wars of the Emperor Justinian*. Procopius's Greek title, *Anekdota* (or "unpublished things"), was

my many shortcomings and offenses, and the loss of the illusions that make up my imaginary self. When one writes one's body, one never knows what one will discover, for, as Paul Ricoeur has pointed out, one comes to *be* through storytelling. Nothing would be learned if the self were a given, that is, already known at the beginning of the narrative: "In place of an ego enchanted by itself, a self is born" through stories,[51] and thus creating a narrative identity for oneself is an important pedagogical act.

Unfortunately, the traditional academic institution has been a place where one seldom gets to do this, for it has been and continues to be a place where the cultural strictures of which Cixous speaks are created, taught, and maintained, a place where discourse is tightly controlled or policed through organs such as the five-paragraph essay, the research paper, Turnitin.com, and what Barthes refers to as "the very oppressive, not to say repressive, constraints brought to bear upon students by the myth of the outline and syllogistic Aristotelian development."[52] However, the conjunction of psychoanalysis and feminism has created a space in which to give up control, a space in which not knowing and/or knowing differently is not only acceptable but also necessary. There is no use for pre-packaged knowledge in analysis, whether we are on the couch or in the classroom. The nicely-decorated package of our neuroses must be unwrapped, its contents allowed to spill out if, like Cixous, we are to employ writing (and thinking and speaking) as a means of transformation and if, like Freire, we are to cure the particular type of "narration sickness" from which the classroom suffers, wherein the teacher alienates the student by expounding upon texts and topics that have little or nothing to do with the lived experience of the student.[53] The shadow chapters, in which I use myself and my body's experiences as a pedagogical tool along the lines of Augustine's *Confessions*, are an attempt to enact the feminine writing Cixous describes but also to move into what J. Allan Mitchell would call "a place for safe stumbling," his definition of what the humanities should be.[54] Just what the reader will learn from these shadow chapters is impossible to say ahead of time, but then is it not more fruitful to discover what one will than what one is told to? Will Stockton, for one, would say so, for he suggests in *Burn After Reading* that we "delete all course objectives from our syllabi—all things that seek in advance to tell the student

later translated by Nicolò Alemanni into the Latin *Arcana historia* (or "secret history"). See Bullard, introduction to *The Secret History in Literature, 1660–1820*, 3.

51 Paul Ricoeur, "Life," 132.
52 Barthes, "An Almost Obsessive Relation to Writing Instruments," 181.
53 Freire, *Pedagogy of the Oppressed*, 57.
54 J. Allan Mitchell and Will Stockton, "Time Change/Mode Change," 284.

what he or she will learn."[55] Like Stockton, Kim Paffenroth argues in her discussion of Augustine and modern pedagogy that teachers "must constantly remind themselves that their role is to assist their students in realizing *their own truth*[,]" and she emphasizes the fact that "the students' act of learning is *their own*."[56] The same thing can be said of the analysands' act of analysis: it is their own, for no one knows ahead of time what will be learned from an encounter with the unconscious.

Those of us who study and teach literature, who read and write about it, have chosen to do so because of a powerful relation to language, that gift—or perhaps *exigency* would be a better word—offered to us as a substitute for the loss of the mother's breast. If the unconscious is about the "yes" or the non-binary, then language is about the "no" or the Name-of-the-Father, the function that denies the child access to that originary dyadic bond with the mother. Is this denial a problem? Not at all, for most of us recognize the undesirability of living our lives in the sheltering confines of the maternal bosom, and thus we accept the necessity of acquiring language as that which sutures us into the social fabric. But what we may fail to grasp is the enjoyment afforded by allowing space for the appearance of the unconscious when it spills through or into language, disrupting the comfortable rhythms and patterns of our speech and utter(ance)ly unsettling us. Making room for the unconscious, for *jouissance*, is what Cixous is talking about when she argues that a feminine discourse "even when 'theoretical' or political, is never simple or linear or 'objectivized,' universalized [...]."[57] In fact, the discourse of the personal, particularly the discourse of the hysteric, offers a challenge to the notion of the universal subject and functions as a form of resistance to its normative status. Although the concept of the hysteric has wide-ranging misogynistic currency, I view the hysteric as a heroic figure, using her body to reject an oppressive cultural situation and/or identity when her voice cannot be heard. In fact, many feminists (including me) view hysteria as an incipient form of feminism, for hysterics such as Anna O. became feminists once they found their voices. Not only was Anna O. responsible, at least in part, for the birth of psychoanalysis, but also, in the aftermath of her treatment, she became the leading figure in Germany's Jewish women's movement. Later, Lacan found in his clinical work that the analysand must be hystericized before any fruitful analysis could take place. And thus in our pedagogical work, perhaps we shall find that the classroom must be feminized before

---

55 See Mitchell and Stockton's "Time Change/Mode Change," 162.
56 Kim Paffenroth, "Bad Habits and Bad Company," 10, her emphasis.
57 Cixous and Clément, *The Newly Born Woman*, 92.

fruitful learning can take place. If we (teacher and student alike) write ourselves, make our bodies heard, perhaps "the huge resources of the unconscious will burst out."[58] Perhaps we shall begin to learn and to know differently.

Objection!

Before I give the reader a glimpse of what lies ahead, I would like to address one of the difficulties I have had to wrestle with in writing this book and several objections to my approach that a discerning reader might rightfully make. In attempting to use psychoanalysis to understand Chaucer's pilgrims and, conversely, Chaucer's pilgrims to understand psychoanalysis, I am forced to straddle two intellectual communities that have not always been in accord and that can sometimes be actively hostile toward each other: the literary and the theoretical or, in this case, the Chaucerian and the psychoanalytic. I am sure to annoy Chaucerians when I supply plot summaries that they do not require but that non-Chaucerians do; and I am sure to annoy Lacanians, for example, when I explain terminology that they already understand and use but that non-Lacanians do not. There is no good way around this dilemma, except to ask for the reader's good will and to quote Richard Rorty on Hegel and Heidegger:

> To get through their books, you must temporarily suspend disbelief, get into the swing of the story that is being told, pick up the jargon as you go along, and then decide, after having given the entire book the most sympathetic reading you can, whether to move out into unchartered space. If you lay down those books feeling no temptation to make any such move, you may conclude that Hegel and Heidegger are, at best, failed poets and, at worst, self-infatuated obscurantists.[59]

Of course, I am not comparing myself to Hegel or Heidegger, merely making a plea for the most sympathetic reading a generous and patient reader can give.

The first objection to my approach that might arise for the discerning reader can be put in the form of the following question: is it an anachronistic gesture to make use of a discourse conceived in the nineteenth century to discuss a medieval text? The way I would address this question is by making a distinction between existence and what Heidegger refers to as "ex-sistence." Even before something is given identity by naming—masochism, for example—it can "ex-sist" in the register of the real, a register that Fink defines as *"that which has*

---

58 Cixous and Clément, *The Newly Born Woman*, 97.
59 Richard Rorty, *Philosophy as Poetry*, 29.

not yet been symbolized, remains to be symbolized, or even resists symbolization."[60] Once named, this something (whatever it may be) takes up existence in language or the symbolic register, which is identified with "social reality." Fink explains the shift from "ex-sistence" to existence in this way: "insofar as we name and talk about the real and weave it into a theoretical discourse on language and the 'time before the word,' we draw it into language and thereby give a kind of existence to that which, in its very concept, has only ex-sistence [...]."[61] In other words, meaning now begins to congeal in a way that was impossible before this shift into existence occurred. This does not mean that the object moves out of one register and into another. Instead, it means that the object occupies two overlapping registers, and because of the complexity created by the overlap of real and symbolic, a residue of opacity will always cling to the name, which is simply to say that we can never experience the object named in an unmediated, fully present, fully revealed form. Even a more historicized lexicon such as that of complexion theory, medical astrology, and/or alchemy runs up against the residual opacity of language. If Chaucer's texts were simply the sum of these outmoded theories, we would no longer need or want to read them, but there will always be something irrecoverable—and thus something that creates hermeneutic desire—when we turn our gaze toward the medieval world whether we do so from a historicist, a psychoanalytic, or any other contemporary viewpoint.

Closely related to the issue of anachronism is that of psychoanalyzing fictional characters, about whom, some would argue, we have insufficient information to do so. First, the word "information" is antithetical to analysis, for it names the factual, the non-disputable, the dead matters of knowledge. And, second, no analysis (whether of a fictional character, a person, or a text) has sufficient particulars, and it is precisely this lack that drives the quest for interpretation. The gaps in one's memory and/or in a story are what set the text-reader relationship in motion. In fact, argues Wolfgang Iser, "it is only through inevitable omissions that a story gains its dynamism,"[62] for it is these omissions that draw the reader's imagination into engagement, thus allowing the reader "to 'climb aboard' the text."[63] Like the sentences that were imprisoned upon the pages of my second-grade book report and needed freeing, the pilgrims of *The Canterbury Tales* did not really come alive or take on definition for me until I

---

60 Fink, *The Lacanian Subject*, 25, his emphasis.
61 Fink, *The Lacanian Subject*, 25.
62 Wolfgang Iser, "The Reading Process," 1005.
63 Iser, "The Reading Process," 1004.

began to "cut up" with them. What gives an object in a story density, argues Sartre, is the complexity of its connections to the story's characters: "The more often the characters handle it, take it up, and put it down, in short, go beyond it toward their own ends, the more real will it appear."[64] Is this not true of a reader's interaction with Chaucer's pilgrims? The more we handle them, take them up, put them down, in short, go beyond them toward our own ends, the more real will they appear.

A third objection to my approach that might arise can also be put in the form of a question: is it possible to write autobiography if one is a Lacanian? The answer to this is complicated. The way Lacan has conceived of the subject, traditionally understood as the "self" or the "individual," can be brought to bear quite fruitfully on how we think, talk, and write about the "failure" of autobiography, that is, its inability to tell all and/or to tell the truth. For what happens when we begin to write about ourselves is that we are immediately guilty of what Lacan would call "ego discourse," which is based on the false image one has of oneself, and thus we are immediately in the realm of fiction rather than that of fact. This makes the writing of autobiography impossible, but it is also what makes those who attempt to write autobiography continue to attempt to write it—over and over and over again—as I have done. Perhaps one way to skirt the problem of impossibility, then, is to define autobiography not as a genre but as a practice: it is not a thing that is but a thing that one does. Perhaps another way is to admit that although the being who speaks—that is, the subject —can never be entirely represented in language, this does not mean that the "I" is or should be disregarded. What it does mean is that the "I" occupies a fragile relationship to language and thus to constructed reality. In light of this, one must acknowledge the fragility of any autobiographical enterprise.

A final objection concerns the politics of confession, for women's autobiographical writing is often read as personal confession, and, as Irene Gammel points out in *Confessional Politics*, the "term *confession* is a problematic one for women, as it brings to mind its patriarchal history."[65] While I agree with Gammel, I also believe, as Gammel does, that it is possible to employ the conventions of the confessional self-consciously in order to reclaim one's agency and voice. In fact, if my shadow chapters do read like confessions, that is as it should be, for those four chapters are meant to be read, like the first nine books of Augus-

---

64 Jean-Paul Sartre, "Why Write?," 30–31.
65 Irene Gammel, Introduction, 3.

tine's *Confessions*, as a conversion story embedded in a larger polemical work.[66] There is also a social dimension to the confession, for as Foucault argues, self-writing "offsets the dangers of solitude" by exposing us to the other's gaze: "Confession then is both a communicative and an expressive act, a narrative in which we (re)create ourselves by creating our own narrative, reworking the past, in public, or at least in dialogue with another."[67]

Having, I hope, engaged the reader's sympathy and attenuated possible concerns about my approach, I turn now to brief summaries of each chapter.

In Chapter 1, "The Prick of the Prioress, or Hysteria and Its Humors," I examine the many contradictions in which the Prioress is mired, the most important of which is that between the ladylike way she presents herself to her fellow pilgrims as described in the *General Prologue* and the unladylike spectacle she stages in her tale. Using hysteria as a touchstone, I flesh out (and flush out) the difference between the Wife of Bath's response to authority and the Prioress's, arguing that the Wife of Bath represents the "normal" woman who understands the patriarchal economy of exchange and, because she is a good businesswoman, makes the system work to her advantage. Ultimately, however, she does not subvert the existing order; she simply inverts it by asserting that women want mastery. But if the Wife of Bath directly addresses the question that Freud placed at the center of psychoanalysis—"What does woman want?"—the Prioress has the much more challenging role of acting it out, amplifying and staging the question in the theater of her body. And for the Prioress, as for Freud's hysterics, there is no easy answer.

Chapter 2, "Portrait of the Hysteric as a Young Girl," is a shadow chapter devoted to loss: of body, of mother, and of voice. Perhaps it will come as no surprise to learn that it was my own oscillations between the dutiful (being disgusted) and the disruptive (being disgusting), my own hysterical symptoms, that led to my initial interest in the Prioress and finally to my attempt to write about her. Behind an analysis of the Prioress, then, lies a shadowy analysis of myself. Like Charlotte Perkins Gilman, I have found it cathartic, even curative, to write about

---

66 In Annemaré Kotzé's "The Puzzle of the Last Four Books of Augustine's *Confessions*," her "aim is to show that general literary practice from the time of Plato (and even earlier) as well as a number of specific works [...] offer precedents for the inclusion of an autobiographical section, or what [she] would prefer to call a conversion story, in a larger work that has an apologetic, polemic, or protreptic-paraenetic overall purpose," 66.
67 Tina Besley, "Foucault, Truth-Telling and Technologies of the Self," 66.

my experience of aphasia—a typical hysterical symptom—which began when I heard my mother speak in tongues.[68]

In Chapter 3, "Masochist as Miscreant Minister: The Parable of the Pardoner's Perverse Performance," I argue that Chaucer is making use of the morally and sexually ambiguous Pardoner to agitate for religious and sexual tolerance during a time of political crisis. My argument is composed of three sections. The first argues that the Pardoner's puzzling performance can best be understood through the perverse structure of masochism. The second functions as a pivot point between the first and the third sections, its aim being to show how tightly imbricated the "normal" and the perverse are and thus how much in sympathy they should be. The third relies on the story of Matthew the publican and the Parable of the Tares to argue that the Pardoner's masochism both conceals and reveals a criticism and a provocation of religious and sexual law, a religious and sexual law about which Chaucer may have had his doubts.

Chapter 4, "Confessing Animals," is a shadow chapter focusing on the theme of confession, a carry-over from the previous chapter in which I ask why audiences respond indulgently to the Wife of Bath's confession but not to the Pardoner's. In this chapter, I narrate a scene in which my Mennonite boyfriend and I confessed our sexual misdeeds to each other with disastrous consequences following in the aftermath. I also draw a connection between the trauma of the confessional and the panic attacks that I began experiencing during a two-year teaching stint in the People's Republic of China. Like the central chapter before it, this shadow chapter invites the reader to think about the function of confession and its effect on a reader.

In Chapter 5, "Before There Was Sade, There Was Chaucer: Sadistic Sensibility in the Tales of the Man of Law, the Clerk, and the Physician," I lay out a series of questions that I found difficult to answer until I began using sadism as the lens through which to view them. For example, what is each teller's relationship to law, knowledge, and power? For whom are these tales told and to what end? And although there is a great deal of cruelty in the tales told by the Man of Law, the Clerk, and the Physician, does that mean these pilgrims are sadists? Given the challenges of writing about sadism, the argument I make in this chapter is somewhat different from the one I make in the chapter on the Pardoner in which I argue that he is a masochist. In this chapter, I am less interested in ar-

---

[68] In an essay about hysteria and the famous author of "The Yellow Wallpaper," Diane Price Herndl states the following: "In 'Why I Wrote "The Yellow Wallpaper"?' Charlotte Perkins Gilman claimed that she wrote the story in order 'to save people from being driven crazy.' It also seems to have been part of what saved Gilman, herself, from a life of 'being crazy.'" See Herndl's "The Writing Cure," 52.

guing that the Man of Law, the Clerk, or the Physician is a sadist than I am in arguing that a sadistic sensibility informs each of their tales, thus accounting for the general bemusement that has suffused their reception. Taken all together, these three tales flesh out the portrait of the sadist, each tale giving us a slightly different perspective from which to view him.

Chapter 6, "Sadomasochism for (Neurotic) Dummies," begins with a scene in which my hysterical symptoms have become so severe that they have crippled my sexual relationship with my husband. After narrating this scene, I attempt to explain why we remained together for as long as we did and how I began to recover from my hysterical symptoms after we divorced, namely through the study of psychoanalysis and with the help a fellow graduate student who made use of psychoanalysis in his everyday life.

In Chapter 7, "The Reeve's Paranoid Eye, or the Dramatics of 'Bleared' Sight," I turn from neurosis and perversion to psychosis, focusing on the Reeve's and the Miller's tales and/of doublings. I argue that the Reeve views the world through the lens of paranoia and that the fat, bag-piping Miller is the frightening rival who makes itself known as the Reeve's terrible enjoyment or *jouissance*. I argue further that the tale told by the Miller is a recounting of the Reeve's primal scene, made traumatic by the father's (in this case, Nicholas's and the community's) refusal to validate, through language, the carpenter's understanding of events. I also contend that the Reeve's lengthy prologue is a moment in which the Reeve bemoans the split between his mirror image, an image that appears whole or "together," and his experience of the awkward, uncoordinated limbs that fragment his body. Because the father does not operate for the Reeve, he will always be in search of this figure, constructing him not as the agent that allows for meaningful exchange within the community but as a hostile force that threatens his tenuous connection to the community.

Chapter 8, "Farting and Its (Dis)contents, or Call Me Absolon," is a shadow chapter that focuses on the fart's social status as well as on my own attitude toward and history of farting. Comparing myself to what has been termed the "fart repressed," I explain how I first became "flatuphobic" and how I then overcame my phobia so thoroughly as to be able to make pedagogical use of the concept of the fart to explain Lacan's registers of the real, the imaginary, and the symbolic.

Chapter 9, "Retractor," is my concluding chapter. Playing on Chaucer's "Retraction" at the end of *The Canterbury Tales*, I make use of the concept in terms of the surgical retractor, an instrument used to hold open the edges of a wound. My concluding point is that Chaucer's cut—that is, his work—is a wound that cannot be sutured or closed. Despite scholars' attempts to master the text or have the last word, it stubbornly remains open to further interpretation and speculation, for Chaucer's "Retraction" functions precisely as a retractor.

Chapter 1
The Prick of the Prioress, or Hysteria and Its Humors

I love you, but, because inexplicably I love in you
something more than you [...] I mutilate you.
—Jacques Lacan, *The Four Fundamental Concepts of Psycho-Analysis*

We often speak of love as a mysterious phenomenon, saying things such as "I don't know why I love him. There's just something special about him." That "something special," which we cannot quite locate or determine, is what Jacques Lacan refers to as *objet a*, the thing that is in the beloved more than the beloved, the thing that escapes signification, a kernel of the real. Generally, we are not willing to let the matter rest with what seem to be romantic vagaries, and so we begin a retroactive search for the cause of our love. We say, perhaps with a certain amount of unconscious desperation, "I love him because his body is like a thick knot, because his shoulders are dense, as smooth as baby's skin, because his hair erupts into curls on a particularly humid day, because his eyes are as cold and clear as an ice-blue glacier," and so forth and so on. We can make list after list of reasons, list after list of the beloved's adorable characteristics, but love and/or the identity of the beloved cannot be totally positivized. There is no way to sum it up, to say it all, and if there were, the field of desire would be evacuated. And yet we continually search for the one signifier that would explain this mysterious phenomenon. What this search amounts to, however, is mutilation. As Slavoj Žižek argues, "Word is murder of a thing not only in the elementary sense of implying its absence—by naming a thing, we treat it as absent, as dead, although it is still present—but above all in the sense of its radical *dissection*."[1] In seeking to account for love, then, what one does is to "quarter" the beloved, hack it up into its component parts, reduce its organic whole to a list of fetishized pieces. Love is, one might say, fetishization *par excellence*. Paradoxically, it is this failed search for the final signifier or the impossibility of representing the subject that actually founds or constitutes the subject's identity. It is around the missing part (*objet a*), which representation fails to inscribe, that the subject constructs its fantasies and/or its self-image, not, as Joan Copjec

---

1 Slavoj Žižek, *Enjoy Your Symptom! Jacques Lacan in Hollywood and Out*, 51, his emphasis.

https://doi.org/10.1515/9781501514104-003

points out, "in imitation of any ideal vision but in response to the very impossibility of ever making visible this missing part."[2]

The Prioress, then, is situated at the center of a series of mutilations or "murders," including her own, for what is her portrait but a list of fetishized pieces? If because of its ambiguity, Chaucer's portrait of the Prioress is a failed attempt to represent the "beloved" Prioress, it is also what brings her to life. The garment of the text gapes, and it is in this gap where two edges fail to meet that we see the Prioress emerge, for looking at the Prioress is like looking at something through a kaleidoscope: with one small adjustment of the lens, the picture shatters into something entirely different. What one will find in the following chapter is a series of lens adjustments, one picture of the Prioress shattering into the next.

Dora and the Prioress

In "The Disposition of the Voice," Régis Durand argues that the voices that return to us from the past are "like a powerful current," for "they leave marks. They burn."[3] Like the voices that return to us from childhood, voices that have left their mark, the Prioress's voice returns to us from the fourteenth century. Hers is a voice that is cut off from us through the passage of time—of centuries—but it is a voice that we return to again and again. It is a voice that never gives us the satisfaction of mastery. It, too, is a voice that leaves its mark. That burns us. For she has become the Lady and we, her courtly lovers. She is the inaccessible object around which our desire circulates. And if she is our Lady, our "Domna," then we "domnoyer," we "caress" her, we "play around" her. Just as readings of the petite hysteric Dora, another voice from the past, continue to proliferate like an analysis interminable, so, too, do readings of the Prioress. For what creates mystery also creates desire, the wish to see and understand something that remains hidden from view.

In a discussion of courtly love, Lacan articulates surprise that it emerged "at a time when the historical circumstances are such that nothing seems to point to what might be called the advancement of women or indeed their emancipation."[4] He then uses as an example of these historical circumstances events surrounding the Countess of Comminges, daughter of William of Montpellier, events that took place during the full flowering of courtly love. Peter of Aragon, who

---

2 Joan Copjec, "Cutting Up," 242.
3 Régis Durand, "The Disposition of the Voice," 108.
4 Jacques Lacan, *The Seminar of Jacques Lacan, Book VII*, 147.

was king of Aragon, wished to extend his power north of the Pyrenees, and because the Countess of Comminges was heir to the county of Montpellier, Peter of Aragon wanted her. The obstacle, however, was that she was married to someone else and was apparently not the type to participate in sordid extramarital intrigue. Political machinations and pressure from Peter of Aragon forced her to leave her husband, and although she was returned to him through papal intervention, she was again corralled by Peter of Aragon upon her father's death. Worn down by these machinations, the Countess's husband repudiated her, and she became the wife and property of Peter of Aragon, who mistreated her so flagrantly that she fled to Rome and lived out the rest of her life under the protection of the Pope.

What makes this story odd is its temporal juxtaposition to the flowering of the courtly love tradition, the most important convention of which is the Lady's inaccessibility, for as this story illustrates, women are hardly inaccessible, used as they are as political pawns or objects of economic exchange. Even within *The Canterbury Tales* itself, we have story after story showing the plight of women and the paucity of options for dealing with it. If we think of what the Prioress has been listening to before it is her turn to speak, perhaps her tale's aggressivity will not seem quite so startling, her rage at the plight of women manifesting itself in virulent anti-Semitism and displaced violence against the little clergeon and the Jewish community.[5] The Knight, for instance, speaks of conquering the Amazons and bringing two of them home as prisoners of war. Theseus marries the older of these two Amazons, and he turns the younger one over to whichever knight, Palamon or Arcite, defeats the other in hand-to-hand combat. In both cases, Ypolita and Emelye have little or no say in their destiny. This tale is presented under the guise of courtly romance, but it hardly hides the fact that while Palamon and Arcite have some hope of escaping from their prison, women do not. Far raunchier and more troubling than the *Knight's Tale* is the *Reeve's Tale*, in which women are used as pawns in an ugly game of revenge involving rape, the nocturnal "swyvings" seen by the two clerks as a mere joke upon Sympkyn the miller. Not surprisingly, the degenerate Cook responds with great glee to the Reeve's tale, telling an abbreviated tale that features a woman who is forced to earn her living through prostitution. And the Wife of Bath's prologue explains in great detail the machinations a woman must go through to have her own desires met and the price she pays on and with her

---

5 The concept of aggressivity should be understood not as aggression but as a form of passive-aggression, which is a potent blend of ambivalence, resentment, and paranoia. See Lacan's "Aggressivity in Psychoanalysis" in *Écrits: A Selection*.

body. These, however, are the mildest of the stories involving the subjection of women, the Man of Law, the Clerk, and the Physician offering more cruelly sadistic ones. Even the tale told by the Shipman, which comes just before the Prioress's, hints at the sinister underbelly of domesticity, for the rich merchant's wife is forced to apply to Monk John for money, saying, "[...] if that I hadde a space, / As I have noon, and namely in this place, / Thanne wolde I telle a legende of my lyf, / What I have suffred sith I was a wyf / With myn housbonde [...]" (VII, 143–47). Once Monk John and she have sworn not to tell anyone of their conversation, the wife continues, saying,

Myn housbonde is to me the worste man
That evere was sith that the world bigan.
But sith I am a wyf, it sit nat me
To tellen no wight of oure privetee,
Neither abedde ne in noon oother place;
God shilde I sholde it tellen, for his grace!
A wyf ne shal nat seyn of hir housbonde
But al honour, as I kan understonde;
Save unto yow thus muche I tellen shal:
As helpe me God, he is noght worth at al
In no degree the value of a flye.
But yet me greveth moost his nygardye. (VII, 161–72)

As we learn from the rest of the story, Monk John gives her the money she needs, but she is forced to pay interest, so to speak, by sleeping with him. And when her husband confronts her about the loan, she avoids trouble by saying that he can "score it upon [her] taille" (VII, 416). No doubt, the events narrated in this tale explain why the Prioress begins her own tale with bitter references to "foule usure and lucre of vileynye" (VII, 491), for this is what Monk John and the rich merchant are guilty of.[6]

While women such as Dame Alys and the rich merchant's wife find ingenious ways to cope with the patriarchal order of exchange, not all women do. The Prioress is a case in point. As Juliet Mitchell comments, "Hysteria is the woman's simultaneous acceptance and refusal of the organisation of sexuality under patriarchal capitalism,"[7] but I would amend the final phrase to read simply, "under patriarchy"—hence hysteria's long and venerable history. We may be accustomed

---

6 See Lester Little's *Religious Poverty and the Profit Economy in Medieval Europe* for a discussion of the scapegoating of the Jews during the difficult period of adjustment to the increasingly important money economy. Little's thesis is that the Christians, having been taught to value poverty and work, projected guilt about their own interest in usury onto the Jews.

7 Juliet Mitchell, *Psychoanalysis and Feminism*, 289–90.

to thinking of hysteria as a Victorian ailment, but it has been around for centuries, the oldest known record an Egyptian medical papyrus dating from about 1900 B.C. According to Charles Bernheimer, the Egyptians believed the cause for such curious behavioral disturbances "was the flight of the uterus, which they considered a mobile, independent organism, up and away from its normal position."[8] Given this explanation, the cures they came up with seem perfectly logical if rather humorous: "the woman's sexual parts could be fumigated with fragrant substances to attract the migratory uterus from below, or vile-tasting and foul-smelling potions could be ingested to drive the deviant womb back from above."[9] In medieval times, hysteria was not thought of in physical terms of illness but in supernatural terms of witchcraft or demonic possession. By the eighteenth century, the explanation for hysteria had become attached to the notion of "sympathies" and the nervous system. Because women were supposed to have a more highly impressionable sensibility than men, they were more frequently attacked by the illness. It is not surprising, then, that in the early nineteenth century, moral and ethical components had been added to its etiology: "In the case of hysterics, whose symptoms Pinel associated with 'deviant' sexual conduct (masturbation, prurient stimulation by pornography, irregular menstruation), cure involved, as it had for Plato, Marriage, the Family, and productive Work."[10] By the late nineteenth century, Freud was connecting the medieval theory of possession to his own theories of the foreign body and the splitting of consciousness. And by 1897, his analyses of hysterical patients had convinced him that the "medieval demons" that possessed them were, in fact, close male relatives such as fathers, uncles, brothers, and cousins.

Although the etiology of hysteria changed over the course of time, the treatment remained fairly consistent: "submission to the yoke of patriarchy" or "the reproduction of mothering."[11] Certainly, this was the cure Dora's father had in mind when he brought his eighteen-year-old daughter to Freud and asked that he "bring her to reason." Of course, there was no Freud around during the fourteenth century, but if one were to create a back story for the fictional Prioress as I am attempting to do, one could speculate that the Prioress's father might very well have made the same demand when he dropped her off at the nunnery gates: "bring her to reason."[12] As we know from Graciela Daichman's discussion

---

8 Charles Bernheimer, Introduction, 2.

9 Bernheimer, Introduction, 2.

10 Bernheimer, Introduction, 5.

11 Bernheimer, Introduction, 3.

12 E. Talbot Donaldson argues in *Chaucer's Poetry* that "[c]onvents were often the refuge of well-born women whose fathers were too poor to provide the dowry without which no

of wayward nuns in the Middle Ages, there have been for ages on end social, political, and economic reasons for the well-known medieval maxim—"aut virum
aut murum opertet mulierem habere"—which Daichman translates as "a
woman ought to have either a husband or a wall."[13] Centuries later, this medieval maxim was still in force as we see in the case of Dora.

The problem with Dora was that she had been suffering from a number of
troubling ailments—aphonia, depression, coughing fits—and had lately threatened to commit suicide. As her father explained to Freud, these symptoms
had sprung up after an incident that had taken place two years earlier, while
the Bauers and their friends the K.s had been vacationing together in the
Alps. The story, as Dora told it, was that Herr K. had propositioned her, she
had slapped him, and then she had hurried away. Later she had told her father
of the incident and encouraged him to break off his friendship with the K.s, but
he had refused to do so, assured as he was that Dora's story was nothing but a
fantasy—"the result of a mind overstimulated by erotic books."[14] What Freud
found in his sessions with Dora did not quite mesh with Philip Bauer's version
of the story. In fact, as Claire Kahane explains,

> [...] the story that emerges from Freud's text is a melodrama of sexual politics riddled with
> illness and infidelity. Dora's father, engaged in an affair with Frau K., hands Dora over to
> Herr K. in return for his complicity, and although for many years Dora herself has raised no
> objections, even suppressing a sexual advance by Herr K. when she was fourteen, in the
> crucial scene at the lake, Dora refuses to be any longer a passive object in the circle of ex-
> change.[15]

Although Freud believes Dora's perceptions of the intrigue that has gone on
around her, he cannot deny the fact that she exhibits hysterical symptoms,
and because hysterical symptoms are a means of compromising between an expression and a repression of sexual wishes, he knows that there must be at play
an unconscious desire on the part of Dora. The challenge for Freud is to figure
out what that unconscious desire is: "Since hysterics suffered from gaps in
their memories, holes in their stories—the sign of repression—Freud's aim was
to fill those gaps."[16] And he did this by listening carefully to what his analysands

---

woman was considered marriageable," 1044; however, Hardy Long Frank takes issue with Donaldson in "Seeing the Prioress Whole." According to Frank, Donaldson "does not take into consideration either the small numbers of nuns or the fact that [...] nuns also needed dowries," 116.
13 Graciela S. Daichman, *Wayward Nuns in Medieval Literature*, 13.
14 Claire Kahane, Introduction, 20.
15 Kahane, Introduction, 20–21.
16 Kahane, Introduction, 21.

said in verbal discourse or through symptoms, which he treated as parts of the narrative, that is, as signifiers in their own right.

What Freud first proposes to Dora is that, despite her protestations, she really is in love with Herr K. and has only rejected his advances out of jealous pique once it comes to light that he has also made advances toward a young governess in his employ. Dora seems to accept this interpretation, but when she breaks off analysis, Freud is forced to reconsider the evidence. What he finds, on further investigation, is that he has imposed his own attraction to Herr K. onto Dora and has thus been blind to "the strongest unconscious current in her mental life": that of her homosexual love for Frau K.[17] In other words, Dora's bisexuality manifests itself in both attraction to and identification with her father (and/or Herr K.) as well as rivalry with and sexual desire for Frau K.

The sexual politics and intrigue in which Dora finds herself embroiled take place centuries after Chaucer's creation of the Prioress, but Dora's story is not, on the whole, radically different from that of the Countess of Comminges, Ypolita, Emelye, or the Prioress. It is, simply put, the story of a young girl who has no power except what she gains through the disruptive force of her illness.

In my view, it does not seem unreasonable to assume that, like Dora's unwilling entry into analysis, the Prioress first entered the nunnery against her wishes.[18] Everything about her suggests that she or perhaps her parents had planned on another fate, that is, that she had hoped to be (or been told to be) a courtly lady, someone's wife or lover. For, as we learn in her portrait, she has all of the appropriate trappings. She sings and speaks French, in addition to which she eats delicately and dresses elegantly. Because she has the behavioral and sartorial accouterments of the petite nobility, it would seem that she should be the wife of someone like the Knight or the Franklin. But something has obviously gone awry.[19] I say this not because I think that, in taking nun's

---

17 Sigmund Freud, *Dora: An Analysis of a Case of Hysteria*, 110n2.

18 I appear to speak of the Prioress as if she were a real person, and Arthur W. Hoffman as early as 1954 explains why it is easy to find oneself doing so: "Criticism of the portraits in Chaucer's General Prologue to *The Canterbury Tales* has taken various directions: some critics have praised the portraits especially for their realism, sharp individuality, adroit psychology, and vividness of felt life; others, working in the genetic direction, have pointed out actual historical persons who might have sat for the portraits; others, appealing to the light of the medieval sciences, have shown the portraits to be filled, though not burdened, with the lore of Chaucer's day, and to have sometimes typical identities like case histories." See "Chaucer's Prologue to Pilgrimage: The Two Voices," 1.

19 In "Seeing the Prioress Whole," Hardy Long Frank takes issue with this view of the Prioress, arguing that "we have failed to grasp that whole—the poet's full fledged characterization of a thoroughly competent, shrewd professional woman of the late fourteenth century," 229. Frank's

vows instead of marriage vows, Madam Eglantyne has won the booby prize but because of what Arthur W. Hoffman refers to as "a sustained hovering effect" that manifests itself as a tension between human nature and sacred obligation: "there are the coral beads and the green gauds, but they *are* a rosary; there are the fluted wimple and the exposed forehead, but the costume *is* a nun's habit; there is the golden brooch shining brightly, but it *is* a religious emblem."[20] Where this much ambiguity exists, ambivalence hovers close by. And as Daichman points out, the medieval nunnery was on the whole an aristocratic institution whose gates were open to any and all upper-class females, but not every young woman who entered its gates did so freely or happily. Although for some young women devotion to the church and an earnest desire to live the religious life motivated entry, for others it was merely an honorable substitute for marriage. Still yet another "group of women, all of them young and just as numerous, seem to have entered the nunnery at the behest of their families and entirely against their will."[21] Most poignant are the words Daichman reports of the fifteenth-century German prelate Johann Geiler on the subject of child-nuns: "some come [into the convent] because, against their own will, they have been cast or thrust in by their parents like puppies for the drowning, for the sole purpose of getting rid of them."[22]

There are, then, a number of striking parallels between Dora and the Prioress: both exhibit hysterical symptoms focused around the rim-structures of nose, mouth, and throat. Both are, with respect to disgust, its subject and object. Ned Lukacher is speaking of Dora when he says, "There is no shortage of disgust when it comes to this case history and to the response it has received in recent years from feminist literary and cultural critics,"[23] but he might just as well be speaking of the Prioress, for there is no shortage of disgust when it comes to her anti-Semitism and the response it has received from scholars of every stripe. Both disturb the family circle in which each is a player—for Dora, the allied Bauers and K.s; and for the Prioress, her fellow pilgrims as well as Chaucer's readers. Both suggest the bisexual figure around which circulates the question of the hysteric: "Am I a man or a woman, and what does that mean?" And both have a strong cathexis to or fixation upon the figure of the Madonna, for as we learn from Dora's fragmented case history, she stands for two hours in rapt attention

---

description of the Prioress is completely unrecognizable to me, and thus it suggests the willful blindness of what I call well-intentioned but misguided "knee-jerk feminism."

20 Hoffman, "Chaucer's Prologue to Pilgrimage: The Two Voices," 8.
21 Daichman, *Wayward Nuns in Medieval Literature*, xiii.
22 Daichman, *Wayward Nuns*, 171.
23 Ned Lukacher, Foreword, xi.

before Raphael's painting of the *Sistine Madonna*, which pictures Mary holding what looks to be a four- to five-year-old Christ in her arms, and the Prioress devotes most of her prologue to praise of the Virgin Mary, praise that spills over into her tale with the devotion shown the Virgin Mother by the little Christian boy.

We know Dora's story—that her real name was Ida Bauer, that she was born in Vienna on November 1, 1882, of Bohemian Jewish ancestry, that one year after leaving analysis she entered into what was to be an unhappy marriage, that the marriage produced one child, and that she died of colonic cancer in New York City in 1945—but we can only make one up for the Prioress.[24] Perhaps she was forced, like the Countess of Comminges, to flee the cruelty of a husband and take sanctuary in the convent. Or perhaps as a young girl she had no wish to marry, given what she knew or had observed about the trials of domestic life, and considered a vocation in religious life her only alternative. Or perhaps because of an unexpected pregnancy, she was flung into the convent like a puppy for the drowning, simply to get her out of the public eye.[25] Whatever the case may be, when we see her on pilgrimage to Canterbury, we recognize immediately that she is someone whose personal development has been severely circumscribed by circumstance. Everything about her, from her delicate table manners to her indelicate tale, underscores this impression. As Louise O. Fradenburg has fruitfully commented, "The obstructed passages of the Jewish ghetto and the cut throat of the little clergeon [...] together constitute the very narrow space allotted by the tale to human aspiration and change and growth."[26] How could the Prioress tell a tale of human aspiration, change, and growth when, as a woman, each of these things has been denied her? Whether Chaucer was simply creating a fictional character or basing his portrait on someone he knew as John Manly argues in *Some New Light on Chaucer*, in giving us the Prioress, Chaucer has given us, unwittingly or not, an accurate rendering of the incompatible syntheses women must forge when confronted with the limitations imposed on them by a patriarchal society.

---

24 Although Judith Ferster connects Chaucer, feminism, and psychoanalysis in fruitful ways, she advocates suppressing the most important part of psychoanalysis when she says that the "impulse to invent a past cause for present symptoms is a natural result of human—as well as clinical—curiosity, but in literary study it is easy and dangerous." See "'Your Praise Is Performed By Men and Children,'" 152.

25 For just such an argument, see Maurice Cohen, "Chaucer's Prioress and Her Tale: A Study of Anal Character and Anti-Semitism," 242, and Wolfgang E. H. Rudat, "Gender-Crossing in the *Prioress' Tale*," 13.

26 Louise O. Fradenburg, "Criticism, Anti-semitism, and the *Prioress's Tale*," 212.

Prosthetic Body and Rim-Structure

When one thinks of the hysteric, what may come to mind is the dramatic creature that New York physician E. H. Dixon wrote of in the 1840s: "Let the reader imagine the patient writhing like a serpent upon the floor, rending her garments to tatters, plucking out handsful of hair, and striking her person with violence—with contorted and swollen countenance and fixed eyes resisting every effort of bystanders to control her."[27] Or perhaps what one calls to mind is the three-ring circus of Charcot's amphitheater and the attached "living pathological museum" at the Salpêtrière, where the "leading ladies" of hysteria were paraded before interested audiences, experimented on, and photographed. One might even remember the parallel that Freud drew between the medieval theory of possession and his early ideas about hysteria, conjuring up images to match. Given what the Prioress says of herself in her prologue, however, the more appropriate if far less sensational image to call to mind is that of the "child-woman," the portrait of the hysteric that emerged from the nineteenth century's mostly male medical literature. According to Carroll Smith-Rosenberg, nineteenth-century physicians described the hysteric "as highly impressionable, labile, superficially sexual and exhibitionistic. She was given, they insisted, to dramatic body language and grand gestures. She had strong dependency needs, a masochistic or self-punishing behavior pattern, and decided ego weaknesses."[28] In this description, Smith-Rosenberg sees a resemblance to Karen Horney's 1934 description of the masochistic female personality:

> Insecure, afflicted with anxieties, the masochistic woman demanded constant attention and expressions of affection, which she sought to secure by appealing to pity. She displayed inferiority feelings, weakness, and suffering. Such a self-image and pattern of object relations necessarily generated hostile feelings [in the masochistic woman], but feelings which the masochistic woman was unable to express directly because they would have jeopardized her dependency relationships. [...] Weakness and suffering, therefore, already serving many functions, now also act as a vehicle for the indirect expression of hostility.[29]

Viewing the Prioress as an hysterical child-woman with something resembling, at least in part, a masochistic female personality would help explain the many contradictions that exist among her portrait, prologue, and tale. For exam-

---

27 Carroll Smith-Rosenberg, *Disorderly Conduct*, 201.

28 Smith-Rosenberg, *Disorderly Conduct*, 212.

29 Karen Horney, "The Problem of Feminine Masochism," 252–54. It is important to distinguish between masochism, clinically defined, and the masochistic female personality. They are not synonymous.

ple, it would explain the fact that while the Prioress is an important church official with many responsibilities in convent as well as community, she describes herself in the guise of a helpless infant, incapable of speech. It would also explain the exhibitionism suggested by her clothing and jewelry as well as the wild shifts between warm tenderness and cold brutality. For while she may seem restrained in her portrait, there is nothing restrained in the dramatic language and grand gestures of her tale, which is nothing if not an appeal to pity or an attempt to tug on her fellow pilgrims' heartstrings. And, finally, the feelings of inferiority, weakness, and suffering suggested by her identification with the little clergeon manifest themselves in hostile feelings that cannot be expressed directly but must take indirect form, the massacred Jews a stand-in for the real butt of her hostility. But of this I shall have more to say later.

In "Flavit et Dissipati Sunt," Copjec points out that from the very beginning, the theory of hysteria was the theory of mimesis: "It is this fact which Lacan recalls in his elaboration of the mirror phase, which can only be seen as the grounding of the thetic, the positing and positioning of the ego and the object in the theatrics of the Imaginary."[30] According to Lacan, mimesis is a matter of self-dispossession, but it is this very self-dispossession that allows the subject to become inserted into the world, that enables the "I" to connect to socially constructed situations. For without this self-dispossession, or the split between the subject and its mirror image, there would be no lack and hence no desire, desire being set in motion at the moment the subject takes on an image: "The subject, that is, desires insofar as it is other, finds itself exteriorized in an image. Thus alienated from itself, the subject has, henceforth, a mediated relationship to itself and must seek validation by recognition from another."[31] According to this theory, mimesis is the means by which the divide between the alienated subject and its other is concealed. This mediated relationship is different for everyone, but the hysteric's problem is that she does not know from whom to seek validation or as what, precisely, she should be recognized. If the imaginary, or what Lacan refers to as the site of images, is the precondition of the unconscious, then the hysteric's dilemma is not caused by a lack of images or representations, as Luce Irigaray and Michèle Montrelay have suggested, but by a series of conflicting images. For as Freud points out in his discussion of hysterical attacks as projected fantasies, the patient often undertakes "the parts played by both persons appearing in the phantasy, that is, through *multiple identification*."[32]

---

30 Joan Copjec, "Flavit et Dissipati Sunt," 33.
31 Copjec, "Flavit et Dissipati Sunt," 35.
32 Freud, *Dora*, 121, his emphasis.

We see the Prioress's multiple identification and/or identities in the portrait Chaucer-the-pilgrim presents us with. His very first line, for example, creates a double image of the Prioress that creates double vision in the reader: "Ther was also a Nonne, a PRIORESSE [...]" (I (A), 118). Although E. Talbot Donaldson argues that naming the profession twice raises "her nunliness to a higher mathematical power, as it were,"[33] I would argue instead that the need to repeat—repeat with a difference, in this case—creates doubt rather than certainty and, further, that what is implied by the word "nun"—obedience, submission to the order of the convent—is undermined by the word in apposition to it, "prioress," a title that entails power and/or dominance. Both signifiers contain equally compelling connotative information, but because they seem to contradict each other, the reader is left uncertain as to which term is most representative. And the next line offers no clarification, only further ambiguity: "That of hir smylyng was ful symple and coy [...]" (I (A), 119).[34] While the word "symple" suggests that her smile is innocent or artless, the word "coy" introduces the possibility of ambiguity or artifice.[35] And "[h]ire gretteste ooth" is perhaps the crowning touch, for when she swears, it is by "Seinte Loy," a French saint of the sixth century who swore never to swear. By employing this oath, the Prioress, like the fetishist, manages to engage in a disavowal of sorts: she both swears and swears not (to swear).[36]

The next line of the portrait, "And she was cleped madam Eglentyne" (I (A), 121), has created perhaps the most potential for multiple identities, for it has led to a good deal of speculation as to why Chaucer assigned the Prioress this particular name. Many readers such as Priscilla Martin see "Eglentyne" as a "fragrant name" lifted from the pages of a love poem.[37] Laura Kendrick supports this view when she says, "The word *eglantine*, especially in conjunction with the phrase 'simple and coy' (which is often applied to the shepherdesses of *pastourelles*), suggests the sexual quest and love-making outdoors—especially with

---

33 E. Talbot Donaldson, *Speaking of Chaucer*, 60.

34 Florence Ridley supports this view, saying that the "key to both description and ensuing tale lies in [this] couplet [...], for these lines establish at once the basic ambiguity which Chaucer sustains throughout." See *The Prioress and the Critics*, 22.

35 The OED's second definition of "coy" in its adjectival form is used of a person: "Displaying modest backwardness or shyness (sometimes with emphasis on the displaying)," and, in this case, I read the word with emphasis on the displaying.

36 As Richard Rex points out, even those who swore "only by saints [were] not innocent of false swearing or free from sin," for oath-takers "were commonly and vehemently denounced for dismembering Christ." See *"The Sins of Madame Eglantine" and Other Essays on Chaucer*, 109, 108.

37 Priscilla Martin, *Chaucer's Women: Nuns, Wives, and Amazons*, 33.

a peasant girl (a 'wild rose')."[38] Richard Rex, on the other hand, argues that although the name might have been immediately understood by Chaucer's audience as the name of a romance heroine, it also links the Prioress to a notorious red-light district in which was located a brothel called "The Rose."[39] And Maurice Cohen surmises that Chaucer may have named the Prioress after Belle Aiglentine, a French romance heroine forced into marriage because of a suspected pregnancy.[40]

If we look into the etiology of the word *eglantine*, we find further ambiguity rather than clarity: from Old French comes the word *aiglent*, which refers to the sweet brier with its pink flowers and prickly stem, and from Latin come the words *aculeus*, a sting or prickle, and *acus*, a point or sting. Although the Prioress is described in the *General Prologue* as gentle and attractive (in other words, as a pink flower), in her tale we find the sting or prickle of violence and ugliness. We also find in her name the suggestion of the bisexual figure: the lush petals of the rose and its phallic thorns and stem, the feminine and the masculine housed in one body. While some scholars claim that the Prioress represents the epitome of femininity, it would be more accurate to say that her description exhibits such an excess of femininity that one is led to wonder what is hidden beneath her habit.[41]

Just as important as the name itself, however, is the fact of her being named, for she is one of only two pilgrims named in the *General Prologue*, and this fact cannot be without significance. As Lacan argues in *Seminar II*, the "power of naming objects structures the perception itself,"[42] and thus we must attend to the Prioress's name and to the implications of her being named with ears pricked. There is an odd contradiction at work between the two, for while the name "Eglentyne" suggests sexual ambiguity, to name the Prioress is to submit her to the law of language, which insists that every speaking subject line up on one side or the other of the sexual divide. Theoretically, a person with a penis can line up on the side of woman, and a person with a vagina can line up on

---

38 Laura Kendrick, *Chaucerian Play*, 149.
39 See Rex's *"The Sins of Madame Eglantine."* In "A Neo-Revisionist Look at Chaucer's Nuns," Henry Ansgar Kelly sheds doubt on this, however, when he argues that "while [Rex] does establish that the priory owned a garden next to a property called the Rose, he does not cite evidence that the Rose, either then or later, was a brothel," 124.
40 Cohen, "Chaucer's Prioress and Her Tale: A Study of Anal Character and Anti-Semitism," 242.
41 In *Disorderly Conduct*, Smith-Rosenberg supports this view of hysterical femininity when she argues that the hysterical woman embodies a "perverse or hyper-femininity," 198. She also notes that hysteria has often been referred to as "a stark caricature of femininity," 207.
42 Jacques Lacan, *The Seminar of Jacques Lacan, Book II*, 169.

the side of man. Biological difference does not constitute sexual difference. Language does. According to Lacan's formula of sexuation, "[O]n the side of man *all* aspects of any individual are functions of the phallus, while [...] on the side of woman *not-all* characteristics are functions of the phallus."[43] This is why we can speak of Man as a universal concept, but we cannot speak of woman as such. It is because some part of her is not subject to the phallic function that patriarchal society has been so urgent and persistent in its attempts not only to "symbolize" her but also to fix her in place—with chastity belts, laws, walls, and names. Traditionally, for example, a woman was christened with her father's name and then, upon marriage, forced to adopt her husband's, and thus she dropped out of sight as a subject, becoming simply a "function" of phallic man.

In naming the Prioress, Chaucer seems to have been working at cross purposes with himself, attempting to repress the instability of gender through naming while simultaneously subverting the rules of language and sexual difference through ambiguity. But if Chaucer is crazy, he is crazy like a fox. For in creating the Prioress, he has created a much more disruptive and troubling character than Dame Alys even though the talkative and imposing Wife of Bath is generally supposed to be the woman who challenges the status quo, and the Prioress, the one who quietly submits to it. Unlike the Prioress, the Wife of Bath has accepted her place in the order of exchange and has learned how to make it work to her advantage. She is, one might say, the epitome of the "normal" woman who quickly learns that something is amiss but uses what she has learned to cope with that fact. Dame Alys knows that, within a patriarchy, woman is an object of commerce. Well educated in the economy of object exchange, Dame Alys has become a good businesswoman, exchanging sex for money and moments of personal freedom. Of course, one might argue that her tale suggests otherwise, that she upsets the patriarchal apple cart in her answer to the question, "What does woman want?" But does she? By saying that women want mastery, is she not simply inverting the already existing order? Perhaps this, along with the fact that she defines herself within the rubric of marriage, one of patriarchy's most powerful institutions, is why the Wife of Bath is not ultimately an offensive character. While the Wife of Bath directly addresses the question that Freud placed at

---

43 Jonathan Scott Lee, *Jacques Lacan*, 176. To clarify this further, it is helpful to note how Ellie Ragland-Sullivan glosses Lacan's discussion of sexual identity in *Seminar XX:* "Although masculine and feminine traits characterize both sexes, ensuring that there be no pure feminine or masculine essence, the assumption of a gender identity elaborates fantasies around *jouissance* experiences that keep any subject from being fulfilled by her or his desires. Insofar as difference identifies itself to law—a no to the chaos of psychosis—it is what Lacan called the phallic part." See *Lacan and the Subject of Language*, ed. Ellie Ragland-Sullivan and Mark Bracher, 51.

the center of psychoanalysis, it falls to the Prioress to take up the much more challenging role of acting it out, amplifying and staging the question in the theater of her body. And for the Prioress, as for Freud's hysterics, there is no easy answer.[44]

"In every human being a vacillation from one sex to the other takes place," says Virginia Woolf's Orlando, "and often it is only the clothes that keep the male or female likeness, while underneath the sex is the very opposite of what it is above. Of the complications and confusion which thus result every one has had experience."[45] With respect to the Prioress, the complications and confusion manifest themselves in a vertiginous spiral of questions that we as readers pose about the Prioress but that she might pose herself if she could get access to the unconscious: is she a nun or a prioress? Does she passively submit or actively dominate? Should her smile be simple or coy? Is she innocent or guilty? A martyr or a murderer? A saint or a slut? A religious woman or a romance heroine? The real thing or a masquerade(r)? An hysteric or a hypocrite? A girl or a woman? A boy or a man? A Christian (same) or a Jew (other)? And does she dare to have a body? By way of ambiguity—just what type of *amor* the Prioress advertises through her golden brooch is impossible to say—Chaucer shows how deeply the divide between the spiritual and the carnal has affected the Prioress.[46]

As a number of historians have demonstrated, "[T]he Middle Ages was anything but a purely metaphysical time period. It was, on the contrary, a moment of history governed by what we might call an incarnational aspect."[47] The word had been made flesh, and thus ordinary life for medieval folk would have been, by our contemporary lights, extraordinarily "bodily."[48] Given this, even the most de-

---

44 Although I appreciate H. Marshall Leicester's adroit treatment of *The Canterbury Tales*, I disagree with his contention that the Wife of Bath challenges male definitions while the Prioress does not. In my view, she does not, as Leicester asserts, refuse carnality and competition, nor does she tell a tale appropriate to a good, pious, and docile woman. Like the hysteric, the Prioress exhibits an uneasy relation to sexual identity, which causes general discomfort for both herself and those around her. See Leicester's *The Disenchanted Self.*

45 Virginia Woolf, *Orlando*, 189.

46 Edward Condren supports my contention in "The Prioress: A Legend of Spirit, a Life of Flesh" when he argues that the Prioress's "literal language reveals her conscious thoughts of piety while her fleshly metaphors suggest her subconscious [sic] preoccupation with her physical nature," 199. And in "Chaucer's Prologue to Pilgrimage: The Two Voices," Arthur W. Hoffman argues that the Prioress's portrait seems "to define the Prioress as woman, and strongly enough so that tension between the person and her office, between the given human nature and the assumed sacred obligation is put vividly before us," 8.

47 Linda Lomperis and Sarah Stanbury, Introduction, viii.

48 Lomperis and Stanbury, Introduction, ix.

vout religious women must have occasionally wondered what to do with their bodies.[49] If they were to imitate Christ, for example, how could they do so with a female body?[50] And why, if they were to imitate the Virgin Mary, had their bodies been endowed with the possibility of registering sexual desire and pleasure? Surely, in many cases, the body must have been seen as an encumbrance or, worse still, as an affront, and for those who entered the convent unwillingly, questions addressing the body and its necessities must have been even more bewildering. This, I think, goes a long way toward explaining one of the most ambiguous aspects of the Prioress—the meaning of her clothes. As the narrator tells us,

> Ful fetys was hir cloke, as I was war.
> Of smal coral aboute hire arm she bar
> A peire of bedes, gauded al with grene,
> And theron heng a brooch of gold ful sheene,
> On which ther was first write a crowned A,
> And after *Amor vincit omnia*. (I (A), 157–62)

Commenting on this description in language that points toward the Prioress's affect, doubling, and contradiction, Priscilla Martin aptly notes that the words used to describe her suggest

> [...] a daintiness, a preoccupation with effect, a fondness for worldly objects unbecoming to a religious [woman]. She has a flair for dress which can make even her nun's habit stylish. Her rosary, of fine coral with a gold pendant, doubles as a bracelet. Her wimple [...] becomes more decorative than decorous: contrary to the rules, it reveals her high forehead, a particularly admired feature in this period.[51]

Not quite sure who or what she is, the Prioress, like Orlando, uses her clothes prosthetically to keep her female likeness, while underneath something very dif-

---

49 In her discussion of the *Prioress's Tale*, Kathleen M. Hobbs argues that the "Prioress plays out the unique predicament of the medieval monastic woman, as she must acknowledge her status as a daughter of Eve, doing penance for an inherited and inescapable sin, while she must simultaneously strive to meet the impossible requirements of the Marian ideal. Such a predicament forces the ecclesiastical woman to wallow in her inescapably bodied femininity while trying desperately to meet the standards of a monolithic dogma that requires her disembodiment." See "Blood and Rosaries," 187.
50 Caroline Walker Bynum has pointed out that some medieval mystics viewed Christ's body as feminine since his mother was the source of his physicality, but it is not clear to me just how widely shared this view was among the general populace. See Bynum's *Holy Feast and Holy Fast*, 265.
51 Martin, *Chaucer's Women*, 33.

ferent is being played out. There is, then, a pronounced artificiality about the Prioress. Too much attention is given to external signs of femininity, but this is the only way to mask or camouflage either her lack of it or her confusion about what it means.

In 1929, Joan Riviere translated the philosophical question "*Was will das Weib?*" into a psychoanalytic question, "What is the essential nature of fully developed femininity?" Using as her object of study the bisexual woman, or what Ernest Jones referred to as an "intermediate type," she then attempted to answer the question she had posed, stating quite unequivocally that there is no difference between genuine womanliness and the masquerade. According to Riviere, the capacity for womanliness exists equally in the most completely heterosexual and homosexual woman, but in the former it develops as a primary mode of sexual enjoyment while in the latter it is used as a means of avoiding anxiety. Although Riviere does not explicitly say so, it seems to me that the subject of her study is precisely the hysteric, whose anxiety about her sexual identity and its multiplicity is often manifested in an excessive femininity "behind which man suspects some hidden danger."[52] Given Riviere's conception of womanliness, the Prioress could be said to represent one of the intermediate types who wears feminine garb and acts the coquette in order to hide the anxiety that accompanies both her problematic sexual identity and her troubled relation to sexuality itself.

Oddly, or perhaps not so oddly, Lacan moves quite seamlessly in his *Ethics* seminar from a discussion of *das Ding* and the extreme good it brings the subject, something so good, in fact, that the subject defends against it through symptoms, to a discussion of an hysteric named Emma who had a phobia connected to her clothes. After relating a bit of her case history, Lacan concludes that Emma's neurosis is related to an early memory involving sexual attraction but that "the path of truth is suggested in a masked form, in the deceiving *Vorstellung* of her clothes."[53] For our purposes, the word "*Vorstellung*" can be most appropriately translated, here, as "presentation" or, better yet, "performance." Thus, the deceiving presentation or performance of the Prioress's clothes is a symptom of her desire to express herself sexually as well as her desire *not* to, the typical symptomatic paradox of the hysteric, whose memory of a sexual trauma or fantasy returns again in adulthood along with the ambivalent sexual feelings that accompany it. As Lacan argues, "Human defense takes place by means of something that has a name, and which is, to be precise, lying about evil. At

---

52 Joan Riviere, "Womanliness as a Masquerade," 43.
53 Lacan, *The Seminar of Jacques Lacan, Book VII*, 74.

the level of the unconscious, the subject lies. And this lying is his [or her] way of telling the truth of the matter."[54]

Because something in the history of the Prioress's body could not be formulated, except by way of symptoms, her body has not been symbolized or sexualized in any normative sense. As Monique David-Ménard might put it, she has both no body and too much body, for her symptom(s), or her hysterogenic body, becomes "a kind of prosthesis for the lack of an erotogenic body."[55] She is neither/nor at the same time that she is both/and—hence the impossibility of "fixing" herself as anything other than a disruption or a spectacle. I can only agree when Stephanie Gaynor speaks of the Prioress's body as "grotesque"[56] or when Kathleen M. Hobbs calls it "abject."[57] For the Prioress's is a body under scrutiny, a body in pain, and her body's impossibility is clearly registered in the opposition between her portrait (the repressed) and her tale (the return of the repressed). This opposition between the repressed and the return of the repressed finds its parallel in Freud's hysterical patient who, as he described it, "pressed her dress to her body with one hand (as the woman) while trying to tear it off with the other (as the man)."[58] Observing hysterical attacks such as this led Freud to conclude that a hysterical symptom expresses both a feminine and a masculine unconscious fantasy. In other words, the hysteric does one thing with one hand and quite another with the other. So, too, does the Prioress, for in telling her tale, she violates and/or does violence to her own feminine code as laid out in her portrait. There, we learn what a dainty and delicate eater she is and that she seems to have an aversion to the sloppy spillage which often accompanies the activity at table. We learn, too, of her concern for mice, weeping if she saw one caught in a trap, dead, or bleeding, and for her small hounds, bitterly weeping if one died or were hit with a stick. What puzzles, then, is not so much the tale itself as the incompatible synthesis of tale and teller. In short, why does someone who seems disgusted by grease, gravy, and violence toward small creatures revel in detailing several gruesome murders, including that of a child whose neck is cut to the bone and whose body is thrown into the privy, where "thise Jewes purgen hire entraille" (VII, 573)? If the Prioress is careful to avoid spillage, why would she choose to tell a tale that includes the spilling of blood, the breaking and shattering of bones, the mutilation and degradation of the body, and an explicit reference to the place where people "spill" the

---

54 Lacan, *The Seminar of Jacques Lacan, Book VII*, 73.
55 Lukacher, Foreword, xiv.
56 Stephanie Gaynor, "He Says, She Says," 387.
57 Hobbs, "Blood and Rosaries," 187.
58 Freud, *Dora*, 151.

body's refuse? In short, why would someone who avoids dipping her fingers too deeply into the gravy appear quite willing to splatter blood and gore and excrement in the faces of her assembled audience?[59]

The answer is that the Prioress, like Dora, is the "patron saint of disgust," both object and subject of it. That is to say, in her portrait she is disgusted, while in her tale she disgusts. In fact, according to Ned Lukacher, Freud's theory of hysteria is his attempt to describe "an epistemology of disgust."[60] In a letter to Fliess that begins with a reference to labor pains and the birth of a new piece of knowledge, Freud not only feminizes himself by participating in the vacillation from one sex to another but also begins to theorize a connection between repression and disgust: "To put it crudely, the current memory stinks just as an actual object may stink; and just as we turn away our sense organ (the head and nose) in disgust, so do the preconscious and our conscious apprehension turn away from the memory. This is *repression*."[61] In Dora's case, she is disgusted by pleasure at the same time that she gets enjoyment from her disgust: for example, she is disgusted by Herr K.'s kiss, the idea of fellatio, the heavy breathing and ejaculatory material that accompany sexual intercourse, and yet through symptoms such as aphonia, a chronic cough, asthmatic breathing, and a vaginal discharge, her own body mimics, and thus enjoys, these sensations.

The same can be said of the Prioress, for if we look carefully at the Prioress's portrait, we see a similar focus on (or elision of) the rim-structures of nose, mouth, and throat:

Ful weel she soong the service dyvyne,
Entuned in hir nose ful semely;
[...]
At mete wel ytaught was she with alle;
She leet no morsel from hir lippes falle,
Ne wette hir fyngres in hir sauce depe;
Wel koude she carie a morsel and wel kepe
That no drope ne fille upon hire brest.
In curteisie was set ful muchel hir lest.
Hir over-lippe wyped she so clene
That in hir coppe ther was no ferthyng sene

---

59 In "The Prioress: A Legend of Spirit, a Life of Flesh," Edward Condren sees much more ambiguity and (perhaps) irony in the description of the Prioress's table manners than I do: "We are not surprised that so delicate a dinner companion 'ne wette hir fyngres in hir sauce depe.' But we wonder if *depe* might not be an adverb, giving the quite different meaning that she did not wet her fingers deeply in the sauce—perhaps she stopped short of her rings," 194.
60 Lukacher, Foreword, vii.
61 Sigmund Freud, *The Origins of Psychoanalysis*, 232, his emphasis.

Of grece, whan she dronken hadde hir draughte.
Ful semely after hir mete she raughte. (I (A), 122–23, 127–36)

Because singing and eating are considered two of the most pleasurable of human activities but also two of the most sensuous, it is important to examine the Prioress's relationship to these activities. Let us begin with the nose. Rex points out that the "Prioress's performance of the divine service is linked by juxtaposition to her pronunciation of French, which she speaks with the same nasality evident in her singing."[62] The conclusion he draws from this nasality is that her singing is "an affectation rather than an act of devotion: she intones the office in her nose rather than in her heart."[63] He supports his assertion by referring to the monastic tradition, which held that singing through the nose indicated a lack of devotion. Perhaps what Rex says about the monastic tradition is true, but given that the Prioress may have entered the convent unwillingly, a lack of devotion to the divine service would hardly be surprising. Arguing instead that her nasality represents a hysterical symptom, I leave it to others to decide whether the Prioress is lacking in devotion or whether, as Manly suggests, the Prioress is simply avoiding unnecessary strain on her vocal chords.[64] Because the hysteric's nose interferes with her sexual development, the nose will play a leading role in the theater of her body.[65] As Lukacher explains, the hysteric's sexual body smells so disgusting to her that she would prefer to have no body at all, and thus the hysteric's disgust prevents the sexualization of her body from proceeding normally. Because disgust is the central affect of the hysteric, it is of interest to note that Kant assigned disgust to the "lower" senses of taste and smell, arguing that these senses are not connected to the cognition of objects but to the production of pleasure. Perhaps because incorporation through smell is even more intimate than incorporation through mouth or throat, as Kant argues, dis-

---

62 Rex, *"The Sins of Madame Eglantine,"* 110.

63 Rex, *"The Sins of Madame Eglantine,"* 110. In "A Neo-Revisionist Look at Chaucer's Nuns," Henry Ansgar Kelly comments on this, too, making reference to Conrad of Zaubern's treatise *De modo bene cantandi* in which he "condemns singing through the nose as a rusticity on the same level as adding extra *h*'s to the beginning of words and mangling vowels—for instance, saying *aremus* ('let us plough') instead of *oremus* ('let us pray')," 127. Kelly also makes reference, via Rex, to St. Bernard's Sermon 47 on the Song of Songs, which "demands a manly voice from his monks, cautioning them against emitting a womanish sound 'with a lisping nose' (*balba de nare*), a phrase from Persius. It is picked up by Robert Chartreux in the fourteenth century, in *Le chastel perilleux*, addressed to nuns: they are not to sing 'in a half-voice, with a feminine voice, that is, from the nose' (*a demye voix d'une voix femenine, c'est a dire du nez*)," 127–28.

64 John M. Manly, *Some New Light on Chaucer*, 216–17.

65 Lukacher, Foreword, xiv.

gust will have the ability to provoke both desire and indignation.[66] And thus the Prioress's nose will be both the site of pleasure and unpleasure, a site of ambivalence where the two collide in the experience of *jouissance*, that terrible enjoyment from which the neurotic subject shrinks. Instead of singing from an abstract place known as the heart or the soul, the Prioress sings through a very concrete place known as the nose. Might it be the case, asks Barthes, "that music is an access to *jouissance* [...]?"[67] Perhaps the Prioress has been taught by rigorous singing teachers that the discipline of breathing is the key to the art of vocal music. But, as Barthes argues, the lung is "a stupid organ"; it "swells but gets no erection."[68] Rather than experiencing the music in her lungs, the Prioress opts for experiencing it through the rim-structure of the nose, allowing the voluptuousness of the music and words to move across her vocal chords and then, channeling it upward, vibrate in her nostrils like something alive and pulsing. And, too, as long as she sings and speaks through her nose, it is impossible to smell anything bad. Thus, her nasality acts both as a means of obtaining a forbidden pleasure and as a means of avoiding unpleasure, blocking as it does the entry of external olfactory sensations.

In her tale, however, singing becomes not a defense—the little clergeon's song passes through his throat rather than his nose—but a provocation, and thus all of the smells that the Prioress turns away from return to haunt her. Not only do we have the stink of the privy but also the stink of the body, for, as Rex points out, the burial of the little clergeon takes place with an uncharacteristic amount of haste. As the Prioress tells us, "Upon this beere ay lith this innocent / Biforn the chief auter, whil the masse laste; / And after that, the abbot with his covent / Han sped hem for to burien hym ful faste [...]" (VII, 635–38). This haste, argues Rex, suggests that the little clergeon's body has begun to stink, either because it has lain all night on the dung heap or because decay has set in, and thus Chaucer appears to be working against the hagiographical tradition of the sweet-smelling martyr. Adding to the evidence for the body's stench is the "greyn" that the Virgin Mary lays upon the dead child's tongue, for Rex argues that what is being referred to here is cardamom, which was frequently used in the Middle Ages as a breath freshener.[69] Because the nose

---

66 Immanuel Kant, *Anthropology From a Pragmatic Point of View*, 50.

67 Roland Barthes, *Image—Music—Text*, 179.

68 Barthes, *Image—Music—Text*, 183.

69 Rex, *"The Sins of Madame Eglantine,"* 40. Of course, this is not the only interpretation of the "greyn," which has been and continues to be a subject of contention among scholars. Other interpretations include a salve for the throat, a prayer bead, a eucharistic wafer, and, for Bruce W.

plays such a powerful role in the Prioress's hysterical drama of disgust, it does, of necessity, find its way into the drama of her tale, for she displaces disgust with her own body's smells onto the body of the little clergeon.

As for the Prioress's relationship to the act of eating, what we see in her portrait is a fixation on the rim-structure of the mouth and a concern for containment, not a subtle reference to her indulgence of gluttony as Gaynor argues.[70] "In the drive," asks Lacan, "is not this mouth what might be called a mouth in the form of an arrow?—a mouth sewn up, in which, in analysis, we see indicating as clearly as possible, in certain silences, the pure agency of the oral drive, closing upon its own satisfaction."[71] The Prioress's behavior toward food, manifested through what might be called her "sewn up" mouth, has more in common with that of the anorectic than the glutton—a body consuming itself, its lips closing upon its own pleasure—for the anorectic's obsessive focus is food, which symbolizes, as Caroline Walker Bynum points out, both "physicality and control."[72] The anorectic's refusal to eat, argues Bynum, is her means of exerting control over a body that, because of its "painful or embarrassing excretions," has gotten out of control.[73] Although Bynum would not advocate calling the Prioress an anorectic (nor would I, for the Prioress is described in the *General Prologue* as "nat undergrowe"), she does argue that there are striking parallels between the modern syndrome and the behavior of medieval women. As she points out, "[R]efusal to eat ordinary [non-eucharistic] food was often accompanied, as it is in modern anorectics, by frenetic attention to feeding others."[74] This clearly describes the Prioress, who cherishes her small hounds, feeding them bits of food perhaps taken from her own plate,[75] while denying herself the pleasure that accompanies eating. She allows no bit of food to fall from her mouth, nor does she allow her fingers to sink very deeply into the sauce. Nothing gets on her clothes, and her upper lip is wiped frequently and thoroughly so that no greasy residue turns up in or on her cup. What this fastidious behavior suggests is an aversion to spillage, an abhorrence of the sloppy, sensuous aspects of eating. To the crumbs, the drips, the sticky fingers, the stained clothing, the greedy

---

Holsinger, "the miraculous affirmation of body as the very instrument of devotion." See his *Music, Body, and Desire in Medieval Culture*, 289.

70 Gaynor, "He Says, She Says," 376.

71 Jacques Lacan, *The Seminar of Jacques Lacan, Book XI*, 179.

72 Caroline Walker Bynum, *Fragmentation and Redemption*, 140. Robert Boenig comments, too, on the centrality of food in the *Prioress's Tale*. See his *Chaucer and the Mystics*, 77, 83.

73 Bynum, *Fragmentation and Redemption*, 140.

74 Bynum, *Fragmentation and Redemption*, 141.

75 Ridley, *The Prioress and the Critics*, 23.

gobbling, the thirsty slurping, the licking of the lips or fingers, the Prioress would turn her head away in hysterical disgust. (One can easily imagine the Prioress's response to other types of spillage such as semen, menstrual blood, urine, pus, and mucus.) And what are these crumbs, drips, stains, this stickiness if not what Lacan refers to as *lamella*? Stating that the lamella is something membranous and "extra flat," he compares it to the amoeba but says that it is a bit more complicated: "It is the libido, *qua* pure life instinct, that is to say, immortal life, or irrepressible life, life that has need of no organ, simplified, indestructible life. It is precisely what is subtracted from the living being by virtue of the fact that it is subject to the cycle of sexed reproduction."[76] When Lacan speaks of lamella as something that is subtracted from the living being, he is talking about extra-corporeal "supplements" of the body such as the voice and the feces, which operate through the mechanisms of incorporation and expulsion and which divide the body into the exterior and interior while belonging to neither.[77] If it is the lamella as libido or as pure life instinct that the Prioress turns away from in disgust, then excuse her from the dinner table, ask her to tell a story, and see what happens. Instead of being disgusted, the Prioress disgusts. Like the bulimic who binges and purges, the Prioress eats in the portrait and vomits in the tale. And thus all of the smells and spills the Prioress has avoided, all of the repression in which she has engaged, everything that has been nicely contained comes pouring out when she is forced to rip out the stitches of her "sewn up" mouth, open it, and speak. In this respect, she is not unlike the "holy anorexics" that Rudolph Bell has written about, women whose pursuit of saintly perfection led them to acts so extreme as to evoke disgust in those around them. The seventeenth-century Italian abbess Orsola Giuliani, for example, regularly vomited when forced to eat normal convent food but, upon "seeing an opportunity for self-abasement,"[78] ate a bowl of minestrone contaminated with "pieces of rodents, clumps of hair and similar refuse."[79] She also ate willingly "when a fat leech crawled around in her soup spurting out blood."[80]

Even more revolting, however, is the Prioress's tale of murder in which a child's throat is cut and his body thrown into the privy, after which a Jewish community is ravaged by revenge. Put in more disgusting detail, a child's bleeding body is tossed amidst what Georges Bataille would call that "nauseous, rank and heaving matter, frightful to look upon, a ferment of life, teeming with

---

76 Lacan, *The Seminar of Jacques Lacan, Book XI*, 198.

77 Mladen Dolar, *A Voice and Nothing More*, 81.

78 Rudolph Bell, *Holy Anorexia*, 76.

79 Bell, *Holy Anorexia*, 77.

80 Bell, *Holy Anorexia*, 77.

worms, grubs and eggs."[81] No doubt, the gash in the child's neck is a thorough-
fare for, a red highway down which travels, the teeming matter. But there is
more. Once the child's body is discovered and the murderers rounded up, punishment is meted out in the most violent of ways. Although there has been much
discussion regarding the Prioress's use of the word "drawe," some arguing that it
simply means to be dragged along behind the horse rather than to be torn apart
by horses, the fact that equine quartering is mentioned not once but twice in the
tale just prior to hers suggests that what she means is quartering. (In both cases,
it is the rich merchant's wife who makes reference to this type of punishment,
first saying, "Though men me wolde al into pieces tere" (VII, 136) and next saying, "And but I do, God take on me vengeance / As foul as evere hadde Genylon
of France" (VII, 193 – 94). The reference, here, is to Ganelon, who betrayed Roland in the *Chanson de Roland* and was torn to pieces by horses.) Once the Jewish bodies have been drawn and quartered, however, all that is left for public
viewing are the fragmented remains of bodies torn apart by Christian law. So,
yes, the word has become flesh, the Prioress seems to say, but it is also the
word that mutilates the flesh.

How are we to understand this shift from one pole to the other, from the Prioress's ability to be disgusted to her ability to disgust? There are several possible
answers to this question. First, it may be the case that the Prioress is even more
like Bell's holy anorexics than has been suggested, for as Susan Morrison states
in her book on sacred filth, saints such as Catherine of Siena and Catherine of
Genoa "eat filth—from putrid water to pus—to overcome the naturally repulsed
instincts of their bodies, prove their sanctity, and show that they cannot be reduced to their bodies."[82] Perhaps the Prioress's filthy speech is an attempt to
overcome the aphasia that so often characterizes hysteria, her putrid and pus-
like story of murder and massacre, an attempt to show that she can conquer
her body's lingual weaknesses.

Second, if, as Morrison argues, "[p]ilgrimage can be understood as a sacred
ritual wherein prohibited and tabooed filth becomes refigured[,]"[83] might it be
the case that, in the context of pilgrimage, speaking filth has a similar function
to eating filth? By way of answer, let us turn to Anthony Bale's *Feeling Persecuted*. Comparing medieval readers to fans of the contemporary horror film, Bale
cites a number of similarities between medieval and contemporary horror, the
most important of which is a "a focus on extremes of emotion" such as love

---

81 Georges Bataille, *Erotism*, 56.

82 Susan Morrison, *Excrement in the Late Middle Ages*, 75.

83 Morrison, *Excrement*, 74.

and hate "and graphic moments of physical violence."[84] For our purposes, the most useful definition of the word "horror" comes from the Latin "horrēre," which means to shudder or tremble. Horror is, as James Twitchell argues, "a moment of ecstatic dread," in which theologians such as Rudolf Otto "located the sense of awe that leads to the evolution of spiritual consciousness. In fact [...], Otto even argued that it is from this shiver ('daemonic dread') that the visionary and mystical experience ('*mysterium tremendum*') emanates."[85] Although some viewers might argue that the violence in many contemporary horror films is gratuitous, the violence in a medieval text served an important hermeneutical function, for, according to the writings of the thirteenth-century Dominican aesthetic theorist John of Genoa, "sentimental and violent images should be used 'so that the mystery of the incarnation and the examples of the Saints may be *more active in our memory* [...].'"[86] In juxtaposing the sentimental and the violent, then, the Prioress appears to be following the directives laid out in his *Catholicon* for edifying and horrifying one's audience: "To imagine pain, to think of terror, to place oneself at Christ's Passion, in exile, or in another moment of persecution and violence, and to feel afraid was edifying *because* it was disturbing."[87] Because Christ's crucifixion came to be seen throughout medieval Europe as a "specifically 'Jewish' crime," Bale argues that Christians represented Jews through moral allegory suffused—as is the Prioress's tale—with disgusting images of violence, bloodiness, and torture.[88] "To adopt the pose of a victim, or to identify with a martyr" as the Prioress does, "was, paradoxically, one of the most empowering kinds of subjectivity available in medieval culture," for if one took seriously the words of Matthew 5:10 ("Blessed are they that suffer persecution for justice' sake: for theirs is the kingdom of heaven"), persecution became the path to salvation.[89]

And, third, we can understand the Prioress's shift from one pole to the other through the drive, that silent but deadly force that compels us to do things that are not in our best interests and that are often harmful to us and those around us. According to Lacan, it is the movement outward and back that is fundamental to the drive, and, as he points out, Freud designates these two poles with the verbs *beschauen* and *beschaut werden*, to see and to be seen. It is important to remember, however, that the circularity of the drive has not two but three stages: the outward movement, the backward movement, and the return into the circuit.

---

84 Anthony Bale, *Feeling Persecuted*, 18.
85 James Twitchell, *Dreadful Pleasures*, 10 – 11.
86 Bale, *Feeling Persecuted*, 21, his emphasis.
87 Bale, *Feeling Persecuted*, 22, his emphasis.
88 Bale, *Feeling Persecuted*, 16, 23.
89 Bale, *Feeling Persecuted*, 24.

It is with the third stage that a new subject appears. There is, properly speaking, no subject of the drive; the subject appears only as the drive manifests its circular course. What I am suggesting by these references to the circularity of the drive, and the mouth in the form of an arrow, is that the Prioress's portrait and tale represent the movements outward (repression) and back (the return of the repressed) and that what is created by these movements is the spectacle of the (holy?) hysteric.

The Breast and An Erotics of the Divine

Hobbs's "Blood and Rosaries" argues that in the Prioress's tale, the speaker "simultaneously affirms and denies her gender, identifying with both the Virgin Mary and the little clergeon,"[90] but I would argue that this simultaneous affirmation and denial—a hysterical form of gainsaying that attempts to efface difference—is located in her prologue. For in the portrait there is an "affirmation" of femininity through use of the masquerade or the deceiving *Vorstellung* of her clothes and in the tale a "denial" of it through overt identification with the little Christian boy and covert identification with the (male) Jews, identifications that I shall explain shortly. There is, then, an opposition between portrait and tale that reaches a kind of makeshift compromise in her prologue. It is here that we first hear her voice, a voice tentative yet ecstatic that wants to fly in the way the mystics do but that does not quite get off the ground. In fact, hers is a voice that sounds eerily like a medieval Hélène Cixous, yearning for a fusion of language and the maternal body: "Voice. Inexhaustible milk. Is rediscovered. The lost Mother. Eternity: it is the voice mixed with milk."[91] Or, like the voice that Durand speaks of, the disposition of the Prioress's voice "has to do with the return to origins, to the dream of an Ur-language, a corporeality of language."[92] *Here* is the voice that leaves its mark. That burns us. The reason for this profound effect is that her voice recounts a loss suffered, the loss we all suffer when we become speaking beings, and it is a voice full of desire for more than what the dry, cracked ground of the symbolic has to offer. Her voice moves us because it both longs for and, at least momentarily, becomes "the bearer of some unfathomable originary meaning which, supposedly, got lost with language."[93] Unfortunately, this voice is, as Mladen Dolar reminds us, "a structural

---

90 Hobbs, "Blood and Rosaries," 187.
91 Hélène Cixous and Catherine Clément, *The Newly Born Woman*, 93.
92 Durand, "The Disposition of the Voice," 102.
93 Dolar, *A Voice*, 31.

illusion, the core of a fantasy that the singing voice might cure the wound inflict-
ed by culture, restore the loss that we suffered by the assumption of the symbolic
order."[94] It is this illusion, however, that has given rise to the voice as sacred instrument holding out the promise of "an ascent to divinity, an elevation above
the empirical, the mediated, the limited, worldly human concerns."[95] Given
that the language of the *Prioress's Tale* shows us that "there is nothing really
new to learn," that "we have not really gone anywhere and nothing [of interest
or importance] has really happened to us,"[96] this promise of ascent and elevation
would be hard for the Prioress to let go of—hence her passionate outburst of
something akin to both plea and song.

The Prioress's prologue is a patchwork of bits and pieces taken from the
Psalms and the liturgy of the Blessed Virgin, but the way these bits and pieces
have been stitched together tells us a good deal about the speaker. In fact,
this patchwork prologue is the *point de capiton*, as Lacan would call it, for not
only does it connect portrait to tale but also it shows us how to read them. If
the portrait and tale are located on the horizontal axis—that is, if they are linear
or narrative in some sense—then the prologue is located on the vertical axis. In
other words, it does not function as part of the signifying chain in quite the same
way that the portrait and tale do; it is instead their support, the button that keeps
the upholstery of the Prioress's portrait and tale attached to the literary framework. It is the one moment in which we see the Prioress let go of something
that she has been containing, the one moment in which the tight rein she
keeps on herself appears to momentarily loosen. Here, she opens her throat
and "sings" without any of the nasality of the portrait. In doing so, might she
be using music to efface what Bruce W. Holsinger refers to as the "sensual
and epistemological boundaries between sexual and other modes of experience
in the flesh"?[97] For she seems to know and to use to her advantage the fact that,
as Holsinger points out, the history of sexuality has been hopelessly entangled
with that of musicality for centuries.[98] If she denies herself the sensuality of eating, perhaps in her song-like praise of the Virgin, she allows herself some ecstatic if not orgasmic pleasure.

Although the Virgin Mary is the focus of the Prioress's prologue, praises to
her taking up twenty-nine of the thirty-five lines that precede the tale itself,
the Prioress begins with an address to Christ: "O Lord, oure Lord, thy name

---

94 Dolar, *A Voice*, 31.
95 Dolar, *A Voice*, 31.
96 Fradenburg, "Criticism, Anti-Semitism, and the *Prioress's Tale*," 214.
97 Bruce W. Holsinger, *Music, Body, and Desire*, 10.
98 Holsinger, *Music, Body, and Desire*, 10.

how merveil- / lous / Is in this large world ysprad [...]" (VII, 453–54). What is of interest in this address is that her reverence for Christ, shown rather cursorily, is connected to his name—the name being representative of the law, the register of the symbolic, or the Name-of-the-Father. But she moves quickly from the name (or the word) to the flesh, saying, "For noght oonly thy laude precious / Parfourned is by men of dignitee, / But by the mouth of children thy bountee / Parfourned is, for on the brest soukynge / Somtyme shewen they thyn heriynge" (VII, 455–59). Not only are men of dignity capable of praising the Lord but also children sucking on the breast. In fact, the Prioress's view seems to be that to suck on the breast *is* a means of praise. Here, she sounds very much like theologian, mystic, and ecclesiastical activist Catherine of Siena, who "described the soul ascending to God as a baby reaching for the maternal breast."[99] Perhaps, for the Prioress, this is what is meant by the corporeality of language: tongue and teeth on breast, voice mixed with milk, the orality of the hysteric resolved in an erotics of the divine.

Mention of the breast leads directly into the Prioress's ecstatic praise of the Virgin Mary and a rare burst of alliteration, which seems akin to speaking in tongues: "O mooder Mayde, O mayde Mooder free! / O bussh unbrent, brennynge in Moyses / sighte [...]" (VII, 467–68).[100] What she concentrates on are the contradictions and paradoxes of the Virgin's position. But, as the Prioress says a few lines later, even this rapturous praise is inadequate for expressing the true value of the Virgin: "Lady, thy bountee, thy magnificence, / Thy vertu and thy grete humylitee / Ther may no tonge expresse in no science [...]" (VII, 474–76). The being of the Virgin cannot be grasped through science, that is, through the language of facts, reason, or sense itself, for she "ex-sists" in the Heideggerian sense of the word, standing outside of or apart from what we know as "reality." What the Prioress seems to be suggesting is that the Virgin has escaped castration and thus difference, that she has not surrendered her *jouissance* in exchange for language, that she is precisely *das Ding*, the good "thing" of which Lacan speaks. Within discourse, argues Lacan, the subject can only assume either a male or a female position, but because the hysteric does not know which position to take up, does not know how to choose, whether to choose, or why she should be forced to choose, she desires escape from the realm of signification. In fact, one of the most typical symptoms of hysteria is aphasia. Anna O., for example, the famous hysteric who came up with the term "talking cure," lost for a time her ability to

---

99 Bynum, *Holy Feast and Holy Fast*, 250.

100 In *The Gift of Tongues*, Christine F. Cooper-Rompato argues that speaking in tongues was not a sporadic or isolated phenomenon but "a vital part of later medieval religious culture," 2.

speak her native tongue. In the interim, she put sentences together out of a number of languages and in doing so rendered herself nearly unintelligible. Unlike Anna O., the Prioress has not lost her tongue, nor are her sentences nonsensical. But it is clear from what she says in her prologue that she yearns for some means of expression beyond or outside a discourse where there are no positive terms, only relations of difference, and this is why the figure of the Virgin Mary is so important to her.

Like Dora, the Prioress is fascinated by a figure that embodies the resolution to the hysterical conflict: the Madonna is both virgin and mother, unsullied by involvement in the primal scene of sexuality but able to give birth nevertheless. Like the painting of the Virgin Mary that Dora stations herself in front of, which shows "a Madonna who is still, as it were, *Virgo intacta*,"[101] the image that the Prioress seems to have before her eyes in the prologue to her tale is the Virgin Mary as "a mayde alway" (VII, 462).[102] The Prioress's prologue is thus a passionate denial of sexual difference, an enactment of what Lukacher describes as "the hysterogenic body's movement toward totalization [...]."[103] Obviously, the figure of the Virgin Mary will be for her a powerful icon, for the Virgin's body is a place where contradiction and paradox reside, where difference is attenuated. The miracle of the pregnant but virginal Mary is that she can be simultaneously subject and other, one and two, male and female, and even, as Wolfgang E. H. Rudat argues, Christian and Jew.[104]

In her praise of the Virgin Mary, what the Prioress points to is a feminine *jouissance* that cannot be located in experience and thus escapes the symbolic order. The Virgin's *jouissance*, and the *jouissance* for which the Prioress appears to long, is one that is liberated from the binary oppositions characterizing the symbolic system of language, one that uses paradox, contradiction, and even *mi-dire* (or half-saying) in order to convey a powerful and shattering experience that loosens all the bonds of linguistic captivity. Unlike phallic *jouissance*, woman's *jouissance* involves access to the order of the real, the register of the sublime. But this is an experience that cannot be spoken of through the usual channels of language. It is in the texts of the mystics, says Lacan, where one can find a description of *jouissance* that moves beyond the phallic "*jouissance* of the idiot," or mere organ pleasure. In saying this, perhaps he had in mind the intoxicated and intoxicating words of the Flemish mystic Hadewijch:

---

101 Mary Jacobus, *Reading Woman*, 138.
102 Nevill Coghill's Modern English translation puts it even more directly, calling the Virgin Mary that "whitest lily-flower" who bore Christ "all without the touch of man," 187.
103 Lukacher, Foreword, xvii.
104 See Rudat's "Gender-Crossing in the *Prioress' Tale*," 12.

Then he gave himself to me in the shape of the sacrament, in its outward form, as the custom is; and then he gave me to drink from the chalice ... . After that he came himself to me, took me entirely in his arms, and pressed me to him; and all my members felt his in full felicity, in accordance with the desire of my heart and my humanity. So I was outwardly satisfied and fully transported. And then, for a short while, I had the strength to bear this; but soon, after a short time, I lost that manly beauty outwardly in the sight of his form. I saw him completely come to nought and so fade and all at once dissolve that I could no longer recognize or perceive him outside me, and I could no longer distinguish him within me. Then it was to me as if we were *one without difference.*[105]

If nothing else, these words suggest the *jouissance* that the child has access to before it is forced to give up the breast, encounter its mirror image, suffer castration, and live *with* difference. We also have, from an anonymous biographer, the words of Alice of Schaerbeke, a thirteenth-century mystic who contracted leprosy and had to be sequestered from the convent for fear of contagion: "And when she had learned from what she experienced to take refuge in the most secure harbor of God, she ran to Christ's breasts and wounds, in every tribulation or anguish, every depression or dryness, like a little child drinking from its mother's breasts, and by that liquid she felt her members restored."[106] Here, we see Christ becoming mother, gender difference dissolving in the image of the breast. As stated earlier, the breast is also mentioned by Catherine of Siena, who says, "We must do as a little child does who wants milk. It takes the breast of its mother, applies its mouth, and by means of the flesh it draws milk. We must do the same if we would be nourished. We must attach ourselves to that breast of Christ [...]."[107] And in the *Showings* of the great female theologian Julian of Norwich, the motif of Jesus-as-mother looms large, for she continually refers to "our precious Mother Jesus" who gives birth to us through suffering and who feeds us at "his blessed breast through his sweet open side."[108]

Although I am not suggesting that the Prioress is among the ranks of the mystics, the words she uses in her prologue are not unlike theirs, and we know that there were a number of fourteenth-century English mystics whose writings were extremely popular in the late Middle Ages, especially among the middle classes, the country gentry, the merchants, and the craftsmen. These mystic writings concerned themselves with individual spiritual culture, emphasizing personal religion, the possibility of direct access to God, and reliance on the inner light rather than on authoritative tradition. Unsettled by war, pestilence,

---

105 Bynum, *Fragmentation and Redemption*, 120, my emphasis.
106 Bynum, *Fragmentation and Redemption*, 133.
107 Bynum, *Fragmentation and Redemption*, 196.
108 Bynum, *Fragmentation and Redemption*, 164.

and social change, medieval folk were beginning to seek a faith based on the heart and individual conscience rather than on obedience to the laws of the church, for, according to A. R. Myers, it "was widely felt that the spirit of official Christianity was now too mechanically legal and authoritarian. Even the grace of God had become so strictly confined to prescribed ecclesiastical channels that it had the appearance of law."[109] The Prioress's prologue suggests quite strongly that she is, if not a mystic herself, deeply sympathetic to the concerns expressed in the mystics' writings.[110]

The Beating Fantasy and Orphic Song

Many scholars have argued that Chaucer is satirizing the Prioress, using her incompatible syntheses to suggest hypocrisy, a lack of charity, and downright cruelty—her tender concern for mice and hounds appearing ridiculous when coupled with her utter disregard for human life. Allen C. Koretsky, for example, states that "Chaucer has created the appalling irony of a seemingly gentle nun preaching hatred while expressing her devotion to the mother of Christ."[111] But I believe that Chaucer is more sophisticated and generous in his treatment of the Prioress than Koretsky suggests. If we were to mimic Saint Augustine's interpretation of Psalm 48 as depicted in the Luttrell Psalter, which depicts Jewish violence against Christian bodies, we might see in the Prioress's tale something different from what it seems to be at first glance. As J. Allan Mitchell has argued, the parable is an enigma, "provocative rather than directly persuasive because it challenges an audience to think through the terms of comparison being made rather than to apply it immediately in action without reflection."[112] And thus perhaps it is not the Prioress that Chaucer is satirizing but the institutions of patriarchy and church, which oppress anyone considered to be a grotesque or abject other, whether woman or Jew. If we look closely at the Prioress's story, a story for

---

109 A. R. Myers, *England in the Late Middle Ages*, 70–71.

110 In "Sense and Sensibility in the 'Prioress's Tale,'" Carolyn P. Collette argues that the Prioress's "concern with emotion, tenderness, and the diminutive are part of the late fourteenth-century shift in sensibility, which, following the so-called triumph of nominalism, produced the flowering of English mysticism, a highly particularized, emotional style in the arts, and the ascendancy of the heart over the reason in religious matters. In both her portrait and her tale the Prioress reflects these developments as she focuses on the physical, tangible, often diminutive—mice, dogs, and little children—as objects of her 'tendre herte' and symbols of her understanding of Christian doctrine," 138.

111 Allen C. Koretsky, "Dangerous Innocence," 23.

112 J. Allan Mitchell, "Chaucer's 'Clerk's Tale' and the Question of Ethical Monstrosity," 4.

which she has requested guidance from the Virgin *mother* rather than from God the *father* or Christ the *son*, we see that beneath the attack on the Jews is an attack on the patristic and paternal fathers who have ordered her life and the lives of all "others" who are subject to their power, rules, and laws. The phallic imagery used by the Prioress in her account of what leads the Jews to kill the little Christian boy lends support for this argument: "Oure firste foo, the *serpent* Sathanas, / That hath in Jeus herte his waspes nest, / *Up swal*, and seide, 'O Hebrayk peple, allas!'" (VII, 558–60). Represented as an up-swelling serpent, Satan is, as Cohen argues, "the negative father imago par excellence."[113] Rudat makes a similar argument when he asserts that, through his use of sexual terms, Chaucer is satirizing the religious conflict between Christians and Jews in order to launch an attack on the sexually repressive practices of the church, particularly as they impacted women.[114]

As Bynum has pointed out, "[C]riticism of corrupt clergy was—in the eyes of both women and men—the special role of religious women" and even though "the function of pointing out uncomfortable truths to society was sometimes seen as possession by demons rather than an inspiration by Christ, all agreed that—whether demonic or divine—such criticism was particularly female."[115] It falls to the Prioress, then, to state the uncomfortable truth of the corruption, oppression, and repression that arise out of a patristic and patriarchal society. She has asked the Virgin to guide her song, but she is not singing when she tells her tale. She is saying something that might be articulated in this way: "Look at me. Look at the kind of spectacle created by the demands of our institutions. Look at what these divisions—male/female, Christian/Jew—have bequeathed us: the violence of gender difference bleeding into the violence of religious difference." And while it is said of the Prioress that she "peyned hire to countrefete cheere / Of court, and to been estatlich of manere, / And to ben holden digne of reverence" (I (A), 139–41)—in short, to identify with the hegemonic forces that hold her in thrall—it is not with the powerful court figures that she identifies but with the lowliest of beasts and humankind. Because the Prioress has no power to determine her own destiny, forced as she is to capitulate to the laws of patriarchy, which say that every woman must belong to a father, husband, or church, she feels like a small and helpless creature. Of course, she *pains* herself to *counterfeit* the behavior of the court, but she *identifies* with the trapped

---

113 Cohen, "The Prioress and Her Tale," 242.
114 Rudat, "Gender-Crossing in the *Prioress' Tale*," 12–13.
115 Bynum, *Fragmentation and Redemption*, 136.

mice, over which she weeps, and her small hounds.[116] One is merely a performance, part of the masquerade; the other, however, represents what she perceives to be her real place in society: that of a trapped mouse or a dog begging for food. Of necessity, then, her story will be heavily coded—as is the hysteric's—for she must appear dutiful even as she disrupts.

A close look at portrait and tale reveals that in both mention is made of corporal punishment, specifically, beating. In the portrait, for example, the narrator says of the Prioress and her hounds, "But soore wepte she if oon of hem were deed, / Or if men smoot it with a yerde smerte [...]" (I (A), 148–49). And in the tale, the little Christian boy, determined to learn a hymn of praise to the Virgin Mary despite all obstacles, says, "Now, certes, I wol do my diligence / To konne it al er Christemasse be went. / Though that I for my prymer shal be shent / And shal be beten thries in an houre [...]" (VII, 539–42). What we have, here, are the two conscious phases of what Freud calls the "beating-phantasy." In phase one, the child being beaten by the father is someone else—in this case, the small hounds. In phase three, the child being beaten by the father, or a father substitute such as a teacher, is always a boy—in this case, the little Christian boy. These two phases are often seen as sadistic since the possessor of the fantasy gets onanistic pleasure from the thought of some other child's being beaten. It is through the Prioress's prologue, however, that we can construct the repressed middle phase of the fantasy, which is masochistic in its content: "I am being beaten by my father"—in this case, the patriarchal fathers. I mention the beating-phantasy to counter the claim that the Prioress's aims are ultimately sadistic and to suggest again her lack of identification with the patriarchal fathers and the powers that be. Holsinger lends support for this reading when he argues that "the clergeon himself effectively fantasizes the violence of his pedagogical discipline—'I shal be beten'—in a percussive alliteration just as he vows that he 'wol it konne'; the threat and promise of violence seem to be the very conditions for the learning of the antiphon."[117] Through identification, the Prioress's and the clergeon's violent fantasies of being beaten overlap.

---

116 In "Sadism and Sentimentality," Merrall Llewelyn Price argues that each time Chaucer uses the word "countrefete," it "contains the implication of fraudulent or unsuccessful reproduction," and thus the implication is that the Prioress "is at best inexactly simulating courtly behavior," 198.

117 See Holsinger's *Music, Body, and Desire*, 271. Merrall Llewelyn Price, on the other hand, argues in "Sadism and Sentimentality" that the Prioress's "disproportionate concerns with bodily hygiene" are an indication that she is stuck in the anal stage of psychosexual development, the stage "to which is often ascribed 'sadism or sentimentality, or a combination,'" 199. But she un-

Like the mice and hounds, the little clergeon is small and helpless. As has been pointed out by numerous scholars, the Prioress clearly identifies with him because of what she says in her prologue:

My konnyng is so wayk, O blisful Queene,
For to declare thy grete worthynesse
That I ne may the weighte nat susteene;
But as a child of twelf month oold, or lesse,
That kan unnethes any word expresse,
Right so fare I, and therfore I yow preye,
Gydeth my song that I shal of yow seye. (VII, 481–87)

She says in these lines that her ability is so weak, she would fare about as well as a twelve-month-old child in declaring the great worthiness of the Virgin Mary. And how does she speak of declaring this worthiness? Through song. Perhaps the Prioress chooses song as a means of speaking about or praising the Virgin because she believes, as did Saint Augustine himself, that "the jubilation expresses what cannot be expressed by words, the singers are so overwhelmed with joy that they abandon words and give way to their heart."[118] Song, unlike proper speech, is closely connected to Julia Kristeva's conception of the *genotext*, which operates in a space where the subject is not yet split, where it does not yet communicate through the differential signifiers of the symbolic. In a nicely articulated Kristevan reading, Corey Marvin argues that there is a link between the little clergeon's early stages of language acquisition and what Kristeva might refer to as the pre-symbolic "maternal space" of the Virgin Mary.[119] According to Marvin, Kristeva's pre-symbolic maternal space is located

---

dercuts this when she argues that the Prioress's avowed linguistic capacity corresponds more to the oral than the anal stage.
118 Dolar, *A Voice*, 49. On the other hand, Saint Augustine was well aware of the dangerous seductiveness of song, for he says, "Yet when it befalls me to be more moved with the voice than the words sung, I confess to have sinned penally, and then had rather not hear music," 48. Because the tale "repeatedly emphasizes that it is the aural quality of the song, not its semantic content, that entrances and overpowers," as Andrew Albin points out in "The *Prioress's Tale*, Sonorous and Silent," 94, one cannot help wondering whether Chaucer is commenting on the anxious debates regarding polyphonic music that were taking place during the fourteenth century. According to Clair Olson in "Chaucer and the Music of the Fourteenth Century," the "fourteenth century was primarily a time of polyphonic music," the church having developed out of "the simple monadic plainsong […] an increasingly complex polyphonic music," 65. And, as Dolar argues, rather weighty problems were caused by polyphony, for "when several voices sing at the same time, and follow their own melodic lines, the text becomes unintelligible," 49.
119 Corey J. Marvin, "'I Will Not Thee Forsake,'" 40.

"in the little clergeon's engagement with the melodies, sounds, and rhythms of the *Alma redemptoris mater.*"[120] As the Prioress says in her tale, upon hearing the *Alma*, the little Christian boy learns the words and music by rote, not knowing what the Latin words mean, only that they are a hymn to the Virgin Mary. The realm of sense or meaning is occluded by the experience of what Barthes might call the "grain" of the voice, which he describes as something "manifest and stubborn" that is "beyond (or before) the meaning of the words."[121] The song the child sings is the equivalent of Kristeva's *geno-song*, which Barthes describes as "that apex (or that depth) of production where the melody really works at the language—not at what it says, but the voluptuousness of its sounds-signi-fiers, of its letters."[122] Even though the meaning of the song is a mystery to him, the little Christian boy "song it wel and boldely, / Fro word to word, acordynge with the note. / Twies a day it passed thurgh his throte [...]" (VII, 546 – 48).[123] This is his access to *jouissance*, for it is in the throat, says Barthes, rather than in the lungs or elsewhere that the materiality of the body collides with language. Is it any wonder, then, that the throat will be the site of the child's fatal wound?

Although the Prioress states in her tale that the Jews are responsible for the death of the little Christian boy, the real culprit of the tale is Satan. There is no indication that the Jews have been disturbed by the little clergeon's song until Satan stirs them up by suggesting that the boy's song is a provocation and by asking them the following question: "Is this to yow a thyng that is honest, / That swich a boy shal walken as hym lest / In youre despit, and synge of swich sentence, / Which is agayn youre lawes reverence?" (VII, 561– 64). As we find in the book of Genesis, when God first creates Adam and Eve, they are said to be "one flesh" and thus unashamed of their nakedness. It is only after Satan encourages Eve to eat the fruit of the tree of the knowledge of good and evil that she and Adam understand their nakedness differently and grow ashamed of their exposed bodies. In other words, it is only after eating the for-bidden fruit that Adam and Eve experience sexual difference and the strife that

---

120 Marvin, "'I Will Not Thee Forsake,'" 42–43.
121 Barthes, *Image–Music–Text*, 182.
122 Barthes, *Image–Music–Text*, 182.
123 Interestingly, J. Stephen Russell in "Song and the Ineffable in the 'Prioress's Tale'" argues that the little clergeon's song would resemble glossolalia or speaking in tongues were it seen in the context of modern Christian denominations: "A person gifted with the charism of tongues— at least the ones of my acquaintance—do [sic] not understand their words in a linguistic sense: they know what they are saying generally but could not, say, put their sentences in the passive voice or the past tense. The charism of tongues is, like the boy's song, a language between hearts, a 'speech' that bypasses the verbal or cognitive level and communicates movements of the soul directly," 185.

follows in its wake. What the Prioress's tale implies, then, is that division and/or difference creates violence and that the one who encourages division and points out difference is the one responsible for the violence that follows. In short, the Jewish community is no more responsible for the division between Christian and Jew than Eve is for the division between male and female. For behind both Jewish community and Eve stands the great divider, Satan. Perhaps for the Prioress the real evil is being obliged to give up access to *das Ding*, the thing that stands outside signification, the thing that does not know the human world of binary oppositions and sexual difference, the thing that, like the mother, is "the object forever lost around which the subject and his desire revolve."[124]

Because of the Prioress's longing for an enjoyment beyond the signifier, it might be possible to argue that Chaucer is using the Prioress and her obvious interest in song to illustrate a debate that had been raging for centuries regarding the source of music: God or Satan? The introduction of polyphony into sacred music was particularly worrisome, for when voices harmonize rather than sing in unity, they obscure the words of the liturgy. Seeing musical invention such as polyphony as morally ruinous, Pope John XXII issued a decree in 1324 reprimanding and instructing musicians to cease and desist who "intoxicate the ear without satisfying it"; who "dramatize the text with gestures"; and who prevent devotion "by creating a sensuous and indecent atmosphere."[125] The pope's decree did little to stop the spread of polyphony, however, for J. Stephen Russell notes that the *Alma* was particularly popular in the fourteenth century for polyphonic settings.[126] But not everyone was driven by the obsession to "pin down the voice to the letter, to limit its disruptive force, to dissipate its inherent ambiguity."[127] The twelfth-century abbess and mystic Hildegard of Bingen, for example, composed a musical morality play entitled *Ordo virtutum* in which the soul is tempted by Satan and rescued by personified virtues that sing: "In a most curious *tour de force*, the Devil is the only masculine and the only speaking role, being confined just to words, to mere *logos*. An inherently non-musical creature, the Devil is the Devil because he cannot sing."[128] Clearly, the Prioress is on the side of the voice and not the signifier, for her Devil is hostile to song, inciting the Jews to murder the singing clergeon. Robert Sturges supports my contention

---

124 Lee, *Jacques Lacan*, 164.
125 See his *Docta sanctorum Patrum*, www.cengage.com/music/book_content/049557273X_wrightSimms/assets/ITOW/7273X_10b_ITOW_John_XXII.pdf.
126 Andrew Albin makes reference to Russell's comment on the *Alma* in "The *Prioress's Tale*, Sonorous and Silent," 92n2.
127 Dolar, *A Voice*, 49.
128 Dolar, *A Voice*, 50.

when he argues that "the Prioress is more concerned with the bodily, acoustic properties of her voice than with what she is singing [...]."[129] In the Prioress's musical morality play, then, the little clergeon represents an orphic Christ figure,[130] while Satan represents those such as Pope John XXII who believe as Plato does that "the core of the danger is the voice that sets itself loose from the word, the voice beyond logos, the lawless voice."[131]

Although the child's throat is cut unto his "nekke-boon," he continues his song, saying to the abbot who performs the mass, "I synge, and synge moot certeyn, / In honour of that blisful Mayden free / Til fro my tonge of taken is the greyn [...]" (VII, 663–65). In this song between-two-deaths, we see the shadowy contours of Ovid's tale of Orpheus, the great poet and singer so attached to his wife that he was willing to descend into the underworld to search for her. Like the Prioress, he, too, is guilty of looking back to a "pre-lapsarian" moment before loss or division had occurred, before he had been cut off from his beloved by the bite of a serpent (read allegorically, another incarnation of Satan). As Ovid tells us, upon suffering this loss, Orpheus rejects the love of women, of difference, and is punished by the Thracian women who murder him, leaving his limbs scattered, his head and lyre floating down Hebrus's seaward flow. But, like the little Christian boy who continues to sing even after his throat has been cut, Orpheus's severed head and his lyre continue their mournful song until Phoebus intervenes. And just as the Prioress's tale ends with the reunion of the little clergeon and the Virgin Mary, the shade of Orpheus finally finds its way back to Eurydice.[132] Perhaps this is the child's and/or the Prioress's attempt to re-find a relation to *das Ding* somewhere beyond the law. If so, the proper *moralitas* for the Prioress's tale might be stated thus: the law cuts, but the grain of the voice lives on.

---

129 Robert Sturges, *Chaucer's Pardoner and Gender Theory*, 92.

130 Similarly, in *Excrement in the Late Middle Ages*, Morrison views the little clergeon "as the symbolic equivalent of the consecrated Host [...]," 87.

131 Dolar, *A Voice*, 45.

132 In *Chaucer's Pardoner*, Sturges draws a similar parallel between the little clergeon and Orpheus when he argues that the *Prioress's Tale* "corrects the misogyny of Ovid's and most medieval commentators' versions of the Orpheus story" by conflating "[s]ong, the feminine, and eternal life [...] in a new form of spirituality [...]," 122.

The Joke of the Host and the Prick of the Prioress

Both the performance of the Wife of Bath and that of the Prioress can be spoken of in terms of the theatrical, but while Dame Alys gives a performance that we, if not her fellow pilgrims, can easily applaud, the Prioress leaves her audience in a state of confusion, ill at ease with what they have seen and heard, uncertain of what their response should be: "Whan seyd was al this miracle, every man / As sobre was that wonder was to se, / Til that oure Hooste japen tho bigan [...]" (VII, 691–93).[133] After a moment or two of stunned silence, the Host takes it upon himself to cover the awkwardness, and he does this not by addressing the Prioress—in fact, no one says a word to her—but by beginning to joke. The fact that he responds this way is particularly revealing in that it suggests a certain kind of distress on his part, or what Freud would call unpleasure. Clearly, his reaction to the Prioress's tale is quite different from his reaction to the other pilgrims' tales. For example, when the Miller drunkenly insists on speaking, Harry quite bluntly orders him to pipe down. And when the Physician has finished his tale, Harry's response is honest and quick, for he says, and rightly so, that the tale has made him ill, and he turns to the pretty Pardoner (a stand-in, perhaps, for a nurturing woman or a nurse) to request "triacle" or medicine. Then there is the case of the Knight's interruption of the Monk and Harry's echoing of the Knight's sentiments. In each of these cases, the response is direct and immediate. Harry voices his displeasure to the teller or in front of the teller and then asks for something else, something "nice." But after the Prioress finishes, everyone is silent until Harry begins to joke. Why tell a joke directly on the heels of such a seriously unfunny tale?

---

133 Albert B. Friedman argues in "The 'Prioress's Tale' and Chaucer's Anti-Semitism" that when "the Prioress is done a hush of sobriety falls over the company—precisely the edifying effect she had intended, and a response which the tale, considering the immediate audience, thoroughly deserves," 118. But there are a number of scholars who, like me, read the silence differently. The view closest to my own is Julia Bolton Holloway's belief, expressed in "Convents, Courts and Colleges," that the silence suggests "disapproval and discomfort," 205. In "The *Prioress's Tale*, Sonorous and Silent," Andrew Albin argues that the pilgrims' silence is "deeply troubling," 110. Lawrence Besserman, in "Ideology, Antisemitism, and Chaucer's *Prioress's Tale*," emphasizes the ambiguity of the pilgrims' response, which is in keeping with the ambiguity that surrounds everything the Prioress is, does, and says. Like Besserman, William A. Quinn draws attention to Chaucer-the-pilgrim's "own seemingly reticent and certainly enigmatic reaction (*CT* 7.696–97)." See "The Shadow of Chaucer's Jews," 301. Echoing Albin, Besserman, and Quinn, Bronwen Welch argues that the pilgrims' silence points to their confusion regarding how they should respond. See "'Gydeth My Song,'" 147.

In his book, *Jokes and Their Relation to the Unconscious*, Freud theorizes humor as "a means of obtaining pleasure in spite of the distressing affects that interfere with it; it acts as a substitute for the generation of these affects, it puts itself in their place."[134] Moreover, he states that the "pleasure of humor [...] comes about [...] at the cost of a release of affect that does not occur: it arises from an *economy in the expenditure of affect*."[135] Because what the Prioress has spoken of—castration, mutilation, and death but also feminine *jouissance*—creates anxiety in her listeners, Harry takes it upon himself to displace or at least to diminish the anxiety through his jokes. His jokes, however, fail to completely dispel his anxiety, for a residue remains, which we see clearly exhibited in the next lines: "And thanne at erst he looked upon me, / And seyde thus: 'What man artow?'" (VII, 694–95). In asking this question, it seems that Harry is really asking, "What *kind of* man are you?" or perhaps "Are you a *man* at all?" Ultimately, of course, he would like to ask this of the Prioress—"What *kind of woman* artow?"—but he is registering his discomfort at the level of the unconscious, and so the question gets displaced or misdirected. Instead of directly responding to the Prioress, Harry relieves (or relives) his own castration anxiety through projection and/or aggressivity aimed at the diminutive Chaucer-the-pilgrim. In other words, instead of recognizing his own "cut," Harry cuts his fellow traveler.

Although the Prioress does not speak about mastery or sexuality as the Wife of Bath does, she nevertheless succeeds in calling into question the sexuality of her fellow travelers. Of course, many of the tales and their tellers make it a point to question the virility of their rivals (for example, the Miller's and the Reeve's tales are told to this end, each one recounting a story of cuckoldry), but the Prioress's tale goes much further, working insidiously on her fellow pilgrims at the level of the unconscious, subliminally insinuating into their psyches its traumatic effects. Because the tale is not aimed at anyone in particular, it pierces everyone in general: like the unconscious, which alienates the subject from any position of certainty and exposes the fictional nature of the sexual categories to which every subject is assigned, the Prioress pricks or jabs a hole in the supposed subjective integrity and/or sexual identity of her fellow pilgrims. The effect of this prick is made manifest in the drama that follows her tale—the interaction between Chaucer-the-pilgrim and the Host—which is a comic repetition of the events the Prioress has just narrated.

Like the young Christian boy in the Prioress's tale whose song in praise of the Virgin Mary provokes the Jewish community to commit murder, so, too,

---

134 Sigmund Freud, *Jokes and Their Relation to the Unconscious*, 293.
135 Freud, *Jokes*, 293, his emphasis.

does Chaucer-the-pilgrim's "drasty rymyng" provoke murderous impulses in Harry. Here, of course, I speak of murder metaphorically, but the effect is the same: Harry's wish is to silence the "song" of the elf-like pilgrim, for just as Chaucer-the-pilgrim is coming to the climax of his *Tale of Sir Thopas*, Harry cuts in and says,

> "Namoore of this, for Goddes dignitee,
> [...] for thou makest me
> So wery of thy verray lewednesse
> That, also wisly God my soule blesse,
> Myne eres aken of thy drasty speche.
> Now swich a rym the devel I biteche!
> This may wel be rym doggerel [...]." (VII, 919 – 25)

But like those of the Jews, Harry's insults do not stop there. What do the Jews do with the boy once his throat has been cut? As the Prioress tells it, "I seye that in a wardrobe they hym threwe / Where as thise Jewes purgen hire entraille" (VII, 572–73). That is to say, they add insult to injury by tossing his body into the privy. Is this not what Harry does to Chaucer-the-pilgrim, albeit metaphorically, when he says, "By God [...] for pleynly, at a word, / Thy drasty rymyng is nat worth a toord!" (VII, 929 – 30)? In other words, Harry throws the body of his fellow pilgrim's tale onto the dung heap. But, like the continued singing of the little Christian boy even after his throat has been cut, Chaucer-the-pilgrim sings again, too—although this time more prosaically—with the *Tale of Melibee*.

To help explain Harry's response to the spectacle of the Prioress, it is useful to refer to Copjec's "Cutting Up." In her discussion of the death drive and the compulsion to repeat, she says that when Lacan speaks of the way in which language carves up the body, he does not mean that it simply carves out or defines the body. He means that language carves up or divides the body and that this causes the subject to find something lacking in its image: "The subject constructed by language finds itself detached from a part of itself. And it is this primary detachment which renders fruitless all the subject's efforts for a reunion with its complete being."[136] To understand the cut of the signifier, Lacan calls upon us to witness the hysteric, for it was through the hysterical subject that psychoanalysis first realized the essential division of the "normal" subject. As Copjec states, "Lacan is asking us to witness the paralyses and anaesthesias of the hysteric, those blind spots in consciousness, those spaces of an omitted attention which mark the point where something is missing in the hysteric's image of her-

---

136 Copjec, "Cutting Up," 236.

self. The fact that she is constructed by society's language means *to the hysteric* that part of her body will not be visible, or present to her."[137] This explains, at least in part, why the Prioress tells the tale she does. Like the hysteric, the Prioress cannot speak her trauma or tell her story, and thus she manifests the trauma through symptoms, unintentionally, or unconsciously, telling her own story by telling that of the little Christian boy and the Jews. It is her story, the story of her body's cut, the story of a life short-circuited. The body of her story, like the hysteric's body, is transformed into what Catherine Clément refers to as "a theater of forgotten scenes."[138] Whatever her trauma has been, she does not remember it. Unlike the Wife of Bath, who has not forgotten and will never forget her first trip to the marriage altar at the tender age of twelve, the Prioress can only relive her past vicariously, through the tale of the little clergeon. By telling his tale, she "[bears] witness to a lost childhood that survives in suffering."[139] As a subject, then, she can only reside in the breach or in the cut.

Clément's use of the word "theater" is important, too, and not just as a metaphor, for the Prioress's tale, unlike those of her fellow storytellers, is an *act*— specifically, the "feminine act" that Žižek speaks of in "Rossellini: Woman as Symptom of Man." Through the act, the Prioress puts everything at risk—herself, her symbolic identity, and her relationship to the community. Because the act transgresses the limits of one's symbolic community, states Žižek, it is thus always a "crime": "The act is defined by this irreducible risk: in its most fundamental dimension, it is always *negative*, that is, an act of annihilation."[140] Among other things, the Prioress annihilates what Barthes would refer to as the "text of pleasure" that has been woven by the storytellers preceding her, replacing it with what he would call a "text of bliss." In explaining the difference between the two, Barthes argues that the former is connected to a culturally inscribed "*comfortable* practice of reading," and thus it is one "that contents, fills, grants euphoria." The text of bliss, on the other hand, "imposes a state of loss."[141] In upsetting the reader's cultural, historical, and psychological assumptions, and thus the compatibility and coherence of the reader's tastes, values, and memories, it is a text that creates discomfort and creates a crisis in the reader's relationship to language.[142]

---

137 Copjec, "Cutting Up," 235, her emphasis.
138 Cixous and Clément, *The Newly Born Woman*, 5.
139 Cixous and Clément, *The Newly Born Woman*, 5.
140 Slavoj Žižek, "Rossellini," 34–35, his emphasis.
141 Roland Barthes, *The Pleasure of the Text*, 14.
142 Barthes, *The Pleasure of the Text*, 14.

The Prioress's act, which imposes a state of loss, can also be seen as a form of rupture, the exposure of a cut, and Harry's response is an attempt to cover it up; or, as Žižek would say, his masculine activity is a "desperate attempt to repair the traumatic incision of this rupture."[143] Harry is, after all, the Host, the one who has set the stage, through the storytelling contest, for the Prioress's act. And like any self-respecting master of ceremonies, he must make amends for the appalling performance that the audience has witnessed. Before the boos begin, before the rotten tomatoes are hurled, before the audience demands its money back and leaves the theater *en masse*, he must find a way to keep the community together. He does this by means of the sacrifice, the elementary function of which is to mend the split in the Other. The sacrificial victim in this case is the childlike Chaucer-the-pilgrim whom the Host offers up to what Lacan calls the dark God. "Sacrifice," as Žižek explains, "is a 'gift of reconciliation' to the Other, destined to appease its desire. Sacrifice conceals [...] the Other's lack, its inconsistency. Sacrifice is a guarantee that 'the Other exists,' that there is an Other who can be appeased by means of the sacrifice."[144]

The problem with Harry is that he has not read Lacan, and therefore he does not know that the end of analysis occurs when the subject assumes not his or her own lack but that of the Other. Because the Other does not have in its possession what the subject lacks (that is, because the Other is itself castrated, thereby pointing up the fact that castration is the inescapable condition of the human experience), the act of sacrifice is to no avail. No sacrifice to the Other can make up for the lack that exists in the subject. But Harry, were he hurtled into the twenty-first century, would never go knocking at an analyst's door because he chooses—like most of us—to ignore the truth of human experience. That is why the incompatible syntheses of the Prioress are so disturbing to him. That is why he does not engage the Prioress in conversation once she has finished her tale. That is why he is probably glad that most of the time she remains hidden away from society, locked inside the nunnery gates.

---

143 Žižek, "Rossellini," 37.
144 Žižek, "Rossellini," 41.

Chapter 2
Portrait of the Hysteric as a Young Girl

> The voice was put into the very cradle of psychoanalysis, so to speak, as it is after all in its
> nature to accompany the cradle. For the story of the voice [...] is at the very heart of the
> psychoanalytic endeavor.
> —Mladen Dolar, *A Voice and Nothing More*

How I Lost My Body

Like any child, some of the first black marks I put on a page were the letters that
spell out my name. When my fat baby fingers first gripped that thick, lead pencil,
I was wary of the tool and deliberate about the message: I was making an initial
and awkward stab at creating myself through my relationship to language. But
there was a more originary tool, and what was being written was a more originary story.

One can easily imagine the scene as I am forced to do since I have no actual
memory of it: the tile of the bathroom floor, the white porcelain of the tub, the
small wooden frame of the potty used for teaching children the arts of the toilet.
And then there is the child herself seated upon her small throne, legs slightly
apart, head bowed intently over her work. But what is that in her hand, and
what is she doing with it? This primal drama climaxes with the return of the
m(O)ther, suspicious of the silence that calls her to the bathroom.[1] "What's
that child up to?" she wonders. And then she sees. In her daughter's tiny
hand, there is a silver nail resembling a cruel but miniature penis, and it is
aimed directly at her child's genitals. Fear and revulsion crash into each other
and cannot be untangled soon enough to spare the rod as she hauls the child
off the potty and spanks her harder than she ever has before or ever will again.

"Don't do that!" she says. "Do you understand me?" Her sexual hang-ups as
a small-town girl reared during the 1940s and '50s in a Pentecostal church produce the simple black-and-white of "That's bad!"

Perhaps the child wishes for clarification, but because her access to language is still minimal, she cannot ask an important question: "To what does
the 'that' refer?" And further: "For what, precisely, am I being punished?" Or:

---

[1] I am indebted to Bruce Fink for this way of designating the mother function whether real or
imaginary: m(O)ther.

https://doi.org/10.1515/9781501514104-004

"Whatever the 'that' is, Mommy my All, what does it contain that warrants this kind of hurt, these hot tears?"

In "'Civilized' Sexual Morality and Modern Nervousness," Freud argues that the original aim of the sexual instinct is not procreation but pleasure and that we see this aim manifested in the polymorphously perverse delight children take not only in their genitals but also in other parts of their bodies.[2] This auto-eroticism must be curtailed by circumscription, however, in order that the sexual instinct not grow "uncontrollable and unserviceable." In other words, through "civilized" education and training, children are taught to pass from auto-eroticism to object-love and to subordinate their multiple erotogenic zones to their genitals and thus to procreative functions rather than to "perverse" sexual excitations. The problem, as Freud points out, is that this "civilizing" gesture of circumscription frequently goes too far, resulting in an impaired sexual instinct. Although Freud published this essay in 1908, my guess is that not much had changed between then and 1940, the year my mother was born, and, further, that not much had changed between when my mother was born and 1959, the year I was born. Having had her own sexuality driven into submission under the lash of the Pentecostal church with its interdictions against dancing, card playing, drinking, wearing slacks, using cosmetics (especially lipstick), and attending the cinema, how was my mother to have known what to do in the face of her daughter's auto-erotic explorations?

Another "civilized" educational and training ground: just before I enter high school, I replace my glasses with contact lenses, and my mother says that this would be a good time to start plucking my eyebrows. Since I have never done so before, my mother does it for me. Although I derive childish comfort from lying with my head in her lap, her bosom heaving gently as she applies a warm cloth to my forehead to open the pores, the staccato action of the silver tweezers hurts, and I feel as if I have gotten pepper shot up my nose. Clearly, the cost of feminine beauty is pain, and the plucking and arching of the brows seem to be a strange and mysterious rite of initiation into the cult of Femininity, a cult I am not sure I want to join. Not yet, anyway. In college, I quit shaving my armpits and throw away the tweezers. My eyebrows, however, never return to their former fullness. Out of pique, perhaps? After all, when one is

---

2 Sigmund Freud, "'Civilized' Sexual Morality and Modern Nervousness," 17. I use the phrase "sexual instinct," here, because that is how the English translation reads. However, this is a mistranslation, for Freud was not talking about *Instinkt* but about *Trieb*, the former translated as "instinct" and the latter as "drive." I should also note the fact that Freud does not use the phrase "polymorphously perverse" in this essay of 1908, and yet he clearly has the concept in mind as he writes, for he had published "Three Essays on the Theory of Sexuality" in 1905.

lying in the maternal bosom, one expects to receive something from the mother's body, not have something taken from one's own.

Before I leave high school, more lessons are delivered on how to move from being an object of sexual interest to oneself to being an object of sexual interest to another. It is prom night, and I have been "fixed up" with a rotund boy who has fanglike cuspids and a crisp, powder-blue bowtie tucked under his chin. Using silver thread and needle, my mother has made a dress for me with a high waist and a plunging neckline. With my stiletto heels, I am nothing if not an anthropomorphic version of that phallic nail of old. Eyeing me thoughtfully, my mother says, "You need a push-up bra. It'll give you cleavage."

> "I don't want cleavage," I say.
> "Cleavage looks good with that kind of neckline," she argues.
> "I don't want cleavage," I say again.
> "Why not?" asks Mom, truly puzzled.
> "I don't know," I say.

But, in fact, I *do* know. I do not wish to have my rotund, bow-tied date think of me as a Woman or the Opposite Sex or whatever else cleavage might make him think of. I am filled with the desire not to be desired, which is to say, I am filled with hysterical disgust at the thought of myself as desirable and of my date as desiring.

Thirty years later, over dinner, the girl (mature now, or so one would assume) says to her husband, "I may be highly neurotic, but it has nothing to do with my childhood." And she is not joking. She is deadly serious. But, then, after a brief pause in which the words are carefully digested, wife and husband laugh (how else but hysterically?) at the absurdity of the statement.[3]

How I Lost My Mother

In *Jacques Lacan: The Death of An Intellectual Hero*, Stuart Schneiderman describes Freud's first patients as hysterical young women who were "suffering from problems that prevented them from having normal sexual relations, from loving and desiring men, from settling down into good marriages, from bringing up healthy children."[4] I see myself clearly reflected in this simple but elegant

---

3 The anecdotes from my childhood and young adulthood mentioned here appear in slightly different form in "Big Sex: The Story of the Silver Nail and Other Objects of (Mass) Construction."
4 Stuart Schneiderman, *The Death of an Intellectual Hero*, 57.

portrait of the hysteric, for I have suffered from problems that prevented me from having normal sexual relations, from loving and desiring men, and from settling down into a good marriage. The jury is still out on whether I shall have been able to bring up a healthy child. When Schneiderman argues that the major task of psychoanalysis is repairing "the relationships people have, not with other people, but with the dead" and when he further argues that "the dead have far more appeal to the hysteric than anything about the living[,]"[5] he is talking about the dead not necessarily in terms of ordinary reality but in terms of psychic reality. What the hysteric cannot get over—that is, what remains a stumbling block for her—is the narcissistic wound, the loss of a particular relation she enjoyed with the Other, particularly the m(O)ther, before some sort of rupture occurred. As Schneiderman so rightly points out, if "the hysteric has renounced life for something else, then we ought to be more curious about what that something else is."[6] Obviously, for some hysterics that "something else" is the quite literal loss of a parent. Anna O., for example, suffered hysterical symptoms because she was "fixated on the scene of her vigil for her dying father."[7] For others, however, that something else is a figurative loss. In the case of Dora, we might say that she lost her mother to an obsession with housekeeping, while she lost her father to the embraces of Frau K. But a literal loss is no greater or more significant than a figurative one in the psyche's economy, for psychic reality gives equal weight to both types. Although Freud, Anna O., and Dora all focus on the loss of the father, behind their loss of the father lie the shadowy contours of the loss of the m(O)ther, a more originary loss than that of the father and one that bears consideration. When a *méconnaissance* this big occurs (in other words, a failure to register the importance of the mother), it ought to make one prick up one's ears. As Barthes says, "When a great many people agree that a problem is insignificant, that usually means it is not. Insignificance is the locus of true significance."[8] Barthes may not have thought he was speaking about the neglect of the mother when he spoke these lines, but the fact that he died not long after the death of his mother suggests that his words could be applied to the very concern I have posed. As he wrote on May 28, 1978, in what might be called his "journal of suffering" regarding his mother's death, "The truth about mourning is quite simple: now that *maman* is dead, I am faced with death (nothing any

---

5 Schneiderman, *The Death*, 57.
6 Schneiderman, *The Death*, 58.
7 Schneiderman, *The Death*, 58.
8 Barthes, "An Almost Obsessive Relation to Writing Instruments," 177.

longer separates me from it except time)."[9] What can one do in the face of the loss of the m(O)ther but write?

After my mother moved to Los Angeles, leaving hometown and church behind, she became a glamorous woman. She was Ava Gardner and Marilyn Monroe rolled into one—a dark-eyed bombshell like Gardner with the shy but sexy cadence of Monroe. (When my Grandpa McLaughlin first met her back in Cool Springs, North Carolina, he thought Hollywood itself had come to call.) There is a photograph of my mother and me taken in my early childhood that fills me with a mixture of pain and pleasure every time I see it. In the photo, my mother is quite literally holding me at arm's length. Like the white-hatted hero and the black-hatted villain in an Oedipal version of the spaghetti western, I am wearing a white sweater and underpants while my mother is dressed in black cocktail dress and blood-red lipstick. As she smiles at the camera, her teeth dazzling squares of snow-white porcelain, she grips my small arm in an attempt to keep me from getting close enough to mess up her hair or makeup. As the hero of this scenario, I am looking killingly unhappy, as if I know that my villainous mother is about to leave me for something (or, worse yet, some*one*) more interesting. I am heartbroken at the thought that this glamorous woman has something better to do than to attend to me, and I do not want her to leave me even if only for the evening. I want her attention, *all of it*, but that is clearly not what is in store for me, and I am still far too young to be able to fake happiness for the sake of the lens. How can my mother train her beautiful, dark eyes on the camera rather than on me? How can she be happy when I am so desperately sad? These might have been the questions I would have asked if I had had better access to language at the time the photograph was taken. I have seen the faces of unhappy children caught in photographs, but the look of unpleasure registered on my face is different from theirs. I do not have the cranky look of a tired child, nor do I have the sulky look of a child who has failed to get her way. I look distressed in the way one looks when one is out of accord with one's lover. There is surprise, hurt, grief, and disbelief—all of the emotions one feels when one suddenly realizes that even if love is an experience shared by two people, their experiences of love are not the same. "There are the lover and the beloved, but these two come from different countries," states the narrator of

---

9 When Roland Barthes was hit by a laundry van in 1980, he had been grieving the death of his mother for three years. He had also been writing two books, *Camera Lucida: Reflections on Photography*, published shortly before his death, and *Journal of Mourning*, published posthumously. Both books were an attempt to deal with the grief he suffered over the loss of his mother with whom he had lived for most of his adult life. See "A Cruel Country," https://www.newyorker.com/magazine/2010/09/13/a-cruel-country.

Carson McCullers's *The Ballad of the Sad Café*.[10] Less poignant but equally disconcerting is Lacan's statement, "There's no such thing as a sexual relationship."[11] What he means by this is that something always stands between two lovers, which mediates, blocks, and thus skews their interactions. The sexual relationship, in other words, is always mishandled, always a bungled action. According to both McCullers and Lacan, it is a structural impossibility for two people to experience love in the same way, and this is a hard truth to swallow at any age. My beloved mother was my first love, and it was such a powerful love that I have never quite gotten over it. Marilyn McLaughlin was the most beautiful, glamorous woman I had ever known, and she was mine. Or so I thought until she gave birth to my sister Bonny.

I lost my mother on December 14, 1960, the day Bonny was born. By this, I do not mean that my mother died; I simply mean that I registered her turn away from me and to the new baby as a form of loss as painful as death. ("Abandonitis" as Barthes would have called it.) Whatever love she had for me in the aftermath of Bonny's birth was a faded version of the original, or so it seemed to me when I saw the new baby held tightly against her breast, her gaze upon it and it alone. Holding me at arm's length, as she had done in the photograph, was no longer a necessity, for, of necessity, I was now always at arm's length. In other words, two cannot occupy the maternal bosom at the same time. If there is rivalry, it must take place elsewhere. During the years in which my mother was attending to the new baby, in which I ceased to be the center of her life as I had previously supposed myself to be, I was handed off to my father, and most of the photos we have of that era show me in my father's arms. Having been "abandoned" by my mother, it is no wonder that I subsequently transferred my affections to my father. But what would become my Oedipal narrative was not the traditional Freudian one in which a child turns away from her mother and toward her father in rage at having been deprived of the valued phallus. If I felt rage, it was at having been deprived of the valued maternal breast, but it was a rage that masqueraded as grief. Or, perhaps more accurately, rage alone was not responsible for the Oedipal turn but rage mixed with grief, and it was at this time that I began obsessively twisting my hair, wrapping first one lock and then another around and around my index finger until it formed a knot. There was satisfaction in feeling the painful little tug on my scalp and in knowing that my mother would have to untangle the knots for me at bedtime. No doubt, this knotty (and naughty) symptom was both a means of getting my

---

10 Carson McCullers, *The Ballad of the Sad Café*, 25.
11 Jacques Lacan, *The Seminar of Jacques Lacan, Book XX*, 45.

mother's attention and of punishing her for my lack of it. When my youngest sister, Susan, was born, Bonny signaled her distress by pulling her hair out in silky, blonde clumps. The fact that Bonny and I attacked our hair in the ways that we did is not without significance, especially as the body is "overwritten/overridden by language,"[12] and thus a symptom is a linguistically structured entity. While I was "tied up in knots" over the loss of my mother, Bonny was "pulling her hair out" in vexation.

The year Susan was born was the year I walked to and from kindergarten alone, the year my father taught me how to skip, the year I first watched *The Rifleman* and fell in love with both father and son, the year we lived in the Midwest among Mennonites and Quakers, and the year I began hearing the benighted and culturally insensitive Riceland Rice commercial on television, which featured a cartoon version of a young Chinese farmer in western garb driving a combine and singing, "Riceland is nice land so rich and so good. / Riceland grows rice like no other land could. / It's vely nice; it's Riceland!" Although Anabaptists and Asians do not necessarily have much in common, the two became intertwined that year, for Asian figurines decorated many American homes in the 1960s, including our own, and I became friends with a Mennonite boy who both courted and teased me by stepping on the backs of my Hush Puppies. Nevertheless, it would have been difficult to predict that twenty-two years later I would find myself married to a Mennonite and that China would be the place where my hysterical symptoms would reach a tipping point.

How I Lost My Voice

This story is about an inability to speak. As I finish typing that sentence, I realize with dissatisfaction that while it may be an authentic statement, it is not an accurate one. And yet my inability to accurately say what I want to say is illustrative of the condition of aphasia that gripped me from the time I was fourteen until I was well into my forties. What makes the statement inaccurate? First, I speak of "an inability" as if it belongs to no one in particular when, in fact, it belongs to me. *I* was the one unable to speak. *I* was the one crippled by what might have been called hysteria had I been born in Freud's nineteenth-century Vienna. And, second, when I state that this story is about an inability to speak, I hardly capture the magnitude of the problem. Not only was I unable

---

12 Bruce Fink, *The Lacanian Subject*, 12.

to speak, but also I was unable to sing or even to cry, except under exceptional circumstances.[13]

Growing up in the Presbyterian Church was what might be called a "dry" or "parched" rather than a "moist" experience, to use the terms Lévi-Strauss introduces in *The Raw and the Cooked*.[14] Like a typical American therapy session, the service lasted exactly fifty minutes. There was no "short" or "variable" session such as Lacan introduced when he argued for punctuation and the concept of "homework," that is, important psychoanalytic work that takes place between sessions. And the order of worship was implacable in its regularity: we hurtled through the "call to worship," "affirmation of faith," "litany of confession," "assurance of pardon," "the offering," and several hymns in order to allow the minister time to deliver a twenty-minute sermon of biblical exegesis, which was more akin to a lecture one might hear in a history or literature class than a homily. While the minister spoke, no one cried, moaned, trembled, shook, or shouted. The congregation did not punctuate the sermon with hearty "Amens" or sweaty "Hallelujahs." When the organ played, no one clapped, danced, swayed, or sang in parts. We droned in unison to the dismal drone of the organ, which was played (if that term can even be applied, here) by a grumpy, sour, thoroughly unpleasant old woman named Miss Lillian. Memoirist Patricia Hampl recalls her piano-playing Catholic nun as having the oily, round face of an olive,[15] but I recall the organ-playing Protestant Miss Lillian as having the face of a prune with lipstick that sat askew on always-already pursed lips. She played out of duty, not out of love or devotion. Her fingers did not caress the keys but pressed them as if to punish them for making music. Communion did not seem communal. There was no common cup, no chalice full of red, red wine, and no crusty loaves of bread. The members of the congregation drank grape juice out of thimble-sized glass cups that resembled shot glasses or the small, plastic cups used for holding urine samples. (These days, one can shop for communion cups on Google, where one can buy prefilled communion cups with wafers. A box of fifty costs $14.95. Even more surprising is the existence of a company called Living Grace, which sells disposable plastic communion cups, touting their products as "the best value in the industry," for Living Grace offers "top grade quality—never skimping on features—at a discounted price." Some of the selling points of these "quality, low price, recyclable" cups are striking. According to

---

13 While most people probably associate crying with the eyes, I connect it with the voice. I feel tears in my throat long before they leak out of my eyes, and real anguish can only be expressed when tears are accompanied by oral emission.

14 Claude Lévi-Strauss, *The Raw and the Cooked*, 1.

15 Patricia Hampl, "Memory and Imagination," 93.

Living Grace, years of testing and research have gone into producing this cup, which does not make use of "reground low-grade plastic" such as that used by their competitors. The company has also reduced the top flare of the cup to ensure "an easy fit on all communion trays," and it vows that the cup's "smooth, even lip" will not cut or cause discomfort. Plus, these cups are easy to fill, handle, and stack. When one sees ads such as these, one cannot help conjuring up images of the Pardoner's false relics.) Bits of saltine crackers served as "bread." Why not oyster crackers? They, at least, would have had a pleasing shape. (Perhaps the oyster cracker was too closely associated with shellfish and the interdiction against eating it found in the book of Leviticus. Or perhaps the idea of the body's brokenness was kept intact by the saltine cracker's loss of integrity.) My guess is that most of the congregation disliked communion Sunday because it meant getting to the golf course or the lake house later than usual. We kept communion Sundays to a minimum. The biggest dispute among the congregation arose over the question of padding the pews. Should some portion of the church budget be used to buy cushions for its members' tender bottoms and, if so, how big a portion? A committee was formed to settle the dispute. My mother was opposed to the cushions, believing their purchase a misuse of church funds. Perhaps at an unconscious level she had continued to cling to her old Pentecostal upbringing, which had taught her that God was as Jonathan Edwards describes: a wrathful, superegoic figure who would punish her if she grew too comfortable or complacent by sitting on a cushy church pew.

And then one Sunday, the Puthoffs came to church. They had recently moved to town and were "shopping around," as the unfortunate phrase goes, for a "church family." They were not Presbyterian, not by a long shot, but they settled in amongst us. Two years ahead of me in school, Pete was their oldest son, a tall, pudgy, pockmarked boy with lots of smarts who played the trombone in the high school band. There was something oddly, sexually disturbing about his playing the trombone, and if one "Googles" the trombone, one can see why. What one finds is information for the beginning trombone student that would be excellent grist for the mill of Mike Judge's Beavis and Butt-Head, for one reads of "vibrating lips," "telescoping mechanics," "superbones," and "large trumpets."[16] If the thought of Pete's vibrating lips, his telescoping mechanism, his superbone, and large trumpet were not already disturbing enough—I can hear Beavis and Butt-Head snickering even now—one Sunday during the intermission between Sunday school and the worship service, Pete told me he knew how to speak in tongues. Although I was familiar with the concept, I had certainly never encountered any-

---

16 www.beginband.com

one who did it or even claimed to do it. I was skeptical but also intrigued. *Can glossolalia be turned on and off like a faucet?* I wondered, having always assumed that it was a spontaneous act, an utterance occurring during a state of ecstasy. And what about translation? Could he both speak and interpret? This question was raised by the pedant in me, who was unwilling to believe that the act itself had significance before, beyond, or without literal meaning. Clearly, I had already absorbed Saint Augustine's concept of "sinning by the ear," mentioned in his *Confessions.* For Saint Augustine, music becomes dangerous when the voice that accompanies it "sets itself loose from the word" and becomes the "voice beyond logos, the lawless voice."[17]

"Do you want to hear it?" Pete asked. I found his question a curious one, for he spoke of the act of speaking in tongues as if some foreign object were being channeled through his body. I was to hear "it," not "him." Now, of course, I understand that this is precisely the nature of language as Lacan understands it. But, in those days, I believed that language was as much a part of myself as my eye color or internal organs. "Yes," I answered tentatively, feeling that I was assenting to something vaguely obscene such as a peep show. Taking hold of my hand, he said, "We have to find a private place to do it." His phrasing suggested that I would be a participant in the act rather than a mere observer. This bothered me, but I was too curious to draw back, and so I allowed myself to be led into the rec room, which was unoccupied at the moment. Closing the door, he gripped both of my hands and closed his eyes as if great concentration were necessary. After a dramatic pause, he opened his vibrating lips and caused the air surrounding us to hum with the words of an unknown tongue. In the days following this demonstration, I felt ashamed of myself in the same way I was later to feel when a man exposed his penis to me in a public library. As Joan Copjec points out in "The Sartorial Superego," "[I]f the Chinese man mutilates the woman's foot *and* reveres it, it is the foot that wears the mark of this division, not the Chinese man."[18] In this scenario, Pete functioned as the Chinese man, and I functioned as the foot, for I wore the mark of a division between enjoyment and revulsion. In other words, if my only affect had been revulsion, I would not have felt shame. This is, of course, not a bad way of understanding the concept of *jouissance:* terrible enjoyment.

It is impossible to say whether there was a causal connection between the appearance of the Puthoffs and the sudden emergence in our church and community of the Christian coffeehouse scene and its "kissin' cousin," the encounter

---

17 Mladen Dolar, *A Voice and Nothing More,* 45.
18 Joan Copjec, "The Sartorial Superego," 91.

group. For those twenty-first-century readers unacquainted with the forum of the encounter group, its main aim is to get its members to shed "their ordinarily polite social mask and [express] their real feelings. The group usually emphasizes verbal interaction, games, and other activities that encourage open displays of approval, criticism, affection, dislike, and even anger and tears, rather than the tact and inhibition of emotional expression that ordinarily govern our social behavior."[19] If my experience of the Presbyterian Church was "dry" or "parched," as I have said, then my experience of the Christian coffeehouse scene and the encounter group was "moist." In fact, it was so moist as to be positively wet. Everything that was repressed in the church returned in the coffeehouse and the encounter group in the form of what might be called the "ooey-gooey." Talk about an incompatible synthesis: this comingling of two radically different socio-religious cultures was it! Thinking back on it now, I wonder if Pete's glossolalia was contagious, the words of his unknown tongue so many respiratory pathogens that were transmitted like an airborne disease, or if what happened next was merely an outgrowth of the enthusiasm (in the evangelical sense of the word) produced by the coffeehouse and the verbal interactions encouraged by the encounter group. Whichever the case may be, I probably would have reacted less strongly to my second encounter with speaking in tongues if the first had not occurred. This is a perfect example of how one signifier impacts another as in the *fort/da* game. In other words, the first occurrence primed me to experience the second occurrence as traumatic because the first occurrence had no definitive meaning until the second had occurred. If Pete had tossed the cotton reel into the crib, I would soon witness its being pulled back out again, and the utterance of the *da* (its claustrophobic presence, its implacable "here-ness") would continue to resound for years to come.

It was a Thursday night, and the sliding wooden doors that separated the foyer from the living room were closed. But ours was an old house, built around 1900, and so even when the doors were drawn together, there was a sizable crack between them. Having finished my homework, I was roaming around the house —probably a bit bored—bellowing, whinnying, and singing, as I was wont to do. At age fourteen, I was enjoying a major growth spurt, and like my developing body, my voice was finding its range and power.[20] In those days, I was always hungry and always loud. Maybe there is a causal connection between the two

---

19 "Encounter Groups": http://www.mhhe.com/cls/psy/ch14/encount.mhtml.
20 According to Dolar, hearing oneself and/or recognizing one's voice creates the "same jubilatory effects in the infant as those accompanying self-recognition in a mirror[,]" and thus the former operates as a more originary experience than the latter in producing a sense of self. See *A Voice*, 39.

and the teenager is simply an inflated version of the infant crying to be fed. Now, as the mother of a teenaged son, I often wonder how my parents coped with my massive food consumption and the love affair I was having with my voice. That Thursday night, I may have been singing a Johnny Mathis tune such as "Odds and Ends," or Hank Williams's "Hey Good Lookin'," or the "B-I-B-L-E Song," but whatever I was singing, I was singing it full throttle—until, that is, I passed by the living room doors and heard a strange sound issuing from behind them. The hair on the back of my neck registered the uncanny timbre of my mother's voice, which was at once familiar and strange. Peering through the crack, I saw my mother seated on the sofa, her head thrown back and her eyes closed. Was the look on her face one of agony or ecstasy? It was impossible to say. Inarticulate sounds—guttural, gurgling, glottal—were pouring out of her mouth as if her vocal cords were drowning in honey and she was calling for help. Her mouth was open so wide that it looked as if it would never close again, as if her lips would never find their way back to each other, as if her jaw had been jammed open. Was she choking? Singing? No? What, then?

Suddenly it hit me: this strange tongue channeling freely through my mother's receptive body was the Holy Ghost, that part of the trinity that had always made the least sense to me. My mother was speaking in tongues! Whatever had been "inside" tall, pudgy, pockmarked Pete with his "large trumpet" and his glossolalia was now "inside" my mother, but I did not want it to be. The Holy Ghost suddenly struck me as being as intrusive as the aliens' rectal probe later did in Whitley Strieber's *Communion*, and I was as thoroughly shaken as I would have been had I seen my genteel, utterly ladylike mother doing a striptease, downing shots, or rolling up her sleeves to arm wrestle at the local bar. Turning from the door, I went as far away from the living room as possible. I no longer felt like bellowing, whinnying, or singing—not then or ever again. When my parents and their guests emerged from the living room later that night, I did not inquire about their evening together because I did not want to know why the Holy Ghost had chosen to invade our house. Was I the cause of this invasion? By having listened to Pete, had I opened the door and unwittingly invited it in? Had the Holy Ghost leapt from Pete to me like a flea jumping from one dog to another? To devout Christians, my comparison of the Holy Ghost to a vampire or a flea might seem blasphemous, for when we think of the consecrated bread of communion as the "host," it is the communicant who is parasitic, who feeds upon the "host." And thus my encounter with what I understood as the parasitic intrusion of the Holy Ghost may have been my first step away from orthodoxy and toward apostasy.

In *The Origins of Psychoanalysis*, Freud argues that the missing piece of the "hysteria puzzle" turns out to be "things heard in early infancy and only subsequently understood."[21] What Freud is talking about, here, is the primal scene, which plays a foundational role in the way one's sexual identity, behavior, and attitude are shaped. Between the perception of the things heard and the subsequent understanding of them, however, lies a significant time lag. And thus as Mladen Dolar argues, when the moment of understanding finally does arrive, "it is 'always-already' too late," for "there is never a point where one could say, with clear objectivity and equanimity, with calm composure: 'So this is what it was all about, it was my parents having sex [...]. I can see clearly now, there is no need for trauma, *the world is back in joint again.*'"[22] Hearing and seeing my mother's ecstatic experience was a return to the primal scene, and it deeply affected how I understood religion and sex (and their implied relation) for a long time to come.[23] In fact, this was the shattering moment in which my world became seriously *out* of joint, and from that day forward, I refused to sing, except in church, where the drone of the organ and the voices singing in unison with heads bowed over hymnals proved a strong defense against what Dolar refers to as the "acousmatic" voice, a voice that is both obscene and uncanny: "The voice comes from some unfathomable invisible interior and brings it out, lays it bare, discloses, uncovers, reveals that interior."[24] Because the voice reveals something private that should have remained so, the effect (and affect) is shame. The fact that the voice producing this shame was the m(O)ther's voice is not inconsequential, for her voice is the "sonorous envelope" that has been described ambivalently as both "the first nest and the first cage."[25]

As I revisit my confused reaction to my mother's glossolalia, I think I must have registered it as a strange and inexplicable reversal on the part of my mother. She had always delicately swerved away from discussion or apparent recognition of anything connected to the body's functions, and now she was "coupling" with the Holy Ghost in what appeared to be an almost orgasmic encounter. When the minister said, "Eat this bread. It is my flesh," and when he said, "Drink this wine. It is my blood," I had always understood that he was speaking metaphorically. Even as a child who loved the world of make-believe, I was never duped into thinking that I was actually eating the flesh or drinking the blood of Jesus Christ. Communion was simply a symbolic gesture of remembrance. But now the presence of the Holy Ghost had thrown a monkey

---

21 Sigmund Freud, *The Origins of Psychoanalysis*, 193.
22 Dolar, *A Voice*, 137, his emphasis.
23 One might think, for example, of moments in which the divine and the human have "coupled": the Christian God and the Virgin Mary or Zeus and Leda, to name but two.
24 Dolar, *A Voice*, 80.
25 Kaja Silverman, *The Acoustic Mirror*, 72; Dolar, *A Voice*, 41.

wrench into the metaphor. It was no longer symbolic but real. Although I had successfully managed to ignore the disjuncture between the "dry" and "moist" cultures of church and coffeehouse, I could no longer do so after hearing my mother speak in tongues. The incompatible synthesis that had always existed between the two cultures was now visible, and I fell headlong into hysteria, disgust becoming my central affect, a petite form of aphasia on the horizon.

Chapter 3
Masochist as Miscreant Minister: The Parable of the Pardoner's Perverse Performance

As the father of English literature and the most important English poet of the Middle Ages, Chaucer cannot have been a writer given to stereotyping, moral viciousness, or exaggerated piety. He was educated, thoughtful, witty—and not without sympathy for underdogs such as women and perhaps even sexually aberrant men. This much we can surmise from *The Canterbury Tales* alone. And thus what I intend to argue in this chapter is that Chaucer is making use of the morally and sexually ambiguous Pardoner to agitate for religious and sexual tolerance during a time of political crisis. My argument will be composed of three sections. The first, "Father, Mother, Masochist," will argue that the Pardoner's puzzling performance can best be understood through the perverse structure of masochism. The second, "The Perverse Dynamic and the Double Standard," will function as a pivot point between the first and the third sections, its aim being to show how tightly imbricated the "normal" and the perverse are and thus how much in sympathy they should be. The third, "Of Parables and Pardons," relies on the story of Matthew the publican and the Parable of the Tares to argue that the Pardoner's masochism both conceals and reveals a criticism and a provocation of religious and sexual law, a religious and sexual law about which Chaucer may have had his doubts.

Father, Mother, Masochist

Any discussion of Chaucer's unpopular pilgrim, the Pardoner, could fruitfully begin with the word "relic," which is generally defined as a remaining fragment, a surviving part. More specifically, it is defined as a part of the body of a dead person—the remains. But when does a relic become a fetish? The answer is when it falls into the hands of someone such as the Pardoner. In this ecclesiastic's possession, the relic becomes a fetishized object, the remains of a body that never existed.[1]

---

1 Although I began viewing the Pardoner's relics as fetishistic objects long before reading Carolyn Dinshaw's brilliant *Chaucer's Sexual Poetics*, I find Dinshaw's treatment of the Pardoner as a fetishist a nice parallel to my treatment of him as a masochist.

https://doi.org/10.1515/9781501514104-005

If the Prioress is the figure of the masquerading woman, the Pardoner is her mirror image or structural counterpart—the fetishist. For both "disguises"—the masquerade and the fetish—function as a substitute for something that was never there in the first place. In the case of the masquerade, the woman attempts to cover, with the mask of womanliness, her possession of the phallus, which she has "stolen" from the father. In the case of fetishism, the fetishist attempts to construct, through the use of the fetishized object, a maternal penis. And just as their disguises differ, so, too, do their "wounds," the Prioress's manifesting itself on her body through symptoms located around the rim-structures of mouth, nose, and throat, and the Pardoner's manifesting itself outside his body in fetish objects such as the shoulder bone of a sheep. Because the hysteric and the pervert construct their psychical worlds differently from each other, however, it is no wonder that in the narrative of *The Canterbury Tales* their paths will never cross. Instead, the two people with whom the Pardoner interacts are Harry Bailly and the Wife of Bath, or what are for the Pardoner the figures of father and mother.

Father

> The formula of masochism is the humiliated father.
> Hence the father is not so much the beater as the beaten.
> —Gilles Deleuze, *Coldness and Cruelty*

The Pardoner's performance presents a number of questions for Chaucer's readers, four of which I shall tackle in the following pages: 1) Why does the Pardoner first confess to having cheated his congregants with the sale of his false relics and then attempt to cheat his fellow pilgrims? 2) Why does he single Harry Bailly out for derision at the end of his tale? 3) Why does he give such close attention to what the Wife of Bath says? And 4) why do audiences—whether diegetic or extra-diegetic—respond indulgently to the Wife of Bath's confession but not to the Pardoner's? The key to answering these questions lies in a particular understanding of perversion, and thus before these questions can be addressed, it will be necessary to view the etiology of perversion from a clinical perspective. Here, I shall be making use of a number of analysts and psychoanalytic thinkers, some of whom may appear to be out of alignment with one another but whose clinical observations and theoretical insights can, with a little effort, be brought into harmony.

According to Lacanian analyst Jean Clavreul, a child first becomes a desiring subject (that is, first enters language) when he realizes that the mother has no penis.[2] Formerly, the child did not know that there is a difference between mother and father, thinking incorrectly as he does that both are equipped with the same bodily accouterments. The new discovery forces a reinterpretation, which situates the child as the one who did not know. His new knowledge is thus lodged in a previous not-knowing; in other words, there is a before and an after, a past, present, and future. The past involves not knowing; the present involves both a wish to know and the subsequent discovery; and the future entails a relationship between these events or positions with respect to knowledge. The child must learn that someone else knew more about the object of his desire (the mother) than he did. This place of non-knowledge with regard to sex and desire is the place at which the subject locates himself in the signifying chain, a place marked by the desire of the Other (the father).

In the perverse subject, however, this discovery is rejected or disavowed. The child refuses to be the one who did not know, refuses to acknowledge that someone else—namely, the father—had prior knowledge. And so the perverse subject's understanding of the human condition, which he perceives to be the truth, becomes rigid and immovable. He refuses to believe that the thing he loved most was first unknown, then known and lost in one and the same moment. What this means in more concrete terms is that the perverse subject refuses to recognize that the mother does not have a penis. By refusing to recognize this absence or lack, he may then avow its existence elsewhere—in some other part of the body or in some external object. The material object that represents or initiates this disavowal is the fetish. The problem with perversion, however, is that it always hovers near the edge of psychosis, which entails an absolute knowledge outside of time and the field of illusion. For the psychotic, there is no field of illusion because nothing is thought to lie beneath the surface. Nothing is thought to be missing, nothing that creates desire or curiosity. And without curiosity, there is no questioning spirit and little possibility of exchange within the community.

The fetish, then, is the pervert's weapon against psychosis, for it is through the fetish that the perverse subject reconstitutes the field of illusion. In other words, it is only around the fetish that fantasy[3] and some form of desire can

---

2 Jean Clavreul, "The Perverse Couple," 215–33. Because the Pardoner is identified by Chaucer-the-pilgrim as a male, I shall be using the male pronoun "he" to refer to the perverse subject.
3 It is important to recognize that the word "fantasy" is used in psychoanalytic discourse to mean three distinctly different things: conscious fantasies or daydreams, unconscious fantasies, and primal or fundamental fantasies. Here, I am using the word in the first and second senses. As Freud has pointed out, unconscious belief, and thus psychical reality, is determined not by real events but by fantasy.

come into play. One might even say that the fetish is an attempt to make sense and being coincide, for the fetishized object operates both as a representation of something *and* the thing itself. But the fetish is also that which allows the perverse subject to deny the reality of sexual difference between mother and father. In some sense, then, the fetish is both the perverse subject's weapon and wound. Needless to say, the mechanism of disavowal is paradoxical in that through its operation the perverse subject consciously acknowledges the authority of the father's intervention at the same time that he consciously denies it. Disavowal both creates the subject's "pathology" and allows the subject to operate in some manner within the symbolic register.

This is a rough sketch of the etiology of perversion, but there is much more to be said. First of all, the field of perversion encompasses a number of sub-categories, all of which manifest themselves differently from one another. Under the rubric of perversion, for example, fall exhibitionism, masochism, sadism, and voyeurism. But as Freud notes in "The Economic Problem of Masochism," even the field of masochism itself can be divided into three variant forms: "erotogenic," "feminine," and "moral."[4] Like Freud, Parveen Adams distinguishes three separate groups of masochists: the self-flagellating religious men, what she calls the "traditional" sexual perverts, and the contemporary lesbian sadomasochists.[5] Although the Pardoner is a religious man in name if not in spirit, nothing in his behavior suggests the martyrdom requisite of the self-flagellating man of religion. Of the three, the Pardoner most clearly resembles the traditional sexual pervert. But of what does this category consist? Fetishism is always at the heart of the perversions, and fetishism always implies disavowal. Thus, fetishism and disavowal are two of the central ingredients for any type of perversion. What these mechanisms lead to is a transgression of the Oedipal law with its prohibition on incest—the prohibition that sets desire in motion. When there is disavowal, the distinction between a mother who lacks the penis and a father who has it is not made. Thus, the Oedipus complex no longer functions as the moment in which one accepts sexual difference. The paternal phallus, as marker of difference, is disavowed. In the case of the masochist, the father is degraded, eliminated from the symbolic, while the mother is magnified to such an extent that, symbolically, she lacks nothing. And so lack is not the cause of desire, as it is in the case of the so-called "normal" subject, but presence is—specifical-

---

4 As Kaja Silverman notes, however, the distinction among the three erodes during Freud's discussion, with moral and feminine masochism bleeding into each other. See *Male Subjectivity at the Margins*, 188.
5 Parveen Adams, "Of Female Bondage," 251.

ly, the presence of the fetish. There are, however, four other factors of importance in masochism: fantasy (by which is meant conscious fantasy or daydream), suspense, demonstration, and provocation.[6] These factors were isolated by Theodor Reik, one of Freud's most brilliant students, in his attempt to bring a new approach to the study of the perversions, specifically the perversion of masochism.

In introducing the Pardoner, I have called him a fetishist—and certainly he exhibits the characteristics of one—but as I intend to show, the Pardoner is, in fact, a masochist. Having said this, I realize that the first objection to arise in any reader's mind concerns the Pardoner's manipulation of innocent, gullible people. If he is willing to cheat the innocent and gullible without any apparent feelings of guilt, is he not more of a sadist than a masochist? This is a reasonable question, to which the answer is "no." The common understanding of the masochist as a passive victim of the sadist's machinations is far from correct. First, masochism and sadism are not complementary subject positions, and so the masochist and the sadist do not function together as sexual partners. Second, the masochist is, as Adams puts it, "the stage manager in charge of the scenery, the costumes, and the roles."[7] In other words, if he is having his buttocks whipped by a woman in black leather boots, he has written these stage directions into his script and coached his "leading lady" on exactly how best to torment him. The Pardoner's theatrical flair in the pulpit is illustrative of the theatrical element that Reik has observed when the masochist turns fantasy into practice: "The actual scene corresponds thus to the staging of a drama and is related to the phantasies as is the performance to the dramatist's conception. [...] The rules, given in such a scene, are comparable to directions to the stage manager. It is in accordance with the theatrical element in masochism that it seldom becomes a matter of 'deadly earnest' as with the sadistic perversion."[8]

Like the enigmatic Prioress—why, readers ask, does a lady-like woman with an apparently enormous love for small creatures tell the hideous tale of a child's decapitation?—the Pardoner, too, offers up a puzzling performance, one even more puzzling, in fact, than that of the Prioress. As John H. Fisher puts it, the Pardoner seems to be aware of his fraudulent actions during his confession, but then—"motivated by what demon no critic can explain—he invites the pilgrims to buy his pardons."[9] Before I attempt to explain this motivating

---

6 Theodor Reik, *Masochism in Sex and Society.*

7 Adams, "Of Female Bondage," 253.

8 Reik, *Masochism*, 49.

9 Geoffrey Chaucer, *The Complete Poetry and Prose of Geoffrey Chaucer*, ed. John H. Fisher, 215. While I use *The Riverside Chaucer* for all textual citations, I nevertheless find many of Fisher's notes useful.

"demon," it is important to note where the Pardoner's performance takes place: off the road to Canterbury at an unnamed alehouse. There are a number of things that are important about this setting, described so vividly by the Dominican Lorens d'Orléans as "the devil's chapel or school wherein his 'scolers' receive many 'lessouns'" in gluttony, villainy, lechery, swearing and forswearing, lying, and slander.[10]

First, it represents a halt in the forward movement toward Canterbury. That is to say, it suggests the suspension that is characteristic of the masochistic structure. As I have pointed out, the perverse subject's relation to time is different from that of the "normal" subject. Because the pervert's desire to see and/or to know leads to a discovery that he cannot avow, he must suspend time, keep at bay "the dangerous consequence of movement, the harmful discoveries that result from exploration."[11] Obviously, then, there will be a reluctance on his part to admit the before and after of temporality, and so any pleasure he gets comes at the price of delay. Reik has noted the paradoxical nature of the masochist's suspense, arguing that in the dilatory theme of delay one can recognize the contradictory desire for pleasure and self-torment. By prolonging preparatory fantasy and ritual, the masochist delays climax or consummation, and thus what Reik refers to as the masochist's "tension-curve" has a much longer arc than that of the non-masochist.[12] Instead of the pleasure that comes with climax or consummation, the masochist "chooses" *jouissance*, the terrible enjoyment that the "normal" subject tries to avoid. Because *jouissance* is often defined as the satisfaction of the drive, one fruitful way of thinking about the suspension of the masochist is through the concept of the drive. If desire is seen as linear, then the drive can be seen as circular. In desire, the passage of time is acknowledged. Narrative and the concept of history help organize time; in fact, these are two of the "fictions" we live by. But in the drive, the markers of time are erased, and time becomes an endless loop in which terms such as *before* and *after* or *beginning* and *end* are rendered meaningless. If desire functions under the rule of the cut, then drive functions under the rule of no cut.[13] In other words,

---

10 Alistair J. Minnis, *Fallible Authors: Chaucer's Pardoner and the Wife of Bath*, 137.

11 Gilles Deleuze, *Coldness and Cruelty*, 31.

12 Reik, *Masochism*, 60.

13 I am using the word "cut" in a number of ways: 1) Slavoj Žižek speaks of the rule of no cut with reference to Hitchcock's *Rope*, a film in which the camera runs continuously and in which the diegesis suggests the perversion of sadism at play, 2) Lacan speaks of the cut of the signifier. This cut is a reference to the way in which language carves up the body, divides it, and thus creates in the subject a dissatisfaction with its image: something always seems to be missing. This

the "normal" subject has been cut by the father's law in a way that the masochistic subject has not. In his return to Freud, Lacan discovered that although belief in the maternal penis is not without relevance for understanding perversion, more central still is the father's law and how it operates to separate mother and child. While the father's law operates fully in neurosis, it operates only partially in perversion, and thus the perverse subject has never been forced to fully submit to it. What this means, as Bruce Fink explains, is that the father has never insisted that the child give up his mother and the *jouissance* he experiences in her company.[14] The alehouse might be said to represent the figure of the mother vis-à-vis its connection to oral forms of pleasure and sustenance such as eating and drinking. In fact, I would argue that the Tabard Inn represents the real, the unnamed alehouse the imaginary, and Canterbury Cathedral the symbolic.

Second, the Pardoner's demand to stop at the alehouse before starting his tale is a means of suspending the Host's authority. As we know from the *General Prologue*, there is no real narrative—no plot—until Harry Bailly enters the scene. Up to that point, the only thing Chaucer-the-pilgrim has offered is a barrage of description, a Tabard full of characters. Certainly, with this many disparate folk rubbing shoulders at the Tabard Inn, something is bound to happen, but until Harry comes along, we do not know what that something will be. As Harry says, it is no fun to ride along "doumb as a stoon," but without Harry's intervention, that is precisely the manner in which the trip would have taken place, for Harry is the third term needed to break the dyadic bond between Chaucer-the-pilgrim and his companions. It is only with Harry that exchange (that is, dialogue and thus action) becomes possible. And like the father's law, which breaks up the mother-child dyad, Harry's proposal to the assembled group is a means of establishing both a community and the law by which it will be ruled:

> And if yow liketh alle by oon assent
> For to stonden at my juggement,
> And for to werken as I shal yow seye,
> Tomorwe, whan ye riden by the weye,
> Now, by my fader soule that is deed,
> But ye be myrie, I wol yeve yow myn head!
> Hoold up youre hondes, withouten moore
>   speche. (I (A), 777–83)

---

something, which Lacan refers to as "object small a," becomes one of the occluded objects of desire in the subject's signifying chain, and 3) the cut also refers to castration.

14 Bruce Fink, *A Clinical Introduction to Lacanian Psychoanalysis*, 170.

This proposal demands a response, and so once the group has voted its assent, Harry lays out the terms of the agreement, saying, "I wol myselven goodly with yow ryde, / Right at myn owene cost, and be youre gyde; / And whoso wole my juggement withseye / Shal paye al that we spenden by the weye" (I (A), 803–6). Thus, it is determined that Harry will be the governor and judge, and that everyone will be ruled by his governance and judgment. Harry's role within the diegesis is to get the pilgrims safely to Canterbury and back in the merriest of spirits. But his extra-diegetic function is to set time and desire into motion. It is up to Harry to initiate the plot and move it beyond the demonic repetition of the middle, to create what Peter Brooks would call "a forward drive in the signifying chain, an insistence of meaning toward the occulted objects of desire"[15] such as Thomas à Becket's shrine. (According to Robyn Malo, getting access to shrines and/or relics during the Middle Ages was a challenge as they were "jealously guarded and rarely exposed to the public-at-large."[16]) What Harry has to avoid is short-circuiting the narrative by falling prey to the seductive delay of the Pardoner. Like the medieval mermaid or the sirens of Greek mythology, who try to coax passing sailors into shipwreck, the Pardoner is a threat to the movement toward Canterbury, for not only does he stall progress, but also he causes Harry to lose his temper and, with it, the authority to judge that he has been granted.

It is not mere speculation to say that certain of the pilgrims begin to chafe under Harry's rule once the trip gets underway, but the Pardoner is one of the few to actually challenge it. This challenge, however, is offered in the masked form of insolent obsequiousness, rebellious submission.[17] Because Harry functions as father or lawmaker in his capacity as judge, the Pardoner's masochistic project will be to scrupulously apply the law through an excess of zeal, thus demonstrating the law's and/or the lawmaker's absurdity and provoking the very disorder that the law is supposed to prevent.[18] An example of this scrupulous application of the law can be found in the use to which the Pardoner puts the language of Harry's contract: "Now, by my fader soule that is deed, / But ye be myrie, I wol yeve yow myn heed!" (I (A), 781–82). This statement may sound like one that Harry has tossed off without much thought, one that he may not even remember having uttered, but the Pardoner has obviously tucked it away

---

15 Peter Brooks, *Reading for the Plot*, 105.

16 Robyn Malo, "The Pardoner's Relics (And Why They Matter the Most)," 86.

17 Donald Fitz lends support to this observation when he argues that "the Pardoner's early responses to the Host, though ingratiating, may really hold venom, not merely mild mockery, under his guise of agreeableness." See "Reflections in a Golden Florin," 338–59.

18 Deleuze, *Coldness and Cruelty*, 88.

in his memory "male" for future use. Instead of acknowledging the hyperbolic and metaphorical aspects of this statement, the Pardoner acknowledges only their most literal meaning, which might be rendered as "I swear on my dead father's soul that if you're not merry, I will decapitate myself and give you my severed head," a self-castrating gesture *par excellence*. Instead of observing the spirit of the statement, the Pardoner observes the letter. Thus, when Harry turns to the Pardoner asking for medicine, no doubt the Pardoner is happy to oblige, but what he offers up in the end is bitter medicine indeed, for the Pardoner intentionally creates a situation in which anger replaces merriment, forcing Harry to break his oath to the assembled pilgrims and thereby putting both his head and his authority in jeopardy.

Significantly, the Pardoner begins his prologue in this way: "[...] in chirches whan I / preche, / I peyne me to han an hauteyn speche, / And rynge it out as round as gooth a belle, / For I kan al by rote that I telle. / My theme is alwey oon, and evere was— / *Radix malorum est cupiditas*" (VI (C), 329–34). The first thing to note, here, is that he uses the same metaphor for speaking, that of sounding the bell, as the Wife of Bath. After the Man of Law's tale, the Host asks the Parson to preach, but before he can catch his breath, the Wife of Bath intervenes, saying, "My joly body schal a tale telle, / And I schal clynken you so mery a belle, / That I schal waken al this compaignie" (II (B¹), 1185–87).[19] This is, perhaps, a common figure of speech, but it is important that first the Wife of Bath and then the Pardoner are the ones who employ it, for it establishes a rhetorical link between the two and gives rise to two questions: what is Chaucer-the-pilgrim suggesting by linking the spurred Wife of Bath and the effeminate Pardoner? And is the figure of the bell significant?[20] By way of answering the first question, one might recall that from the very beginning of Christian history, the wayward woman and the religious heretic have been coupled. Thus, what one might be left to conclude is that Chaucer-the-pilgrim is suggesting a parallel between a woman who perverts the "proper" order of the marital relation by insisting on her right to rule and a man who perverts the aims of the church by selling

---

19 As stated earlier, I am aware that the Man of Law's epilogue is a problematic link, considered by many scholars to be a canceled or "cut" passage, but I prefer to follow John H. Fisher's lead in assigning these lines to the Wife of Bath rather than to Squire or the Summoner. Because of Dames Alys's obvious concern with the body, as well as her numerous references to it, she seems to me to be a much more convincing speaker of these lines than would be the Squire, the Summoner, or even the Shipman. See *The Complete Poetry and Prose of Geoffrey Chaucer*, ed. Fisher.
20 Bells are mentioned in the Pardoner's tale when he says that before the morning service bell had rung, the three outlaws were sitting in a tavern when they heard a bell clink before a corpse being carried to the grave.

false relics. As for the significance of the word *belle*, as Clair Olson notes, the "ringing of bells was [...] used figuratively to symbolize the spread of a reputation, especially a bad one."[21] Although the word functions as a noun in the phrases of the Wife of Bath and the Pardoner, the way it is used by both speakers calls to mind the intransitive verb "bell," which comes from the Old English word *bellan* and which means to bellow, roar, or make a loud noise, perhaps not unlike that of a deer in rutting season.[22] From the gap between her teeth to her treatise on marriage, everything about the Wife of Bath is suggestive of her lascivious nature; and, as she herself seems to indicate, it is never anything but rutting season when she is around. In terms as clear as a bell, she announces precisely for what kind of flesh she rings her bell—not for old bacon but for fresh, young meat. And although the Pardoner's sexuality is ambiguous, it is *conspicuously* ambiguous as is made apparent by his interest in appearance and fashion. As Chaucer-the-pilgrim points out, the Pardoner's yellow locks are carefully arranged so that they fan out across his shoulders, and to make sure this sight is available for all eyes to see, he wears no hood. The practice of going bareheaded had until quite recently been considered immodest, argues Fisher, and thus the Pardoner appears to be at the front of a new trend.[23] And as René König points out in *A La Mode*, eroticism is both the driving force of fashion and the reason for society's ambivalent attitude toward it. The basic dilemma of fashion is that its adherent must balance desire to attract attention with desire to preserve modesty, and yet "both aims spring from the common root of the sex urge, acknowledged in one, denied in the other."[24] Of the Pardoner's desire to attract attention I shall have more to say later. For now, suffice it to say that sexual impotence and sexual ambiguity are two very different things.

After using the image of the bell, the Pardoner says that everything he tells he knows by rote—that is, by memory alone without understanding or thought. Even the fact that he admits the emptiness of his words and pardons but suggests their potency for those who believe in their magic is a parallel to his own need for the ("magical") fetishized object: "Thus kan I preche agayn that same vice / Which that I use, and that is avarice. / But though myself be gilty in that synne, / Yet kan I maken oother folk to twynne / From avarice and soore to repent" (VI (C), 427–31). What the Pardoner begins with, as he explains his "gaude" to the assembled pilgrims, is a representation of his deception—or a metaphorical acknowledgment of the split in himself brought about by language

---

21 Clair C. Olson, "Chaucer and the Music of the Fourteenth Century," 88.
22 See the OED's definition of "bell," *v.* 4.
23 Fisher, *The Complete Poetry and Prose of Geoffrey Chaucer*, 22n.
24 René König, *A La Mode*, 36.

(the subject is always divided, for while it is excluded from the signifying chain, it is also represented in it)—but what he ends with is deception itself. That is to say, he moves from signifier to signified, from sense to being. For the "normal" subject, there is always an excess of being over sense, but because the Pardoner speaks by rote, he seems to operate solely in the realm of being with little regard for sense. Through the suturing process, which occurs with the intervention of the father, the child is plugged into language and becomes a desiring subject. But because language never seems adequate—the final signifier is always missing even though it is supposed to exist, and thus we are never able to say everything—desire is kept in play. One knows—or one *believes*, I should say—that there is more to what one sees than meets the eye. But what one sees, what one believes to be true, and what one is capable of saying never quite match up, and so one attempts to cover this gap or *béance* through interpretation. As Lacan says, desire *is* interpretation. For the Pardoner, however, desire is problematic because it arises out of lack or loss, and this lack or loss is precisely what he wishes to disavow.

Unfortunately for the perverse subject, the mechanism of disavowal does not eliminate castration anxiety. In fact, it could be supposed, from a logical standpoint if not from a clinical, that the perverse subject will be more susceptible to anxiety than the "normal" subject, for anxiety is not produced by lack or doubt but by a lack of lack, or certainty.[25] The ideal relationship between the subject and *objet a* is one of distance, but when that distance is eliminated—when the subject comes into close proximity with it—anxiety is produced. And this overwhelming proximity is what results when *objet a* is positivized as it is in the case of perversion. There will be a something too much, a suffocating surplus. This suffocating surplus, in Lacan's re-reading of Freud, is the mother's anxiety-provoking demand. Confronted with this demand, the Pardoner must work continuously and repetitively to keep in place the fundamental fantasy that sustains him, a fantasy in which he offers himself to the mother as her imaginary object of desire, the penis/phallus. The problem with the perverse subject's fundamental fantasy, as Fink explains, is that it keeps him fixated in and on the imaginary:

---

25 Reik lends support for this supposition in *Masochism*, for he argues that, because of the preponderance of anxiety that accompanies it, the element of tension that characterizes masochism is different from that which characterizes "normal" sexuality. What Reik discovered was that the masochist does not achieve pleasure through discomfort but through "the *expectation* of discomfort," 59. Anxiety itself thus becomes pleasurable.

If he *is* the phallus for his mother, he will never accede to a symbolic position—that associated with symbolic castration. Rather than becoming someone the mother can be proud
of, he remains someone she cuddles with, strokes, and perhaps even reaches sexual climax
with. He cannot go off to "make a name for himself" in the world, for it is not symbolic
stature that he is able to seek. He remains stuck at the level of serving as his mother's
be-all and end-all.[26]

In eliminating the phallic signifier and its sanction against *jouissance* by answering the mother's demand, the masochist does not achieve the free play of abandon. As Joan Copjec argues, the condition of freedom in fantasy rests on the interdiction or the refusal of *jouissance*. Because the perverse subject rejects this
interdiction, he makes himself subject to what Kant calls the categorical imperative, which means that he will work like a dog for the Other but never receive
recognition.[27] With interdiction, the subject is told, "Do not do this," but with
the categorical imperative, the subject receives commands: "Do this. Do it
again. Do it better, faster, harder. And again. Now!"

Comparing the pervert's frantic activity to repairing a crumbling wall with
Scotch tape, analyst Joyce McDougall notes that the pervert fights a losing battle
with reality every day.[28] The price of winning this battle, or maintaining his fundamental fantasy, is a loss of mobility and an abhorrence of exploration. Thus,
the pervert's actions are characterized by a rigidity and ritual that call to mind
the Pardoner's sermons. The message and/or the relations between speaker
and audience are no longer what is at stake; what *is* at stake is the act of enun-
ciation itself. As the Pardoner himself admits, his theme is always the same and
always has been: *Radix malorum est cupiditas*. For the Pardoner, desire is indeed
the root of evil because the object of desire is unknowable, and to search for it
might entail exploration. In other words, he might find himself in an unexpected
and unpleasant situation, one that brings home to him the threat of castration.
And so the Pardoner never deviates from the successful routine that he has
worked out. Like the fetish, which Deleuze describes as "a frozen, arrested,
two-dimensional image, a photograph to which one returns repeatedly to exor-
cise the dangerous consequences of movement, the harmful discoveries that result from exploration[,]"[29] the Pardoner's ritualistic performance in the pulpit
freezes or arrests movement in the way that compulsively habitual acts do.
Reik, too, has observed the ritualized quality of the masochistic scene, but in

---

26 Fink, *A Clinical Introduction*, 176.
27 This reference to Kant's categorical imperative comes from a series of lectures given by Copjec at SUNY-Buffalo during a course on Lacan and ethics.
28 Joyce McDougall, *A Plea for a Measure of Abnormality*.
29 Deleuze, *Coldness and Cruelty*, 31.

his view the masochist's strict adherence to ritual has less to do with fear than with "lust-value." In comparing the rigidity of rule and order that dominates the masochistic scene to the performance of a religious or magical rite, he argues that a change in the ritual can not only diminish but also destroy its lust-value. If Deleuze and Reik seem out of alignment with each other, here, we have only to recall that the antagonism between pleasure and unpleasure is one of the marks of masochism. As Reik points out, "Masochistic tension vacillates more strongly than any other sexual tension between the pleasurable and the anxious, and it tends to perpetuate this state."[30]

Ironically, the Pardoner begins his ritual of deception by proving his authenticity. As he confesses to his fellow pilgrims,

> First I pronounce whennes that I come,
> And thanne my bulles shewe I, alle and some.
> Oure lige lordes seel on my patente,
> That shewe I first, my body to warente,
> That no man be so boold, ne preest ne clerk,
> Me to destourbe of Cristes hooly werk. (VI (C), 335 – 40)

Once he has established his authority to pardon through official documents licensed by the Pope, he sets to work:

> And after that thanne telle I forth my tales;
> Bulles of popes and of cardynales,
> Of patriarkes and bishopes I shewe,
> And in Latyn I speke a wordes fewe,
> To saffron with my predicacioun,
> And for to stire hem to devocioun.
> Thanne shewe I forth my longe cristal stones,
> Ycrammed ful of cloutes and of bones—
> Relikes been they, as wenen they echoon. (VI (C), 341– 49)

His entire performance from start to finish is an illustration of disavowal: "Yes, I know my actions are fraudulent," he says to himself, "but I must offer up these relics as if they were authentic nevertheless." The Pardoner's deception of innocent, gullible people is a repetition (albeit in reverse) of the traumatic moment in which he discovered himself to have been the one duped. In the traumatic moment of discovery, he was the innocent, gullible one, believing as he did that the mother, too, had a penis. Once the discovery was made, however, he vowed never again to occupy the position of the one who did not know, and the fetish

---

30 Reik, *Masochism*, 59.

is what has allowed him to do this successfully. In other words, the tricks he plays on his congregants are a form of retaliation for the trick played on his psyche.

Although it is commonly assumed that the Pardoner's documents are forged, there is nothing in what he *says* to suggest that they are, and so it would appear that authentic papal bulls sit cheek by jowl with inauthentic sheep and pig bones. I am not attempting to argue that the Pardoner's papal bulls are, *in fact*, authentic—merely that he implies they are.[31] But this humorous, if outrageous, juxtaposition is in keeping with the way that the masochist transgresses or subverts the law. As Deleuze argues, the masochist is a humorist who turns the law upside down by closely adhering to it. In examining masochistic fantasies and rites, Deleuze has discovered that while the masochist strictly applies the law, the result is not what one would expect. Whipping, for example, does not punish or prevent the masochist's erection but invites it, and thus the masochist "stands guilt on its head by making punishment into a condition that makes possible the forbidden pleasure."[32] The law, then, is made to look ridiculous as are the authority figures who enforce it. Unlike the three young men in his tale, the Pardoner is no outlaw, for only by placing himself at the law's very center will he be able to mock it most effectively. As we shall see, however, this mockery is not the final aim of the masochist. It is a cover for something else.

We are now in a position to answer the first of the four questions posed: why does the Pardoner first confess to having cheated his congregants with the sale of his false relics and then attempt to cheat his fellow pilgrims? The answer is that the Pardoner is playing out his masochistic drama, and he is helpless to do otherwise. Returning to the four factors Reik has isolated, we see each of them at work in the Pardoner's performance. First, in his prologue, sermon, and sale of relics, we see the importance of preparatory fantasy in the implacability of his ritual. As Reik argues, "A kind of tradition will develop, which has to be kept as in ceremonies of the church. First this has to be done, then that; words have to be pronounced in a certain manner, and so on. [...] In no other perversion does ritual play a role similar in importance."[33] If Reik is right, the Pardoner could no more deviate from his usual ritual than Harry could quit swearing, and since the sale of relics is part of that ritual, sell those relics he must. Second,

---

31 Because we are told in the *General Prologue* that he is from the Hospital of St. Mary of Rouncivale, which was notorious for producing fraudulent pardoners, doubt is cast on the Pardoner's authenticity.

32 Deleuze, *Coldness and Cruelty*, 89.

33 Reik, *Masochism*, 50.

through the factor of suspense, anxiety becomes an element of pleasure, and thus the masochistic subject intentionally seeks out something he is afraid of. "[He] voluntarily endure[s] a bit of pain in order not to be exposed to it suddenly and without preparation. This is an intentional seeking of foredispleasure, a masochistic activity in miniature."[34] Can we not say that the Pardoner's castration anxiety causes him to seek out Harry's castrating gesture, a "miniature" version of actual castration? It may be possible to think of Harry's insult as a kind of inoculation against the threat of real castration. Third, the importance of the demonstrative is illustrated by the Pardoner's public humiliation. Reik states emphatically that "in no case of masochism can the fact be overlooked that the suffering, discomfort, humiliation, and disgrace are being shown and [...] being put on display."[35] He further argues that the "showing or wanting-to-be-seen is actually a means to invite the sexually gratifying punishment."[36] The fact that the Pardoner calls attention to himself by singing and riding "al of the newe jet" suggests the demonstrative quality that Reik has observed in the masochists he has treated. More important, however, is the Pardoner's gleeful attitude toward his moral failings. Reik has been struck by the fact that "so many masochists are not ashamed of their weaknesses and bad qualities but boast of them."[37] In fact, continues Reik, the "attention of others has to be drawn to the ego by clumsiness, bad behavior, even crime."[38] In discussing Freud's concept of moral masochism, Silverman echoes Reik's comments regarding the demonstrative: "Although the moral masochist seems to be under the domination of a hyperdeveloped conscience, his or her desire for punishment is so great as to pose a constant temptation to perform 'sinful' actions, which must then be 'expiated.'"[39] In fact, continues Silverman, "Freud warns that moral masochism is [...] capable of swallowing up conscience altogether, of perverting it from within."[40] The Pardoner's motivating demon, which has given rise to such bewilderment, is surely what Reik refers to as the "cyclonelike character that is so often associated with masculine masochism, that blind unrestricted lust of self-destruction."[41] In Reik's comments about the psychic phenomena of masochism, he argues that the "demonstrative feature is designed to show or prove some-

---

34 Reik, *Masochism*, 69.
35 Reik, *Masochism*, 72.
36 Reik, *Masochism*, 73.
37 Reik, *Masochism*, 76.
38 Reik, *Masochism*, 79.
39 Silverman, *Male Subjectivity*, 190.
40 Silverman, *Male Subjectivity*, 190–91.
41 Reik, *Masochism*, 216.

thing. [...] But in conspicuously showing something it hides something else. The existence of the demonstrative feature, in itself a puzzle, strengthens the impression of a hidden paradox in masochism."[42] With these comments, we are back in the domain of parable. But what is being hidden by what is being so conspicuously shown can only be discovered by turning to Reik's fourth factor: provocation.

The Pardoner's offer of false relics to Harry is clearly meant to deride and provoke: "I rede that oure Hoost heere shal bigynne, / For he is moost envoluped in synne. / Com forth, sire Hoost, and offre first anon, / And thou shalt kisse the relikes everychon, / Ye, for a grote! Unbokele anon thy purs" (VI (C), 941–45). Although Reik does not believe that provocation is an essential feature of masochism, he nevertheless believes that it has an important relationship to masochism. And it is certainly the case that the Pardoner attempts to provoke Harry, not just when he offers him his relics but also when he mockingly echoes Harry's oath "by Seint Ronyon," sermonizes on the moral perils of swearing, a sin of which Harry is particularly guilty, and comments on the dishonesty of vintners and taverners. As Donald Fitz points out, it would be difficult for Harry not to feel personally attacked by the Pardoner.[43] Why attack a man described by Chaucer-the-pilgrim as impressive, large, and manly, a man likely to hit back? Is not the Pardoner just begging for trouble? This, of course, gets us to the second question originally posed: why does the Pardoner single Harry Bailly out for derision at the end of his tale? The answer to this has already been hinted at in Fink's *Clinical Introduction to Lacanian Psychoanalysis*, a book on theory and technique in which he explains the hidden paradox in masochism. What the demonstrative feature hides from view is the masochist's true aim, which is not to undermine the law but to bring it into existence: "Where the father's desire (to separate his son [from his mother]) is lacking, the masochist uses his own desire to push a father substitute to legislate and exact punishment."[44] As Fink points out, this father substitute must often be "pushed to the breaking point, to a point of intense anxiety, before he explosively expresses his will in the form of commands ('Stop!' for example)."[45] The problem for the perverse subject, however, is that this moment of punishment must be repeated over and over again because the relief received when the Other pronounces the law is only temporary. Some-

---

42 Reik, *Masochism*, 83.
43 Fitz, "Reflections in a Golden Florin," 353. He, too, has commented on both the Pardoner's mockery and attack of the Host.
44 Fink, *A Clinical Introduction*, 187.
45 Fink, *A Clinical Introduction*, 187.

thing has been exacted from him through the explosion, but no genuine separation has been provided in return.

What the Host's hostile response to the Pardoner calls to mind is Slavoj Žižek's discussion, in "Grimaces of the Real," of the two father figures: the father of the symbolic and the father of the real. The father with whom the Pardoner equates the Host is the Oedipal father, the father as lawmaker or the figure of symbolic authority. As part of the symbolic, this father is always "dead," for he knows nothing about enjoyment or the pure life force that Lacan refers to as lamella. He is the ignorant Other outside of whose knowledge the subject can enjoy or *jouir*. But because the Pardoner has ejected this father out of the symbolic, replacing him with a mother who lacks nothing, the form Harry takes in response to the Pardoner's taunt is that of what Mladen Dolar describes as "the bad father, the castrator, the menacing and jealous figure that evokes the father of the primal horde, the father linked with terrible *jouissance*."[46] Instead of being duped into unbuckling his purse and buying one of the Pardoner's relics for the price of a "grote," Harry has been induced to punish the Pardoner's impudence, stating, "But, by the croys which that Seint Eleyne fond, / I wolde I hadde thy coillons in myn hond / In stide of relikes or of seintuarie. / Lat kutte hem of, I wol thee helpe hem carie; / They shul be shryned in an hogges toord!" (VI (C), 951–55). These are punishing words indeed, and yet this explosion of anger is what the Pardoner has been striving for from the start.[47]

Mother

> The masochist is saying, with all the weight of his symptoms and his fantasies:
> "Once upon a time there were three women ... ."
> —Gilles Deleuze, *Coldness and Cruelty*

Having discussed the role the father plays in masochism and the way in which Harry Bailly embodies the figure of the father in the Pardoner's performance, I would like to turn now to the role of the mother, who looms large in the

---

46 Mladen Dolar, "'I Shall Be with You on Your Wedding-Night,'" 10.

47 Susan Morrison argues in *Excrement in the Middle Ages* that "[w]e can read the Host's comment about the Pardoner's breeches being with 'fundement depeint' (VI. 950), an allusion to the underpants of St. Thomas reputed to be on display in Canterbury Cathedral, as making an analogy between the Pardoner's beshitted breeches and relics (false or otherwise). While a privy may be loathsome and foul, the relic contained in the reliquary is to be venerated," 79. What Morrison's argument seems to suggest, then, is that Harry is unwittingly venerating the Pardoner's testicles.

world of the masochist. Because she is his spectator at the decisive historical moments of discovery and subsequent disavowal, her look and its willingness to be seduced will always be a part of the perverse equation. Here, it is important to mention the question raised by Piera Aulagnier: "with what eye does the mother see her child, who looks at her?"[48] What this question points to is, perhaps, the more primary question of the scopophilic drive: "Can the mother believe that her child is looking at her innocently?" asks Clavreul. He answers by asserting that the relation between the look and the eye is one cloaked in mystery. What is certain, says Clavreul, is that the eye will occupy for the perverse subject the place that the phallus or the beloved object occupies for the neurotic or the "normal" subject:

> This eye, which did not consent to recognize itself as deceived or tricked, discovers itself and lets itself be discovered as deceiving. Is the eye there to see, to look, to *jouir*, or better yet, to seduce? It is always there that the pervert will have to employ his charms [spells]. From the side of this "seeing" that proposes itself as true, he will have to reconstitute the illusory.[49]

What Clavreul is talking about in this discussion of the relation between the eye and the look is the dialectic that exists between the rim-structure of the eye and what Lacan refers to as the gaze, one of the many manifestations of *objet a*. Because the perverse subject has been "wounded" through the eye—he sees, at some horrific moment, that there is a difference between mother and father—it will be through the eye that he protects himself from further traumatic discoveries.[50] But his eye will operate as the lure or the *fascinum*, of which Lacan speaks in *The Four Fundamental Concepts of Psycho-Analysis*, and *not* as the desiring eye. In Lacan's formula for fantasy, the split subject takes up some position in relation to the *objet a* as cause of desire: $ \$ \lozenge a $. In perversion, on the other hand, not only are the positions reversed, the perverse subject offering himself to the Other as *objet a* or the object-instrument of enjoyment, but also the rela-

---

48 Quoted in Jean Clavreul, "The Perverse Couple," 226, his emphasis.

49 Clavreul, "The Perverse Couple," 226.

50 It is important to make note of the fact that the eye, or the visual, functions in the realm of space rather than time. I draw this distinction because of what I perceive to be a similar difference between drive and desire. If the drive is seen as pure life force, or lamella, then it is like the amoeba, immortal in its ability to survive any division. This division, which occurs spatially, is a splitting of one into two, two into four, four into eight, and so on—in other words, an endless/ timeless proliferation of life. In desire, on the other hand, the temporal is foregrounded. Think, for example, of lack as the cause of desire and the signifier of lack: the phallus. What better example of the temporal do we have than that of the before and after of penile erection?

tional distance between the two collapses: a$. Because the gaze arrests movement, freezing it through fascination, it is associated with the evil eye or the *fascinum*. (Obviously, Clavreul's use of the word "charm" or "spell" in relation to the pervert is no accident. In fact, it suggests the intersection of the primitive belief in a material object invested with magical power and the perverse belief in a material object invested with phallic power.) And this arrested movement, or suspension, is exactly what the perverse subject seeks in order to keep disavowal in play. If the *fascinum* is anti-movement, the moment of seeing is its corrective. As Lacan says, it "can intervene here only as a suture [...], and it is taken up again in a dialectic, that sort of temporal progress that is called haste, thrust, forward movement [...]."[51]

One way of understanding this intervention of the moment of seeing is to return again to Harry's outraged response to the Pardoner. Perhaps Harry has been seduced or fascinated by the machinations of his "beel amy," but when the pretty Pardoner offers up a false relic—or a fetish—Harry counters with a moment of seeing and thus destroys the spell the Pardoner has cast over his audience. For the Pardoner, then, Harry is a deeply paradoxical partner in perversion while the Wife of Bath is not. But this is because there is an alliance between mother and son in the masochistic structure, the figure of the mother taking on the phallic importance usually associated with the father. Perhaps this is why in the stories of Leopold von Sacher-Masoch, the heroines all have in common certain fetishistic characteristics—they wear furs, they wield a whip, and they treat men as slaves—even though beneath this apparent uniformity, there are three distinctly different types of women: the Grecian woman or the generator of disorder, the sadistic woman, and the cold, maternal, severe woman associated with Nature.[52]

If, as I have asserted, the Pardoner perceives Harry to be the figure of the father, or the authority that must be mocked in order to get it to operate, then he perceives the Wife of Bath to be the phallic mother. Although we are never told precisely how old the Wife of Bath is, we can assume that she is far older than the Pardoner. In fact, as she herself states quite explicitly, her youth is long past:

> But—Lord Crist!—whan that it remem-
> > breth me
> Upon my yowthe, and on my jolitee,
> It tikleth me about myn herte roote.
> Unto this day it dooth myn herte boote
> That I have had my world as in my tyme.

---

51 Jacques Lacan, *The Seminar of Jacques Lacan, Book XI*, 118.
52 Deleuze, *Coldness and Cruelty*, 47–51.

But age, allas, that al wole envenyme,
Hath me biraft my beautee and my pith. (III (D), 469–75)

The apparent incongruity of the perverse couple has often been commented upon and, as Clavreul points out, it is not unusual to have an older woman coupled with a younger man or "the massive woman with an angel of femininity [...]."[53] As I have already asserted, the Wife of Bath is big. She is bright. And her hat, which is as "brood as is a bokeler or a targe," is the perfect cover for the bareheaded femininity of the Pardoner. Even in the early description Chaucer-the-pilgrim gives of the Wife of Bath, one can see emerge a rough adumbration of the Masoch heroine: her large hips and bold, fair face suggest a well-developed and muscular figure; her ten-pound kerchiefs and determination to be first at the church altar hint at a proud nature; and the sharp spurs that adorn her feet attest to an imperious will.

But it is only with her prologue and tale that we see her Masoch-heroine qualities more fully articulated. For example, the Wife of Bath's first act of speech involves superimposing her will upon Harry's authority. He has just asked the Parson to preach and has commanded the assembled group to give him their attention: "'Now! goode men,' quod oure Hoste, / 'herkeneth me; / Abydeth, for Goddes digne passioun, / For we shal han a predicacioun; / This Lollere heer wil prechen us somwhat'" (II (B¹), 1174–77). But this command holds no weight with the Wife of Bath. She breaks in, not simply to voice an objection but to change the course of events: "Nay, by my fader soule, that schal he nat!" (II (B¹), 1178). Once she has announced what is not to take place, she announces what will take place, addressing the Host directly: "And therfore, Hoost, I warne thee biforn, / My joly body schal a tale telle" (II (B¹), 1184–85). It is important to note that the Wife of Bath says her *body* will tell a tale, for through this word choice, she immediately pits the flesh against the word, the experience of the body against the authority of the text. This is, no doubt, an opposition that the Pardoner appreciates, for what is at stake in the drama of perversion is the integrity of the mother's body. Perhaps from the moment he sees the Wife of Bath swathed in voluptuous linens, he thinks of fur. And when he sees her sitting astride her mount at complete ease and in control, sharp tongue and spurs at the ready, he knows that she is his kind of woman, but it is only through her prologue and the Pardoner's interruptions that our understanding of her importance to him becomes clear.

---

53 Clavreul, "The Perverse Couple," 219.

She begins what the Friar will laughingly refer to as "a long preamble of a tale" by announcing as her subject the misery and woe of marriage. Soon after, however, she makes a rhetorical shift to an apology for the connubial relation, asking, "Why sholde men thanne speke of it vileynye?" (III (D), 34). For the Pardoner, the Wife of Bath represents the perfect partner in perversion because of her promiscuity but also because of her connection to the social order and, thus, respectability. Certainly, her character does in large part suggest the lineaments of the wayward woman, but her waywardness manifests itself *within* the bounds of patriarchy's most important institution: marriage. If the mother's look is central for the young pervert, there are two interconnected reasons for this: 1) it is willing to be seduced, and 2) it looks, or refers, to the father or the law. And therein lies its attractiveness for the masochistic subject. Clavreul confirms this, saying that "most important for the pervert is the fact that the Other be sufficiently engaged, inscribed in the social structure, notably as someone respectable, for each new experience to have the sense of a debauchery where the Other is extracted from his system in acceding to a jouissance that the pervert has mastered."[54] What Clavreul is emphasizing, here, is the fact that the perverse operates internally to the very thing it threatens.

The mother, in this case the Wife of Bath, looks two ways, or, more precisely, in two directions: toward the son and toward the father. Perhaps it would not be inaccurate to say she is the pivot point that allows perversion but prevents psychosis. No doubt, the young Pardoner's ears are pricked when the Wife of Bath cuts in on Harry, but the point at which he ejaculates (pun intended) is when the Wife of Bath begins to speak of her husband as the debtor and slave upon whose body she exacts payment:

> An housbonde I wol have—I nyl not lette—
> Which shal be bothe my dettour and my thral,
> And have his tribulacion withal
> Upon his flessh, whil that I am his wyf.
> I have the power durynge al my lyf
> Upon his propre body, and noght he. (III (D), 154–59)[55]

Before she can break into raptures over the Apostle Paul's commandment that a husband love his wife, the Pardoner says, "Now, dame, [...] by God and by Seint /

---

54 Clavreul, "The Perverse Couple," 227.

55 I am indebted to my colleague John Halbrooks for pointing out to me that in the Wife of Bath's paraphrase of Corinthians, she conveniently neglects to mention the part of the Scripture in which Paul insists on the husband's power over the wife's body. In other words, she edits the Scripture to assure her own dominance. See 1 Corinthians 11:3 for Paul's commandment.

John! / Ye been a noble prechour in this cas. / I was aboute to wedde a wyf;
allas! / What sholde I bye it on my flessh so deere? / Yet hadde I levere
wedde no wyf to-yeere!" (III (D), 164–68). On the surface, it appears that the Pardoner is objecting to the thraldom of marriage, but the truth often shows its face
in masked form. As Lacan says, the subject lies at the level of the unconscious,
and "this lying is his way of telling the truth of the matter."[56] Although the Pardoner's words lie, the place at which he interrupts the Wife of Bath tells the truth
of his masochistic fantasy.

Given who he is, it seems unlikely that the Pardoner really has had plans to
marry, but the Wife of Bath does not blow his cover as Harry or one of the other
pilgrims might. Instead, she appears to take him at his word, saying,

> Abyde! [...] my tale is nat bigonne.
> Nay, thou shalt drynken of another tonne,
> Er that I go, shal savoure wors than ale.
> And whan that I have toold thee forth my tale
> Of tribulacion in mariage,
> Of which I am expert in al myn age—
> This is to seyn, myself have been the whippe—
> Than maystow chese wheither thou wolt sippe
> Of thilke tonne that I shal abroche.
> Be war of it, er thou to ny approche;
> For I shal telle ensamples mo than ten.
> "Whoso that nyl be war by othere men,
> By hym shul othere men corrected be."
> The same wordes writeth Ptholomee;
> Rede in his Almageste, and take it there. (III (D), 169–83)

Once again the Pardoner ejaculates with praise, saying, "Dame, I wolde praye
yow, if youre wyl it / were [...] / [...] as ye bigan, / Telle forth youre tale, spareth
for no man, / And teche us yonge men of youre praktike" (III (D), 184–87). His
words to the Wife of Bath are significant in that he defers not to her authority but
to her will and seems to make a distinction between man and young men. Translated into the language of perversion, his request is this: "If it is your will, Moth-
er/Mistress, continue whipping me and do not allow father to stop you." Were
the Wife less obliging, she could respond by saying, "I know what you want,
you sick little pervert, and you're not getting it from me!" But she is, like the
mother of the perverse subject, a willing accomplice.

Engaging in a reversal of the Pardoner's disavowal, the Wife of Bath pretends not to see the tenor or drift of his sexuality although she probably guesses

---

56 Jacques Lacan, *The Seminar of Jacques Lacan, Book VII*, 73.

the truth without really knowing anything of his activities. Thus, to his request she answers, "Gladly, [...] sith it may yow like; / But yet I praye to al this compaignye, / If that I speke after my fantasye, / As taketh not agrief of that I seye, / For myn entente nys but for to pleye" (III (D), 188–92). In other words, what she says to the Pardoner is something to this effect: "I know that *you* like what I'm saying, but the others may not, and so I have to placate them with my apologies." Needless to say, she functions beautifully as the pivot point, giving the Pardoner the "fantasye" he wants while justifying it as mere "pleye" to the rest of the group. Interesting, too, is the fact that in both passages to which the Pardoner responds, the Wife of Bath structures her comments similarly. In the first passage, she mentions the husband as debtor and herself as the one who extracts the debt from his body. She then justifies this practice by referring to the authority of the Apostle Paul. In the second passage, she mentions her role as whip and then speaks of correction, backing her words again by reference to an authority, in this case that of Ptolemy's *Almageste*. What this illustrates is her ability to look in two directions: away from the law and toward it. In both cases, the Pardoner cuts in just as she turns toward it.

Having settled, if only for the moment, the question of the Wife of Bath's relation to the Pardoner—that is, her importance in the perverse performance that he enacts—I would like to turn now to the fourth question that I have posed: why do audiences—whether diegetic or extra-diegetic—respond indulgently to the Wife of Bath's confession but not to the Pardoner's? In order to answer this question, we must examine the similarities and differences between the two confessions, beginning with their placement in the Ellesmere's narrative chain. Both the Wife of Bath's tale and the Pardoner's follow on the heels of what I shall argue is a sadistic narrative. Dame Alys tells her tale just after the Man of Law has told the story of a beautiful young Christian woman, Custance, who is made to suffer heartache, loss, and separation from loved ones despite her steadfast religious faith; and the Pardoner tells his tale just after the Physician has told the story of a young virgin, Virginia, who is put to death by her father in order to protect her virginity and thus her (or, more accurately, *his*) honor. While the means by which their performances are initiated is different—the Wife of Bath overruling Harry's choice of storyteller and the Pardoner deferring to it—both tales operate as correctives or "triacle" to sadism. This in itself suggests a functional parallel between the two, but the performances themselves have a number of internal parallels, not so much on the level of content as on the level of structure.

To begin, let us examine the strategies that the Wife of Bath and the Pardoner use for getting what they want. Not surprisingly, there is very little difference between their techniques. To wit, both lie with the utmost ease and aplomb. And if both are proud of their ability to deceive their "lewed" companions, the Wife of Bath is even more so than the Pardoner, reveling as she does in her skill at pulling the wool over her husband's eyes. She even goes as far as to *equate* womanly wisdom with deceit:

> Thus shulde ye speke and bere hem wrong
> on honde,
> For half so boldely kan ther no man
> Swere and lyen, as a womman kan.
> [...]
> A wys wyf, if that she kan hir good,
> Shal beren hym on honde the cow is wood,
> And take witnesse of hir owene mayde
> Of hir assent [...]. (III (D), 226–28, 231–34)

As for the Pardoner, he says of himself, "I stonde lyk a clerk in my pulpet, / And whan the lewed peple is doun yset, / I preche so as ye han herd bifoore / And telle an hundred false japes moore" (VI (C), 391–94). What he really prides himself on, however, is the theatrical air with which he delivers these "japes": "And est and west upon the peple I bekke, / As dooth a dowve sittynge on a bern. / Myne handes and my tonge goon so yerne / That it is joye to se my bisynesse" (VI (C), 396–99). His lying, it seems, is connected in some manner to the sleight-of-hand of the magician.

Not only are their strategies of deceit similar but so is their lack of remorse at the success of their machinations. Once the Wife of Bath has her husband under her thumb, she does not appear to care at all about his well-being. As she says of her old husbands with a certain callous mirth, "[...] I laughe whan I thynke / How pitously a-nyght I made hem swynke! / And, by my fey, I tolde of it no stoor. / They had me yeven hir lond and hir tresoor; / Me neded nat do lenger diligence / To wynne hir love, or doon hem reverence" (III (D), 201–6). She continues in the same vein, asking, "But sith I hadde hem hoolly in myn hond, / And sith they hadde me yeven al hir lond, / What sholde I taken keep hem for to plese, / But it were for my profit and myn ese?" (III (D), 211–14). The Pardoner is equally callous, for once he has his congregants' money, he does not give a second thought to the state of their souls or to their destination after death:

> Of avarice and of swich cursednesse
> Is al my prechyng, for to make hem free
> To yeven hir pens, and namely unto me.
> For myn entente is nat but for to wynne,
> And nothyng for correccioun of synne.

I rekke nevere, whan that they been beryed,
Though that hir soules goon a-blakeberyed! (VI (C), 400–406)

To make matters worse, both confessors are equally prepared to shamelessly expose the hypocrisy of their actions. As the Wife of Bath admits, she was always
the guilty one and her husband the innocent, and yet she was able to lay the
blame at his feet and make him accept it as his own: "O Lord! The peyne I
dide hem and the wo, / Ful giltelees, by Goddes sweete pyne! / For as an hors
I koude byte and whyne. / I koude pleyne, and yit was in the gilt, / Or elles
often tyme hadde I been spilt" (III (D), 384–88). More specifically, she tells
her audience that she was able to cover her own amorous indiscretions by accusing her husband of infidelity: "I swoor that al my walkynge out by nyghte / Was
for t'espye wenches that he dighte. / Under that colour hadde I many a myrthe"
(III (D), 397–99). The Pardoner, too, admits hypocrisy when he says that the very
sin he preaches against from the pulpit is the very one he engages in himself.
Coupled with his hypocrisy is an arrogant belief in his ability to prevent others
from sinning while he does so himself.

Given the similarity of their strategies, their equally callous attitudes, their
lack of remorse, and their hypocrisy, how is one to explain the difference in
the audience's response to these two characters? The answer, I think, can be
found in carefully examining their confessional prologues, their tales, and the
fit between each pilgrim's prologue and tale. Returning to their prologues, we
find that both pilgrims begin by announcing the subject of their discourse—for
the Wife it is the trials and tribulations of marriage; for the Pardoner it is desire
as the root of all evil—and by suggesting what gives them the authority to speak.
For the Wife it is personal experience: "Experience though noon auctoritee /
Were in this world, is right ynogh for me / To speke of wo that is in mariage; /
For, lordynges, sith I twelve yeer was of age, / [...] / Housbondes at chirche dore I
have had fyve—" (III (D), 1–6). For the Pardoner it is his papal bulls, seals, and
licenses. Structurally, then, it appears that both begin their performances in the
same way, but the effect on the audience is quite different, perhaps in part because of the nature of each pilgrim's authority. While the Wife of Bath offers
the authority of her live flesh, the Pardoner offers the authority of the dead
word. These two types of authority suggest the traditional opposition between
presence and absence, the "full" sense of presence always being privileged
over the "empty" sense of absence. Here, I part ways with Steven F. Kruger,
who argues in his gay reading of *The Pardoner's Tale* that the Pardoner is "consistently associated with the physical," using as evidence the fact that the Pardoner draws attention to the physicality of his body in describing his preach-

ing.[57] However, the physicality to which Kruger refers is associated with the Pardoner's theatrical preaching style and not with his source of authority.

Perhaps this difference in effect can be further explained by saying that while the Wife of Bath gives a performance, the Pardoner gives a performance of a performance. If it is ever possible to arrive at the truth of something or someone, we are one step removed from it while listening to the Wife of Bath's prologue but two steps removed while listening to the Pardoner's. Although both pilgrims appear to be doing the same thing, confiding to an audience the techniques by which they dupe their adversaries, these "confessions" operate very differently. With Dame Alys, Chaucer creates the feeling that she is thinking things out as she goes along, justifying herself at times, laughing at herself on occasion, and sometimes just reminiscing. But with the Pardoner, the confession itself seems rehearsed, part of his act. In other words, his confession is the very means by which he seduces this particular audience. That is to say, he is putting his act (and by "act" I mean technique of deception) into play from the very moment he begins speaking, whereas the Wife of Bath seems to have put aside, for the moment, her act. If the Wife's confession reveals something about her—her desires, her vulnerabilities, her way of operating in the world—the Pardoner's confession conceals something about him.

Another significant difference between these two "operators" is the instrument that each employs to gain access to power. In the case of the Wife of Bath, it is her *"bele chose"* (III (D), 447). In the case of the Pardoner, it is his "male" full of relics. The "magic" that the Wife uses to her advantage is provided by her own body. As she explains,

> I wolde no lenger in the bed abyde,
> If that I felte his arm over my syde,
> Til he had maad his raunson unto me;
> Thanne wolde I suffre hym do his nycetee.
> [...]
> For wynnyng wolde I al his lust endure,
> And make me a feyned appetit;
> And yet in bacon hadde I nevere delit. (III (D), 409–12, 416–18)

The "magic" the Pardoner uses, on the other hand, can be found in the shoulderbone of a sheep. This difference in "magical" instruments accounts, in part, for the difference in the reactions they receive when their tales are said and done. If the Wife of Bath ruthlessly manipulates her husbands, at least she operates within the order of exchange, for she gives her body to the men who give her

---

57 Steven F. Kruger, "Claiming the Pardoner," 132.

their land and money. As she herself implies, servicing her old husbands was, if not entirely loathsome, at least unpleasant. And thus she gives up something of herself and her own desires in order to get the money and/or the freedom she needs to function in her world. She knows that within the western economy of exchange, there is no such thing as a free lunch. Obviously, this system of exchange is not a perfect one, but it is the system one enters when one becomes a speaking and/or desiring subject and submits oneself to the law. Because the perverse subject is not sutured into the symbolic network in the same manner by which the "normal" subject is, his place in the community and within the order of exchange will be somewhat tenuous. For the masochistic subject, any sort of exchange will occur only by means of the secret contract, and that involves a willingness to play the game (and a knowledge of what that entails) on the part of the chosen partner. Needless to say, the people who buy the Pardoner's relics are not his contractual partners. The exchange, therefore, is an empty one.[58]

Yet another significant difference between the Wife of Bath and the Pardoner is their choice of dupe. For the most part, the Wife of Bath performs her deceptions on her old and apparently wealthy husbands.[59] In patriarchal society, these men are the citizens who possess power, both economic and political. When the Wife of Bath first marries, she is little more than a child, carried to the altar at age twelve. What power does a young girl have, one might ask, except in her beauty and her "bele chose"? None. Is it any wonder, then, that she chooses to use her body to get what she needs? And is it any wonder that one can feel sympathy for a young girl in the plight the Wife of Bath describes as "mariage"? No, but it is hard to find much sympathy for the Pardoner, whose dupes are not wealthy, powerful, old men but poverty-stricken women with young mouths to feed. As the Pardoner readily admits, he will have money, wool, cheese, and wheat whether it comes from the poorest page or the village widow.

But there is more that accounts for this difference in response to the Wife of Bath and the Pardoner than their different types of authority, instrument, and

---

58 Just as a placebo can sometimes have curative or palliative effects, it may be the case that, given the intentions of those duped, they win grace despite the Pardoner's false relics, but this is somewhat beside the point. The relation of exchange between duper and duped is always an empty one.

59 In the *Miller's Tale*, we are told that John the Carpenter had not read the *Distichs of Cato*, from which we learn that men should marry their "similitude." Because Cato was considered an elementary text that every schoolboy would know, most medieval readers probably did not feel much pity for an old husband cuckolded by a young wife. In fact, they might have seen him as simply getting what he deserves.

choice of dupe. Using Lacan's distinction between the *je* and *moi*, or symbolic narrative and imaginary identification, we can move somewhat closer to understanding the difference between the Wife of Bath and the Pardoner. What I would argue is that the tale each tells reveals, on the one hand, the repressed fantasy and, on the other, the disavowed fantasy hidden beneath or screened by the conscious and/or subjective experiences of the *moi* contained in the confessional prologues. Upon examination of the Wife of Bath's prologue and tale, the consistency between the two becomes immediately apparent. The question at the heart of her prologue—what does Woman want?—is the same as the question at the heart of her tale. And in both prologue and tale, she answers the question in the same way. This is a woman who, in terms of Lacan's four discourses, has passed through the discourse of the hysteric and taken up the discourse of the analyst. That is to say, she has found a way to maneuver beyond the internal conflict between whatever identity she has assumed for herself (and tries to maintain) and her unconscious desire for a *jouissance* that is at odds with this identity. Like the "hero" Lacan speaks of in *Seminar VII*, the Wife of Bath acts authentically in conformity with her desire. She is, in both prologue and tale, the wise old "wyf" who wins a young man's heart and manages to achieve some measure of marital bliss.

The same cannot be said for the Pardoner, however. There is a gaping discrepancy between the way he characterizes himself in his prologue and the figure that represents him in his tale. He says of himself in his prologue that he "wol drynke licour of the vyne / And have a joly wenche in every toun" (VI (C), 452–53) even if he has to cheat the village widow out of her life's savings. This rather ugly portrait is not unlike the portrait he paints of the "riotoures thre" who "haunteden folye" at wild parties and the gaming tables, in brothels and in taverns. And yet it is not with the rioters that the Pardoner really identifies but with the old man whom the rioters meet upon the road in their pursuit of the false traitor "Deeth." Just as the Wife of Bath identifies with the old "wyf" at the center of her tale, the Pardoner identifies with the old man at the center of his. We know this because of what Deleuze has to say with respect to the ideal Masoch heroine: "the specific element of masochism is the oral mother, the ideal of coldness, solitude, and death, between the uterine mother and the Oedipal mother."[60] This Masoch heroine shows up in the old man's response to the proud rioter's question: "Why lyvestow so longe in so greet age?" (VI (C), 719). After replying that he has unsuccessfully searched the world over for someone

---

60 Deleuze, *Coldness and Cruelty*, 55.

who will exchange his youth for old age, the withered old man says the following:

> Ne Deeth, allas, ne wol nat han my lyf.
> Thus walke I, lyk a restelees kaityf,
> And on the ground, which is my moodres gate,
> I knokke with my staf, bothe erly and late,
> And seye, 'Leeve mooder, let me in!
> Lo, how I vanysshe, flessh and blood and skyn!
> Allas, whan shul my bones been at reste?
> Mooder, with yow wolde I chaunge my cheste
> That in my chambre longe tyme hath be,
> Ye, for an heyre clowt to wrappe me!' (VI (C), 727–36)

The old man's desire to return to the cold bosom of his "Leeve mooder" represents a desire for a return to the dyadic bond between mother and child. Until the Pardoner has given up the mother, he will not be able to assume his desire and act authentically in accordance with that desire. He will continue to wave the papal bull like a flag, preach against desire as the root of all evil, brag about wine and wenches, and sell his false relics—longing all the while to be wrapped in a burial sheet and enfolded in the cold bosom of his "Leeve mooder."

To return to the original question—why do audiences (whether diegetic or extra-diegetic) respond indulgently to the Wife of Bath's confession but not to the Pardoner's?—perhaps it would not be too far afield to answer in this way: the Wife of Bath acts ethically by not ceding her desire, while the Pardoner acts unethically by giving in to death.

The Perverse Dynamic and the Double Standard[61]

One of the most important observations Michel Foucault made in *The History of Sexuality* is that in the nineteenth century a discursive shift occurred, which allows what one does to dictate what one is. After this shift, one no longer simply engaged in homosexual acts, for example, but was now identified as a homosexual because of those acts: "the nineteenth-century homosexual became a personage, a past, a case history, and a childhood, in addition to being a type of

---

61 The argument I am making in this section is an argument I have made in a slightly different form about the way the perverse dynamic operates in Restoration sex comedies. See "Staging Perversion," 51–71.

life, a life form, and a morphology."[62] No doubt, this shift in discourse is partly responsible for our mistaken impression that perversion was an invention of the nineteenth century. Although certain sexual labels may not have existed until then, there were nevertheless certain dynamics, effects, functions, and structures in operation before Richard von Krafft-Ebing, Havelock Ellis, or Sigmund Freud began identifying and naming them. While Krafft-Ebing wrote the famous *Psychopathia Sexualis* and coined the term "masochism," he cannot be credited with the invention of masochism. And while Ellis wrote the first English medical textbook on homosexuality, he cannot be credited with the invention of homosexuality. Nor can Freud, whose *Three Essays on Sexuality* introduced the idea of the "polymorphous perversity" of children, be credited with the invention of perversion. All three men, however, have provided a discourse for analyzing and speaking about sexual behaviors that have been around for centuries.

Like any paradoxical concept, perversion is especially elusive because it slips so easily into what is often considered its opposite: the natural, right, or normal. The reason for this slippage is that when one uses the term "perversion," one generally understands it as a deviation from something, and yet perversion, in its sexological sense, was observed by Freud to be primary while "normal" sexuality was considered secondary. In fact, if perversion is defined as a deviation from the natural or instinctual, then the truly perverse is "normal" sexuality since it entails learned practices that take shape only after the erotic field of the polymorphously perverse body has been divided up into erogenous zones. What Freud does not merely imply but directly asserts is that perversion is natural, while sexual normality is artificial, and yet ironically the label of "unnatural" is always reserved for perversion.

Calling the term "perversion" a misnomer does little to lessen its uncanny effects, however, for what is most disturbing about perversion is its place of origin. According to Jonathan Dollimore, perversion creates such uncanny effects because "it originates internally to just those things it threatens."[63] Using Saint Augustine's answer to the problem of the origin of evil, Dollimore explains how what he calls the "perverse dynamic" operates:

> [...] evil not only erupts from within a divinely ordained order but, more telling still, it erupts from within the beings closest to God, *those who participate most intimately in divinity* [...]. In short, a negation/deviation erupts from *within* that which it negates (divinity) only to be then displaced onto the subordinate term of the God/man binary—and then fur-

---
62 Michel Foucault, *The History of Sexuality*, 43.
63 Jonathan Dollimore, "The Cultural Politics of Perversion: Augustine, Shakespeare, Freud, Foucault," 1.

ther displaced onto the subordinate within man (i.e., woman): *proximity is the enabling condition of a displacement which in turn marks the "same" as radically "other."*[64]

Dollimore argues that this displacement probably explains why perversion, whether "theological or sexual, is so often conceived as *at once utterly alien to and yet mysteriously inherent within* the true and the authentic."[65] This displacement also probably explains why, even in the fourteenth century, one sees evidence that the male homosocial continuum is anything but fluid or flexible and that there is a powerful investment in maintaining differences between men rather than in acknowledging the wide spectrum of experience that the category "man" encompasses.[66] Because an opposition is created *between* men rather than *within* the category itself, the Host's hostile attitude toward the Pardoner seems to be the same as the attitude a modern-day homophobic man adopts toward a gay one. As I have argued elsewhere,[67] what causes the normative subject to view the perverse subject with such revulsion is his unconscious knowledge that the perverse subject is, in fact, more "same" than "other." The fact that Chaucer-the-pilgrim refers to the Pardoner as a "geldyng or a mare" suggests that the Pardoner lacks phallic wholeness, but as Lacan has pointed out, phallic wholeness is a mere fantasy, one masking the reality of the body's brokenness by virtue of its being "zoned, fragmented, pierced, tattooed, peeled open layer by layer, armored, fitted up with prostheses, weighted down by adornments and protective gear, scarred by accident or war, ravaged by disease, withered by age, pumped up with steroids, emaciated by hunger, anorexic, bulimic—and above all, sexed."[68] Inevitably, it would seem, bodies ooze trouble for themselves because of the abiding gap between the imaginary and the real, between fantasy and reality—a gap the body of the Pardoner exhibits but one that Harry wishes to deny regarding his own.[69] As Dollimore says, "The natural/unnatural binary is only ever a differential relation; that is, a difference which is always already one of intimate though antagonistic interdependence. What is constructed as absolutely other is in fact inextricably related."[70] Here, in a nutshell, is the

---

64 Dollimore, "The Cultural Politics," 5, his emphasis.
65 Dollimore, "The Cultural Politics," 4, his emphasis.
66 I am indebted to Eve Kosofsky Sedgwick, here, for her discussion of the male homosocial continuum in *Between Men: English Literature and Male Homosocial Desire*.
67 See "Staging Perversion," 58–60.
68 Joan Copjec, "Montage of the Drives," 12.
69 See my "Gothicizing Apotemnophilia," 145.
70 Dollimore, "The Cultural Politics," 8.

shattering truth of the perverse dynamic, a truth that the dominant ideology seeks to keep repressed at all costs.

One might say that the inadequacy of language and the uncanny nature of perversion work together to vex discussion of this slippery concept, and yet it may be possible to understand more clearly what Dollimore has identified as a paradox if we think of how the term "perversion" is used or fails to be used in certain situations. Take, for example, a fetishist such as Manley Pointer, the young Bible salesman in Flannery O'Connor's short story "Good Country People." Not only is he fascinated by Hulga's artificial leg, but also he wishes to see how she takes it off and puts it on, the story culminating in his theft of the leg. What is implied by the sexually charged scene in which the leg theft takes place is that Manley Pointer is fixated on prosthetics in the way another man might be fixated on a woman's breasts. Although both men mistake a part for the whole, only Manley Pointer will be considered abnormal, perverse, or sick—words often used interchangeably.

Dominant ideology in the heterosexual realm, the realm considered the norm in Western culture, forces women to function as fetish objects or props that support the illusion that men are in possession of the phallus and thus lack nothing. In psychoanalytic discourse, the phallus is distinguished from the penis, which is simply one metaphor among many for the phallus. The phallus is understood as a key signifier (albeit a repressed one), which stands for completeness, unity, wholeness, and immortality—in short, everything the human subject is not. According to Jonathan Scott Lee, "[A] woman's role in man's fantasy life is simply that of being the *objet a* that makes up for the man's castration by language, his lack of the omnipotent phallus. Thus, man's sexual desire is ultimately narcissistic [...], and the object(s) of his desire are precisely those imaginarily detached body parts, those *objets a*—breasts, buttocks, mouths—that trigger his desire and his masturbatory *jouissance*."[71] When fetishism is used to support the status quo of power relations operating in the heterosexual domain, it is seen as perfectly normal. In fact, it is rarely identified as a perversion when it operates in the procreative, heterosexual realm.

Obviously, the contradictions and paradoxes inherent in the West's dominant ideology are not new ones, for one sees the subtle but powerful machinery of the perverse dynamic operating in and around the Pardoner. While it is true that contemporary labels such as "fag," "fairy," or "perv" are absent from *The Canterbury Tales*, we nevertheless register the effects of such name-calling when Chaucer-the-pilgrim comments at length on the Pardoner's hair, ending

---

71 Jonathan Scott Lee, *Jacques Lacan*, 179.

his commentary with the rather snide remark, "Hym thought he rood al of the newe jet; / Dischevelee, save his cappe, he rood al bare" (I (A), 682–83). In a world in which the scopophilic gaze belongs to men, the Pardoner is on the wrong side of the viewing "screen," exhibiting himself as a spectacle, a role traditionally assigned to women. "In their traditional exhibitionist role," as Laura Mulvey points out, "women are simultaneously looked at and displayed, with their appearance coded for strong visual and erotic impact so that they can be said to connote *to-be-looked-at-ness*."[72] The dominant ideology in patriarchal society insists upon a division of labor between active male gaze and passive female image, an ideology that makes men loathe to look at their "exhibitionist like."[73] No doubt it is as much the Pardoner's exhibitionism as his "glarynge eyen," his small voice, and his beardlessness that causes Chaucer-the-pilgrim to conclude that he is a gelding or a mare. And, thus, not only do we see the double standard applied when normative and perverse subjects engage in fetishizing —the former's fetishizing gesture registered as sexually acceptable and the latter's as sexually *unacceptable*—but also we see two kinds of fetishization resulting in very different effects: fetishization of the female body and fetishization of the male. Just as a double standard applies to men whose fetish objects differ, so, too, does a double standard apply when the body being fetishized is male.

Although Robert Sturges argues that the Pardoner's portrait is the most fragmented of all the pilgrims' portraits, "the one who most fully embodies [the] threat of physical dissolution and fragmentation,"[74] each pilgrim's portrait is fragmented to one degree or another, for each portrait dismembers its subject's "organic whole." In other words, the Pardoner is not the only pilgrim treated to dismemberment, but because of his ambiguous sexuality, his dismemberment will be understood differently from that of the other pilgrims. Take, for example, the portrait of the Prioress. As I argued in Chapter 1, there is a fetishizing gesture on the part of Chaucer-the-pilgrim in his description of the Prioress. The question he seems to be trying to answer through his description of her is "What makes the Prioress so attractive?" In attempting to answer this question, he reduces her to a list of fetishized pieces: "Ful semyly hir wympul pynched was, / Hir nose tretys, hir eyen greye as glas, / Hir mouth ful small, and thereto softe and reed. / But sikerly she hadde a fair forheed; / It was almost a spanne brood, I trowe; / For, hardily, she was nat undergrowe" (I (A), 151–56). "Where is the *objet a*, object-cause of desire?" he might be said to ask. "Is it in her wimple?

---

72 Laura Mulvey, "Visual Pleasure and Narrative Cinema," 11, her emphasis.
73 Mulvey, "Visual Pleasure," 12.
74 Robert Sturges, *Chaucer's Pardoner and Gender Theory*, 123–24.

Her well-formed nose? Her grey eyes? Her small mouth? Her broad forehead?" It is impossible to say where it is, for the *objet a* always eludes signification, and yet it is precisely these "imaginarily detached body parts" that give rise to male desire.

The portrait of the Prioress shares many similarities with that of the Pardoner, but it also betrays significant differences that point toward contradiction or double standard. The fetishizing gesture directed at the Prioress triggers desire, while the fetishizing gesture directed at the Pardoner functions as an inside joke at the Pardoner's expense, inciting further ridicule of and contempt for him. As Sturges points out, "We are not allowed an overall impression of the Pardoner's body [...] but experience it in disconnected bits and pieces."[75] Given the particular set of similarities and differences between the two portraits, we can argue that cutting up the female body is considered normal in that there is a shared understanding of what a female body is: something already lacking, castrated, or mutilated because it does not have a penis. Cutting up the male body, however, is an act of aggression meant to threaten or, worse still, punish a masculine body that is supposed to be non-lacking, un-castrated, and un-mutilated but that fails to pull off the illusion of full-blown phallic power. Both portraits might be said to fall under the rubric of the perverse, but one glorifies while the other punishes. In drawing a distinction between these two fetishizing gestures, I am making use of what Mulvey has said about the defense mechanisms of a male spectator confronted with the spectacle of the castrated (female) body.[76] He defends himself against the horror of castration either by glorifying the female body to such a degree that it is seen to lack nothing and be everything or by punishing the female body for the pain it has caused him. Because of the fact that the Pardoner is compared to a gelding or a mare, he represents the same kind of horrifying spectacle as the castrated female body, but because he is a man rather than a beautiful woman, the defensive gesture on the part of the viewer will be a punishing rather than a glorifying one. In calling the Pardoner his "beel amy" when he asks him to speak, Harry has, at least momentarily, brought the male homosocial continuum into view, but the vehemence of antagonism Harry levels at the Pardoner upon being asked to kiss his relics is Harry's attempt to reassert its invisibility.

---

75 Sturges, *Chaucer's Pardoner*, 124.
76 Mulvey, "Visual Pleasure," 13–14.

Of Parables and Pardons

> And as Jesus passed forth from thence, he saw a man, named Matthew, sitting at the receipt of custom: and he saith unto him, Follow me. And he arose, and followed him. And it came to pass, as Jesus sat at meat in the house, behold, many publicans and sinners came and sat down with him and his disciples. And when the Pharisees saw it, they said unto his disciples, Why eateth your Master with publicans and sinners? But when Jesus heard that, he said unto them, They that be whole need not a physician, but they that are sick. But go ye and learn what that meaneth, I will have mercy, and not sacrifice: for I am not come to call the righteous, but sinners to repentance.
> —Matthew 9:9 – 13

> So the servants of the householder came and said unto him, Sir, didst not thou sow good seed in thy field? from whence then hath it tares? He said unto them, An enemy hath done this. The servants said unto him, Wilt thou then that we go and gather them up? But he said, Nay; lest while ye gather up the tares, ye root up also the wheat with them. Let both grow together until the harvest: and in the time of harvest I will say to the reapers, Gather ye together first the tares, and bind them in bundles to burn them: but gather the wheat into my barn.
> —Matthew 13:27 – 30

Written nearly five centuries after *The Canterbury Tales*, Nathaniel Hawthorne's story of "The Minister's Black Veil" provides a key for understanding why the Pardoner's perverse performance should be read as religious parable. "The Minister's Black Veil," explicitly labeled a parable by Hawthorne, tells the story of Reverend Hooper, a puritan minister who startles his congregation by appearing one Sunday morning with a black veil covering his face. Despite the obvious uneasiness the veil creates in his congregation, Reverend Hooper gives no explanation for his having donned it. Instead, he preaches a sermon on the subject of secret sin, and thus the congregation is led to wonder whether their minister has sinned in some egregious (probably sexual) way. Before the day is over, speculation and rumor begin to circulate around the minister's relationship with one of his female parishioners, and because he refuses to disclose the reason he is wearing the veil, the congregation comes to believe the worst of him. This does not make him a failure as a minister, however. As the narrator tells us, Reverend Hooper becomes very efficient with the aid of his black veil: "[...] he became a man of awful power, over souls that were in agony for sin. His converts always regarded him with a dread peculiar to themselves, affirming, though but figuratively, that, before he brought them to celestial light, they had been with him behind the black veil."[77] Even on his deathbed, Reverend Hooper refuses

---

77 Nathaniel Hawthorne, *Selected Tales and Sketches*, 196.

to remove the veil although he removes some of its mystery, if only for the reader, with his final comments to those gathered around his bedside: "when man does not vainly shrink from the eye of his Creator, loathsomely treasuring up the secret of his sin; then deem me a monster, for the symbol beneath which I have lived, and die! I look around me, and, lo! On every visage a Black Veil!"[78] Might not the Pardoner be able to say the same to his fellow pilgrims?

What Hawthorne's parable touches on is an issue that was being widely debated at the time Chaucer was writing *The Canterbury Tales*: hypocrisy. In the 1390s, fierce antagonism had arisen between the orthodox establishment and the Lollards over several questions, one of which was whether the "spiritual ministrations performed by a corrupt man had any validity."[79] The orthodox position was espoused by Saint Augustine in the fifth century when he argued that "ordination confers a supra-human authority on any duly appointed clergyman, which keeps his sacraments safe and secure, despite any human fallibilities he may have."[80] The Lollards, on the other hand, hovered dangerously close to Donatism, a heretical belief that if a priest lives in mortal sin, he cannot properly perform the church sacraments or minister to the members of his congregation. Like any two religious groups in hostile opposition, each accused the other of hypocrisy and thus of heresy, and so it is no surprise that by 1401, Henry IV had passed a statute giving bishops the authority to arrest, question, and imprison those thought to be Lollards as well as to hand them over to the secular authorities for burning at the stake. As a reasonable man, Chaucer must have seen merit in both the orthodox and the Wycliffite positions, and thus it must have pained him to see the debate degenerate into such serious name-calling, for accusations of heresy were no laughing matter.

Although some scholars have viewed both the Pardoner and his tale as perversions of Christ's message and mystery,[81] the argument I am making runs counter to this view. If we recall the story of Matthew, the publican who was called by Jesus to follow him, we might begin to see what use Chaucer is putting the Pardoner to, for there are a number of parallels between publican and pardoner. During the time of Christ, publicans were just as reviled by the Jews as pardoners were by their medieval counterparts. As Merrill C. Tenney notes, publicans were notorious for their rapine and extortion, the means by which they

---

78 Hawthorne, *Selected Tales and Sketches*, 199.

79 Stephen L. Wailes, *Medieval Allegories of Jesus' Parables*, 14.

80 Minnis, *Fallible Authors*, 20.

81 See, for example, Clarence H. Miller and Roberta Bux Bosse, "Chaucer's Pardoner and the Mass," 171.

oppressed the populace while enriching themselves.[82] It was the publican's job to "collect the customs or taxes levied upon export-import goods," and to make matters worse, in Galilee, publicans with Roman citizenship were themselves exempted from paying the taxes they imposed on others.[83] Another practice that made publicans objects of contempt was their habit of advancing "money to those unable to pay, thus converting the tax into a private debt, upon which an usurious interest was exacted."[84] In fact, as Alan D. Campbell asserts, "[t]he Jews had such utter contempt for the publicans that money known to have come from them was not accepted at the synagogue or temple. It is apparent that few publicans would have had a chance to hear Christ's synagogue discourses."[85] And yet Jesus called Matthew, one of the despised *publicani*, to become a disciple. As Jesus sensibly pointed out to the Pharisees, "They that be whole need not a physician, but they that are sick."

Is it mere coincidence that just as Harry smells a Lollard in the wind, the Wife of Bath makes reference to the Parable of the Tares, told only in the gospel of Matthew? "'He schal no gospel glosen here ne teche. / We leven alle in the grete God,' quod she; / 'He wolde sowen som difficulte, / Or springen cokkel in our clene corn'" (II, 1180 – 83).[86] Like many of Jesus's parables, which often turn expectations upside down, the Parable of the Tares shows Jesus responding to evil in an unexpected way. According to Jerome's reading of the parable, which was prevalent during the Middle Ages, Satan has cultivated heresy in the church during a moment in which its leaders have slumbered, but instead of urging the faithful to root out the evil tares, Jesus commands them to allow the tares to grow among the wheat until harvest, at which time both will be dealt with appropriately. Jerome and Pseudo-Augustine give three reasons for Jesus's surprising command: "First, the delay creates a time for penance, in which some weeds may be changed to wheat [...]. Second, delay is necessary because it is extremely hard for men to tell the wheat from the tares and so judgment should be reserved to the Lord to avoid risk of injury to the innocent [...]. Third, delay is desirable because evil contributes to good [...]."[87] The fourth-century church father John Chrysostom offers yet another reason, an interdiction

---

82 Merrill C. Tenney, ed., *The Zondervan Pictorial Bible Dictionary*, 598.
83 Alan D. Campbell, "The Monetary System, Taxation, and Publicans in the Time of Christ," 133 – 34.
84 A. Hausrath, *A History of the New Testament Times*, 188.
85 Campbell, "The Monetary System, Taxation, and Publicans in the Time of Christ," 134.
86 Here I follow John H. Fisher in assigning the words uttered in the epilogue of the *Man of Law's Tale* to the Wife of Bath rather than to the Shipman.
87 Stephen Wailes, *Medieval Allegories*, 106.

against war and bloodshed, saying, "Nor is it right to kill the heretic, for thus one creates irreconcilable conflict [...]."[88] Like Chrysostom, Bishop Wazo of Liège (ca. A.D. 985–1048) took a tolerant approach to heresy, quoting the Parable of the Tares in a letter to Roger, Bishop of Châlons, and arguing that "the church should let dissent grow with orthodoxy until the Lord comes to separate and judge them."[89]

Given what the Pardoner says in his prologue, it seems at first glance that he represents the orthodox position, for he says, "Thus kan I preche agayn that same vice / Which that I use, and that is avarice. / But though myself be gilty in that synne, / Yet kan I maken oother folk to twynne / From avarice and soore to repente" (VI (C), 427–31). And yet the picture one gets of the Pardoner as he preaches to the "lewed peple" is not unlike that of the Lollard as depicted in anti-Lollard art, for the Lollard minister is often represented as a fox luring geese sitting on misericords closer and closer until the fox is able to get its hands on one of them. And thus it is not at all clear which side of the debate, if either, the Pardoner is meant to represent. Orthodox or Lollard, "geldyng" or mare? Because Chaucer has intentionally cloaked him in ambiguity from head to toe, what does seem clear is that Chaucer is making parabolic use of him. As was pointed out in Chapter 1, J. Allan Mitchell calls the parable "provocative rather than directly persuasive because it challenges an audience to think through the terms of comparison being made rather than to apply it immediately in action without reflection."[90] Although the Pardoner does not veil his face as Hawthorne's Reverend Hooper does, he is said to wear on his cap a "vernycle," a small reproduction of the veil Saint Veronica offered Christ to wipe his face as he bore the cross to Golgotha, and to carry a piece of Mary's veil in his bag. Like Jesus's use of the parable, the figure of the veil was commonly used in the Middle Ages to both conceal and reveal.[91] Characterizing medieval poetry as an "allegorical habit of mind in the service of Christian truth," D. W. Robertson, Jr., argues that inconsistencies and contradictions disappear if we assume that an author—in this case, Chaucer—"had in mind a series of higher meanings seen in the light of wisdom [...]."[92] In fact, Stephen Wailes argues that much medieval poetry can appear incoherent if not looked at from the vantage point of allegory or parable.[93] (One might recall Scottish Chaucerian Robert Henryson's treatment

---

88 Quoted in Wailes, *Medieval Allegories*, 106.
89 Jeffrey Burton Russell, *Dissent and Order in the Middle Ages*, 23.
90 J. Allan Mitchell, "Chaucer's 'Clerk's Tale' and the Question of Ethical Monstrosity," 4.
91 Sturges, *Chaucer's Pardoner*, 65.
92 D. W. Robertson, "The Doctrine of Charity in Mediaeval Literary Gardens," 46.
93 Wailes, *Medieval Allegories*, 24.

of the myth of Orpheus and Eurydice as an example. In his *moralitas*, he refers allegorically to Eurydice's would-be rapist as good virtue![94]) Given the difficulty modern scholars have had in making sense of the Pardoner's performance, it seems fruitful to view it through this particular lens. For even more bewildering than the Prioress's hysterical performance is the Pardoner's perverse performance, and this bewilderment has been amply (and aptly) demonstrated by the mound of arguments that scholars have produced regarding the Pardoner's moral and sexual identities.

Writing in the early 1900s, for example, George Lyman Kittredge refers to the Pardoner as the most "abandoned" pilgrim, the "one lost soul" among those headed to Canterbury.[95] By the mid-1960s, however, Edmund Reiss can be found arguing that the Pardoner is Christ-like, "shown being persecuted because he contains within himself all the sins of the world and specifically all the sins in his fellow Pilgrims."[96] Reiss further interprets Harry Bailly's wish to castrate the Pardoner as a representation of crucifixion. Less than twenty years later, however, Martin Stevens and Kathleen Falvey depict the Pardoner as "a kind of Antichrist," seeing in his tale the ingredients of a black mass.[97] And while Nevill Coghill argues that the Pardoner is "a monster of hypocrisy,"[98] Charles Mitchell argues otherwise. He is a con man, admits Mitchell, but not a hypocrite, for hypocrites generally attempt to conceal their evil from others as well as from themselves, and this the Pardoner does not do.[99] As for the Pardoner's sexual identity, Walter Clyde Curry was the first to pin a label on him when, in 1919, he argued that the Pardoner is a *eunuchus ex nativitate*, that is, a man born without testicles.[100] Since then the floodgates have opened, and a myriad of diagnoses from the most complex to the least has poured in. Eric Stockton, for example, refers to the Pardoner as a "manic depressive with traces of anal eroticism, and a pervert with a tendency toward alcoholism,"[101] while Beryl Rowland has labeled him a

---

94 See Robert Henryson, "Orpheus and Eurydice," lines 435–36: "Arestius, this herd that cowth persew / Euridices, is nocht bot gud vertew."
95 George Lyman Kittredge, *Chaucer and His Poetry*, 180.
96 Edmund Reiss, "The Final Irony of the Pardoner's Tale," 266.
97 Martin Stevens and Kathleen Falvey, "Substance, Accident, and Transformations," 155.
98 Nevill Coghill, *The Poet Chaucer*, 160.
99 Charles Mitchell, "The Moral Superiority of Chaucer's Pardoner," 441.
100 Walter Clyde Curry, "Chaucer's Reeve and Miller," 189. The introduction of the Pardoner as eunuch brings to mind the early Christian theologian Origen of Alexandria, who castrated himself in order to devote himself more fully to God and to his religious activities. What is notable for my purposes is the fact that he told and interpreted the Parable of the Tares and that Jerome's Latin translations of Origen's homilies were widely read in Europe throughout the Middle Ages.
101 Eric W. Stockton, "The Deadliest Sin in *The Pardoner's Tale*," 47.

"testicular pseudo-hermaphrodite of the feminine type."[102] In the highly influential "The Pardoner's Homosexuality and How It Matters," Monica E. McAlpine makes a powerful case for the Pardoner's homosexuality,[103] and in his short story "Philostorgy, Now Obscure," Allen Barnett refers to the Pardoner as the "first angry homosexual, [...] the first camp sensibility in English literature."[104] Richard Green, on the other hand, makes a compelling argument for the Pardoner's being a womanizer, a patron of brothel and alehouse.[105] And C. David Benson reminds us in "Chaucer's Pardoner: His Sexuality and Modern Critics" that "effeminacy in the Middle Ages [...] does not necessarily mean homosexuality but also the reverse—too great a concern with women."[106] In short, there is little agreement about who or what the Pardoner is. With so little agreement, we are compelled to admit that the jury is still out on the Pardoner. Clearly, as Jerome and Pseudo-Augustine have argued, it is extremely hard for any of us—other than the Lord—to tell the wheat from the tares.

What all of these speculations regarding the Pardoner's sexuality suggest is that while scholars are deeply divided about one thing, they work in utter accord about another, behaving like children under the influence of the scopophilic drive, desiring, in short, to see the Pardoner's genitals and to satisfy their voyeuristic curiosity about his bodily functions. Of course, Chaucer-the-pilgrim's statement "I trowe he were a geldyng or a mare" (I (A), 691) is largely responsible for setting these speculations in motion. Everyone who has attempted to tackle the question of either the Pardoner's morality or his sexuality has been forced to grapple with this deceptively simple statement, and while each of the words in this statement has been thoroughly worked over, interpreted and re-interpreted, the motives of the pilgrim who utters the statement have seldom been commented upon. Bruce W. Holsinger is one notable exception when he argues that this statement is the *"real* 'symptom' here, a nervously phobic and distancing acknowledgment of widespread medieval anxieties about same-sex polyphonic singing."[107] Might Chaucer-the-pilgrim's statement about the Pardoner be a case of projection? Much has been made of the Pardoner's "glarynge eyen," which are compared to those of a hare; and the hare, as John Boswell has demonstrated, is "associated consistently in medieval writings with homosexual ac-

102 Beryl Rowland, "Animal Imagery and the Pardoner's Abnormalities," 58.
103 Monica E. McAlpine, "The Pardoner's Homosexuality and How It Matters," 8–22.
104 Allen Barnett, *The Body and Its Dangers,* 47.
105 Richard Green, "The Sexual Normality of Chaucer," 351–59.
106 C. David Benson, "Chaucer's Pardoner: His Sexuality and Modern Critics," 342.
107 Bruce W. Holsinger, *Music, Body, and Desire in Medieval Culture,* 177, his emphasis.

tivity, particularly anal intercourse."[108] But what of "the murye words of the Hoost" to Chaucer-the-pilgrim, "Thou lookest as thou woldest fynde an hare, / For evere upon the ground I se thee stare" (VII, 696–97)? Which, if either, more strongly suggests homosexuality: being compared to a hare or being said to be in search of one? Surely, it is a toss-up. And if the Pardoner is described in effeminate terms, so, too, is Chaucer-the-pilgrim, for Harry Bailly compares him to "a popet," and just as Harry metaphorically castrates the Pardoner when he offers to cut off his "coillons" and enshrine them in a hog's turd, he metaphorically castrates Chaucer-the-pilgrim when he cuts off his "Tale of Sir Thopas," saying, "Thy drasty rymyng is nat worth a toord!" (VII, 930). Harry's scatological hostility toward these two pilgrims points, moreover, toward his own problematic relationship to normative masculinity, for his castrating gestures can be read as a defense against unconscious identification with these "castrated" men, emasculated as he is by his own wife on a daily basis. As he tells the Monk, his wife browbeats him from daybreak to nightfall, calling him a "milksop, or a coward ape" (VII, 1910) and suggesting that he and she trade places, she taking his "knyf" and he taking her "distaff" to "go spynne!" (VII, 1907).[109] The hostility and hypocrisy of one emasculated man attempting to emasculate another through name-calling finds its mirror image in the Lollard and anti-Lollard debate with its name-calling and brutality. As Derek Brewer writes of an event at Oxford,

> In the Lollard controversies, one of the disputants on the orthodox [anti-Lollard] side (which was not popular in the university) lost his nerve when he saw, or thought he saw, that twelve of his listeners held weapons concealed under their robes. He believed that death was threatening him unless he got down from the chair in which, according to custom, he was maintaining in public his argument.[110]

Like the Puritans who followed in Wyclif's wake, these Oxford students seem unable or unwilling to accept the idea of intelligent and nonviolent controversy.

Given that the word "Lollard" may have been derived from the Latin word *lolium*, which means "cockle, tares, or darnel,"[111] it seems reasonable to argue

---

108 John Boswell, *Christianity, Social Tolerance, and Homosexuality*, 137n1.

109 Donald Fitz notes, too, that the Host and the Pardoner have the threat of castration in common. See "Reflections in a Golden Florin," 352.

110 Derek Brewer, *Chaucer in His Time*, 140.

111 Terry Jones et al., *Who Murdered Chaucer?*, 222. Although some scholars have argued that the word "Lollard" derives from the Dutch word "lollaert" or "mumbler (of prayers)," Jones and his fellow scholars argue that "the 'lolium' deriviation [sic] seems more consistent with fourteenth-century perceptions of the word," 379n75.

that Chaucer uses the Pardoner to agitate for religious as well as sexual tolerance, for the hypocritical, heretical, and sexual were often bound up together,
especially during the time Chaucer would have been writing *The Canterbury
Tales*. In fact, in Alan J. Fletcher's discussion of the Lollard and anti-Lollard debate, he notes that "aberrant sexual behavior was a standard accusation in heresy charges."[112] While Chaucer has created what many consider a vicious man in
the character of the Pardoner, he makes use of him for a higher meaning as seen
through the wisdom of the Parable of the Tares. Thus, the parabolic message is
not to be found in the "moral thyng" the Pardoner tells but in the role he plays in
the "moral thyng" Chaucer writes. In other words, Chaucer functions toward
those who read *The Canterbury Tales* as Jesus functions toward those who
read his parables. The Pardoner is Chaucer's publican, for what man is more
in need of pardoning than the Pardoner himself? Instead of seeing the Pardoner
as either monstrous or moral, the better alternative is to see something instructive in Chaucer's use of the monstrous *as* moral.[113]

---

112 Alan J. Fletcher, "The Topical Hypocrisy of Chaucer's Pardoner," 120.
113 I am indebted to J. Allan Mitchell's comments on "ethical monstrosity" in the *Clerk's Tale*
for my concluding statements. See his "Chaucer's 'Clerk's Tale' and the Question of Ethical Monstrosity," 17.

Chapter 4
Confessing Animals

> The most defenseless tenderness and the bloodiest of
> powers have a similar need of confession.
> Western man has become a confessing animal.
> —Michel Foucault, *The History of Sexuality*

Door Number Three

One Christmas Eve when I was around ten or eleven, my sister Bonny asked my parents whether we might open one gift that night to whet our appetite for Christmas morning's ritual feast of gifts. They consented, but things got out of control, and we wound up opening *all* of the gifts that were piled under the Christmas tree. When I woke up on Christmas morning—that most joyous day of the year!—I felt like an alcoholic who had fallen off the wagon and gone on a bender. I felt hungover and hangdog. That was a memorable Christmas but not one I can recall without a sense of moral queasiness. I suspect that my parents knew very well what they were doing when they allowed us to sabotage our usual Christmas morning ritual. I suspect that they were teaching us something about the value of self-restraint such as the time my mother allowed me to eat an entire six-pack of Milky Way candy bars in order to illustrate why that kind of self-indulgence is not such a great idea. Losing my virginity just weeks before setting off for college, where I planned to and did, in fact, meet my future husband, created in me that same sense of moral queasiness (magnified times ten), a moral queasiness that not only infected the entirety of my undergraduate days but also continued to cast a somber shadow over my love life for many years to come.[1]

Perhaps if I had not attended a small liberal arts college affiliated with the Mennonite church, I might not have felt like such a moral reprobate for having arrived on campus no longer a *virgo intacta*. But as it was, I felt as if I wore emblazoned upon my forehead the scarlet letter "U" for unchaste. And to make mat-

---

[1] This moral queasiness can also be understood as a particular form of disgust. As William Ian Miller points out in *The Anatomy of Disgust*, there are two main types of disgust: the first creates barriers to unconscious desire, and the second is the result of a conscious desire: "The first is felt before imbibing and works to prevent it; the second is felt after imbibing and works to prevent further indulgence," 119. Clearly, the moral queasiness I felt was of the second type.

https://doi.org/10.1515/9781501514104-006

ters worse, the Mennonite community turned out to be far more insular regarding its Anabaptist identity than I had anticipated, and so at every turn, I was marked as "other." Knowing full well that I was Presbyterian, a faculty member's wife said to me, "I'm a Mennonite first and a Christian second." Her comment stung like a slap, and my face continued to burn for the next four years. Less violent but perhaps more insidious was a social activity called the "Mennonite game" in which two Mennonites meeting for the first time attempted to establish their kinship relations. The game functioned as a kind of icebreaker, and while it was as useful to a Mennonite as walking a Yorkipoo in a public park, it was as useful to me as a hole in the head, trepanation notwithstanding. Being both a non-virgin and a non-Mennonite, I was doubly other and thus doubly alienated from my fellow co-eds, and every year I vowed to transfer. Instead of doing so, however, I returned to campus every fall, foolishly hoping that my ideal, and thus my imaginary, Mennonite was not a mere fantasy.

Why did I idealize the Mennonites? The answer to this question is complicated, but it explains two things: why being treated as other was so painful and why I chose to stick it out amongst the Mennonites nevertheless. Having been born in 1959 and seeing footage of the Vietnam War as well as my parents' reactions to it, I internalized my parents' respect for traditional peace churches and organizations such as the Pax Program, created by the Mennonites as an alternative to serving in the military. As a fourth grader living on the Yoder Road, named by the Amish who settled there in 1927, I created along with my sister Bonny the Tree House Peace Club. After school we would climb into our tree house, taking our after-school snacks with us, and sing Joan Baez songs. I was eleven when the Kent State shootings occurred. The Mennonite as ego ideal worked at the level of the symbolic, but perhaps what was more powerful still was the Mennonite as object-cause of desire. The year our family lived in the Midwest with Mennonites and Quakers as our next-door neighbors, I became enamored of *The Rifleman*, a western that featured the handsome Chuck Connors as Lucas McCain and the young heartthrob Johnny Crawford as his son, Mark. It may be the case that despite McCain's rifle, he and his son became inextricably linked with Mennonite men as objects of desire. This is pure speculation, however, for the object-cause of desire operates at the level of the unconscious, and yet it would explain why the unpleasure of being other was overridden by something I could not have identified at the time and that would only become visible later with the help of psychoanalysis and its practice of free association.

When I met Philip my senior year and we fell in love, I thought my decision to stay had been vindicated and that I might gain entry into the coveted Mennonite community, after all. We dated for three months, at the end of which we declared ourselves so much in love that it was time for the "confessional." I do not know if this phenomenon still exists, but in those days it was apropos of serious dating or engagement. According to the ritual, the couple agreed to confess to each other all previous sexual activities and encounters to make sure there were no ugly surprises lurking in dark corners. The confessional functioned as a kind of sexual résumé, but in the case of a young, unmarried woman, the less prior experience for the "job," the better.

Philip went first. Being a devout Mennonite as well as the son of a minister, his list was relatively short. Then it was my turn. As I began to reel off my list of "indiscretions," I felt a sudden chill descend upon the room. Before I was finished, Philip had leapt off the bed and grabbed my tennis racquet, which was standing in the corner.

"I don't want to hear anymore!" he said, swinging the racquet through the air as if to swat away my unwanted words.

Is he going to hit me? I wondered, too stunned by his reaction to speak. But, no, the Mennonite church is a traditional peace church and its members devoted to nonviolence. In fact, as a child, Philip had received a set of army men as a party favor, and, seeing Philip playing with them, his father had gathered them up, taken them into his study, and cut off all of their weapons with his pocketknife. In doing so, however, he had also cut off their hands and arms. Upon returning the miniature soldiers with amputated limbs, he had said to Philip, "*Now* you can play with them." Once they had been "castrated," however, they were no longer of interest to Philip. They were ruined, and he no longer wanted to play with them.

"I don't want to see you anymore," Philip said at last, throwing the racquet onto the bed in a gesture of disgust. What he was reacting to may not have been merely the content of the confessional but the southern voice in which it had been delivered. As Mladen Dolar has pointed out, the operation through which the signifier uses the voice as its vehicle for sense making creates a remainder that cannot be made sense of. It is a "a leftover, a cast-off—shall we say an excrement of the signifier?"[2] Someone with an accent such as mine makes the interlocutor aware of the materiality of the voice and thus of its excremental dimension. In the confessional monologue, my voice brought home to Philip the fact that the voice deprives one of distance and autonomy and that the voice that was invading his ear, just as a fart invades the nose, was that of the exotic other: southerner, non-Mennonite, non-virgin, and "castrated" woman. Like the little amputated army men, I was ruined, and he no longer wanted to play with me.

---

2 Mladen Dolar, *A Voice and Nothing More*, 20.

Although the Pardoner obviously means to provoke Harry with his offer of false relics, I had no conscious intention of provoking Philip with my offer of what might be called sexual relics.[3] And yet my words had the same impact on Philip that the Pardoner's had on Harry. My words to Philip, like the Pardoner's to Harry, were an affront to his sense of his own morality and masculinity. More importantly, however, my words, like the Pardoner's, suggested to my interlocutor that he was a sucker, beguiled by a pretty face, a "beel amy," into trusting that what I had to offer was "triacle," not treachery. And thus if I had begun my confessional as the Wife of Bath, I ended it as the Pardoner, a disenchanted Philip no doubt wishing to have my ovaries enshrined in a hog's turd. Like an obsessional neurotic, I can recall the event, but I cannot recall how I felt in the days that followed. This is, of course, a perfect example of repression, event and affect having come untethered from each other. I can only surmise that Philip's disgusted rejection of me must have triggered the same sense of shame I had felt in the aftermath of Mrs. Gorham's reprimand. Although there was no worthy knight to step in and ask us to kiss and make up, eventually Philip did ask to resume our relationship. The question, of course, is why. William Ian Miller supplies a good answer when he says of disgust that it "must always repel in some sense or it is not disgust. Repulsion, however, might bring in its train affects that work to move one closer again to what one just backed away from. These affects could range from curiosity, to fascination, to a desire to mingle."[4] As an exotic other, I was indeed a curiosity, and it was Philip's fascination, his desire to mingle with otherness, that led him back to me with a request to which I should have answered, "No," thereby saving us three rocky years of courtship, eight years of an almost sexless marriage, a painful divorce, and, many years later, an annulment.[5]

Not long after we had resumed our relationship, we were reclining on his bed in the aftermath of having played tennis.

"Hey, I heard a funny joke the other day," said Philip.

"Oh, I love jokes. Tell it!" I urged, unaware that this was an ambush. It was a surprisingly crude joke coming as it did from Philip, but it was also extremely funny, and so I laughed. Sitting up very abruptly, he said, "Why are you laugh-

---

3 On the other hand, I have often thought that there is an element of something other than contrition or regret when one confesses one's sexual "misconduct" to one's partner. It is a way of shifting one's own pain (say, of guilt) to the other's shoulders, and thus it is ultimately a selfish act masquerading as a generous and honest one.

4 Miller, *The Anatomy of Disgust*, 111.

5 Many years after our divorce, Philip left the Mennonite church and became a practicing Catholic.

ing?" to which I replied, "Well, if you think about what that looks like, it's pretty funny."

"How do you know what 'that' looks like?" he asked, leaping off the bed and grabbing his tennis racquet. If the release of *Groundhog Day* had not been twelve years in the future, I would say that this moment resembled nothing if not a scene from it, for Philip began wildly swinging his tennis racquet as if to ward off knowledge of my carnal knowledge. I should have said, "If you had let me finish my confessional, you would know how I know what 'that' looks like," and washed my hands of this relationship once and for all, but instead I allowed myself to be ushered out of his room and told yet again that he did not want to see me anymore. When he asked a second time to resume the relationship, he put a set of rules in place that I would have to abide by, most of which involved censorship but one of which involved disavowal. As if we were living during what Foucault has identified as the seventeenth century's age of repression regarding sexual discourse, there was now to be a screening out of certain words, a policing of certain types of statements and affective responses (in short, no laughing at lewd jokes or merriment over ribald comments; in fact, no recognition of knowledge regarding the content of lewd jokes or ribald comments), and a "control over enunciations as well: where and when it was not possible to talk about such things became much more strictly defined; in which circumstances, among which speakers, and within which social relationships."[6] What this meant was that I had to be vigilant about censoring myself, both in my own enunciations and in my responses to those of others. Spontaneity became a thing of the past as I was forced to keep myself in check and under surveillance at all times. In fact, I grew so self-conscious that, at times, I was positively aphasiac. Much later, a friend who had observed the pervasive effects of Philip's superegoic stringency would say to me, "You're like a big dog on a short leash."

According to Foucault, the confession is "a ritual that unfolds within a power relationship, for one does not confess without the presence (or virtual presence) of a partner who is not simply the interlocutor but the authority who requires the confession, prescribes and appreciates it, and intervenes in order to judge, punish, forgive, console, and reconcile [...]."[7] Even more importantly, however, he argues that the "one who listened was not simply the forgiving master, the judge who condemned or acquitted; *he was the master of truth.*

---

6 Michel Foucault, *The History of Sexuality*, 18.

7 Foucault, *The History*, 62.

His was a *hermeneutic* function."[8] The one who listened to the confession had the power not only to "decide what was to follow after it, but also to constitute a discourse of truth on the basis of its decipherment."[9] I have no doubt that Philip interpreted my acknowledgment of previous sexual activities and encounters as an avowal of a set of truthful facts. But as the celebrated nineteenth-century biologist and geologist Louis Agassiz once said, "Facts are stupid things until brought into connection with some general law."[10] In this case, the general law that had to be brought into connection with the facts was a moral law, and Philip as the listening subject was the one with the power to bring it to bear. Having interpreted my sexual history as immoral and thus me as in need of reprimand and reformation, he decreed that I should have to pay penance by refraining from sex for the next three years. The fact that he was willing to sacrifice his own sexual needs in order to help me pay penance should have given me pause, but at the time I saw it as a courageous and loving gesture on his part.

This three-year abstention was not merely a way to pay penance for my lack of chastity, however; it was also a way to reclaim my virginity. At least, that is how Philip saw it. For me, it was merely a symbolic gesture—like the eating of broken saltine crackers and the drinking of grape juice on communion Sundays—but for Philip it more closely resembled transubstantiation. Just as the bread and wine consumed during the sacrament of the Eucharist *really became* the body and blood of Jesus Christ for those who held to the doctrine of transubstantiation, so, too, was my lost maidenhead *really to be* restored. This, it seems to me, was a form of disavowal on Philip's part, a form of disavowal that I was willing to submit to while knowing full well that it was a form of disavowal. But why? Jean Clavreul might say that as the pervert's partner, I pretended to be doing nothing other than submitting to Philip's disavowal because of something I called "love."[11] Because of this pretense, however, Clavreul would see me as "even more in question" than Philip himself, for the relationship between the one engaged in disavowal and the object of his disavowal is sustained only when this disavowal "has the power to fascinate the other."[12] The word "fascinate," here, should be understood in the sense of "captation." Although Lacan did not coin the term, he adopted it for use in 1948, and for him it suggests not merely being captivated by one's image but, more darkly, being held captive

---

8 Foucault, *The History*, 67, my emphasis.

9 Foucault, *The History*, 67.

10 Samuel Scudder, "Learning to See," 664.

11 Jean Clavreul, "The Perverse Couple," 218.

12 Clavreul, "The Perverse Couple," 218.

by the power of the image—the image in this case was that of Philip as (ego) ideal Mennonite. Never had I pleased my parents as much as I did the day I told them we were engaged. But to *what* were we engaged? Exotic other and Mennonite church, a way out and a way in.

Three years later, I had become one of the young women of whom Freud speaks in his critique of "civilized" sexual morality. Here, we find Freud arguing against complete abstinence before marriage, noting that the "injurious effects" of such a regime are "particularly apparent where women are concerned."[13] The point he makes is well grounded in common sense. If one tells a girl for three— or, worse yet, eighteen or twenty-one or twenty-five—years of her life that sex is bad and then sends her down the church aisle saying it is now good, one is bound to run into resistance, for as Freud points out, "when the girl is suddenly allowed by parental authority to fall in love, she cannot accomplish this mental operation and enters the state of marriage uncertain of her own feelings."[14] In my case, the picture Freud paints is not entirely accurate, for on my wedding night, it was not parental authority but Philip's that said it was now okay to "fall in love," Freud's euphemistic way of saying to "feel sexual desire," and I was not in the least uncertain of my feelings. After three years of having lived in the same house and slept in the same bed with a man with whom I had never made love, I knew very well that I was entering into marriage completely averse to having sex with my husband. And thus my wedding night was not spent in the throes of passion but in a welter of mortification in both the secular sense of humiliation and the Christian sense of "putting one's sin to death." The reward for submitting to a "civilized" morality that preaches abstinence is, as Freud points out, a choice between one of three evils: unappeased desire, infidelity, or neurosis. For better or worse, I "chose" door number three.

Supercaving

I had my first panic attack in the fall of 1986, two years after Philip and I married and a mere two weeks after we had arrived in the People's Republic of China to teach English at an agricultural university in rural Sichuan Province. We had traveled to China under the auspices of the Mennonite Central Committee's China Educational Exchange Program and had been placed in the mountainous village of Ya'an, located approximately eighty-five miles southwest of Chengdu,

---

13 Sigmund Freud, "'Civilized' Sexual Morality and Modern Nervousness," 24.
14 Freud, "'Civilized' Sexual Morality," 25.

Sichuan's capital. At that time, Ya'an was considered a village even though its population was well over 100,000. (Now, it has a population of one and a half million.) Philip and I were the only resident "big noses" or "foreign devils" as the Chinese used to, and perhaps occasionally still do, refer to white Westerners, and Ya'an was still a "closed" area, which meant, among other things, that we were not allowed to visit the homes of anyone living outside the university's compound. I had done some world traveling before landing in China and had even lived in Africa as a child, but no place had ever seemed as foreign to me as this country did. Before I went to China, the "inscrutable Chinese" had been a mere cliché, but after arrival it became a disconcerting reality because of my inability to get an immediate handle on my surroundings and to identify with the people who occupied them.[15] Although I did not realize it at the time, the opportunity to live in China allowed me to overcome, at least in part, the narcissism and over-identification that accompanies familiarity and sameness, and that was an important developmental moment for me. It was the moment in which I became an adult.

The most enigmatic and thus anxiety-provoking person in my new landscape was Ma Wen, the director of the university's Foreign Affairs Department. She functioned as what might now be called our "handler," for she was responsible for conveying all of the upper administration's communiqués to us as well as for making sure we understood the "dos and don'ts" of our position as foreigners in a closed area. Although she was a woman of small stature with slender, brown hands and a face that would have radiated beauty had she found more occasion to smile, I would be giving a very wrong impression of her if one were to assume that by "small" I mean "weak." Ma Wen was a powerful woman, and engaging her in conversation, however banal or benign at a surface level, was like playing an intricate game of chess with a very skilled opponent.

Back in the States, I was known as a pretty good communicator, but with Ma Wen, I felt bereft of all the tools one needs for reliable communication, and so when she issued an invitation to a faculty party, Philip and I read the invitation—delivered not by paper but by word of mouth—very differently from each other. (Ambiguity is one of the characteristics of the inscrutable.) I thought the invitation was a casual one and that attendance was optional. Philip thought it was an official one and that attendance was mandatory. In hindsight, I realize that his interpretation was probably the correct one, but at the time, I thought

---

15 Although any cliché can be insulting because of its stereotyping banality, calling the Chinese people "inscrutable" is not an insult. In fact, it suggests that Chinese culture is complex and not easily understood—and thus not easily assimilated, appropriated, and/or dismissed.

otherwise. Having been subjected to the curious gaze of our fellow villagers and shouts of "Waìguórén!" or "Dà bízi!" every time we set foot out of our apartment, I was weary of being a spectacle and did not want to go to the party. A social gathering such as a party is supposed to be fun, I argued, and if one is forced to attend against one's wishes, then it is no longer fun and its purpose has been undermined. Philip argued that sometimes one has to do things one does not feel like doing when decorum calls for it and that he was certain we would ruffle the feathers of a number of administrators if we failed to attend the party. The argument started as a tropical storm but quickly turned into a hurricane.

"Why did you even come here?" Philip asked bitterly. "Why don't you just go back to the States?"

I do not recall how I answered those questions, but I can still hear him in my mind's ear saying with terrible finality, "Don't talk to me. I don't want to hear anything more from you." An uncanny sense of repetition suffused the air, and that silencing tennis racquet of yore swam into view. Feeling truly alone for the first time since our arrival, I suddenly realized how much I had been relying on Philip for companionship and emotional support 7,500 miles from home in a village with no other foreigners and only a handful of people who could speak passable English. I also suddenly realized just what an ordeal it would be to go home. These were the days before the Internet and cell phones had made quick communication and travel easy, and thus if one wants to get a sense of just how cut off I felt at Philip's moment of dismissal, I can only compare it to what the young Ukrainian caver Emil Vash encountered after joining the expedition to find the deepest cave on earth. Rappelling down the yawning pits of Krubera Cave, one of which was 500 feet deep, and wiggling through excruciatingly tight passages called "meanders," Vash finally made it to the camp at 1,400 meters below the surface only to find that in order to descend to the next camp at 1,840 meters, he would be forced to traverse a short but hazardous tunnel flooded with water. According to James M. Tabor, author of *Blind Descent*, this particular tunnel "was just short enough that scuba equipment was not *absolutely* essential. But it *was* long and tight enough to stretch a breath-hold dive to its extreme limits."[16] Although the tunnel was only ten feet long, it was just eighteen inches wide, and "its walls were rough and spiked with protrusions that could easily snag a caver."[17] As Tabor notes, "It would not take long to drown in those conditions. [Vash] would do well to be able to hold his breath

16 James M. Tabor, *Blind Descent*, 236, his emphasis.
17 Tabor, *Blind Descent*, 238.

for sixty seconds in water that cold. Throw in the added factors of oxygen-devouring panic and wild attempts to extricate oneself, and the probable time before drowning dropped considerably."[18] To get a rough sense of just how deep Vash was, one has only to imagine three Empire State Buildings stacked on top of each other, and to get a rough sense of just how claustrophobic a cave's passages can be, one has only to read Tabor's description of the Sinusoida Meander as "a series of cramped, narrow, winding passages that, on a map, look like the nasal passages of a giant with a badly deviated septum."[19]

So there I was, feeling, for all intents and purposes, as if I were in a giant's nasal passage 1,400 meters below the earth's surface with a supercaving buddy who had just told me to get lost and then swum away into the narrow entrance of the tunnel. What happened next is, again, best explained in terms of a supercaving phenomenon known as "the Rapture." No doubt, many have heard of the scuba diver's "rapture of the deep," another name for nitrogen narcosis, which is a feeling of euphoria that comes over a diver at depths below one hundred feet. The supercaver's rapture, however, creates the opposite of euphoria. It is an extremely unpleasant reaction to darkness and depth, described by those who have suffered it as akin to a panic attack on meth. According to Tabor, the amount of darkness and depth that we can tolerate differs from one person to the next, but when one's limit is reached,

> a switch clicks in the brain and that individual is gripped by "the Rapture." It manifests as the biggest panic attack ever. [You] need to get out; and [you] need to get out NOW. No time for safety precautions. No consideration for the lives of your colleagues. It's fight and flight in overdrive. It's uncontrollable and [you] have to leave NOW! This, naturally, is a bit of a problem, when you are a week's arduous journey from the surface and there's no way back without a lot of skill and self-control.[20]

The problem with this type of panic is that, even if it is brought on by something external, it is experienced internally, and thus one cannot be rescued from its clutches by anyone other than oneself. One is buried alive in one's own head, and, just as one cannot be air lifted out of a supercave, one cannot be air lifted out of one's head.

Obviously, I was not reacting to the darkness and depth of a supercave but to something dark that had lain buried deep in our relationship until our arrival in China: the traumatic effects of the confessional, a shattering event that produced

---

18 Tabor, *Blind Descent*, 238.
19 Tabor, *Blind Descent*, 235.
20 See http://endlesscancun.blogspot.com/2011/01/cheve-caving-equivalent-of-climbing.html.

its full impact years later. This is an example of Freud's concept of latency vis-à-vis what he refers to as traumatic neurosis. According to Freud, the factor of surprise or fright—"the name we give to the state a person gets into when he has run into danger without being prepared for it"[21]—is one of the central causes of ordinary traumatic neuroses, but because the event cannot be made sense of at the time it occurs, its effects are delayed and manifested in forms not obviously associated with the event. In other words, the memory of a traumatic event can be regained in symptomatic form when triggered by a similar event. The symptomatic form in my case was that of a panic attack, and, like the compulsion to repeat, the initial panic attack was not an isolated event but the beginning of a general siege. If we had not gone to China, it might have taken longer for the symptoms to emerge so blatantly, but because we were in a place as foreign and as difficult to navigate as a supercave, we were ill prepared to cope with the yawning pits, tight meanders, and flooded tunnels of our relationship. We were ill prepared for a pilgrimage into the psyche.

Siren Call

Perhaps one can imagine the scene: I am a young woman lying on a twin-sized bed on the fifteenth floor of a tourist hotel overlooking the Pearl River in Guangzhou, China's third-largest city. It is the summer of 1987, and I am reading Doris Lessing's *The Summer Before the Dark*, a novel in which a woman named Kate is coping with the prospect of being alone. Kate's children have grown up, and her husband is involved in business that has taken him far away from home. In the absence of her family, Kate is forced to confront what she sees as the threat of annihilation. Given how suggestible hysterics are, this is not good summertime reading for me as I am lying on the bed overlooking the Pearl River, for fall is fast approaching and with it, perhaps, the dark. Although I am only twenty-eight and have no children, I am identifying far too heavily with Kate. *Wasn't there another Kate, an American Kate, who drowned herself to escape her plight? No, I confuse Kate with Edna.* In fact, with each turn of the page, I grow more and more uneasy. My husband has gone out to tour the city, and I do not know when he will return. I do not feel lonely without him but abruptly and inexplicably afraid. (As Freud so rightly states, what makes this kind of fear so traumatic is that it arrives without warning.) I do not desire my husband's company, only the company of someone—anyone at all would do—to take my mind off the pos-

---

21 Sigmund Freud, *Beyond the Pleasure Principle*, 6.

sibility of annihilation, by which Lessing and I mean the disintegration of the self. This potentially disintegrating self might be reflected in the large picture window that looks out onto the Pearl River were I standing rather than lying on the bed, but because my visage has become uncanny, I have begun to avoid confronting it in or on reflective surfaces. The window, however, is not merely a reflective surface, it is a wall (far too thin and fragile a wall) protecting me from falling into and drowning in China's third-longest river, which has the second-largest volume of water of China's three biggest rivers: the Yangtze, the Yellow, and the Pearl. Thinking of all that water and what is in it—fresh-water eels, for example—is enough to make me tremble. Even the word "volume" has a kind of weight and gravity that sits heavily on my heart.

I read another page of Lessing's novel, and although I attempt to read with concentration, an unwanted and thoroughly revolting thought crowds in. *What if a live eel—?* (Even hysterics can have obsessive thoughts and often do.) *What if a live eel—?* My heart rate increases, and my palms begin to sweat. I glance away from the novel to look at the window, its clear pane suddenly striking me as menacing rather than protective. *I don't want to see what's down below*, I think to myself. I do not want to see that muddy Canton river-water in which swims the *san yu*. (Better to say it in Mandarin than in English.) Should I draw the drapes? I would, perhaps, if I could, but there are no drapes to draw. The window is unadorned like much of Maoist China. Mao and the Anglo-American Puritans would have made good bedfellows with their proclivity for the austere. I read another page and feel my throat and lungs constrict in the way that signals panic and thus difficulty breathing. The window now has invisible sirens hunkering down on its sill, sirens that sing voluptuously, "Come to the window." But as the woman lying on the bed overlooking the Pearl River, I know that answering their call involves sure and utter destruction. If I were to approach the window, I know what the sirens would sing next: "Jump!" Losing myself in the pages of the book is no remedy for what frightens me because losing myself is exactly what I am afraid of. *I don't want to jump there are sure to be eels*, I say to myself, one thought stepping on the (h)eels of the other, but I (f)eel the pull, the ineluctable pull, and so I drop Lessing's novel and, extending both arms outward as if I am making a snow angel on the white sheets, clutch the sides of the bed. I am holding on for dear life, praying that the water and the *san yu* will go away. *What if a live eel—?* My heart pounds, and it feels as heavy as a brick. My pulses racing, my body sweating, and my head's contents sliding sideways as if on board a capsizing ship, I know with certainty that if I stay on this bed in this room, I will crash through the window and fall into the river down below, and then the question of the live eel will no longer be hypothetical. Although I could not have articulated it then, what I shall later understand is that this "will to death" is the function of the drive, that thing (for lack of a better word) that makes us act against our own self-interest. In holding onto the bed, I am fighting *against* the drive and *for* desire. But the bed is not strong enough to hold me. (It may be that the bed itself wants to expel me for not doing in the bed what I am supposed to do as a wife. Unlike the Wife of Bath, I am not a "normal" woman, nor have I been able to find ingenious ways to cope with the patriarchal order of exchange.) If I stay where I am, the window will pull and the bed will push, forcing me to jump into the muddy Canton river-water below. "The window will pull, and the bed will push" becomes a catchy little tune that nearly seduces me, but then I have an inspiration: I shall go into the bathroom, which has no window or bed, take my pants off, and sit on the toilet. *There's no way I'm going out the window with my pants down.* I shall wait there until my husband returns, and then the window, the bed, the river down below, and the *san yu* will no longer threaten me. Funny how shame regarding the body can save me even in moments of what seem like insanity. My impulse, as it turns out, is a good one because my husband returns before I have sat very long on the toilet, and with his return the window loses its sinister aspect and the sirens fall silent. I am safe, at least for the moment, but I am forced to ask, *When did I become afraid of myself?*[22]

The southwestern city of Chongqing serves as the economic center of the upstream Yangtze basin, a major manufacturing center and transportation hub. Among the ex-pat community of the 1980s, however, it has a very bad reputation because of its pollution. It is like a pressure cooker, a city with a lid on it. Every day is overcast, and every night is starless because of the layer of smog cloaking the skies. I know of the city's reputation before my husband and I travel there, but passing through the city is unavoidable. We spend the day in Chongqing, and although I am on edge, I have been able to hold it together until we return to the train station. (Like the Swede from Stephen Crane's "The Blue Hotel," I am anticipating the worst and, in anticipating it, giving rise to it.) Now, it is dusk, which is, in some respects, a meaningless concept since the gloom of the city makes every moment of the day seem like dusk. The train station is packed

---

22 Apparently, I am not alone in this hysterical impulse to throw myself out of a window. The hysteric Alice James, sister of William and Henry James, wrote the following in her diary: "As I used to sit immovable reading in the *library* with waves of violent inclination suddenly invading my muscles, taking some one of their myriad forms such as throwing myself out of the window, or knocking off the head of the benignant pater as he sat with his silver locks, writing at his table, it used to seem to me that the only difference between me and the insane was that I had not only all the horrors and suffering of insanity but the duties of doctor, nurse, and strait-jacket imposed upon me, too." See Claire Kahane's *Passions of the Voice*, 39.

with people, more crowded than any place I have yet encountered in the world's most populated country. Travelers are lying, sitting, and standing, occupying every inch of space in the train station's vast "parking lot" of flesh. As late as 1985, China produced a total of only 5,200 cars. Moving through the station, it is next to impossible to avoid stepping on someone's hand, tripping over luggage, or jostling up against someone. And then the lights go out. A power outage extinguishes every light in the station, and all I can see is the ashy-orange glow at the tip of a thousand Tianma cigarettes. Because of the outage, the trains will be delayed. Because of the outage, my husband and I shall have to ride in third class, which means that he will stand in the aisle with the men, while I shall sit on something akin to a hard wooden church pew with the women and children. But that is hardly the problem. That is hardly the worst of it. The real difficulty is managing the time between now and the train's departure because the panic is quickly rising. I feel buried alive—back in the bowels of Krubera Cave—hemmed in by the people, the cigarette smoke, the inky darkness, and the sheer chaos of the train station. Babies are crying, chickens are clucking and shitting, and people are shouting at one another as they are wont to do in a place where it is difficult to make oneself heard. "I can't breathe," I say to my husband, my entire body beginning to shake in the way it does when the panic takes hold. He tries hard to reassure me, but he does not know, cannot know, the horror I feel. As Elaine Scarry has pointed out, one of the most devastating aspects of physical pain is its isolating effect. Pain is often difficult, if not impossible, to articulate, and thus a person in pain can rarely, if ever, communicate the experience of that pain to someone else.[23] Pain alienates. The same thing can be said of emotional and/or psychical pain. It has the same isolating, alienating effect as physical pain. It cuts one off from those around one, and it even cuts one off from oneself. Despite this fact, I try to tamp the horror down by thinking rationally about the situation, but there is no way to reason or think my way out of this. The part of my psyche that signals danger has already sent its message out to the body, and thus my body is in full reaction(ary) mode.

"Let's go to the tourist hotel and have a drink," suggests my husband. "There will be light there and space for you to breathe."

As we walk into the hotel lobby, I see a stout, middle-aged woman moving toward the bar. The stout, middle-aged woman is elegantly dressed, and she is speaking German. I know German; it is not a tonal language. Its syllables do not slip up and down and sideways. The sounds of "ich" or "dich" do not make my teeth rattle and my head buzz like the Mandarin sounds of "r," "c,"

---

23 Elaine Scarry, *The Body in Pain*, 4–11.

and "z." I think to myself, *If it gets really bad, I'll fling myself at her feet and hold onto her legs. I'll become a small child clinging to its mother. She will pick me up, and I'll be safe.* And I am not joking. This is a real thought, a real remedy in case I slide too close to the edge.

Chapter 5
Before There Was Sade, There Was Chaucer: Sadistic Sensibility in the Tales of the Man of Law, the Clerk, and the Physician

> Nietzsche stated the essentially religious problem of the meaning of pain
> and gave it the only fitting answer: if pain and suffering have any meaning,
> it must be that they are enjoyable to someone.
> —Gilles Deleuze, *Coldness and Cruelty*

> [I]f the Chinese man mutilates the woman's foot *and* reveres it,
> it is the foot that wears the mark of this division, not the Chinese man.
> —Joan Copjec, "The Sartorial Superego"

Nietzsche's statement has led Deleuze to argue that if pain and suffering are enjoyable to someone, we are left with three possibilities as to who that someone might be: the normal answer is the God or gods who direct our lives; the perverse answer is either the person doling out the pain or the person receiving it. For Deleuze, "the normal answer is the most fantastic, the most psychotic of the three."[1] And yet this seems to be the answer provided by each of the men who tell tales in which women are both mutilated *and* revered just as the female foot was in the Chinese practice of foot binding.[2] The coupling of mutilation and reverence immediately suggests the perverse mechanism of disavowal: "I know very well that I'm mutilating you, but nevertheless I revere you." If foot binding seems to be a far cry from anything that occurs in *The Canterbury Tales*, however, allow me to bring it closer by recalling to mind Saint Augustine's etymology of the word "religion," which is derived from *ligare* (to bind),[3] and by asserting that the metaphorical "feet" in question, here, are Custance, Griselda, and Virginia, three Chaucer heroines who are, if not literally mutilated, abused as well as revered by patriarchy's representatives—emperor, marquis, and knight but also lawyer, clerk, and physician—who rule church, state, family, and even the human body. The men who tell their tales represent in turn law, theology, and medicine or what Kant refers to as the higher faculties, the word "higher" in this case meaning closer to power. According to Kant, the foundation for these higher faculties are "statutes" or certain types of written documents such as the law, the

---

1 Gilles Deleuze, *Coldness and Cruelty*, 118.
2 For example, if we read the *Clerk's Tale* as allegory, we see Walter as God and Griselda as Job. See D. W. Robertson, Jr., *A Preface to Chaucer*.
3 See Sarah F. Hoyt's "The Etymology of Religion," 126.

https://doi.org/10.1515/9781501514104-007

Bible, and medical regulations, each of which originates not in reason but in the arbitrariness of a superior power or external legislator. These higher faculties are the support for what Louis Althusser will later call Ideological State Apparatuses (or ISAs), and while Ideological State Apparatuses are different from Repressive State Apparatuses (or RSAs) such as governments, courts, police, and armed forces, they are bound up with each other through the violence that both give rise to.[4] And thus it seems appropriate to briefly recount the events that led to Thomas à Becket's murder in 1170, for the violence of his death set in motion a steady stream of pilgrims and penitents to Canterbury Cathedral.

According to Harold J. Berman, the interpenetration of legal and religious thought that had manifested itself by the time Chaucer was writing had taken on a new form in the eleventh century with the onset of what he calls the Papal Revolution. Berman gives it the name of "revolution" because the reforms that Pope Gregory VII proposed suggested a radical new vision: "one single universal government patterned after the government of the world by God and attempting, so far as possible, to realize that government on earth."[5] One of the important concepts of this radical new vision was that of "right order,"[6] whereby the so-called higher organs would rule the lower. This concept was based on certain suppositions about the nature of the universe that can be articulated as follows: because the heavens are higher than the earth and thus rule events on earth, the same should be the case in the world of human affairs. God is higher than man, and some men, because of their God-given qualities or God-appointed offices, are higher than others. All men are higher than women because women lack the God-given reason that men possess. But in the great chain of being, women are set above the lower orders of creation—the beasts of the animal kingdom, for example—because even with the little reason women possess, they have more than a mere beast does. What the reformers, led by Pope Gregory VII, hoped to do was to transfer this idea of right order into the political and legal realms. The pope, then, would be the head of this single universal government, the church beneath him, and beneath the church the legal authorities. At the bottom of this hierarchy was the smallest governing unit, that of the household with husband or father as its head.

---

4 See Louis Althusser, *Lenin and Philosophy and Other Essays*, 85–126.

5 See Patricia J. Eberle, "Crime and Justice in the Middle Ages," 23.

6 It is, I think, important to point out that Pope Gregory VII did not see his vision as "new" or particularly "radical." The reforms he had introduced were not, in his view, novelties or inventions but simply a return to the teachings of the holy founding fathers. His claim was that a number of wicked practices had sprung up in the church over the past centuries and that by recovering the practices of primitive Christianity, he was adhering to the true tradition of the church.

Unfortunately for the reformers, not everyone was happy with this new vision, particularly not the present emperor, Henry IV, who did not like the idea of giving up control of the church.[7] Needless to say, conflict ensued. Although the reformers did succeed in undermining the moral authority of secular government, saying that royal power was not of divine origin and thus in certain circumstances need not be obeyed, the fight over control of the church continued into the next century. In England, for example, Henry II continued to assert his royal supremacy over the church, appointing his friend Thomas à Becket archbishop of Canterbury in an attempt to consolidate his position. As we all know, he failed to achieve the hoped-for result when Becket denounced the Constitutions of Clarendon as an illegal usurpation of powers rightly belonging to the church. During the next six years, the conflict continued until Becket was murdered. Even his martyrdom did not bring an end to the conflict, however. For over the next two centuries, the ideal for which Becket became a martyr— one system of law based on a hierarchy with God at the top and the individual household at the bottom—came to co-exist with a number of practical applications. That is to say, the legal system became more and more complex, with the secular and ecclesiastical courts often duplicating each other as well as coming into conflict. But, as Berman argues, the one long-lasting outcome of the Papal Revolution was the notion of "reforming the world by means of law, law reorganized and rewritten where and when necessary but based on a consistent and coherent ideal of justice and bearing within itself the principles of its own further growth."[8]

This is a very brief sketch of the events that led to Becket's martyrdom, but it is ample enough to remind us of the way in which Canterbury Cathedral came to be the site of medieval pilgrimages. All who go to Canterbury follow in the footsteps of the repentant Henry II, who was forced to walk barefoot to the cathedral and to retract the portions of the Constitutions of Clarendon that offended the church. It is hard to know with what view of the law or with what degree of genuine religious piety each of Chaucer's pilgrims travels toward Canterbury, but

---

7 As R. H. C. Davis points out, the imperialists did not try to "erect a theory of the supremacy of the 'State' against the 'Church.' The reason for this was that, in the eleventh century, the Church was regarded as being far more than the spiritual power. It denoted the body of Christ, or whole community of Christendom, of which the Papacy and the Empire were but the two executive arms. Consequently, the quarrel between Gregory VII and Henry IV was considered not as a struggle between two independent institutions but as a schism in the Church, and the aim of the pamphleteers was merely to demonstrate that this schism had been caused by the opposing party." See *A Medieval History of Europe*, 247.

8 See Eberle, "Crime and Justice in the Middle Ages," 24.

there is a certain irony in the fact that the three representatives of the higher faculties make the pilgrimage under the authority of a lowly tavern-keeper, brushing shoulders and, in one case, even sparring with the outspoken Wife of Bath along the way. This is hardly a manifestation of the rule of right order.

It was this irony that gave rise to a series of questions, many of which seemed difficult to answer until I began using sadism as the lens through which to view them: what is each teller's relationship to law, knowledge, and power? Or, better yet, what does each teller *perceive* his relationship to be? And what is his attitude toward the tale he tells? Does he identify with any of its characters? If so, which one(s)? For instance, does the Clerk identify with the cruel marquis or the cruelly tortured Griselda? For whom are these tales told and to what end? Are they directed at a particular pilgrim such as the Wife of Bath, who defies right order at every turn? Or is the aggressivity that is displayed in the tales displaced? That is to say, would these tellers prefer to torture Harry, the upstart tavern-keeper? And is "torture" the appropriate word? Although there is a great deal of cruelty in the tales told by the Man of Law, the Clerk, and the Physician, does that alone make these pilgrims sadists, and, if so, are the male characters in their tales sadists as well? If so, what does that make their female counterparts?

These are the questions I hope to answer in the pages that lie ahead, but I feel compelled to say something about the complexity involved in doing so. Like masochism, named after the nineteenth-century Austrian novelist Leopold von Sacher-Masoch, sadism was named after the eighteenth-century French novelist the Marquis de Sade. But unlike Sacher-Masoch's novels, which received little attention until the publication of Deleuze's *Coldness and Cruelty*, Sade's novels have received a great deal of attention from a number of different readers.[9] Each of these readers has provided us with a unique take on Sade, but sometimes one reader's take comes into conflict with another's. And therein lies part of the challenge in attempting to use sadism as a homogeneous concept. Another part of the challenge lies in distinguishing literary sadism from clinical, for the two are not necessarily identical. Perhaps the easiest way to mark the difference is to remind ourselves, as Bruce Fink advises us, not to "confuse conscious fantasies with concrete activity"[10]—or, for that matter, not to confuse conscious with *un*conscious fantasy.

---

9 The following list represents only a fraction of the many who have been drawn to write about Sade: Surrealists such as André Breton, Guillaume Apollinaire, and Paul Éluard, postwar French literary figures such as Georges Bataille, Maurice Blanchot, and Pierre Klossowski, and theorists such as Jacques Lacan, Michel Foucault, Roland Barthes, and Philippe Sollers.
10 Bruce Fink, *A Clinical Introduction to Lacanian Psychoanalysis*, 180.

As I have already pointed out, the category of perversion has many sub-categories, all of which operate differently from one another. However, there is obviously some overlap among the perversions, for each is a manifestation of what Lacan has identified as the perverse structure. Based on Lacan's work and that of clinicians such as Clavreul and Fink, we can identify certain common features shared by fetishism, masochism, and sadism, the most important of which is the perverse subject's relationship to Oedipal law. Whereas in psychosis the law is fully absent and in neurosis fully present, in perversion the law is neither fully absent nor fully present, and thus the perverse subject's unconscious aim is to bring the law into existence in order to put the brakes on the onslaught of *jouissance*. The perverse subject presents what appears to be a paradox, however, for in his attempts to make the lawgiving Other appear, he looks like a "no-holds-barred, jouissance-seeking" machine.[11] What makes the sadist even more peculiar than the masochist or the fetishist—and thus easier to misdiagnose—is the fact that in making "the Other lay down, stipulate, [or] mandate" the law, "the sadist himself plays the role of Other and victim simultaneously."[12] No doubt, this peculiarity accounts for the emergence of Krafft-Ebing's faulty concept of "sadomasochism."

Given the challenges of writing about sadism, the argument I intend to make in this chapter is somewhat different from the one I made in the chapter on masochism. In that chapter, I argued that the Pardoner is a masochist and that everything about him from his pouch full of relics to his provocation of Harry Bailly supports that diagnosis. In this chapter, however, I am less interested in arguing that the Man of Law, the Clerk, or the Physician is a sadist than I am in arguing that a sadistic sensibility informs each of their tales, thus accounting for the general bemusement that has suffused their reception. Taken all together, these three tales flesh out the portrait of the sadist, each tale giving us a slightly different perspective from which to view him.

---

11 Fink, *A Clinical Introduction*, 180.
12 Fink, *A Clinical Introduction*, 192.

The Fat Lady Against the "Holwe" Men

> "True libertines" observed Sade, "believe that sensations
> communicated through the auricular organs are the most acute."
> —Georges Bataille, *Literature and Evil*

As Morton Bloomfield commented in his discussion of the *Man of Law's Tale* in a 1972 issue of the *PMLA*, there are several tales—among which are the Man of Law's, the Clerk's, and the Physician's—that "are the embarrassment of the *Canterbury Tales*[,]"[13] and he argues that although we cannot afford to ignore them, they fail to create sympathy in us, and, worse still, they make us feel uneasy and apologetic. Bloomfield further argues that not only is it difficult to take pleasure in these tales despite their delightful poetry, but also it is impossible to see the rationale for them. Forty-eight years later, scholars are still having the same difficulties with these tales that Bloomfield had. Echoing Mary Flannery's pained outcry in her discussion of the *Physician's Tale*—"What's the *point* of it?"[14]— we, too, might ask, "What's the *point* of them?" Back in 1972, Bloomfield believed, as I now do, that if we could locate the cause of our discomfort, we would be in a better position to understand the paradox inherent in moralistic tales that fail to deliver coherent moral messages, or, at the very least, we would be put "into a better frame of mind for reading them."[15] While Bloomfield's attempt to locate the cause of his unease took him in the direction of Christian comedy, mine has taken me in a darker direction to a Sadian[16] world in which "nature is cruel and indifferent, in a state of 'perpetual movement' that abandons man to the law of the jungle, where the guilty sacrifice the innocent, where the strong dominate and tyrannize the weak."[17] One of the many differences that Deleuze points out between masochism and sadism is that while the masochist educates, the sadist instructs. (Perhaps the easiest way to understand the difference between these two words is to substitute the word "train" as a synonym for "instruct." When one engages in training, one engages in the repetition of exercises or methods. Education, by contrast, does not necessarily do so. And while education is a continuous process, training has a definitive end point.) Unlike masochism, which creates a pedagogical relationship between

---

13 Morton Bloomfield, "The Man of Law's Tale," 384.

14 Mary C. Flannery, "A Bloody Shame," 346, her emphasis.

15 Bloomfield, "The Man of Law's Tale," 384.

16 The word "Sadian" has been spelled in various ways by various writers. I have chosen to follow the lead of American scholar Jane Gallop in my spelling.

17 Carolyn Dean, *The Self and Its Pleasures*, 175.

the masochist and the one punishing him, "sadism is characterized by its refusal to teach."[18] As Deleuze has noted, "[S]adism aims to demonstrate and overpower, not mould and reshape."[19] Perhaps this difference in the two perversions explains why a masochist such as the Pardoner is able to tell a tale that has moral meat on its bones, a tale from which everyone who hears or reads it can learn something, while the three tellers of sadistic tales fail to teach us anything at all, except for the dubious lesson that virtue generally goes unrewarded. Like Edgar Allan Poe and the eighteenth- and nineteenth-century writers who were influenced by the Marquis de Sade, the Man of Law, the Clerk, and the Physician seem to agree that the death or suffering of a beautiful and virtuous woman "is, unquestionably, the most poetical topic in the world[.]"[20] But because these tales do not come from the lips best suited for this topic—"those of a bereaved lover"[21] —it becomes, in the hands of these three pilgrims, the most sadistical topic in the world. Just as Sade's language "repudiates any relationship between speaker and audience[,]"[22] so, too, does the storytelling of the Man of Law, the Clerk, and the Physician. All contracts are broken and all bets are off when a Sadian character speaks.

Joseph Bentley asks a very pertinent question in "Satire and the Rhetoric of Sadism": "what is the relation between violence as a means to personal satisfaction and violence as a means to moral improvement?"[23] His answer, I believe, moves us a little closer to understanding the motives underlying these moralizing tales which are bereft of moral content, for Bentley draws upon Freud to "conclude that noble motives are very often ignoble (or idnoble) motives in disguise. The final implication of the principle is that all acts of reformatory violence, religious, moral, legal and literary, spring from 'sadistic' impulses and are but rationalized ways of justifying one's pursuit of the atavistic pleasure of inflicting pain."[24] Of course, one might object that while these pilgrims may not be particularly virtuous themselves, there is really nothing to suggest that they are particularly evil. Fair enough. But in writing about the Marquis de

---

18 David Sigler, "The Rhetoric of Anti-Pedagogical Sadism in Jacques Lacan's 'Seminar VII,'" 72.
19 Sigler, "The Rhetoric of Anti-Pedagogical Sadism," 72.
20 Edgar Allan Poe, "The Philosophy of Composition," 794.
21 Poe, "The Philosophy of Composition," 794.
22 Deleuze, *Coldness and Cruelty*, 19.
23 Joseph Bentley, "Satire and the Rhetoric of Sadism," 389.
24 Bentley, "Satire and the Rhetoric of Sadism," 389. While voluntary flagellation such as that practiced by eleventh-century theologian Peter Damian may have salvific effects, sadism of the sort that Bentley refers to does not. Bruce W. Holsinger devotes a chapter of his *Music, Body, and Desire in Medieval Culture* to the relationship between pain and religious practice.

Sade, the French writer and literary critic Jean Paulhan argued that what was most notable about Sade was his façade of normality:

> Criminals are in general curious people, more curious than law-abiding people. I mean unusual, giving more food for thought. And though it may happen that they utter nothing but banalities, they are more surprising to listen to, owing precisely to this contrast between the dangerous content within and the inoffensive appearance without. Of all this the authors of detective stories are very aware: no sooner do we begin to suspect the honest country lawyer or the worthy pharmacist of having once upon a time poisoned a whole family, than the slightest thing he says warrants our most avid attention, and he needs but predict a change in the weather for us to sense he is meditating some new crime.[25]

One might recall the good-boy attitude and good looks of serial killer Ted Bundy. It was hard to reconcile the seeming normality of Bundy with the brutal rapes, kidnappings, and murders he committed, and this apparent incongruity between being (dangerous content within) and seeming (inoffensive appearance without) is what allowed him to get away with murder for as long as he did.

In a review of Mario Praz's *The Romantic Agony*, a book in which Praz examines the influence of the Marquis de Sade on the Romantic literature of the eighteenth and nineteenth centuries, Albert Fowler argues that Sade believed "[v]irtue exists only as a restraint to be broken, an essential condition of sadistic pleasure,"[26] and thus, in Sade's world, "sin is the normal state of nature, virtue the artificial reaction of human reason."[27] This belief can be found in Diderot's *The Nun* (*La Religieuse*), a novel in which his continual trumpeting of his heroine's virtue "seems to be used to add spice to the anguish of her persecution, and anticipates Sade's method with his *Justine*."[28] Before there was Diderot, however, there were the Man of Law, the Clerk, and the Physician, each of whom presents a blazon of his heroine's beauty and virtue before telling of the anguish she is made to suffer through no fault of her own. In the case of each tale, its original source (or sources) is modified in such a way as to heighten the cruelty and injustice that rains down upon the heroine's head. For example, the Man of Law's Custance is depicted as more saintly than she is in Trivet. And, according to J. Burke Severs, the Clerk accentuates Walter's cruelty by refashioning Petrarch's apologetic and colorless sergeant as a "harsh, crude, cruel, unfeeling creature who rudely snatches the little child from its crib, and with malevolent grimace seems to express a will to murder it before the very eyes of its

---

25 Jean Paulhan quoted in Dean, *The Self and Its Pleasures*, 179.

26 Albert Fowler, "Sensibility Since Sade," 244.

27 Fowler, "Sensibility Since Sade," 245.

28 Fowler, "Sensibility Since Sade," 244.

mother."[29] In fact, the extended expressions of pity for Griselda and the unnecessary nature of Walter's cruelty are all Chaucer's additions, not to be found in Petrarch. And, as Thomas B. Hanson argues, "[c]learly, by elevating the character of Virginia to a heroine and then ignoring her in the moral epilogue to the tale the Physician alters the tale considerably from its originals. In most contexts his advice to forsake sin would be well taken, but as the reduction of his tale of Virginia it can be seen only as the cruelest of ironies: she forsook sin and was forsaken despite her virtue."[30] With Hanson's comment, we find the perfect parallel to the tale of Virginia: that of Sade's *Justine*, generally considered his most scandalous work. In this novel, the orphaned and abandoned Justine holds fast to her virtue only to be repeatedly beaten, raped, and betrayed by those whom she trusts.

Sade's belief also manifested itself in the works of Byron, who brutalized and morally tortured his wife. In the words of his character Manfred, "I loved her, and destroy'd her," words which "became the motto of the fatal heroes of Romantic literature [...]."[31] Before there was Manfred, however, there was Walter, the Italian marquis who brutalizes and morally tortures his wife in the *Clerk's Tale*. And then there is the "unctuous piety" of Richardson's *Clarissa*, the 1,500-page novel in which the virtuous Clarissa Harlowe falls into the clutches of the libertine Richard Lovelace. Before there was Richardson, however, there was the Man of Law, who seems to delight in coupling moralizing commentary with sexual titillation. In telling of Custance and Alla's wedding celebration, for example, he dwells at length on the fact that, as a new bride, Custance will be forced to have sex with Alla, "For thogh that wyves be ful hooly thynges, / They moste take in pacience at nyght / Swiche manere necessaries as been plesynges / To folk that has ywedded hem with rynges, / And leye a lite hir hoolynesse aside, / As for the tyme—it may no bet bitide" (II (B¹), 709–14). And he enjoys punning on words such as "spille" (II (B¹), 587) and "prikke" (II (B¹), 1029) in relation to Custance's encounters with the men who desire her with "foul affeccioun" (II (B¹), 586).[32]

---

29 J. Burke Severs, *The Literary Relationships of Chaucer's "Clerkes Tale,"* 229.

30 Thomas B. Hanson, "Chaucer's Physician as Storyteller and Moralizer," 137.

31 Fowler, "Sensibility Since Sade," 243.

32 W. W. Allman and D. Thomas Hanks, Jr., find more than titillation in the Man of Law's puns. They "find knife-work associated with eroticism, even in so pious a tale as the Man of Law's." And while they use the word "pious" to describe the tale, they rightly argue that "the conjunction of an overstated profession of horror at impurity—someone else's, of course; indeed, a woman's—figured as at once moral and sexual, acts as a critique of the piety of the teller of this devotional tale." See their "Rough Love: Notes Toward an Erotics of the 'Canterbury Tales,'" 48.

Although the *Wife of Bath's Tale* and the *Clerk's Tale* are considered part of the marriage group, made complete by the *Merchant's Tale* and the *Franklin's Tale*, I find it equally fruitful to consider the tales the Wife of Bath and the Clerk tell as part of a perverse complex for which I have coined the phrase, the "domestic abuse group." This group of tales is set in motion by the Man of Law, after whom the Wife of Bath tells her tale, followed shortly by the Clerk and, finally, the Physician. What we have in this four-tale complex are three tales of obedient, patient, virtuous women flanking a tale in which a husband strikes but then is made to submit to his wife. Given what we know of the Wife of Bath from her confessional prologue, it is little wonder that the Man of Law's tale will provoke a response from her, for Custance has nothing in common with the much less flattering but more realistic portrait the Wife of Bath paints of women. Using herself as an example, Dame Alys says that women like sex and that they can be good cheaters and liars when necessary. She even goes as far as to divulge strategies for manipulating one's husband so that one can have one's cake and eat it, too. In short, what she says of women is more in keeping with the women Jankyn reads about in the book that gets (wo)manhandled than with what the Man of Law says. And thus, like Sheila Delany and numerous other readers, the Wife of Bath obviously sees Custance as unattractive and artificial because of "the somewhat repulsive masochistic qualities of extreme humility and silent endurance."[33] Although I do not believe that Custance is a masochist in the clinical sense of the word, I am certainly sympathetic to Delany's attitude toward her, and, like most readers, I find the Wife of Bath a much more attractive and far less artificial character than Custance. Unlike Custance, who allows herself to drift quite literally from one bad situation into another, the Wife of Bath takes control of her life, refusing to behave with the extreme humility and silent endurance that characterize Custance. The Wife of Bath's prologue is thus a corrective to Custance's lament, "Wommen are born to thraldom and penance, / And to been under mannes governance" (II (B¹), 286 – 87).

If the Wife of Bath makes clear what the grounds of combat are—that is, the opposition between authority and experience, man and woman—then it is obvious which pilgrims will antagonize, and be antagonized by, her: the Man of Law, the Clerk, and the Physician, all of whom have power in what one might call the realm of symbolic "fictions." (One cannot eat a civil law; one cannot taste a

---

33 Sheila Delany, "Womanliness in the Man of Law's Tale," 63. Delany is using the word "masochistic" in its popular sense, here, unlike the way in which I am using it. And thus I shall argue that because Custance participates in a sadistic narrative, she cannot be a masochist. She is what Deleuze will refer to as the "essence" of the sadistic scene.

church doctrine; one cannot smell a medical treatise.) Their ability to function rests entirely upon society's willingness to submit to authority, hence their focus on blind obedience in the tales they tell. The Wife of Bath's world, on the other hand, is that of things that can be bought and sold, touched, tasted, and felt. Even in Chaucer-the-pilgrim's descriptions of these four pilgrims, we see an opposition between what might loosely be called the symbolic and the real or the conjectural and the empirical. The Man of Law, for example, is described as someone who is "discreet" and "of greet reverence[,]" but then this assessment is undermined by the next line, in which Chaucer-the-pilgrim says, "He semed swich, his wordes weren so wise" (I (A), 313). And a few lines later he says, "Nowher so bisy a man as he ther nas," but he again undercuts the veracity of the statement by adding, "And yet he semed bisier than he was" (I (A), 321–22). Seeming rather than being, Chaucer-the-pilgrim suggests, is the key to the Man of Law's success, but there is no seeming about the Wife of Bath. What you see is what you get unless, of course, you happen to be one of her beguiled, old husbands. As for the opposition between the Wife of Bath and the Clerk, it might be articulated as that between being and nothingness, for unlike the Wife of Bath, who is described in all the materiality of the flesh, Chaucer-the-pilgrim uses the word "holwe" to describe the Clerk. Placed next to the Wife of Bath, the Clerk looks like the mere ghost of a man. According to Chaucer-the-pilgrim, the Wife of Bath wears red stockings and an enormous pile of linen on her head. She is a big woman with a broad forehead and a gap between her teeth—all in all, a physically imposing person. She is bright and colorful, perhaps even a bit vulgar but *real*. The Clerk, on the other hand, is described in terms that make him appear thin and threadbare. Even his horse is described as "leene [...] as is a rake" (I (A), 287). It is as if the Clerk wishes to deny the materiality of his body and become all intellect. And just as his body is thin and wasted from hours of study, so, too, is his voice. As Chaucer-the-pilgrim says, "Noght o word spak he moore than was neede" (I (A), 304). Until Harry prods him into speech, he is silent, but this is hardly surprising since he spends all of his money on and time with silent interlocutors: books. As for the Physician, we learn from the *General Prologue* that in his diet he observes measure and that he engages in no pleasurable superfluities. We also learn that he is tightfisted, saving rather than spending the gold he wins in pestilences. What this niggardly attitude suggests is that the Physician does not allow himself much physical pleasure. Unlike the Wife of Bath, who appears to deny herself nothing, the Physician denies himself a great deal. And while Dame Alys can both experience and speak her desire, he cannot, except, as we shall see, in disguised and perverted form.

Clearly, then, these hollow men feel threatened by someone as confident and full of vitality as the Wife of Bath, a woman whose Ellesmere portrait shows her wielding a whip and riding astride her horse rather than side-saddle as the Prioress and the Second Nun do. As we learn in the *General Prologue*, she has engaged in extensive travel, and thus she appears not only independent but also worldly wise: "And thries hadde she been at Jerusalem; / She hadde passed many a straunge strem; / At Rome she hadde been, and at Boloigne, / In Galice at Seint-Jame, and at Coloigne. / She koude muchel of wandrynge by the weye" (I (A), 463–67). Not only has the Wife of Bath traveled far and wide, but also she knows how to hold her own in the company of others, for "[i]n felaweshipe wel koude she laughe and carpe" (I (A), 474). And while the Pardoner may eye the spurs on her boots with perverse delight, the Man of Law, the Clerk, and the Physician will eye them very differently. As Deleuze argues in trying to untangle the mess that has been made of the perversions—specifically, the mess made by linking sadism to masochism in the form of sadomasochism—the "concurrence of sadism and masochism is fundamentally one of analogy only [...]."[34] Because the way these two perversions develop and operate is entirely different, "their common organ, their 'eye,' squints and should therefore make us suspicious."[35] Although each of these perverse pilgrims will see reflected in the Wife of Bath's spurs an image of a powerful mother figure, the masochist will embrace this image while those with a sadistic sensibility will not, for they equate the mother with secondary nature, which must be vanquished by the primary nature of the father. If, in masochism, the mother is glorified and the father humiliated, in sadism the father is exalted while the mother is negated.[36]

Having drawn the Wife of Bath out with his tale of Custance, the Man of Law will leave the abuse of her to the Clerk and the Physician, who attempt to "draw and quarter" Dame Alys through their sadistic treatment of Griselda and Virginia. As French writer, translator, and artist Pierre Klossowski argued in a 1933 article on Sade, the figure of the mother is of central importance as a Sadian victim, and yet "the apotheosis of this maternal victim is [the maidenly] Justine."[37] And, thus, Klossowski is led to state in his 1967 re-edition of *Sade My Neighbor* that the "secret motif of hatred of the Mother ... could be closer to the resentment directed at the virgin than one might admit."[38] Although the Wife of Bath may be

---

34 Deleuze, *Coldness and Cruelty*, 46.

35 Deleuze, *Coldness and Cruelty*, 46.

36 Given the argument I have made in the chapter on the Pardoner as masochist, I cannot agree with Roland Finger when he argues that the Wife of Bath revels in sadistic tendencies. It may be the case that the Wife of Bath enjoys engaging in physical power struggles, but this does not make her a sadist. See Finger's "Cracking the Whip," 65.

37 Jane Gallop, *Intersections*, 85.

38 Quoted in Gallop, *Intersections*, 87.

the most important target of sadistic aggression, she is not the only target. Men such as Harry Bailly, Petrarch, and even Chaucer himself come under attack, but of this I shall have more to say in the discussion of each tale.

"Holwe" Man Number One: The Man of Law

> Evil is justified not because there is no God but as a means of avenging man against an evil God. It is consequently the cruelty of God that justifies, even necessitates, the cruelty of man, abandoned by a father who ravages, abuses, and condemns his children to destroy their own creatures or be destroyed in turn.
> —Carolyn Dean, *The Self and Its Pleasures*

It is appropriate to begin with an examination of the Man of Law as literary sadist because his tale sets in motion a series of violent acts that will culminate in the monstrous crime of filicide occurring in the *Physician's Tale*. Placing the Man of Law's tale together with those of the Clerk and the Physician allows us to see in operation the implacable crime machine of which Clairwil fantasizes in Sade's *Juliette, or Vice Amply Rewarded*. This mechanized crime will be, as she says, "perpetually effective, even when I myself cease to be effective, so that there will not be a single moment of my life, even when I am asleep, when I shall not be the cause of some disturbance."[39] Seeing in Sade "a surprising affinity with Spinoza—a naturalistic and mechanistic approach imbued with the mathematical spirit[,]"[40] Deleuze finds in Clairwil's statement "the clue to the meaning of repetitiveness in Sade's writing and of the monotony of sadism."[41] We see a similar form of repetitiveness and monotony in the Man of Law's rehearsal of Custance's misadventures and in the Clerk's rehearsal of Walter's testing of Griselda, the cumulative and climactic effect of which is a father's destruction of his family, the theme upon which "sadistic fantasy ultimately rests[.]"[42] The Man of Law, the Clerk, and the Physician operate like runners in a relay race: when one man finishes his tale, he hands the baton off to the next man, and thus one is able to perpetuate the violence of domestic abuse even as another "sleeps." The perfect Sadian narrative would have no end, in fact. The play of pain would continue *ad infinitum*. It would be an endless loop of one crime after another and hence a manifestation of the suspension that characterizes the perver-

---

39 Quoted in Deleuze, *Coldness and Cruelty*, 28.
40 Deleuze, *Coldness and Cruelty*, 20.
41 Deleuze, *Coldness and Cruelty*, 28–29.
42 Deleuze, *Coldness and Cruelty*, 59.

sions. Obviously, the Man of Law, the Clerk, and the Physician do not quite achieve the perfect Sadian narrative with its endless loop of crime, but the Man of Law's narrative perpetuates itself and continues to disturb even when he ceases to speak. In other words, if the Man of Law's tale draws to a close because another pilgrim must have his or her say, it is brought to life again through the Clerk's tale. The patient Custance is reconstituted in the form of the long-suffering Griselda, and the long-suffering Griselda is resurrected in the form of the martyred Virginia. Because there is both a diegetic and an extra-diegetic repetition of torture, Harry Bailly finally puts an end to this "play of pain" by calling for "triacle" from the Pardoner. It is not simply the Physician's tale that has done his heart harm but the cumulative effect of three sadistic narratives.

As I argued in Chapter 3, the Pardoner as masochist views Harry Bailly as the father who must be humiliated and the Wife of Bath as the mother who is glorified. If the Man of Law is a sadist, it is clear that he will view the Wife of Bath with hostility, but how will he view Harry Bailly? We can begin to answer this question by examining the exchange that takes place between Harry and the Man of Law. After the Cook has finished his tale, Harry turns to the Man of Law and asks him to tell a tale, a request to which the Man of Law assents. What is striking about the Man of Law's response, however, is that while he makes a point of bowing to Harry's authority, he also carefully avoids saying that he is in Harry's debt. Instead, he speaks of his obligation to the contract or to the law itself, not to Harry as a fellow pilgrim. While Harry uses words that suggest a contractual relationship between the group, the Man of Law, and himself—"Telle *us* a tale anon, as forward is. / *Ye* been submytted, thurgh *youre* free assent, / To stonden in this cas at *my* juggement" (II (B[1]), 34–36)[43] —the Man of Law does not. Instead, his abstract language and use of the personal pronouns "I" and "my" negate the other to whom he is indebted: "To breke forward is nat myn entente. / Biheste is dette, and I wole holde fayn / Al my biheste [...] / For swich lawe as a man yeveth another wight, / He sholde hymselven usen it, by right" (II (B[1]), 40–44). If he were not talking to the Host, we would have no idea with whom the contract has been made, for all the Man of Law says is that he will keep *his* promise, the ownership falling to himself. Unlike the language that Harry uses, which creates a relationship of dialogic exchange, the language the Man of Law uses eliminates exchange and his relation to the other. The fact that the Man of Law concedes to the form of the law while rejecting its content and/or its function is in keeping with the institutional aspect of sadism, however, which tends "to render laws unnecessary, to replace the system

---

43 Emphasis mine.

of rights and duties by a dynamic model of action, authority and power."[44] As we shall see in his tale, the institution of the church as God's representative degrades all laws, setting itself above the law by establishing itself as a superior power.

While contractual relations are of importance in the novels of Sacher-Masoch, they are of no importance in Sade's, and thus what the Man of Law's language resembles is that of one of Sade's libertines, who, as Georges Bataille has pointed out, renounce the relationship between speaker and interlocutor. Although there are important differences in the way that Bataille and his friend and fellow writer Maurice Blanchot understood Sade, one thing they appear to have agreed upon is the sadist's negation of the other. In writing about Bataille and Blanchot in her book on Sade, Jane Gallop states that the "Sadian libertine destroys any particular person in the context of a preliminary denial of the reality of *autrui*. This preliminary annihilation, necessary preface to any particular negation, frees the libertine from being locked into a dialectic of recognition with his victim."[45] In a solipsistic world, the law would be unnecessary because there would be no need to define the boundaries between one subject and another. The other would simply not be thought to exist. But in Chaucer's world and ours, the other does exist, and it is through the exchange of language that we form relationships between ourselves and others. Because the law structures these relationships and gives them meaning, the law, for the sadist, is connected to secondary rather than primary nature. According to Sade, the mother represents secondary nature, "which is composed of 'soft' molecules and is subject to the laws of creation, conservation and reproduction; the father by contrast [...] represents primary nature, which is beyond all constituted order and is made up of wild and lacerating molecules that carry disorder and anarchy; *pater sive Natura prima*."[46] But if Harry represents a figure of authority—in short, a *father* figure—why would the Man of Law treat him as his victim? In answering this question, we must again distinguish between the "dead," or benign Oedipal father, and the "live," or obscene anal one. Because the sadist views the father as a "primitive anarchic force,"[47] the father whom he will exalt is not the Oedipal father of ordered society, the one who passes the law down to his children, the one who knows nothing of *jouissance*. Instead, the father who will be exalted is the obscene anal father who is beyond the law and who is thus neither moral nor immoral but amoral, situated as he is in the violence of the founding

---

44 Deleuze, *Coldness and Cruelty*, 77.

45 Gallop, *Intersections*, 43.

46 Deleuze, *Coldness and Cruelty*, 59.

47 Deleuze, *Coldness and Cruelty*, 60.

moment.[48] In Sadian narratives, therefore, it will be the Oedipal father who is murdered, for he is thought by the sadist to have departed from his true nature and function.

Once the Man of Law has "murdered" Harry through negation, he launches an attack on another figure of authority, Chaucer himself. He begins this attack by suggesting that Chaucer's poetic ability leaves much to be desired, grudgingly complimenting Chaucer's literary prowess when he says that because Chaucer has told all of the stories, there is none left for him to tell. In his refusal to repeat a story that Chaucer has told, he refuses a relationship of debt to Chaucer just as he has refused a relationship of debt to Harry. But there is more to his refusal than a mere refusal of the debt that he would incur by borrowing one of Chaucer's stories. There is also a refusal of the central theme of Chaucer's stories, each of which is about desire and passion (of one stripe or another) and each of which contains one or more characters who engage in strong emotion. The refusal of stories that contain desire, passion, and strong emotion is in keeping with the apathy of the sadist, for, as Deleuze points out, Sade contrasts the cool "self-control of the pornologist" with the "deplorable 'enthusiasm' of the pornographer."[49] Sade condemns feeling—all feelings, including those we might associate with cruelty or evil—because it drains the sadist of the energy he needs to achieve a pure state of "impersonal and demonstrative sensuality."[50] According to Sade, violence must be meted out in cold blood. And, metrically speaking, the violence of the Man of Law's tale *is* meted out in cold blood, for, as Bloomfield has noted, Chaucer uses "a repetitive, stanzaic metrical unit," here, "rather than [...] the flowing style of the pentameter couplet of the vast majority of the tales."[51] The effect of this "cool" medium, argues Bloomfield, is a sense of detachment on the part of the reader.[52] And this sense of detachment, created at least in part by metrics, may explain our discomfort with a tale such as the Man of Law's. The fact that this cool stanza form—rhyme royal—is a highly compressed form, eight lines compressed into seven, may also create a sense of discomfort, not un-

---

48 I am referring here to Derrida's argument in "Force of Law: The 'Mystical Foundation of Authority'" in which he argues that there is a double bind regarding the founding of authority: "On the one hand, it appears *easier* to criticize the violence that founds since it cannot be justified by any preexisting legality and so appears savage. But on the other hand, [...] it is *more difficult*, more illegitimate to criticize this same violence since one cannot summon it to appear before the institution of a preexisting law: it does not recognize existing law in the moment that it founds another," 40, his emphasis.

49 Deleuze, *Coldness and Cruelty*, 29.

50 Deleuze, *Coldness and Cruelty*, 51.

51 Bloomfield, "The Man of Law's Tale," 389.

52 Bloomfield, "The Man of Law's Tale," 389.

like a foot being squeezed into a shoe too small for it. Given all of the anguish Custance suffers, most readers probably believe that they should feel deep sympathy for her, and yet most readers do not. As Robert Dawson comments, "[F]ew critics really seem to like Custance very much," and thus there is a "general coolness" in critics' attitudes toward her.[53] This general coolness on the part of readers puts them in the uncomfortable position of identifying with the apathetic sadist vis-à-vis Custance and her many trials and tribulations.

After both complimenting and complaining about (revering *and* mutilating) Chaucer's many stories, the Man of Law begins cataloguing them:

> Whoso that wole his large volume seke,
> Cleped the Seintes Legende of Cupide,
> Ther may he seen the large woundes wyde
> Of Lucresse, and of Babilan Tesbee;
> The swerd of Dido for the false Enee;
> The tree of Phillis for hire Demophon;
> The pleinte of Dianire and of Hermyon,
> Of Adriane, and of Isiphilee— (II (B¹), 60–67)

With this catalogue, we encounter clinical perversion akin to that of the Pardoner, for what is this catalogue, which continues on for nine more lines, but fetishized knowledge? Like the law, which is empty of meaning for the Man of Law, this list serves no purpose, except to prop up his perverse fantasy. He collects knowledge like the Pardoner collects relics, and he uses this fetishized knowledge to disavow his literary castration: "I may not have a tale to tell, but I can name all of the tales that have been told," his list seems to say. More importantly, at the end of this extensive catalogue, the Man of Law mentions two stories that Chaucer has not told—that of "thilke wikke ensample of Canacee, / That loved hir owene brother synfully" (II (B¹), 78–79) and that of "Tyro Appollonius, / How that the cursed kyng Antiochus / Birafte his doghter of hir maydenhede" (II (B¹), 81–83).[54] And thus we are once again in the presence of disavowal, for what the Man of Law says quite explicitly is both that Chaucer has told all of the stories and that he has failed to do so.

The question that inevitably arises is why the Man of Law mentions these two tales of incest only to dismiss them as tales to which he says, "Fy!" Obvious-

---

53 Robert B. Dawson, "Custance in Context," 294 and 295.

54 Although it is not relevant to my argument, it is worth noting that the Man of Law's mention of the two stories of incest functions as an inside joke at the expense of Gower, who does tell these stories. The gist of the joke is that while Chaucer has told all the stories, at least he has not, as Gower has, written any revolting stories about incest.

ly, he does not object to their content enough to have avoided reading them, for as he says of the latter, "That is so horrible a tale for to rede, / Whan he hir threw upon the pavement" (II (B¹), 84–85). If he really thinks Chaucer was wise not to have included these stories in his literary repertoire and if he is sincere when he protests that he would not tell this kind of story either, why does he mention them in the first place? I would argue, along with Lacan, that his protest is a lie that speaks the truth, for in telling the tale of Custance, he does, in fact, tell a tale of incest between father and daughter, the unholy alliance upon which literary sadism rests. The story of Apollonius of Tyre was widely popular in the Middle Ages, argues Elizabeth Archibald in *Incest and the Medieval Imagination*,[55] and as early as 1927, Margaret Schlauch found traces of what she calls the "Incestuous Father plot" in the *Man of Law's Tale*.[56] Even more damning is Carolyn Dinshaw's chapter on the Man of Law in *Chaucer's Sexual Poetics*, published in 1989. There, Dinshaw makes a very compelling case for finding more than mere traces of incest in his tale:

> The suggestions of incest at the close of the tale are subtle, but the presence of incest in its suppression at the beginning renders these suggestions compelling at the end. Recalling to the reader's mind the position of daughter vis-à-vis father in the Man of Law's description of incest in Apollonius of Tyre (Antiochus raped his daughter "whan he hir threw upon the pavement" [85]), Constance falls onto the street at her father's feet when she sees him at last in Rome [...]. Thus reunited, the two live together "Til deeth departeth hem" (1158), the phrase echoing late-medieval marriage vows "to hold and to have, at bed and at burd, for farer for lather, for better for wars, in sekenes and in heil, *to dethe us depart*."[57]

Not only does Dinshaw make a case for father-daughter incest, but also she makes a case for mother-son incest "*in potentia*."[58] Regarding the potential mother-son incest in the Man of Law's tale, I would argue that while it may function as a kind of pseudomasochistic sub-plot to the central (and sadistic) plot of father-daughter incest, what is most important about the two mothers for my purposes is not their potentially incestuous desires but the Man of Law's treatment of them. Like Sade's hatred of the mother—it was, in fact, his mother-in-law who turned him in to the authorities for his treatment of her daughter—the Man of Law's is directed against both mothers-in-law, and he appears to delight in their gruesome deaths, Donegild slain by her own son and the "cursed wikked Sowdanesse" and her fellow Muslims burned, slain, and brought to mis-

---

55 Elizabeth Archibald, *Incest and the Medieval Imagination*, 61.

56 Margaret Schlauch, *Chaucer's Constance and Accused Queens*, 5.

57 Carolyn Dinshaw, *Chaucer's Sexual Poetics*, 101–2, her emphasis.

58 Dinshaw, *Chaucer's Sexual Poetics*, 106.

fortune by a "senatour" sent to Syria by the Roman emperor. The mother as victim is central to the Sadian narrative, and so it is no surprise that neither mother survives. The exception, of course, is Custance, who bears a child to Alla and thus becomes a mother during the course of the tale. There is good reason for Custance's survival, however, but of this I shall have more to say later.

Directly on the heels of the Man of Law's comments regarding Chaucer and the stories he has told, he gives a disquisition on the horrors of poverty. If what Chaucer-the-pilgrim says of him in the *General Prologue* is true, this is a man who is not poor but financially very well off. As John H. Fisher argues, it "is hard to see how the poverty motif makes an appropriate introduction to [...] MLT."[59] And, indeed, it is puzzling that an apparently wealthy man would make the following moan:

> O hateful harm, condicion of poverte!
> With thurst, with coold, with hunger so con-
> > founded!
> To asken help thee shameth in thyn herte;
> If thou noon aske, with need artow so woundid
> That verray nede unwrappeth al thy wounde
> > hid!
> Maugree thyn heed, thou most for indigence
> Or stele, or begge, or borwe thy despence! (II (B¹), 99 – 105)

There are two explanations for the Man of Law's comments, however, one literary and the other clinical. First, as Barthes tells us in *Sade / Fourier / Loyola*, money is important in the libertine society of Sade's narratives "because it guarantees the spectacle of poverty; Sadian society is not cynical, it is cruel; it does not say: there must be poor in order that there be rich; it says the opposite: there must be rich in order that there be poor [...]."[60] Second, the Man of Law's comments tell the story of Oedipal conflict and suggest the way in which he has been wounded by it. As Oedipal father, Chaucer is the one who has written all of the stories; he is the one who "hath al" and the one in relation to whom the Man of Law, poverty-stricken, "hast to lite." Chaucer is the one who says "no" to stories of incest just as the Oedipal father's "no" represents the law that interdicts *jouissance*. What we see in the Man of Law's prologue is thus a son reacting against the authority of the Oedipal father, a character reacting against his *makar*. Like the perverse Pardoner, the Man of Law refuses to be the one who did not know, the one who lacks and thus desires. And so in true sadistic fashion, he trans-

---

59 See his note in *The Complete Poetry and Prose of Geoffrey Chaucer*, 84.
60 Roland Barthes, *Sade / Fourier / Loyola*, 23 – 24.

gresses Chaucer's law, speaking the unspeakable. In so doing, he thumbs his nose at his creator, saying, "[…] I recche noght a bene / Though I come after hym with hawebake" (II (B¹), 94–95). Like his "murder" of Harry, the Man of Law kills Chaucer off, replacing him with an unnamed merchant from whom he has gotten the tale he tells. What is puzzling is why the figure of the merchant plays such a prominent role in the Man of Law's prologue and tale. In his discussion of poverty, for example, he points to the merchants as those who play the game of chance with winning throws:

> O riche merchauntz, ful of wele been yee,
> O noble, o prudent folk, as in this cas!
> Youre bagges been nat fild with ambes as,
> But with sys cynk, that renneth for youre
>   chaunce;
> At Cristemasse myrie may ye daunce! (II (B¹), 122–26)

He then goes on to say, "Ye seken lond and see for yowre wynnynges; / As wise folk ye knowen al th'estaat / Of regnes; ye been fadres of tidynges / And tales, bothe of pees and of debaat" (II (B¹), 127–30). Although Chaucer may not be a father of tidings or news in the way a merchant is, he certainly is a father of tales. Why does the Man of Law reject Chaucer's tales only to conclude his praise of merchants by saying that if it were not for a merchant he had met long ago, he would have no tale to tell? In other words, why does he replace one tale-telling "father" with another? Or does he? In answering these questions, we must examine the story itself, for it is there that we shall find a clue.

Not only is it a merchant who is responsible for the tale the Man of Law tells, but also it is with a group of merchants that his tale begins: "In Surrye whilom dwelte a compaignye / Of chapmen riche, and therto sadde and trewe, / That wyde-where senten hir spicerye, / Clothes of gold, and satyns riche of hewe" (II (B¹), 134–37). As the Man of Law narrates, these merchants of Syria venture to Rome, where they hear about the beauty and goodness of the emperor's daughter, Custance. Upon returning to their own country, they are full of "tidynges of sondry regnes," which the sultan is eager to hear. And thus is it through the ear and by the merchants that the sultan is fatally injured:

> Amonges othere thynges, specially,
> Thise marchantz han hym toold of dame Cus-
>   tance
> So greet noblesse in ernest, ceriously,
> That this Sowdan hath caught so greet plesance
> To han hir figure in his remembrance,

That al his lust and al his bisy cure
Was for to love hire whil his lyf may dure. (II (B¹), 183–89)

Once the sultan has determined that he must have Custance, he calls his "privee conseil" together to figure out how this union is to be achieved. When there is some speculation as to the difficulties of arranging a marriage between a Christian and a Muslim, the sultan replies,

"Rather than I lese
Custance, I wol be cristned, doutelees.
I moot been hires; I may noon oother chese.
I prey yow hoold youre argumentz in pees;
Saveth my lyf, and beth noght recchelees
To geten hire that hath my lyf in cure,
For in this wo I may nat longe endure." (II (B¹), 225–31)

Within the first two hundred lines of the story, a connection is established between the Man of Law and the sultan with respect to their merchant "friends." In both cases, the wealth of the merchants—whether that of goods or of news—creates the desire to possess in those around them. Although the Man of Law appears to speak to some unnamed other in his prologue, using the second-person "you," this rhetorical trick is merely a veiled reference to himself:

Thow blamest Crist and seist ful bitterly
He mysdeparteth richesse temporal;
Thy neighebor thou wytest synfully,
And seist thou hast to lite and he hath al.
"Parfay," seistow, "somtyme he rekene shal,
Whan that his tayl shal brennen in the gleede,
For he noght helpeth needfulle in hir neede."

Herke what is the sentence of the wise:
Bet is to dyen than have indigence[.]" (II (B¹), 106–14)

If we replace the personal pronoun "you" with "I," then it is the Man of Law who blames Christ for inequitably distributing the goods and who hates his neighbor for his good fortune. And who is this neighbor but the merchant, for directly on the heels of the "sentence of the wise" comes the Man of Law's address to the merchants, which at first glance seems to be praise but on further examination turns out to be condemnation. Because the Man of Law juxtaposes the wealth and good fortune of the merchants to the bitterness of poverty, we can only assume that, on the day of reckoning, it is the tail of the wealthy merchant that he hopes to see burn in live coals. And his choice of words is important, for it can easily be argued that the Man of Law means "tayl" to be read two ways: tail and tale.[61] Like the serpent that tempted Eve, these merchants tempt with their wares and their words, and thus what the Man of Law wishes to suggest through his disquisition on poverty is something akin to the maxim that the Pardoner trots out in every sermon: desire is the root of all evil. For what the merchants, or those at the center of the world of exchange, set in motion is desire. And, of course, their world of exchange is a world of contractual relations, not the Sadian world of institutions, and thus it is a world that can only be reviled by those with a sadistic sensibility.

Because the sultan's desire for Custance dovetails with her father's desire to spread Christianity, the emperor agrees to give the sultan Custance's hand in marriage. These arrangements are made by treaty and negotiation, neither of which Custance is allowed to take part in. Although it is clear that Custance does not want to marry the sultan and leave her home for Syria, there is no attempt to reason with her or to convince her that this marriage is in everyone's best interest, for the sadist's negation of the other is connected to his belief in the violence of reasoning. As Deleuze argues,

> [N]othing is in fact more alien to the sadist than the wish to convince, to persuade, in short to educate. [...] He is not even attempting to prove anything to anyone, but to perform a demonstration related essentially to the solitude and omnipotence of its author. The point of the exercise is to show that the demonstration is identical to violence. It follows that the reasoning does not have to be shared by the person to whom it is addressed any more than pleasure is meant to be shared by the object from which it is derived.[62]

The solitude and irresistible power of Custance's father are suggested by the silence with which he greets her piteous outburst on the day of her departure, an outburst in which she refers to herself as his wretched child and bemoans the fact that she will never see her parents again. His silence is clearly a form of negation, for through it the emperor repudiates his relation to Custance, thereby also demonstrating the apathy of the sadist. Although we see the emperor issue no imperatives—"Imperatives abound in the work of Sade [...],"[63] says Deleuze— we nevertheless feel the effects of them in both Custance's resigned statement, "Allas, unto the Barbre nacioun / I moste anon, syn that it is youre wille" (II (B[1]), 281) and in the Man of Law's "But forth she moot, wher-so she wepe or synge" (II (B[1]), 294).

---

61 With the *Shipman's Tale*, we get a triple pun with "tally." I thank Bill Quinn for pointing this out to me.
62 Deleuze, *Coldness and Cruelty*, 18–19.
63 Deleuze, *Coldness and Cruelty*, 17.

What happens next is rather odd. It is as if the passion lacking in the diege-sis of the tale jumps the tracks and gets expressed in the Man of Law's extra-die-getic apostrophe. In a moment of passion most unlike the apathy of the sadist, the Man of Law declaims the unnatural placement of the stars on the night of Custance's departure:

> O firste moevyng! Crueel firmament,
> With thy diurnal sweigh that crowdest ay
> And hurlest al from est til occident
> That naturelly wolde holde another way,
> Thy crowdyng set the hevene in swich array
> At the bigynnyng of this fiers viage,
> That crueel Mars hath slayn this mariage.
>
> Infortunat ascendent tortuous,
> Of which the lord is helplees falle, allas,
> Out of his angle into the derkeste hous!
> O Mars, o atazir, as in this cas!
> O fieble moone, unhappy been thy paas!
> Thou knyttest thee ther thou art nat receyved;
> Ther thou were weel, fro thennes artow
>   weyved. (II (B¹), 295 – 308)

While there may be passion on the part of the Man of Law, authentic or feigned, it is futilely directed at an absent other, the unmoved mover, and thus it creates no dialogic exchange or affective response. It is an onanistic passion that fails to arouse the passion of his readers. But, then, perhaps what looks like the Man of Law's passion regarding Custance's hard lot is something else entirely. What he seems to imply is that when things—either women or the constellations—are out of their natural place or order, disaster follows, and thus his impassioned com-mentary about planetary misalignment may be nothing more than a thinly dis-guised swipe at the Wife of Bath, who has traveled a great deal and thus has re-fused the rule of right order by refusing to stay in place.

The travel that Custance undergoes is quite different from that of the Wife of Bath, however, for it suggests the suspension one finds in perversion. While sus-pension is a form of stasis, in sadism it is created through repetition rather than through the rigidity of masochistic ritual. Like the travel that occurs at every turn for Custance, we "travel a great deal in some of Sade's novels," says Barthes. And yet despite the depictions of faraway lands, he continues, what we encounter on Sade's every shore "is always the same geography, the same population, the same functions; what must be gone through are not the more or less exotic contingencies, but the repetition of an essence, that of crime [...]."[64] From Syria to Northumberland, what Custance encounters is the same landscape populated with the same people: men who covet her and mothers who wish to be rid of her—in short, people who are willing to commit crimes in order to satisfy their desires. And like the descriptions that Sade gives of his libertines' objects of debauchery, the portrait we get of Custance is what Barthes would call a "rhetorical" one, for it "paints nothing, neither the thing nor its effect: it does not make visible [...]; it characterizes very little (sometimes the color of the eyes, the hair); it is content with naming the anatomical elements, each of which is perfect; and since this perfection, in good theology, is the very essence of the thing, it suffices to say a body is perfect in order for it to be so [...]."[65] Although Custance's anatomical elements are not named, perfection is her very essence, for the common voice of every man says the following of her:

> "Oure Emperour of Rome—God hym see!—
> A doghter hath that, syn the world bigan,
> To rekene as wel hir goodnesse as beautee,
> Nas nevere swich another as is shee.
> [...]
> In hire is heigh beautee, withoute pride,
> Yowthe, withoute grenehede or folye;
> To alle hire werkes vertu is hir gyde;
> Humblesse hath slayn in hire al tirannye.
> She is mirour of alle curteisye;
> Hir herte is verray chambre of hoolynesse,
> Hir hand, ministre of fredam for almesse." (II (B¹), 156–68)

This blazon of Custance depicts an institution of holiness, not a woman made of flesh and blood. Nor should it, for this rhetorical portrait is in keeping with Sade's need for institutions rather than the contractual relations of Sacher-Masoch. Perhaps if Custance were less of a cardboard character and more realistically portrayed—if she were given, for example, the wide hips and the broad forehead, the gapped teeth and spurred boots of the Wife of Bath—she would appear more lifelike and, if more life-like, more full of desire. As it is, because Custance is a character drawn from the hagiographical tradition, she betrays no desire at all, except to maintain her pious obedience to God, and thus her relationships (such as they are) are not manifested on a horizontal plane but on a vertical one. Seldom do we find Custance showing real love, compassion, or concern

---

64 Barthes, *Sade / Fourier / Loyola*, 15.
65 Barthes, *Sade / Fourier / Loyola*, 22.

for her fellow human beings. Even in her relationship with Hermengyld, the love appears to flow in only one direction: from Hermengyld to Custance. And when Custance shows maternal tenderness for her child, it is in the context of his likeness to Christ—that is, as an innocent punished for the sins of others. In short, Custance and her father operate by the same standards: God and/or the church comes first and human relationships come second, if at all. Each of the characters who express desire, on the other hand, winds up dead by the end of the Man of Law's tale. But, again, this is in keeping with the apathy of the sadist. The ones left standing at the tale's end will be those whose actions are not governed by feeling. The sultan, the young knight, the steward, and Alla feel desire for Custance as a woman, not as an institution such as the Christian church. They feel her loveliness; they suffer for want of it; they are willing to go to great lengths to get it; and, ultimately, they die.

The question that must be answered now is what role Custance plays in the Man of Law's sadistic narrative. Is she its victim? If so, does this make her a masochist? The answer to these interrelated questions is a complex one, for while Custance is a victim, at least in some sense of the word, she is not quite the same kind of victim as the sultaness, Donegild, or even Custance's own mother. As Deleuze argues, "In sadism [...] the mother becomes the victim *par excellence*, while the daughter is elevated to the position of incestuous accomplice."[66] One way to distinguish between these two types of victims is to look at the way each is treated in the Man of Law's narrative. When the Man of Law speaks of either mother-in-law, his hostility is palpable. In speaking of the sultaness, for example, he says,

> O Sowdanesse, roote of iniquitee!
> Virago, thou Semyrame the secounde!
> O serpent under femynynytee,
> Lik to the serpent depe in helle ybounde!
> O feynded womman, al that may confounde
> Vertu and innocence, thurgh thy malice,
> Is bred in thee, as nest of every vice! (II (B¹), 358–64)

Although it could be argued that she is just as steadfast in her faith as Custance is in hers, the Man of Law undercuts religious devotion as the motive for the massacre when he says, "This olde Sowdanesse, cursed krone, / Hath with hir freendes doon this cursed dede, / For she hirself wolde al the contree lede" (II

---

66 Deleuze, *Coldness and Cruelty*, 59–60.

(B¹), 432–34). As for Donegild, she leaves the Man of Law bereft of words to express his contempt for her:

> O Donegild, I ne have noon Englissh digne
> Unto thy malice and thy tirannye!
> And therfore to the feend I thee resigne;
> Lat hym enditen of thy traitorie!
> Fy, mannysh, fy!—o nay, by God, I lye—
> Fy, feendlych spirit, for I dar wel telle,
> Thogh thou heere walke, thy spirit is in helle! (II (B¹), 778–84)

Whatever the motives for their actions are, both mothers are murdered and thus negated. As for Custance's mother, she is negated through neglect. She is mentioned once, briefly, at the beginning of the tale, but by the tale's end, she has completely disappeared without comment or explanation. Custance, on the other hand, is like the character of O in Pauline Réage's *Story of O.* As one might recall, no matter how many times O is beaten, whipped, branded, or sodomized, she retains her beauty, youth, and appeal. But this is because the Sadian narrative fetishizes the (in)corruptible flesh of the maidenly heroine. (The word "corrupt" comes from the Latin *corrumpĕre*, meaning to destroy, spoil, or bribe, a Latin word that disavows itself, coming as it does from *cor*, which means "together," and *rumpĕre*, which means "to break into pieces.") Not surprisingly, the concept of (in)corruptible flesh suggests disavowal: yes, the body can be broken apart, but it nevertheless remains whole. Although O is corrupted or broken apart by the violent sexual activities that take place in the château at Roissy, she remains incorrupt or together. The same can be said of Custance. Despite the fact that she is in the midst of the sultaness's slaughter of the sultan and a group of Christians, despite the fact that the sultaness sends her off alone in a rudderless vessel, despite the fact that it is many years before her vessel reaches land, despite the fact that she is accused of murdering Hermengyld and forced to stand trial, despite the fact that she gives birth to a child whom her mother-in-law misrepresents as a monster, despite the fact that she is led to believe that her husband Alla is responsible for banishing her and her child from his kingdom, despite the fact that Donegild thrusts her out to sea again in her rudderless vessel, despite the fact that she drifts for more than five years before nearing land, despite the fact that a wicked steward climbs aboard her vessel and tries to rape her— *despite all of this!*—she remains the same Custance from start to finish. She is the Teflon heroine, fetishized and disavowed by the Man of Law but never— no, never—negated, and this is because her central role is that of (incestuous) daughter and not of mother.

Although the emperor appears only briefly at the beginning and end of the Man of Law's tale, he nevertheless plays an important role in its narrative, for it is he who puts Custance into circulation, and everywhere she goes, destruction and death follow in her wake. In many respects, Custance herself functions as something akin to Clairwil's crime machine, for she creates a violent disturbance every time she comes into contact with another human being. It is not until Custance is returned to her father as incestuous ally—that is, until she has come full circle and stopped circulating—that the disturbances cease. What we might say, then, is that Custance is both victim and ally of the sadist. As victim, is she a masochist? And as ally, is she a sadist? The answer to both of these questions is "No." As Deleuze compellingly argues, the Sadian victim "cannot be masochistic, not merely because the libertine would be irked if she were to experience pleasure, but because the victim of the sadist belongs entirely in the world of sadism and is an integral part of the sadistic situation. In some strange way she is the counterpart of the sadistic torturer [...]."[67] Deleuze's distinction "between the [sadistic] subject (the person) and the [sadistic] element (the essence)" allows us to understand how Custance can be part of the sadistic situation and yet not be a sadist herself, for in her role as ally, she is the element of sadism and not its subject.[68] And yet as integral to the sadistic situation and in some strange way counterpart to the sadistic torturer, she is impossible for the reader to identify or sympathize with.

Before turning to an examination of the next hollow man, I would like to return to one of the questions with which I began. What is the Man of Law's relationship to law, knowledge, and power, and, in turn, to the tale he tells? If we are to believe the Man of Law, he (like the emperor and Custance herself) adheres to "Cristes lawe deere" (II (B1), 237), but of what does this law consist? In his letter to the Galatians, the Apostle Paul refers to the law of Christ when he exhorts the Galatians to "bear one another's burdens, and so fulfill the law of Christ."[69] According to some scholars, this is an allusion to the commandment to "love thy neighbor as thyself." But Christ's law as articulated by the Man of Law has nothing to do with the New Testament laws that govern human relationships. It has only to do with the power of God to perform miracles, eight of which occur in the story of Custance. After narrating each miracle, the Man of Law asks the same question, "What law kept Custance alive?" and supplies the same answer, "God's law, which man is not equipped to understand."[70] The first miracle, for

---

67 Deleuze, *Coldness and Cruelty*, 41–42.
68 Deleuze, *Coldness and Cruelty*, 42.
69 Galatians 6:2, English Standard Version.
70 See *The Canterbury Tales*, trans. Nevill Coghill, 136.

example, occurs at the Syrian wedding banquet when everyone except Custance is slaughtered. "Why was she not slain?" the Man of Law asks, to which he answers with another question: "Who succoured Daniel in the lion's den?" The second miracle occurs when Custance is kept safe in her vessel on the sea. "Why was she not drowned?" the Man of Law asks. Again, he answers with a question: "And who kept Jonah in the fish's maw / Till he was spouted up at Nineveh?"[71] To the question, "Why did she not starve to death during her three-year sojourn on the sea?" the Man of Law replies with the story of the five loaves and two fishes that fed a crowd of thousands. And when Custance is attacked by the lustful steward, the Man of Law asks, "How could this feeble woman have the strength / Against this scoundrel?"[72] The answer, not surprisingly, is yet another question: "How did David have the strength to kill Goliath?" The Man of Law, who seems to revel in miracles, sums up his theology in this way:

> God liste to shewe his wonderful myracle
> In hire, for we sholde seen his myghty werkis;
> Crist, which that is to every harm triacle,
> By certeine meenes ofte, as knowen clerkis,
> Dooth thyng for certein ende that ful derk is
> To mannes wit, that for oure ignorance
> Ne konne noght knowe his prudent purveiance. (II (B¹), 477–83)

This passage tells us a great deal about the Man of Law's relationship to knowledge, law, and power. Although he is a collector of knowledge, he does not use it to understand the world around him. Unlike the Wife of Bath, who uses her powers of reasoning to understand the Scriptures and who actually engages in interpretation when she quotes Ptolemy's proverbs, the Man of Law is helpless before the "prudent purveiance" of Christ. The Man of Law's God, like the "primitive anarchic force" of which Deleuze speaks, is beyond the laws of "secondary nature," the laws of creation, conservation, and reproduction. He is a force that cannot be understood but must simply be obeyed. It would seem, then, that the Man of Law's unstated but implied take on God resembles that of Sade as articulated by Klossowski: God's cruelty necessitates that of man.

In telling the tale of Custance, the Man of Law is telling his own tale, for where nothing is interdicted—that is, in the realm of the obscene anal father— everything is interdicted. A subject who rejects the benign Oedipal father winds up working overtime for the cruel and sadistic father associated with

---

71 Coghill, *The Canterbury Tales*, 136.
72 Coghill, *The Canterbury Tales*, 149.

the superego. There will be no end to the list of imperatives imposed or sacrifices required. And this is a position that the Wife of Bath will not tolerate, hence her rude intervention when Harry asks the Parson to preach. She must offer up an alternative to the superegoical power to which the Man of Law subjects Custance and, ultimately, himself. The bell the Wife of Bath rings to awaken all of her companions is what will later be the slogan of the Enlightenment: "Dare to know! Have the courage to use your own reason against any kind of imposed or external authority [...]."[73] Although the Wife of Bath claims that her tale will "not ben of philosophie, / Ne phislyas, ne termes queinte of lawe" (II (B¹), 1188 – 89), what she engages in during her prologue is akin to the "lower faculty" of philosophy, which pursues knowledge of the truth. Whatever the existing laws decree, the Wife of Bath understands that as a woman of reason, she can make an appeal for changing them. The Man of Law, on the other hand, does not question the power that holds him in thrall. He simply obeys it. To question it would be to admit doubt or uncertainty, and this is something the perverse subject cannot do. He lives with a rigid and implacable knowledge, a knowledge that refuses to recognize the prior "not-knowing" out of which understanding comes. Because the Man of Law fetishizes knowledge, he occludes the truth instead of exposing it. As Jean Clavreul points out, "[T]he activity, the knowledge, and the interests of the pervert must above all be *rigorously of no use*, to lead nowhere."[74] Here, then, we find literary and clinical sadism in close alignment, for the tale the Man of Law tells is of no morally edifying use, nor does it lead anywhere but back to where it started. In the worst sense of the expression, all (of the Man of Law's) roads lead to Rome.

"Holwe" Man Number Two: The Clerk

> Sade's work refuses what Bataille called the "trickery" of the state because it names violence, refuses to pretend that it is somehow outside of the proper limits of what we refer to as civilization, and insists, on the contrary, that violence structures all our political and social institutions.
> —Carolyn Dean, *The Self and Its Pleasures*

As if finally recognizing the irony of his position as judge and the possibility of his authority's being undermined by someone more learned than he, Harry Bail-

---

73 This is Mladen Dolar's translation of Kant's starting point in his text on the Enlightenment. See Dolar's "The Legacy of the Enlightenment," 47.

74 Jean Clavreul, "The Perverse Couple," 226, his emphasis.

ly takes an aggressive approach when he turns to the Clerk to ask him to speak. In his request that the Clerk tell something merry, he compares the Clerk to a young bride, accuses him of sophistry, and demands that he keep his high style in check and speak plainly. If Harry expects to be challenged, his expectations are disappointed when the Clerk submits rather obsequiously to him, saying, "Hooste, [...] I am under youre yerde; / Ye han of us as now the governance, / And therfore wol I do yow obeisance, / As fer as resoun axeth, hardily" (IV (E), 22–25). Unlike the Man of Law, who refers to the contract but not to Harry, the Clerk stresses his submission to the Host in terms that suggest the punishment authority metes out through use of the yardstick. Even more suggestive is Coghill's modern English translation in which the Clerk says, "Sir, I kiss the rod!"[75] And thus the Clerk's language not only reflects the language that Griselda and her father will use in his tale but also a strangely paradoxical aspect of Sade's language, which is, as Bataille has pointed out, *"essentially that of a victim."*[76] According to Bataille, "Only the victim can describe torture; the torturer necessarily uses the hypocritical language of established order and power."[77] Bataille's understanding of Sade's paradoxical language is complemented by Deleuze's psychoanalytic explanation of the sadist's ability to act as both sadist and victim, identifying as he does with both positions. While the masochist expels his superego, projecting it onto his torturer, the sadist expels his ego, projecting it onto his victim. Because the ego is the site of feeling, the sadist's apathy can be explained by the ego's expulsion and projection, for once the sadist's ego has dissolved and been expelled into the external world, the sadist becomes pure superego. "The sadist has no other ego than that of his victims[,]" Deleuze states emphatically, arguing that this fact "explains the apparent paradox of sadism, its pseudomasochism."[78] Thus, what looks like masochism on the part of the sadist is not masochism but pseudomasochism.

Similarly, what looks like submission on the part of the Clerk is pseudosubmission, for the tale he tells is anything but merry, and although he might be said to use plain language in the telling of his tale, his message is so obscure that its meaning continues to mystify and divide Chaucer scholars in their understanding of it. In a brief survey of the tale's reception, for example, J. Allan Mitchell notes that it "is an offensive monstrosity to some, an alluring and subtle fable to others, and to still others an artistic failure or deliberate caricature[.]"[79]

---

75 Coghill, *The Canterbury Tales*, 339.
76 Cited in Deleuze, *Coldness and Cruelty*, 17, his emphasis.
77 Cited in Deleuze, *Coldness and Cruelty*, 17.
78 Deleuze, *Coldness and Cruelty*, 124.
79 J. Allan Mitchell, "Chaucer's 'Clerk's Tale' and the Question of Ethical Monstrosity," 2.

But whatever reception the tale receives, argues Mitchell, it "remains a moral challenge."[80] The same can be said of Sade's narratives and, in fact, *has* been said. For example, while Klossowski believed that Sade maintained moral categories in his writing, Blanchot believed that the logic of Sade's works leads inexorably "to the ruin of all moral categories and therefore away from the moral conscience [...]."[81] And while Angela Carter argued in *The Sadeian Woman* that Sade was a "moral pornographer," Andrea Dworkin castigated Carter's book, calling it "a pseudofeminist literary essay."[82] As Carolyn Dean succinctly and wittily summarizes the polarizing forces surrounding the infamous marquis, "[...] depending on whom one listens to, Sade is hard as stone (as an unwitting executioner) or a hard moralist in the Kantian sense (which means of course that one is hard for somebody else's good, as the philosopher of the bedroom always insisted)."[83] Filtered through Dean, Bataille's comment regarding Sade's refusal of the state's hypocrisy makes of Sade an ethical writer if not a moral one, but of this I shall have more to say later.

While the Clerk's and the Man of Law's interactions with Harry Bailly differ, both men engage in metaphorical parricide of the Oedipal father. Like the Man of Law, who admits to having gotten his tale from a merchant, the Clerk also cites an external source: Francis Petrarch. While many of the other pilgrims are either creative storytellers or plagiarists, the Man of Law, the Clerk, and the Physician are neither, for each one makes a point of attributing his tale to someone else. Whether this is merely in keeping with their relationship to a certain kind of paternal authority or a means of shirking responsibility for the events that take place in their narratives, I do not know. Perhaps the two go hand in hand. In any event, the Clerk begins his tale by referencing Petrarch and praising him in what appears at first to be an unqualified and unambiguous way. At least initially, then, there is a noticeable difference in the Man of Law's opening remarks and those of the Clerk. While one skirts his obligation to Harry, disavows Chaucer, and bites the hand of the merchant who feeds him, the other obsequiously declares his obedience to Harry and lauds Petrarch as a "worthy clerk" whose "rethorike sweete / Enlumyned al Ytaille of poetrie [...]" (IV (E), 32–33). His adulation of Petrarch is undermined, however, by what Barrie Ruth Straus refers to as the Clerk's "excessive zeal in declaring Petrarch, the father of his story, 'nayled in his cheste'" (IV (E), 29) and in declaring Petrarch's proheme irrele-

---

80 Mitchell, "Chaucer's 'Clerk's Tale,'" 2.
81 Dean, *The Self and Its Pleasures*, 189.
82 Andrea Dworkin, *Pornography*, 84.
83 Dean, *The Self and Its Pleasures*, 195.

vant, thereby enacting "the violence of parricide against the text and the Host."[84] Just as the Man of Law negates or "murders" both Harry and Chaucer, the Clerk negates or "murders" both Harry and Petrarch—Harry, by agreeing to his demands while flagrantly flouting them, and Petrarch, by announcing both his death (not once but thrice) and his proheme's irrelevance.

The Clerk's tale, like that of the Man of Law, begins in what is now called Italy, but we are not introduced to Griselda right away. Instead, the central character appears to be Walter, a marquis who is lord of a region in western Italy called Saluzzo. The Clerk begins his narrative by telling of the marquis's position with respect to his vassals, saying, "And obeisant, ay redy to his hond, / Were alle his liges, bothe lasse and moore. / Thus in delit he lyveth, and hath doon yoore, / Biloved and drad, thurgh favour of Fortune, / Bothe of his lordes and of his commune" (IV (E), 66–70). He then moves into a description of Walter's noble descent, faulting him only for his lack of interest in the future. Like the perfect libertine—or, clinically speaking, like the perverse subject who does not recognize the before and after of time—Walter "considered noght / In tyme comynge what myghte hym bityde, / But on his lust present was al his thoght […]" (IV (E), 78–80). His subjects, however, understand the vicissitudes of the temporal; they look at the past and future, to which Walter turns a blind eye, and what they see worries them. Until they approach him with the request that he marry, it appears that the marquis's will and theirs have been one and the same. But as time passes, Walter's subjects grow uneasy, thinking as they do that perhaps Walter intends to hawk and hunt forever, allowing all other concerns to slide. Consequently, they go to him with this plea:

> "Boweth youre nekke under that blisful yok
> Of soveraynetee, noght of servyse,
> Which that men clepe spousaille or wedlok;
> And thenketh, lord, among youre thoghtes wyse
> How that oure dayes passe in sondry wyse,
> For thogh we slepe, or wake, or rome, or ryde,
> Ay fleeth the tyme; it nyl no man abyde (IV (E), 113–19)

But they do not stop there. They drive their point home by reminding the marquis that even though he is still young, he cannot escape the menace of age:

> "And thogh youre grene youthe floure as yit,
> In crepeth age alwey, as stille as stoon,
> And deeth manaceth every age, and smyt

---

84 Barrie Ruth Straus, "Reframing the Violence of the Father," 124.

In ech estaat, for ther escapeth noon;
And al so certein as we knowe echoon
That we shul deye, as uncerteyn we alle
Been of that day when deeth shal on us falle." (IV (E), 120–26)

Although Walter agrees to their request, allowing them to appoint the day on which the wedding vows will be solemnized, this exchange with his subjects has clearly disturbed him. Not only is he forced to recognize that he and his subjects are not one—that their desires are different from his and, in this case, diametrically opposed—but also he is forced to look death and/or castration in the face. And thus Walter quickly consents to his subjects' request in order to silence this troubling "other" voice, immediately setting about to construct an edifice that will keep at bay any further traumatic discoveries, an edifice of which Griselda is the central supporting beam.

What the Clerk describes in these early passages is the construction of the perverse structure. The blissful period before Walter's subjects come forward is akin to the dyadic bond that exists between mother and child before the father intrudes as the third term, separating the child from the mother's breast and insisting on the child's acquisition of language. Walter's subjects' request, which shatters the dyadic mirroring that has been occurring, is the traumatic moment in which the child is forced to reckon with its mother as other, separate, and different from itself. Because some children accept this sudden reckoning while others do not, we have neurotics, perverts, and psychotics of all stripes. No one goes unscathed, not even libertines such as the Marquis de Sade or the Marquis of Saluzzo, but the way these two noblemen suture (in the surgical sense of the word) their narcissistic wounds is through perversion, specifically the perversion of sadism. We see sadism writ large in Walter's decision to marry Griselda and most painfully in his treatment of her after she becomes a mother.

Like the striking disparities that exist between partners in perversion ("Thus we find the athlete linked with a puny little kid, the refined intellectual with the hillbilly, the massive woman with an angel of femininity, the immoral alcoholic with a saint, the vicious dirty old man with the prepubescent adolescent, the sociably respectable person with the hobo," notes Clavreul.[85]), there are a number of striking disparities between Walter and the woman he chooses to take as his bride, the most notable of which is their social status and wealth. Walter is of noble descent; Griselda is a peasant. His is the wealthiest of households; hers is not merely a poor household but the poorest of the poor. The Clerk goes to great lengths to emphasize the vast difference in station between the two. In de-

---

85 Clavreul, "The Perverse Couple," 219–20.

scribing their respective homes, for example, he says of Griselda's that it stood not far from the marquis's palace in a "throop" in "which that povre folk of that village / Hadden hire beestes and hir herbergage, / And of hire labour tooke hir sustenance, / After that the erthe yaf hem habundance" (IV (E), 200 – 203). In contrast to the simplicity of Griselda's humble farming community is Walter's opulent palace, which on his wedding day "put was in array, / Bothe halle and chambres, ech in his degree; / Houses of office stuffed with plentee / Ther maystow seen, of deyntevous vitaille / That may be founde as fer as last Ytaille" (IV (E), 262– 66). As Kristine Gilmartin notes in "Array in the 'Clerk's Tale,'" the word "array" is used several times in the Clerk's narrative but not in Chaucer's original sources. This deviation prompts Gilmartin to argue that "Chaucer has thus particularly underlined [...] the social distance between the splendid Walter and the simple Griselda."[86] This marked social distance between Walter as libertine and Griselda as object is representative of the highly coded Sadian society that one finds in novels such as *The 120 Days of Sodom* and *Justine*. In these novels, Barthes argues, two great social classes exist: the haves and the have-nots. Again, as Barthes has pointed out, Sadian society is not cynical but cruel, and thus money "in no way designates what it can acquire (not a *value*), but what it can withhold (a site of separation)."[87] In short, says Barthes, "wealth is necessary because it contrasts with misfortune."[88]

We see one particularly poignant example of wealth contrasting with misfortune on Griselda's wedding day. After Walter and she emerge from Janicula's house, the "richely arrayed" Walter presents her to the assembled crowd and demands his ladies-in-waiting to strip her of her "olde geere" and dress her in new:

> "This is my wyf," quod he, "that standeth
>   heere.
> Honoureth hire and loveth hire, I preye,
> Whoso me loveth; ther is namoore to seye."
>
>   And for that no thyng of hir olde geere
> She sholde brynge into his hous, he bad
> That women sholde dispoillen hire right
>   theere. (IV (E), 369 – 74)

What makes this scene humiliating is that Griselda is stripped right before the assembled crowd, not in the privacy of her own home, and what makes it doubly

---

86 Kristine Gilmartin, "Array in the 'Clerk's Tale,'" 235.
87 Barthes, *Sade / Fourier / Loyola*, 24, his emphasis.
88 Barthes, *Sade / Fourier / Loyola*, 24.

humiliating is the attitude with which the ladies-in-waiting strip Griselda: "Of which thise ladyes were nat right glad / To handle hir clothes, wherinne she was clad" (IV (E), 375–76). This scene would not be out of place in the best of Sadian narratives, for, as Barthes comments, "when in a group the naked brushes up against the clothed (and thereby contrasts with it), that is, outside of orgies, it serves to mark particularly humiliated persons [...]."[89]

Later in the tale, we see a particularly poignant example of money designating what it can withhold when Griselda is stripped of her finery and sent back to her father's house. To Walter's command that she return to Janicula, Griselda asks that she not be turned out of the palace naked: "Ye koude nat doon so dishonest a thyng, / That thilke wombe in which youre children / leye / Sholde biforn the people, in my walkyng, / Be seyn al bare; wherefore I yow preye, / Lat me nat lyk a worm go by the weye" (IV (E), 876–80). The marquis grants her meager request, saying, "The smok [...] that thou hast on thy / bak, / Lat it be stille, and bere it forth with thee" (IV (E), 898–91). The smock that the marquis allows Griselda to wear home is a basic undergarment for which the word "sherte" is often used interchangeably. As Laura Hodges explains in her reading of Griselda's smocks, to wear a "smok" or a "sherte alone" is to be "presented in a state of virtual nakedness, bereft of all usual signs of social rank and, on occasion, suffering humiliation."[90] Seeing Griselda's virtual nakedness, Janicula hurries to meet her, attempting to cover her with "hire olde coote," but "on hire body myghte he it nat brynge, / For rude was the clooth, and moore of age / By dayes fele than at hire mariage" (IV (E), 913, 915–17). Directly before this description of Griselda's journey from the marquis's palace to Janicula's humble cottage comes a description of her children's journey from Bologna to Saluzzo. The juxtaposition of the pomp and circumstance under which the children ride toward Saluzzo and the abjection under which Griselda walks home heightens the contrast between wealth and misfortune, but it also shows Griselda devolving into the role of victim *par excellence* while her daughter "is elevated to the position of incestuous accomplice."[91] In fact, the tale's father-daughter alliance is made emphatic through doubling: Janicula and Griselda mirror Walter and his daughter, the latter two becoming a "couple" just as the former two are reunited. Walter's final test of Griselda, whereby he proposes to marry his own daughter, functions as a cruel joke expressing Walter's unconscious desires and thoughts, particularly those concerning sexuality and aggression. Walter

---

89 Barthes, *Sade / Fourier / Loyola*, 19–20.
90 Laura F. Hodges, "Reading Griselda's Smocks in the *Clerk's Tale*," 84.
91 Deleuze, *Coldness and Cruelty*, 60.

can say, "Just kidding!" and have Griselda believe him, but he cannot do the same with those who have been steeped in Freud's ideas regarding jokes and their relation to the unconscious.

Social status and wealth are not the only disparities that exist between Walter and Griselda, however. Spending his days hawking and hunting, Walter is irresponsible and frivolous, pursuing only his own pleasure. Griselda, on the other hand, spends her days spinning and tending sheep, her only moments of idleness occurring when she sleeps. She is dependable and hardworking, devoting herself not to selfish pursuits but to her elderly father. Griselda is, in every way imaginable, Walter's disparate other, but this fact is disavowed through Walter's insistence on Griselda's absolute obedience to him. In fact, he makes it a condition of the marriage alliance that she submit to his will completely:

> "I seye this: be ye redy with good herte
> To al my lust, and that I frely may,
> As me best thynketh, do yow laughe or smerte,
> And nevere ye to grucche it, nyght ne day?
> And eek when I sey 'ye' ne sey nat 'nay,'
> Neither by word ne frownyng contenance?
> Swere this, and heere I swere oure alliance." (IV (E), 351–57)

What he demands of her, in short, is that she never differ from or oppose him. His "no" is to be her "no." His "yes" is to be her "yes." Without pause or reflection, Griselda agrees to this condition, saying, "Lord, undigne and unworthy / Am I to thilke honour that ye me beede, / But as ye wole youreself, right so wol I" (IV (E), 359–61). Griselda gets her lines right from the very start: if it seems good to you, then it seems good to me. In other words, his "good" is her "good." Walter's condition is a form of sadistic negation, for in being asked to agree to Walter's erasure of her will or desire, Griselda is essentially being asked to negate herself. This is, if possible, even more sadistic than Walter's negating her himself, for he forces her to be complicit in her own negation.

While there are many similarities between the sadistic narrative of the Man of Law and that of the Clerk, one of the very real distinctions to be made between the two is the way in which the marriages of Custance and Griselda take place, and yet both marriages share perverse characteristics. In the Man of Law's tale, Custance has no say in her marriage to the sultan. In the Clerk's tale, on the other hand, the marquis makes a point of asking first Janicula and then Griselda whether his marriage proposal is acceptable. It may seem, then, that the marquis's approach is more in keeping with the contractual relations of the masochist than with the institutions of the sadist, but I would argue that this apparent deviation from sadism is merely apparent, marking as it does the difference between literary sadism and clinical. For while Deleuze's study of Sade's and Sach-er-Masoch's novels has caused him to emphasize the sadist's need for institutions and the masochist's need for contractual relations, Clavreul's clinical practice has not. According to Clavreul, the terms and conditions of the perverse relationship—whether it be sadistic or masochistic—are contractual, made in secret and thus known only to those involved, and yet this secrecy does not necessarily signify the absence of a third party. While in a normal relationship, a third party must be present to sanction its authenticity by signing or countersigning a marriage document, in a perverse relationship, a third party will be present "only insofar as he is blind or an accomplice or impotent."[92] And thus if Walter and Griselda were entering into a normal love relationship, the proper third party would be Walter's subjects, who are neither blind, complicit, nor impotent. But because the marquis knows that his subjects expect him to marry a member of the nobility, he chooses Janicula instead, who is as ready as his daughter to negate himself. When Walter approaches Janicula, he takes him aside—out of the sight and hearing of his subjects, who would, no doubt, raise objections to the proceedings—to tell him of his wish to marry Griselda. Given that Janicula and Griselda live in more abject poverty than anyone in their village, the marquis is pretty much guaranteed Janicula's assent, and indeed, Janicula's reply is very similar to that of his daughter: "'Lord,' quod he, 'my willynge / Is as ye wole, ne ayeyns youre likynge / I wol no thyng, ye be my lord so deere; / Right as yow lust, governeth this mateere'" (IV (E), 319 – 22). Asking Janicula for permission is, of course, a request that cannot be refused, and thus it serves to underscore Walter's authority.

Once Janicula's complicity is assured, the marquis suggests entering his humble cottage for a "collacioun" or conference. The Clerk narrates it thus:

> "Yet wol I," quod this markys softely,
> "That in thy chambre I and thou and she
> Have a collacioun, and wostow why?
> For I wol axe if it hire wille be
> To be my wyf and reule hire after me.
> And al this shal be doon in thy presence;
> I wol noght speke out of thyn audience." (IV (E), 323 – 29)

On the surface, everything the marquis says sounds perfectly gallant, but his words are empty, for he knows that Janicula's presence is meaningless and that, once inside Janicula's little cottage, no one will contradict him. Because

---

92 Clavreul, "The Perverse Couple," 218 – 19.

his subjects are gathered in a throng about the house, the marquis must move the conference indoors in order to maintain the secrecy requisite of the perverse alliance. Once the pact is made, the marquis presents Griselda to his subjects, saying to them, "This is my wyf [...] that standeth / heere. / Honoureth hire and loveth hire, I preye, / Whoso me loveth; ther is namoore to seye" (IV (E), 369 – 71). These words set the tone for the events that follow. The marquis does not demand love for her because of who *she* is but because of who *he* is. He says that his subjects must love her because she is his, because they love him. Then he has her stripped of everything that is hers, and thus Griselda enters her new life with Walter as nothing more than his echo.

Without opposition from Griselda or his subjects, everything runs smoothly for Walter until the birth of his and Griselda's first child. Then, suddenly, the marquis feels compelled to test his wife in the cruelest of ways. The sudden emergence of Walter's "merveillous desir his wyf t'assaye" (IV (E), 454) raises three important questions: 1) why does it emerge when it does, 2) what is its purpose, and 3) is it, in fact, a "desir," or this a misnomer?

The fact that Walter's sudden "desir" to test his wife coincides with the birth of their first child is significant for two reasons, both of which help to explain why this "desir" emerges when it does. First, the fact that Griselda is not barren but able to give birth announces her sexual difference from Walter in a rather stark way. Consequently, Griselda's delivery of their first child is a betrayal of the condition under which she and Walter married. What the marquis wanted from the outset was a negation of the other. That is why he exacted a promise from Griselda not to express her difference from him in any way, shape, or form and had her stripped of all physical reminders (such as her clothes) of her previous autonomy. And, second, like the father who separates mother and child, the baby creates triangulation, rupturing the dyadic bond that has existed between Griselda and the marquis. The baby is a third party—not like Janicula but like the marquis's subjects—with its own set of needs, demands, and desires, a third party who may be blind in the way that all babies are but who is not complicit or impotent. And so Walter must get rid of it in order to maintain the dyadic bond between himself and Griselda and to keep their perverse alliance intact.

The marquis does not take the baby away from Griselda himself, however. Instead, he masks his own cruelty with the supposed cruelty of the big Other —that is, his subjects[93]—telling Griselda that they resent being ruled by someone

---

93 The marquis's subjects function as the big Other in much the same way that the Burmese natives do in George Orwell's "Shooting an Elephant": "Here was I, the white man with his

of such low birth: "And though to me that ye be lief and deere, / Unto my gentils ye be no thyng so. / They seyn, to hem it is greet shame and wo / For to be subgetz and been in servage / To thee, that born art of a smal village" (IV (E), 479–83). He then suggests that, in this matter, his hands are tied, saying, "I moot doon with thy doghter for the beste, / Nat as I wolde, but as my peple leste" (IV (E), 489–90). Like the sadist of whom Slavoj Žižek speaks in *Looking Awry*, the marquis is acting, here, "in the position of the object-instrument, the executor of some radically heterogeneous will," tormenting Griselda not "for his own pleasure, but for the enjoyment of the Other [...]."[94] Thus, the one thing that now belongs to Griselda, having been nourished by and introduced into the world through her body, is taken away from her by the marquis's "suspecious" sergeant, the theft of her baby a sadistic repetition of the original stripping Griselda has undergone at the hands of the marquis's ladies-in-waiting. Now as then, however, Griselda responds with utter compliance: "Lord, al lyth in youre plesaunce. / My child and I, with hertely obeisaunce, / Been youres al, and ye mowe save or spille / Youre owene thyng; werketh after youre wille" (IV (E), 501–4). She then reissues her commitment to Walter, saying, "Ther may no thyng, God so my soule save, / Liken to yow that may displese me [...]" (IV (E), 505–6).

Once the baby has been removed, the marquis observes his wife to see whether there is any change in her behavior toward him, but no matter how carefully he searches, he can find no trace of rancor in her. Griselda continues to operate in the same humble and obedient way as before, never mentioning her daughter or even uttering her name. Life goes on as if the child had never existed. Four years go by in this suspended state, and then Griselda gets pregnant again and bears a baby boy. This time the child is allowed to remain with its mother until it is two, but then Walter again approaches his wife, voicing his concerns as the concerns of his subjects:

> "Now sey they thus: 'Whan Walter is agon,
> Thanne shal the blood of Janicle succede
> And been oure lord, for oother have we noon.'
> Swiche wordes seith my peple, out of drede.
> Wel oughte I of swich murmur taken heede,

---

gun, standing in front of the unarmed native crowd—seemingly the leading actor of the piece; but in reality I was only an absurd puppet pushed to and fro by the will of those yellow faces behind. I perceived in this moment that when the white man turns tyrant it is his own freedom that he destroys," 909.

94 Slavoj Žižek, *Looking Awry*, 108–9.

> For certeinly I drede swich sentence,
> Though they nat pleyn speke in myn audience." (IV (E), 631–37)

To this, Griselda says exactly what she has said all along, "I wol no thyng, ne nyl no thyng, certyan, / But as yow list" (IV (E), 646–47), reminding him that when she first came to him, she left her will and all her liberty behind and took his clothing. Therefore, she concludes, he may do as he pleases and she will obey. As before, the marquis has Griselda's two-year-old boy taken away by his sergeant, and then he waits to see whether she will complain or "grucche," but he waits in vain. As the Clerk puts it, her will and his remain as one, undivided.

Still, the marquis is not satisfied with his tests of Griselda. He must try her further, and thus he hits on the idea of divorce, requesting from Rome a counterfeit papal bull ending their marriage and granting him permission to remarry. In open audience one day, the marquis springs his latest test on Griselda, saying that it is the will of the people that he take a new wife and that she is even now on her way to Saluzzo. Who is this new wife to be? No one knows except Walter that it is his twelve-year-old daughter, whom he has kept hidden away in Bologna under the care of his sister. If the marquis's previous tests were meant to cause Griselda private pain, his present test is designed to cause her public humiliation, but like her response to pain, Griselda's response to humiliation is to accept it without complaint. The final blow comes when the marquis sends for Griselda, asking her to make arrangements for the arrival of his new bride: "I have no wommen suffisaunt, certayne, / The chambres for t'arraye in ordinaunce / After my lust, and therfore wolde I fayn / That thyn were al swich manere governaunce. / Thou knowest eek of old al my plesaunce [...]" (IV (E), 960–64). To this cruel request, Griselda says, "Nat oonly, lord, that I am glad [...] / To doon youre lust, but I desire also / Yow for to serve and plese in my degree / Withouten feyntyng, and shal everemo [...]" (IV (E), 967–70). Even when the marquis taunts Griselda by pointing out the beauty of his new bride, Griselda answers with unflagging humility and good will.

Having reviewed each of the ways in which Walter tests Griselda, it is now possible to answer the question regarding the tests' purpose by way of Fink's clinical expertise in Lacanian analysis. According to Fink, the sadist's goal is not merely to harm his victim but to create anxiety in her first by identifying and then by threatening to take away *objet a*. In explaining what he means by this, Fink uses the example of a B-grade movie in which the villain captures and trusses up the hero "in such a way that if he tries to free himself, his beloved falls into a pool of boiling acid. In this way, the hero is forced to contemplate the imminent loss of what is most precious to him: his cause of desire, the woman who for him embodies object *a*."[95] In the case of Walter and Griselda, Walter is the villain and Griselda, the hero. In threatening to take away her children, for example, Walter is pressing Griselda to contemplate the loss of what is most precious to her or, in other words, what constitutes her object-cause of desire. Because it is Oedipal law that establishes the object-cause of desire (*objet a*), the sadist, for whom Oedipal law does not operate properly, "plays the part of the Other in his scenario *in order to make the Other exist*, and seeks to isolate for his victim the object to which the law applies."[96] In contrasting the masochist and the sadist, Fink argues that while the masochist "has to orchestrate things in such a way that his partner enunciates the law even though he is the one pulling the strings, the sadist's own will can play the part of the law. In a sense, the sadist plays both parts: legislator and subject of the law, lawgiver and the one on whom the exaction or limit is imposed."[97] Because the symbolic Other's castrating and/or separating function does not ineradicably exist for the sadist as it does for the neurotic, the sadist will be forced to enact castration and/or separation over and over again, and this is the purpose of Walter's testing of Griselda. Each time he tests her, he is attempting to identify what is for Griselda *objet a*, for he believes as does the sadist that "it would be the symbolic Other's will to wrest the object from him, to take away his jouissance, if only the Other really existed."[98] Paradoxically, then, the sadist enjoys staging "the very operation (castration) that is supposed to require a loss of jouissance. He derives satisfaction from the enactment of the very operation which demands that he separate from the source of his satisfaction."[99]

In explaining from a clinical standpoint the relationship between the mother and the perverse subject—whether it be sadistic or masochistic—Fink argues that perversion results when the child is unable to identify and name his mother's desire and thus to see her as a lacking subject. As long as her desire goes unnamed, the child will be treated to her suffocating demands and forced to function as her *objet a*. As Fink says of Freud's little Hans, he was able to raise the question of what his mother wants, but he was never able "to answer it with anything other than himself: 'She wants me.'"[100] And thus little Hans could not translate his mother's "unbearable presence and demands (the mother as real)

---

95 Fink, *A Clinical Introduction*, 190–91.
96 Fink, *A Clinical Introduction*, 191, his emphasis.
97 Fink, *A Clinical Introduction*, 191.
98 Fink, *A Clinical Introduction*, 191.
99 Fink, *A Clinical Introduction*, 192–93.
100 Fink, *A Clinical Introduction*, 197.

into a speakable, bearable reality (the mother's desire as named) [...]."[101] What this means is that little Hans was faced with an anxiety-provoking and claustrophobic lack of lack created by his mother, from whom his father had never managed to separate him. Little Hans's perverse relationship with his mother gives us yet another way to think about Walter's relationship with Griselda, for she functions as mother while Walter functions as child. In his tests of her, he is thus attempting to identify and name Griselda's desire, a desire that is never identified and named except in the way little Hans's was.

Thinking of Griselda as mother and Walter as little Hans also sheds light on the rather surprising comment that the Clerk makes at the end of his tale: "This storie is seyd nat for that wyves sholde / Folwen Grisilde as in humylitee, / For it were inportable, though they wolde [...]" (IV (E), 1142–44). Here, the Clerk sounds more like an analyst (or a Petrarchan allegorist) than a sadist, for he states that it would be intolerable if wives behaved as Griselda did, especially, I would add, in their role as mothers. Because Griselda's desire (as mother) has never been identified, Walter (as child) will be treated to her suffocating presence. And thus his staging of castration can be understood as his attempt to create a lack that allows space for his emergence, development, and growth. Castration becomes, in this scenario, a means by which the perverse subject defends against the suffocating presence of the mother, and what is more suffocating than an echo? To put it in slightly different terms, we can argue that what the perverse subject desires are the dialectical comings and goings of the *fort/da* game, of which only one term has been properly articulated. In the hands of the sadist, little Ernst's cotton reel, which stands in for a mother who comes and goes, represents a mother who comes but never goes, a mother whom he wishes to "toss away" in order to create breathing space in a claustrophobic psychic scenario.[102] Because the father has failed as representative of the (always absent) phallus, or the law- and thus space-maker, the sadist must become his own law- or space-maker.

While it is certainly true that the moment Griselda becomes a mother is the moment her victimization begins, like Custance, she is a rather unusual victim in that she is both the tortured and fetishized object *par excellence*. From a clinical standpoint, what is at stake for the perverse subject is the integrity of the mother's body—and ultimately his own—and thus the sadist's fantasy will revolve around repeated attempts, the success of which lies precisely in their failure,

---

101 Fink, *A Clinical Introduction*, 201.

102 This would go a long way toward explaining why the mother is the sadist's victim *par excellence*.

to corrupt or break apart the maternal body. Nothing the marquis does to Grisel-da corrupts or breaks her apart. He takes everything from her—her clothes, her maidenhead, her children, her marriage and high position, her dignity—but she remains unbroken from start to finish. Like the activity of the perverse subject, the marquis's continual tests are *rigorously of no use:* they lead nowhere. As Lacan says in his discussion of the ethics of psychoanalysis, in "the typical Sa-dean scenario, suffering doesn't lead the victim to the point where he is dismem-bered and destroyed. It seems rather that the object of all the torture is to retain the capacity of being an indestructible support."[103] What one finds in analysis, continues Lacan, is "that the subject separates out a double of himself who is made inaccessible to destruction, so as to make it support what [...] one cannot help calling the play of pain."[104] Lacan's concept of the sadistic subject's double is akin to Deleuze's concept of the victim as the sadist's counterpart and/or ex-pelled ego, and thus we can understand Griselda in each of these three ways: as Walter's counterpart, expelled ego, and/or double. She is, as Lacan might say, what is in the marquis more than the marquis, his excess sprout of enjoyment, the *thing* that *enjoys* through suffering.

Having attempted to explain the purpose of Walter's tests, we must now de-termine whether "desir" is the appropriate word to use in describing the force behind these tests. As Thomas A. Van argues in his reading of the *Clerk's Tale*, Walter's testing of Griselda is a game that has gotten out of control, for Walter "moves, or is driven, from one test to the next, as though each result opens up a new level of inquiry, whether or not in the light of common sense he would ever have wanted to go that far."[105] While the word "driven" is left unex-plored in Van's analysis of Walter's motives, his unwitting reference to Freud's concept of the drive is a useful one, for the drive describes the force behind Wal-ter's sadistic actions far better than desire does. As the Clerk so insightfully states, "But ther been folk of swich condicion / That whan they have a certein purpos take, / They kan nat stynte of hire entencion, / But, right as they were bounden to that stake, / They wol nat of that firste purpos slake" (IV (E), 701–5). What the Clerk is describing in these lines is the drive, not desire, for de-sire is set in motion by lack or loss and is thus linked to the Oedipal law in its search for something that is prohibited or unavailable.[106] Renata Salecl usefully

---

103 Jacques Lacan, *The Seminar of Jacques Lacan: Book VII*, 261.
104 Lacan, *The Seminar of Jacques Lacan: Book VII*, 261.
105 Thomas A. Van, "Walter at the Stake," 218.
106 I have explained this difference between desire and the drive in similar terms in "Staging Perversion," 62–63.

states the differing logics of desire and drive in this way: in desire, the subject says to himself, "It is prohibited to do this, but I will nonetheless do it."[107] Drive, on the other hand, does not concern itself with prohibitions or transgressions of the law, and thus a subject following the dictates of the drive would say, "I do not want to do this, but I am nonetheless doing it."[108] Because Walter has absolute power over Griselda, testing her is not prohibited by anyone, nor do his tests transgress any law. And, thus, his tests do not operate through the logic of desire but of drive. Walter appears to be driven to test Griselda against his better judgment as well as his own best interests, for not only do his subjects begin to hate him for what he has done to Griselda—"where as his peple therbifore / Hadde loved hym wel, the sclaundre of his / diffame / Made hem that they hym hatede therfore" (IV (E), 729–31)—but also Walter himself appears to be genuinely pained by it. For instance, when he agrees to allow Griselda to wear a smock back to her father's house, the Clerk says, "But wel unnethes thilke word he spak, / But wente his wey, for routhe and for pitee" (IV (E), 892–93). Like being bound to a stake, the drive is a constant pressure that produces the painful satisfaction Lacan refers to as *jouissance*. As Jacques-Alain Miller says, "With the drive you can always ask, who is driving? Is there a pilot in this drive? In some sense, the drive seems to go adrift (*à la dérive*). But in fact it is desire that drifts, whereas the drive knows its way."[109] What, then, is the relationship between perversion and the drive? According to Miller, the drive is by its very nature perverse. Perversion is the norm of the drive.

Before turning to an examination of the *Physician's Tale*, I would like to return to Bataille's comment regarding Sade's refusal of the state's "trickery." According to Dean, Bataille argues that Sade's work is both a critique and an indictment of the state, for it "names violence, refuses to pretend that it is somehow outside of the proper limits of what we refer to as civilization, and insists, on the contrary, that violence structures all our political and social institutions."[110] Bataille further argues that violence is fundamentally a "profound silence [...] for violence never declares either its own existence or its right to exist; it simply exists."[111] In giving violence a voice, Bataille argues, Sade "deconstructs this cultural fantasy that violence is outside or elsewhere [...]."[112] If Bataille's take on Sade is correct, then perhaps it is possible to argue that Chaucer is doing some-

---

107 Renata Salecl, "The Satisfaction of Drives," 106.
108 Salecl, "The Satisfaction of Drives," 106.
109 Jacques-Alain Miller, "On Perversion," 316.
110 Dean, *The Self and Its Pleasures*, 187.
111 Georges Bataille, *Erotism*, 188.
112 Dean, *The Self and Its Pleasures*, 187.

thing similar in the *Clerk's Tale*, for feminist scholars such as Harriet Hawkins, Patricia Cramer, and Barrie Ruth Straus have argued that the *Clerk's Tale* reveals the violence inherent in patriarchal institutions such as marriage and the family. Straus, for example, argues that Walter's behavior is not aberrant but consistent with "the inherent violence of the structure of the family in patriarchal culture."[113]As an example of this violence, she cites Walter's first test, in which he takes Griselda's baby daughter away: "In doing so, he reveals that the nature of social fatherhood consists in the prerogative of the father to use and abuse women and children, treating both as his property, with which he can do anything he likes."[114] Writing in 1975 during the second wave of the feminist movement, Hawkins argues that throughout the tale, "Chaucer may be criticizing those social assumptions which enable Walter to demand that Griselda render unto him the service due only to a deity" and further that "Chaucer is making his own 'modest proposal' about the potential suffering inherent in the assumption that one human being should have godlike power over another. For, after all, the relationship between Walter and Griselda simply carries to its logical conclusion the orthodox medieval assumption that a wife should have no will apart from that of her husband."[115] Writing in 1990 as third-wave feminism was being ushered in, Cramer argues that the "contemporary importance of the sexual power relations presented by 'The Clerk's Tale' is reflected in current feminist theories about pornographic fantasies and practices similar to those enacted by Walter and Griselda."[116] And, like Hawkins, Cramer believes that the tale's "peculiar power" resides in its portrayal "of tyranny and submission to tyrannical authority," both of which continue to plague us today.[117]

In fact, one could argue that what the story of Walter and Griselda offers us is a cautionary tale about the downside of obedience, Chaucer acting as a medieval precursor to Stanley Milgram. In "The Perils of Obedience," Milgram points out how deeply ingrained obedience is and how easily it can sabotage one's moral and ethical sensibilities. And thus perhaps the reason that some readers have viewed the *Clerk's Tale* as "an offensive monstrosity" is because Griselda puts obedience to her husband above the lives of her children. "What kind of mother would *do* that?" these readers ask. Milgram supplies an answer to this question when he argues that in order "[f]or a person to feel responsible for

---

113 Straus, "Reframing the Violence of the Father," 130.
114 Straus, "Reframing the Violence of the Father," 128–29.
115 Harriet Hawkins, "The Victim's Side," 345, 352.
116 Patricia Cramer, "Lordship, Bondage, and the Erotic," 495.
117 Cramer, "Lordship, Bondage, and the Erotic," 492. Here, she is quoting Harriet Hawkins.

his actions, he must sense that the behavior has flowed from 'the self.'"[118] Because Griselda has been asked and has agreed to negate herself, she has no self from which responsible behavior can flow. As Milgram argues, the "most far-reaching consequence [of obedience] is that the person feels responsible *to* the authority directing him but feels no responsibility *for* the content of the actions that the authority prescribes."[119] And thus while readers of the *Clerk's Tale* can find Griselda responsible for the content of the actions that Walter prescribes, she herself cannot, for in obeying Walter she believes she is simply doing her duty as loyal wife. Obeying one's husband has, for centuries, been seen as the normal role of women, and yet in the *Clerk's Tale* the normal becomes the perverse. And thus what feminists such as Straus, Hawkins, and Cramer as well as social psychologist Milgram seem to suggest is that the normal and the perverse are much closer to each other than we are generally willing to admit. For example, it was not sadists drawn from the fringes of society who were willing to shock their "student" counterparts most aggressively in Milgram's experiment but ordinary people. *Ordinary people like Griselda.*

"Holwe" Man Number Three: The Physician

> Because the libertine, in Sade most often acting as a sadist, requires evidence of others' misery in order to feel pleasure in his own fortune, he is dependent on others for his status as master.
> —Carolyn Dean, *The Self and Its Pleasures*

As John Berger argues in "Ways of Seeing," once the camera was invented, it changed the way we understood the visual world. For when it becomes possible to reproduce a work of art, its uniqueness is undermined. If the original work of art manages to retain something of its uniqueness despite its reproducibility, this is only because it is now considered the original of a reproduction: "It is no longer what its image shows that strikes one as unique; its first meaning is no longer to be found in what it says, but in what it is."[120] Although no camera existed during the time Chaucer was writing, we may nevertheless use Berger's ideas about reproduction to think about the role the eye plays in the *Physician's Tale*. For it is only after Apius sees Virginia in the street that a counterfeit image, or a reproduction, is created. In short, after Apius's optical lens captures

---

118 Stanley Milgram, "The Perils of Obedience," 443.
119 Milgram, "The Perils of Obedience," 442.
120 John Berger, "Ways of Seeing," 61.

Virginia's beautiful contours, he develops a reproduction via his churlish accomplice, Claudius. With the introduction of Claudius's "cursed bille," two images of Virginia come into existence: the virtuous daughter and the stolen "thral." As Berger rightly points out, once reproduction is possible, the meaning of the original changes. That is, Virginia's uniqueness (her value as a work of Nature's art) is no longer about what she does for or says to the viewer—that is, it is no longer about her beauty or her goodness—but about what she is. In other words, it is now about her authenticity, legitimacy, and/or her line of descent.

Like the squabbling National Gallery and the Louvre—each claiming that its *Virgin of the Rocks* is the original—Virginius and Claudius both claim ownership of the virgin Virginia, and for Virginius, it comes down to the hateful question of paternity, which is, or at least was before DNA testing, a mystical estate. Because his ownership of Virginia has been called into question, so, too, has his legitimacy as a father. And while both he and Claudius claim that they can bring witnesses in to give proof of ownership, there is no eye powerful enough to guarantee paternity. The only guarantee a man such as Virginius has is his wife's word. And thus the eye may be responsible for setting this drama in motion, but it is helpless to bring it to a just close. Given the subject matter of the *Physician's Tale*, one cannot help but be reminded of the two young knights from the *Knight's Tale* who are wounded in the eye by the sight of the lovely Emelye walking in the garden below their tower prison. Apius, too, is wounded in the eye by the sight of Virginia, and this wound prompts him to wound Virginius in the public eye. These two men's responses to their respective wounds are quite different, however. Although both seek possession of Virginia, Apius fetishizes or reveres the "wounding" object, while Virginius punishes or mutilates it. And these differing responses give rise to a question not unlike that asked at the end of the *Franklin's Tale*. Perhaps it could be articulated thus: tell me, who is the biggest art lover—the man who kills himself when he sees Nature's art defaced or the man who defaces it?

I have begun my discussions of the Man of Law and the Clerk by examining their interactions with Harry Bailly, but because the Physician has no interaction with Harry until his tale has ended, it is more fruitful to begin my discussion of the Physician by referring to the tale told just prior to his. The *Franklin's Tale*, which revolves around the concepts of honor and generosity, is about the relationship between a man's good name and the virtue of his wife, or, articulated slightly differently, between man's *name* and woman's *body*. The same can be said of the *Physician's Tale*, for Virginius's name, and thus his honor, is inextricably bound up with his daughter's hymen. In the *Franklin's Tale*, the trouble that Dorigen gets herself into is finally resolved by the reciprocal generosity of husband, wife, lover, and magician. But, as if to cancel out or negate the groundswell of generosity that has put an end to Dorigen's anguish, the Physician takes up the subject matter of his fellow pilgrim's tale and gives it a sadistic twist. For like Sade's libertine, the Physician requires evidence of others' misery in order to experience pleasure. And thus in replacing the Franklin's knight with Virginius, the knight's wife with Virginius's fourteen-year-old daughter, the lustful squire with a lustful judge, the unnamed magician with the judge's churlish accomplice, and—most importantly—optical duplicity with optical duplication—the Physician creates what might be called the "perverse" twin of the Franklin's tale of compassion.[121] Aping the central plot of the Franklin's tale in which Aurelius attempts to get Dorigen into bed, the Physician's tale is devoted to Apius's plot to rob Virginia of her maidenhead. But there is one very big difference in these stories: their outcomes. While both women ultimately retain their honor, Virginia loses her head when her father decapitates it and carries it by the hair to the lecherous judge as he sits in open court. When Apius sees that the object of his desire has been mutilated, he orders his men to take Virginius and hang him (the only sound judgment in the entire story, as far as I can see), but the knight's many friends surge forward to save him, and the judge winds up in jail, where he kills himself. Virginius's friends then round up Claudius, the judge's accomplice, with the aim of hanging him, but here is the moment of supreme generosity: "[...] Virginius, of his pitee, / So preyde for hym that he was exiled; / And elles, certes, he had been bigyled" (VI (C), 272–74). Clearly, Virginius's pity is supposed to echo the moment of generosity that sets off the domino effect of generosity illustrated in the *Franklin's Tale*, which begins with Arveragus and ends with the magician, and yet it does not. It only makes the Physician's narrative more sadistic and Virginia's death more senseless.

Except as the gruesome climax to the four tales that make up the "domestic abuse group," nothing about the *Physician's Tale* makes any obvious or immediate sense. R. Howard Bloch is emphatic in his denial of the tale's sense-making potential when he argues that the "characters of The Physician's Tale act so inexplicably and even illogically that not even the weight of psychologistic Chaucerian criticism can recuperate their intent."[122] Unlike Bloch, I believe that the concept of sadism makes it possible to understand the characters' behavior in the *Physician's Tale*, particularly that of Virginius, but I nevertheless agree that because of the characters' strange behavior, the tale "seems to raise more questions than it answers [...]."[123] If nothing about the Physician's tale seems to make

---

121 Here, I use the word "perverse" in its popular, not in its psychoanalytic, sense.
122 R. Howard Bloch, "Chaucer's Maiden's Head," 22.
123 Mary C. Flannery, "A Bloody Shame," 346.

much sense, however, there is a good reason for it: his tale is not about what he says it is. Like the teller himself—a counterfeit doctor whose inability to deal with cause and effect renders him not only impotent but also downright injurious as a healer[124]—the Physician's tale is itself a counterfeit, for it is not about the rewards of virtue (apparently, there are none) but about something akin to what Bataille calls Sade's "impossible desire," which he could only liberate through self-destruction.[125]

The Physician begins his tale by naming his source, the Roman historian Titus Livius, and by introducing a character central to his story: "Ther was, as telleth Titus Livius, / A knyght that called was Virginius, / Fulfild of honour and of worthynesse, / And strong of freendes, and of greet richesse" (VI (C), 1–4). The line that immediately follows this introduction is strangely but tellingly articulated. Instead of saying, "This knyght and his wyf hadde a doghter," the Physician says, "This knyght a doghter hadde by his wyf [...]." The Physician's oddly worded statement estranges husband and wife by placing their daughter between them. And thus this simple but oddly worded statement is extremely important, for it accomplishes three things: 1) it establishes the relationship that will be the focus of the Physician's tale, 2) it perverts the Franklin's loving couple by transforming it into the incestuous alliance of father and daughter upon which sadism rests, and 3) it announces the theme most prevalent in sadism, the paternal and patriarchal, by calling attention to Virginius's uncertain fatherhood. Because the Physician makes it a point to say the knight had a daughter *by his wife*, one is led to doubt the veracity of his statement. The name is a man's only guarantee that a child is his own, and it is not really a guarantee at all, especially in the case of a name such as Virginia, which smacks of overcompensation, a protesting too much. Thus, the name—who is named and when and who is not named and why—plays an important role in the Physician's tale. The knight's wife remains unnamed, for example, but then she is a mother, and we have already seen how mothers fare in sadistic narratives. After line 5, she is only mentioned once in the course of the story, apparently not having been pre-

---

124 According to Emerson Brown, Jr., "[...] the Physician as storyteller reveals himself to be unable to apply a skill which is singled out in the General Prologue as essential to the process of healing. The responsibility for Virginia's death, unmistakably clear in the sources, is now spread among so many different and etiologically incompatible people and forces that the 'cause' is, in effect, no longer 'yknowe.' This failure to deal with causality in the storytelling game of the pilgrimage reflects back to the General Prologue sketch to undercut Pilgrim Geoffrey's confidence that the Physician did indeed know 'the cause of everich maladye.'" See Brown's "What Is Chaucer Doing with the Physician and His Tale?" 137.
125 Dean, *The Self and Its Pleasures*, 187.

sent for her daughter's beheading. Although the Physician spends the next sixty lines describing the beauty and virtue of Virginius's daughter, she is not named until line 213, when death is nearly upon her. Even the names of the false judge and his accomplice are given before we learn the central character's name and that it is merely a feminized version of her father's. The refusal to name Virginia until just before her death is a form of sadistic negation as is the feminized version of her father's name, which makes Virginia nothing more than a patronymic echo.

On the heels of the introduction of the knight comes a discourse on art's inability to counterfeit Nature, a deviation from Livy during which mention is made of Pygmalion. "Who kan me countrefete?" asks Nature, answering that "Pigmalion noght, though he ay forge and bete, / Or grave, or peynte [...]" (VI (C), 13–15). Although the Physician passes over Nature's reference to Pygmalion without comment, it is worth pausing to note the incestuous alliance of father and daughter that the myth of Pygmalion and Galatea implies. As Galatea's creator, Pygmalion is her father. And like Frankenstein's creature, Galatea is brought to life in the body of an adult but with all the knowledge and guile of an infant. She is thus simultaneously Pygmalion's "infant" daughter to be molded and shaped as he wishes *and* his paramour. Although the Physician *appears* to use Pygmalion to prop up Nature's claim that she cannot be counterfeited, what he does *in fact* is to enhance the theme of sadism with a second father-daughter alliance. Perhaps it is true, as Nature asserts, that Zeuxis, the Athenian artist who so skillfully represented a cluster of grapes that birds attempted to peck at it, would be unable to create a counterfeit of Virginia, but what Nature fails to take into account is the power of words. The desiring eye does not bear the power to see the truth, but it does possess the power of imagination, and thus the "artful" Apius can and does counterfeit Nature's work through the reproduction created by Claudius's lie. In the hands of the Physician, Nature herself is made a mockery of, for she is equated with the secondary nature of the mother rather than the primary nature of the father, and thus what she creates must be destroyed.

While Nature is said by the Physician to "forme and peynte" Virginia, the description we get of her actually comes from the Physician himself. If the Physician believes as Tertullian does that "[s]eeing and being seen belong to the self-same lust" and that "every public exposure of a virgin is (to her) the equivalent of rape[,]"[126] then his lengthy and public blazon of Virginia is a form of rape. As Bloch has argued, "[T]he rhetoric of excessive praise, absent both in

---

126 Tertullian, "On the Veiling of Virgins," 28, 29.

Livy and Jean de Meun, [excites] the desire of the reader even before Apius enters upon the scene[,]," and thus the Physician "incites, in fact, the very thing which the tale seems morally to denounce [...]."[127] Not only is the Physician's blazon a form of rape and an incitement to rape, but also it is a way of prostituting Virginia. As Nancy Vickers has convincingly argued, the blazon creates a commercial relationship involving "an active buyer, an active seller, and a passive object for sale."[128] Generally, the buyer and seller are both male, while the object for sale is female. In taking inventory of or itemizing Virginia's favors, the Physician as seller takes control of her body and her public image, putting her up for sale at the same time that he implicitly identifies with Apius.

The Physician's blazon also provides him with an opportunity to launch an attack on the Wife of Bath, who is nothing if not visible and who thrives on seeing and being seen. The first sign we have that his words are directed at Dame Alys comes when he equates the virtue of virginity with that of discreet speech:

As wel in goost as body chast was she,
For which she floured in virginitee
With alle humylitee and abstinence,
With alle attemperaunce and pacience,
With mesure eek of beryng and array.
Discreet she was in answeryng alway;
Though she were wis as Pallas, dar I seyn,
Hir facound eek ful wommanly and pleyn,
No countrefeted termes hadde she
To seme wys, but after hir degree
She spak, and alle hire wordes, moore and
        lesse,
Sowynynge in vertu and in gentillesse. (VI (C), 43–54)

As the Wife of Bath points out in her prologue, not everyone is cut out to be a virgin, and although she has no quarrel with virginity, she freely admits that she has no taste for sexual abstinence. Let the virgins be "breed of pured whete seed," she says, but as for herself, she is content to be called "barly-breed" (III (D), 143–44). In short, the Wife of Bath is not an advocate of virginity, nor is she a woman who can be silenced. She will take her pleasure, and she will speak her mind, neither of which can be said of Virginia. The Physician continues his description of Virginia, saying, "Bacus hadde of hir mouth right no maistrie; / For wyn and youthe dooth Venus encresse / As men in fyr wol casten oille

127 Bloch, "Chaucer's Maiden's Head," 35, 36.
128 Nancy Vickers, "'The blazon of sweet beauty's best,'" 97.

or greesse" (VI (C), 58–60). But, again, this is nothing more than a thinly veiled response to the Wife's comments about her jollity when under the influence of wine: "How koude I daunce to an harpe smale, / And synge, ywis, as any nyght-yngale, / Whan I had dronke a draughte of sweete wyn" (III (D), 457–59). She then recounts an incident in which a man strikes and kills his wife because she has been drinking. Calling him a foul churl, Dame Alys says that she would not have been daunted by such a husband to give up wine, for "after wyn on Venus moste [she] thynke, / For al so siker as cold engendreth hayl, / A likerous mouth moste han a likerous tayl" (III (D), 464–66). Like the Physician, she draws a connection between wine and lechery, but, unlike the Physician, she sees this connection as desirable. Clearly, the Wife of Bath could never be part of a sadistic scenario because she is a desiring subject who might just get a little too much pleasure out of being spanked.

For the Physician, it is an easy leap from wine to wickedness, a leap he makes when he says of Virginia that she had often feigned illness in order to escape company that was likely to treat of folly, company such as might be encountered at feasts, revels, and dances, occasions which are little more than opportunities for dalliance: "Swich thynges maken children for to be / To soone rype and boold, as men may se, / Which is ful perilous and hath been yoore. / For al to soone may she lerne loore / Of booldnesse, whan she woxen is a wyf" (VI (C), 67–71). With the word "wyf," the Physician finally points the finger at Dame Alys, who speaks with relish of her penchant for seeing and being seen in her gay scarlet gown at vigils and processions, at sermons and pilgrimages, at miracle plays and marriages. Unfortunately for Virginia, however, even if a girl avoids bad company and dresses in quiet, modest colors, a pretty face is always in danger of being gazed upon with desire.

Once the word "wyf" has been uttered, the floodgates open, and the Physician admonishes those in charge of girls to watch them well. First, he addresses the governesses, and, second, he addresses the fathers and mothers, saying,

> Youre is the charge of al hir surveiaunce
> Whil that they been under youre governaunce.
> Beth war, if by ensample of youre lyvynge,
> Or by youre necligence in chastisynge,
> That they ne perisse; for I dar wel seye
> If that they doon, ye shul it deere abeye.
> Under a shepherde softe and necligent
> The wolf hath many a sheep and lamb torent. (VI (C), 95–102)

These lines make no sense in the context of the Physician's tale because it is not about a girl who goes astray through improper training or negligent surveillance.

In fact, the Physician undermines his own *moralitas* when he says in the lines that directly follow his address to governesses and parents, Virginia "[s]o kepte hirself hir neded no maistresse, / For in hir lyvyng maydens myghten rede, / As in a book, every good word or dede / That longeth to a mayden virtuous, / She was so prudent and so bountevous" (VI (C), 106–10). To what end does he admonish parents to be watchful of their daughters if the tale he tells is not that of a girl in need of a watchful eye? Like a wolf in sheep's clothing, the apparently superfluous lines in his tale turn out to be significant, for they alert us to keep our eyes peeled for funny-looking sheep.

The next section of the Physician's tale is a narration of Virginia's fateful trip to town, where she is seen and immediately desired by Apius. She does nothing to draw attention to herself, however, for unlike the Wife of Bath she is not traipsing around town unescorted, coquetting and showing off her gay clothes. Instead, like a religious devotee, she is headed toward the temple in the company of her mother.[129] Contrary to what the Physician says, a parent's presence is no protection at all for a beautiful, young girl, for the judge spots her and determines that he must have her. The scheme that Apius concocts for getting access to Virginia is to have his accomplice, Claudius, bring a suit against Virginius, accusing the knight of having stolen Virginia away from his household and of having taken her into his own, where he calls her his daughter and pretends that she belongs to him. Apius, of course, rules in Claudius's favor and commands Virginius to hand Virginia over to the custody of the court.

If Apius is a wolf, at least he does not wear sheep's clothing. From the moment he is introduced into the narrative, we know full well the kind of unsavory fellow he is. He may be an unscrupulous, lowdown rascal, but he is not a counterfeit. The real counterfeit, the wolf in sheep's clothing to which the Physician refers, turns out to be none other than Virginius himself. I assert this for two reasons: 1) as soon as Apius hands down his judgment, Virginius immediately guesses that Apius is behind the false suit and that his aim is a lecherous one. How could Virginius so easily guess another man's desire unless it were his own? And 2) although Virginius seems to concern himself with his daughter's honor, it is really his own with which he is concerned. To have his paternity called into question brings dishonor to his name, and thus he is compelled to destroy the thing (that is, the girl) that has caused the dishonor. As in the *Franklin's Tale*, there is in the *Physician's Tale* a domino effect, sparked this time not by forgiveness but by blame. Although Virginius says to his daughter that she does

---

129 Although the Physician does not give voice to an accusation, the fact that Virginia is in her *mother's* company when Apius spies her is surely meant to be significant.

not deserve to "dyen with a swerd or with a knyf" (VI (C), 217), he explains to her that she must nevertheless do so, bemoaning the fact "that evere Apius the say!" (VI (C), 227). Setting aside, for the moment, Tertullian's misogynistic notions about seeing and being seen, there is a troubling ambiguity to this line, for it can be interpreted in two significantly different ways. The first reading makes Apius the owner of the look, while the second reading puts Virginia in possession of it. If Virginia is the one who looks, then Virginius can make her responsible for kindling Apius's desire, for, as we have learned from film theorists such as Linda Williams, to look is often interpreted as to desire.[130] So-called "good girls" are usually blind, oblivious to the fact that they are the recipients of a voyeuristic gaze, oblivious to the fact that they are desired. Is there, then, an accusation embedded in the knight's ambiguous phrasing? If so, this would account for his having set up a counterfeit court in the privacy of his own home, where he, like the exalted Sadian father who is beyond all laws, hands down a sentence that suggests guilt on the part of Virginia: "Take thou thy deeth, for this is my sentence" (VI (C), 223).

Although the Physician gives Livy credit for the tale he tells, his handling of the encounter between father and daughter is significantly different from that of his source text in two ways: first, according to the source text, Virginius kills his daughter in the public realm of open court. In the Physician's account, on the other hand, Virginius kills her in his feudal hall, which functions much like the libertine's "solitary," a place in the Sadian retreat "where the libertine takes some of his victims, far away from all, even friendly, eyes, where he is irrevocably alone with his object [...]."[131] And, second, according to the source text, no discussion takes place between father and daughter. In the Physician's account, on the other hand, Virginius and his daughter have a brief conversation before he beheads her. This "conversation," however, is one that makes a mockery of conversation, for although it is Virginius himself against whom the suit has been brought by Claudius, Virginius says to his daughter, "Thus hath he falsly jugged the to-day" (VI (C), 228). What this line and the line before it ("that evere Apius the say") do is to shift responsibility away from its proper source, whether it be Apius or himself, and toward his daughter. Significant, too, is the shift of pronouns from the second-person "thou" to the first-person "I" or "my" in the following passage:

> "Ther been two weyes, outher deeth or shame,
> That thou most suffre; allas, that I was bore!

---

130 Linda Williams, "When the Woman Looks," 83.
131 Barthes, *Sade / Fourier / Loyola*, 16.

For nevere thou deservedest wherfore
To dyen with a swerd or with a knyf.
O deere doghter, endere of my lyf,
[...]." (VI (C), 214–18)

Like the narcissist, Virginius requires everything (except responsibility, of course) to revolve around himself: his suffering, not Virginia's; his pain, not his daughter's; his loss, not hers. As for the reasoning Virginius uses in explaining to Virginia why she must die, it in itself is a form of violence. Like the reasoning the emperor uses for sending Custance to Syria or the reasoning Walter uses for taking Griselda's children away, Virginius's reasoning is no more "shared by the person to whom it is addressed than pleasure is meant to be shared by the object from which it is derived."[132] "For love, and nat for hate, thou most be deed," says Virginius, a sentence as illogical as Apius's is when he passes judgment without allowing Virginius to answer Claudius's false claim.[133] To Virginia's very legitimate question, "Is ther no grace, is ther no remedye?" (VI (C), 236), Virginius answers, "No, certes, deere doghter myn" (VI (C), 237), prompting Virginia to negate herself by agreeing to her own death. Like Griselda, who pledges unflagging obedience to her husband's will, Virginia does the same with her father, saying, "Dooth with youre child youre wyl, a Goddes / name!" (VI (C), 250).

There is what I would call an ugly dog-in-the-manger quality to the character of Virginius. Because he is Virginia's father, he cannot take her maidenhead, and so he takes her head instead. As Daniel Kline has argued, Virginius's "murderous act [is] as perversely violent as if he had deflowered her himself."[134] But I would go further, arguing that in the privacy of his "solitary," Virginius recognizes and satisfies his own incestuous desire by beheading his daughter, the beheading standing in for defloration. Although Kline argues that Virginius's use of synecdoche—"My pitous hand moot smyten of thyn heed" (VI (C), 226)—distances him from her murder, I would argue that it does the opposite, drawing him closer to both his incestuous desire and her murder than if he had said, "My pitous *swerd* moot smyten of thyn heed." Unlike Virginius's sword or knife, his hand is attached to his body in the same way that his genitals are, and thus to say that his hand will do the deed is to create intimacy between their bodies. And like a husband exposing the bloody sheets of his nuptial bed, Virginius carries his daughter's decapitated head to court and publicly presents it to the judge.

---

132 Deleuze, *Coldness and Cruelty*, 19.
133 See Bloch, "Chaucer's Maiden's Head," 23.
134 Daniel T. Kline, "Jephthah's Daughter and Chaucer's Virginia," 96.

In killing his only child, Virginius effectively destroys his family and his future. And thus it would seem that Virginius is compelled to act by the same kind of death wish that Bataille saw in Sade's writing: "In an endless and relentless tornado, the objects of desire are invariably propelled towards torture and death. The only conceivable end is [the] possible desire of the executioner to be the victim of torture himself. In Sade's will [...] this instinct reached its climax by demanding that not even his tomb should survive: it led to the wish that his very name should 'vanish from the memory of men.'"[135] With the beheading of Virginia, Virginius has effectively beheaded himself, for without progeny, his name will vanish from the memory of men. And with the telling of his tale, the Physician, too, reveals a death wish, for just as we expect a father to love and protect, not kill, his daughter, we expect a physician to heal, not hurt, those around him. And yet what the Physician offers to his fellow pilgrims is, like the severed head the knight offers to Apius, poison, not palliative. If he is remembered at all by his fellow pilgrims, it will be as the quack who told the sadistic story of child abuse and murder.

---

135 Georges Bataille, *Literature and Evil*, 95.

Chapter 6
Sadomasochism for (Neurotic) Dummies

> My rule of thumb: the more religious, puritanical
> or fundamentalist the territory, the kinkier it gets.
> —Susie Bright, *Susie Bright's Sexual Reality*

China's Aftershocks

Before Philip got to the front door, I saw him coming and picked up the book I had been trying unsuccessfully to read. As he put his key into the lock, I slid more deeply into the nylon sleeping bag and held the book up close to my face. I wanted him to know that his arrival was an interruption, and the only way to signal that was to appear to be doing something.

"Good book?" he asked, hanging up his jacket and dropping into the armchair across the coffee table from where I was lying.

"It's alright." I was noncommittal, still holding the book between us.

"Remind me not to read it," said Philip, noticing the scant number of pages pinched between my left thumb and forefinger.

I lowered the book. Even if I had not been reading with real focus, it irritated me that for Philip the speed at which I consumed the book indicated its value.

"What's for supper?" he asked, abruptly switching topics.

"I don't know," I said. I had eaten at the restaurant where I worked as a waitress and was not hungry. Besides, I missed the sweet Chinese wine and eating with chopsticks at every meal. A fork and knife seemed too harshly metal after the gentle wood of the chopstick.

"Shit," said Philip. He got up from his chair and went into the kitchen. I heard him open the refrigerator, move containers around, and then slam it shut with such violence that the bottles lined up in the door rattled and banged together.

"Shit!" he said again, this time with more force, and I had a sudden image of Philip wrapping my severed head in Saran Wrap and placing it in the refrigerator like a piece of cut-up watermelon. Returning to the armchair's embrace, he stared at me with accusing eyes.

"The fridge is empty," he said.

"Well," I began tentatively, "we could go to the store and—"

"*We?*" he said, incredulous. The word had never sounded nastier.

https://doi.org/10.1515/9781501514104-008

After a makeshift supper that did not really satisfy either of us, I crawled back into my sleeping bag and picked up my book again. Philip took a long bath and then came into the living room to towel off. I knew that I was supposed to watch with mounting desire, but I did not glance up from the pages of my book. Once Philip was dry, he twisted the towel into a whip and made popping noises with it until I was forced to respond.

Knowing that I did not want to know, I asked, "What do you want?"

He smiled, full of hope that my question was really meant to be answered, and rotated his hips so that his waterlogged penis flapped back and forth between his legs. It made a soft smack as it slapped first against the left thigh and then against the right.

"I want to go to bed with you," he said, beginning to swell.

"I'm not ready to go to bed yet," I said.

Philip dropped the towel to the floor and moved toward the couch, where he began to unzip the sleeping bag. "It's been a long time," he said. "We haven't done it once since we've been back."

I let him unzip the bag but said, "I'm not in the mood."

"You're never in the mood," he said, kissing my neck. "But I could get you in the mood if you'd let me."

I removed his hand from the depths of the sleeping bag and gently pushed at his face, which had moved from my neck to mouth. His touch, the touch of my husband, was repellant to me, but I had become expert at concealing an impulse to recoil, except that lately I had developed an odd little cough which erupted every time he tried to kiss me.

"Maybe later," I said, hoping he would be tired before long and that I would not have to turn him down again. The thought of his obvious desire filled me with rage, but I smiled at him with a tranquil face and understood that out of despair he would continue to ask and to hope.

He put on his pajamas and sat in the armchair, a newspaper spread across his lap. Soon, he was asleep. When a small snore erupted from his mouth, I looked up and examined his face.

At breakfast this morning, Philip was very quiet. I said, "I don't think you're very happy here in the People's Republic." And he said, "No, I'm not terribly happy here at the moment." I asked him why, and he gave a few vague answers, but when I pressed him, he told me he thought there was a rat in the apartment. He said he looked at the pear core this morning, and he thought he saw that a small bite had been taken out of it. He revealed all of this information at breakfast just as I was drinking my scalded milk and eating my steamed bread. Neither Philip nor I could quite finish, as one can well imagine.

I told him that I really doubted a rat was sharing our living quarters—maybe a mouse but not a rat. Nevertheless, when we returned from breakfast at the dining hall, we both went into the kitchen to examine the pear core. We had to hurry back to the apartment to arrive ahead of the little cleaning lady, who would have dumped out all evidence of a poaching rodent. Upon looking at the core, I decided that a bite had not been taken out of it and that there was no rat. However, as we were being shown to our offices today, Philip saw a dead rat on the staircase leading up to our floor. Wang Moxi was with us, and when Philip commented on the rat, Wang Moxi said that Sichuan has a lot of rats because of all of the grain grown here. Unfortunately, Philip pointed out the dead rat shortly before lunch, and so when we went into the dining hall, we again found ourselves unable to eat.

One might suppose we are being too squeamish, and probably we are, but the sights and smells in the streets are sometimes overwhelming. Plus, everybody hacks and spits because of the humid weather in this province and because of all the red pepper that is consumed. These unsavory things combined with the rat scare have made us a little less than enthusiastic about eating. And then tonight at supper, Philip's nose started bleeding.

"We have very different ways of coping with loneliness and fear," I said to myself as I turned back to my book. "He bleeds."

Two hours later, I had shifted from a sitting position to a sleeping position on the couch, and Philip had begun to stir. He folded up the newspaper, stood, and stretched.

"Time for bed," he said, moving toward the bathroom.

I heard him open the medicine cabinet and get out the toothpaste. I decided to wait until he was finished in the bathroom. Then I would get up.

Philip appeared in the doorway. "Come and brush your teeth," he said around a mouthful of toothpaste. The authority in his voice annoyed me, and I slid further down into the sleeping bag.

"I'm too tired to brush my teeth," I said in my most childish voice. "Will you brush them for me?"

Philip returned to the bathroom to spit out the toothpaste and rinse his mouth with water from the tap. I heard him relieve himself in a heavy stream that splashed against the toilet bowl, and then he blew his nose. I had come to loathe the sound of these bedtime rituals.

"Is Baby sleepy?" asked Philip, coming into the living room with my toothbrush in one hand and the toothpaste in the other. My lower lip stuck out in a pout, I nodded solemnly as he squeezed the sea-green paste onto the bristles of the brush. This was a game we had played before, and although I continued to employ it on occasion, I hated it because it did not work in the way that I wanted it to. Originally, I had thought that being babyish would call up the usual taboos, making me unappealing enough that Philip would go to bed and leave me alone, but the only purpose it served was to delay the inevitable request.

"Does Baby want Daddy to brush her teeth?" he asked in the voice an adult uses to speak to a child. I nodded vigorously and opened my mouth. Philip stuck the toothbrush in and began scrubbing away at my molars. I twisted my head this way and that, moving my tongue to one side and then the other so that he could brush the insides of my teeth.

"I wish you'd be like this in bed," said Philip. "Want to spit?" he asked, holding an empty cup to my lips.

"I swallowed it," I said, shaking my head.

"How obliging of you," Philip muttered.

"But I want a drink of water," I said miserably, forcing the ugly game to continue.

Philip rose from the couch and went into the kitchen to fill the cup. When he returned, he put his hand behind my neck and the cup to my lips.

"That's enough," I said after a few sips.

"Okay," said Philip, "time for Daddy to put Baby to bed." He took my hand and placed it on the hard flesh between his legs, but I jerked my hand away and plunged both arms inside the sleeping bag.

"Pretend I'm a quadriplegic."

"Is Baby playing a new game?"

"I can't feel anything from the neck down," I said, reflecting briefly upon the occasional intersection of fiction and fact.

Philip lifted me up and carried me to the bed, where he lowered me onto the right side. He plumped up the pillow beneath my head and then began to unzip the sleeping bag, but I stopped him.

"No, I want to stay inside the bag."

He shrugged and climbed into bed, jerking the covers irritably. "It'd be nice to sleep together sometime." Inside my cocoon, I remained as silent as a sphinx.[1]

---

1 A fictionalized version of this brief narrative appears in "The Very Small Things That Fall," a short story about the celebration of our first Valentine's Day upon Philip's and my return from China.

The Sphinx Speaks

If these bedtime games sound perverse, there is good reason, for what Freud discovered in his analysis of Dora is that the "motive forces leading to the formation of hysterical symptoms draw their strength not only from repressed normal sexuality but also from unconscious perverse activities."[2] "China's Aftershocks" may read like fiction—in fact, I first published it as part of a short story because I wanted to distance myself from the reality of our debased sexual relations—but it perfectly illustrates behavior on my part that is typical of the hysteric, for as Bruce Fink has found in his clinical practice, the hysteric resists being the source of sexual satisfaction for her male partner, keeping his desire unappeased while fantasizing that he is getting his sexual kicks from some other woman.[3] The hysteric, like the obsessional, takes as her motto, "The Other will never get off on me!"[4] This neurotic stance is quite different from that of the perverse subject, who devotes himself to the Other's *jouissance*; and while there was certainly a masochistic tinge to my sexual fantasies, at least on this score it would have been impossible to mistake me for a pervert.[5] Hysterics are often said to be suffering from sexual repression, and yet sexual matters are for them a central preoccupation, and they are generally quite knowledgeable about them. As Freud points out in the Dora case, "[W]here there is no knowledge of sexual processes even in the unconscious, no hysterical symptom will arise; and where hysteria is found there can no longer be any question of 'innocence of mind.'"[6] Although it is true that I was disgusted by the idea of having sex with my husband, it is also true that I got onanistic pleasure from a rich fantasy life. In typical hysterical fashion, I pictured my husband as the desiring one, but this did not mean as some feminists might argue that I occupied no position of desire. What Fink stresses and what I know to be true from personal experience is the hysteric's identification with her male partner: she "desires *as if she were him*. In other words, she desires as if she were in his position, as if she were a man."[7] In short, what excites her is imagining her partner in bed with another woman. Had I been able to share this fantasy with Philip, we might have been able to cobble together some sort of serviceable sex life, but given my aphasia, speaking of such a thing was impossible.

---

2 Sigmund Freud, *Dora*, 44.

3 Bruce Fink, *A Clinical Introduction to Lacanian Psychoanalysis*, 127.

4 Fink, *A Clinical Introduction*, p. 128.

5 Here, I am using the word "masochistic" in its popular and not in its clinical sense.

6 Freud, *Dora*, 42.

7 Fink, *A Clinical Introduction*, 124, his emphasis.

Perhaps anyone reading about our relationship would be hard pressed to understand why we continued to see each other after the debacle of the confessional and, more puzzling still, why we remained together as a married couple for as long as we did. Knowing that I was averse to having sex with Philip, why did I marry him? And once I had proven averse to having sex, why did he not seek divorce? (If we had lived during Chaucer's time, Philip could have taken me to court for denying him conjugal relations, and the court would have awarded him sexual reparation.[8]) There are a number of explanations that I could offer, but none is as satisfactory as what might be called the psychological bottom line: we were neurotic dummies, made so, at least in part, by our "civilized" moral and religious upbringings, ensnared in a nasty little "sadomasochistic" game of discipline and punish. Here, I am using Krafft-Ebing's neologism like Patricia Cramer does when she refers to Walter and Griselda as a couple who engages in sadomasochistic rituals of dominance and submission, for as she argues, "Walter's sadistic command of Griselda's acquiescence parallels relations of dominance and submission idealized in Christian dogma and institutions, the patriarchal family, and monarchies and other governments led by tyrants."[9] After the confessional, for example, Philip, like an early church father, disciplined and punished me for my unchaste behavior, and I, like Griselda, patiently submitted to what might be called his patristic and patriarchal abuse. But after we married, our roles were reversed, and I began (unconsciously) punishing Philip for his treatment of me by refusing to have sex with him, a refusal that he, like Griselda, (mostly) patiently submitted to. Perhaps if Freud's *Sexuality and the Psychology of Love* had sat on the shelf above my childhood bed instead of the Bible, I might have been less of a neurotic dummy, in all senses of the word, and more conscious of the abusive game Philip and I were playing with each other. Alas, my father as a bequeather of books was well acquainted with Dr. Spock but not with his most significant influence: Sigmund Freud.

---

8 According to Elizabeth Makowski's "The Conjugal Debt and Medieval Canon Law," by adopting "a debt-model of conjugal relations, the canonists maintained that each partner owed marital coitus to the other. The lawyers emphasized the mutually binding character of this obligation, and consistently defended the right of spouses to exact their marital due, insisting that this duty could be abrogated only by mutual consent," 99.

9 Patricia Cramer, "Lordship, Bondage, and the Erotic," 492. As I have pointed out, the term "sadomasochism" is a misnomer as far as psychoanalysis goes, and Deleuze has done a splendid job of showing why. However, the term does have its place in popular discourse, and so I use it here as shorthand for a dynamic involving cruelty on the part of one and a willingness to put up with that cruelty on the part of the other.

One of the dumber beliefs I held as a young girl—and one that I would wager is still quite common—was that a marriageable man would possess a certain set of admirable qualities and that as soon as I found one possessing the full set, I would be filled with desire and fall deeply in love. My set included qualities such as good looks, intelligence, wit, honesty, and mechanical know-how, and Philip was the first man I met who possessed everything on my wish list. (I created this list long before I knew anything about *objet a* and the difficulty of identifying what creates desire, and so I did not know that it is rarely a quality such as good looks or intelligence that sets desire in motion but the enigmatic *objet a* associated with the gaze or the voice. In other words, I may have thought I was responding to a man's good looks or intelligence when, in fact, I was responding to the way he looked at me or the way his voice hit my ears. A case in point was my immediate and strong sexual attraction to Eric M., a fellow college student who possessed very few of the qualities on my wish list and who I would have sworn up and down was not my "type.") Philip was a man of parts as they used to say in the eighteenth century, and I was enamored of that fact. One might even say that, like a good little fetishist, I took more satisfaction in his parts, in a Philip-in-parts, than in the whole.[10] Philip was like the living room of our apartment: each piece of furniture was exquisite, but I did not enjoy spending much time there. I would often pause in the doorway to survey the beauty of the room's décor and then make my way to the kitchen, where I would nestle down at the table with my books and papers. What I needed was a man like a kitchen, and that is what I got when I finally gave myself permission to ask Philip for a divorce.

Before we divorced, however, we tried therapy in an attempt to repair our sex life, stumping one therapist after another because we did not fit the stereotype of a couple whose marriage was in trouble: "You two appear to respect each other and to communicate well," they would say. "So what's the problem?" In short, they saw nothing wrong with our relationship, and so they were unable to help us. What these therapists did not know is that there is a structural difference between desire and love and that one does not often find them in the same place. I liked Philip, perhaps even loved him, and certainly felt affection for him, but I did not desire him, and trying to persuade me that I did would have been like trying to persuade a gay man that he is straight. In fact, one of the practices for which Lacan criticized American analysts was that of steering their analysands toward normative heterosexuality, believing as they did that those who cannot find sexual satisfaction and love in one and the same partner

---

10 Here, I am using the word "fetishist" in its popular and not in its clinical sense.

would be able to do so through therapeutic intervention. Because Lacan understood the structural differences between love and desire, he did not believe it was his job to bring about a fusion of the two but to aid in shoring up his analysands' libidinal economies. According to Lacan, neurosis is not the outcome when an analysand fails to find love and desire in the same person but when "the analysand gives up the pursuit of desire and sexual excitement, say, for the sake of an ideal such as 'the perfect love.'"[11] This is what I did in choosing to marry the perfect man of parts, and this is why most matchmakers fail in their mission to fix people up.

Paradigm Shift

My decision to enter the Ph.D. program at SUNY-Buffalo in the fall of 1990, two years after our return from China, was the beginning of the end for Philip and me. As I began taking classes with Joan Copjec, who was then director of the Center for the Study of Psychoanalysis and Culture, I began learning the language of psychoanalysis and speaking it at home. Philip was actively hostile to my new language acquisition, referring to it as jargon, at best, and gobbledygook, at worst. For me, however, reading Lacan's seminars with Copjec at the helm was a mind-bending experience, and, for the first time, I felt that my intellectual pursuits were destined to have a profound impact on my personal life. Unfortunately, the fact that I was being steeped in an academic culture that valued literary experimentation and theoretical rigor whereas Philip was working at a nine-to-five job meant that we were inhabiting worlds that had little in common. One thing I never explained to Philip and that might have made him more sympathetic to psychoanalysis was that it represented what might be called the antidote to my undergraduate experience as a non-virgin and non-Mennonite. Being marked as "other" at my undergraduate institution had been cause for alienation, but now my alterity placed me in good company. With psychoanalysis, the other (as Other) suddenly had gravitas and importance: for Freud, the Other is the discourse of the unconscious, and when it speaks through bungled actions or slips of the tongue, it speaks the truth. For Lacan, the Other might be said to steal the show from the subject, running "the unlikely gamut" from the Other as language to the Other as demand, desire, and *jouissance*.[12] In fact, one of the most famous lines of Lacan's oeuvre is "the self is

---

11 Fink, *A Clinical Introduction*, 128.
12 Bruce Fink, *The Lacanian Subject*, xi.

an other,"[13] a simple but uncanny statement that I found remarkably liberating. Instead of the claustrophobic, essentializing, and tyrannical tautology of the self as self, the concept of the self as other opened up space for existence, mystery, and play (in both the sense of "slack," or "give," and "role-play").[14]

Another thing I never explained to Philip and that might have seemed like an accusation had I done so was Lacan's lack of moralizing in his clinical practice. In "The Direction of the Treatment," as I have pointed out, he notes that while the analyst directs the treatment, he or she "must not direct the patient. The direction of conscience, in the sense of the moral guidance that a Catholic might find in it, is radically excluded here."[15] What this means is that when Lacan diagnosed one as a neurotic, pervert, or psychotic, no moral judgment was implied, simply a need to distinguish between three structurally different subject positions in order to determine the appropriate analytic treatment. Because the history of hysteria has included a great deal of moralizing regarding women's sexuality, Lacan's exclusion of moral guidance in his brand of psychoanalysis was good news to me, far better than that of the Calvinistic gospel, and, like a zealous missionary, I wanted to spread it far and wide.

What those who are hostile to Freud and his French disciple fail to recognize is the important paradigm shift that occurred when Freud returned to Vienna after having studied in Paris with the renowned neurologist Jean-Martin Charcot. Because Charcot emphasized the visual aspects of hysteria, the figure of the hysteric became a spectacle for prurient eyes, forced as she was to occupy center stage in the amphitheater of the Salpêtrière and to submit to the curious and titillated gaze of the male doctors in the audience. One has only to view André Brouillet's famous painting, *A Clinical Lesson at the Salpêtrière*, to recognize the sexual theatricality of this pedagogical *mise-en-scène*. When Freud shifted emphasis away from the visual and toward the aural register, the figure of the hysteric ceased to be a spectacle and became instead a figure of sympathy. As Mladen Dolar argues, desire itself is inherently aural; it is what causes dialectical exchange, what causes us to speak and to be heard. This is why the ear played a more central role for Freud than the eye, for Freud found it analytically fruitful to listen to the fragmented narratives his hysterical patients shared with him. In

---

13 Lacan gives the poet Rimbaud credit for having uttered it first.

14 Understanding one's self as an other does not entail shirking responsibility for one's actions, however. As Freud stated, "Wo Es war, soll Ich werden," translated by Lacan as "Where it was, there I must come to be." In other words, whatever trauma one has suffered, one must come to grips with it, placing oneself in the driver's seat and ceasing to blame everyone else for what ails one.

15 Jacques Lacan, *Écrits: A Selection*, 227.

fact, the relationship between Freud and his analysand included a visual occlusion, whereby the analysand, who lay on a couch, faced away from her analyst. And, thus, from Charcot to Freud, there was a significant shift from one method of treatment to another. "The stress fell," as Rachel Bowlby argues, "not on the patient as a bodily spectacle for assembled observers, but on her words to a single trusted interlocutor. Here the rehearsal of the symptoms is not didactic (for an audience) but therapeutic (for the patient)."[16]

Sitting in a seminar room at SUNY-Buffalo, I was in the same position as Freud's analysand when I underwent a paradigm shift not unlike Freud's. It began with a voice, the faceless voice of a student who sat behind me. The question he posed was smart and provocative, but that was not what made my ears prick up with desire. It was the timbre of his voice, a voice that caressed the ear like certain textures such as silk caress the skin. My mother would later say his voice sounded as if it had baby powder on it, and although it never would have occurred to me to put it that way, I knew exactly what she meant. His voice was the aural equivalent of a powdered baby's bottom. Who could resist falling for *that?* In shifting away from the visual to the aural, I left the concept of the wish list behind, rejecting what might be called the eye of judgment for the voice of analysis. Everything changed when I divorced Philip and set about getting to know the owner of that irresistible voice, a Canadian filmmaker and foundling who would later become my second husband and the father of my child.[17] His name was Mike, and, for me, he came to embody psychoanalysis because he put it into practice in his everyday life.

With Mike, what I had perceived as my sexual shortcomings and hang-ups were now being perceived *other*wise. For example, my sexual history was no longer cause for judgment but for *jouissance,* and our conversations about it were not confessional but alchemical, turning the base metal of my problems into psychoanalytic gold. Instead of occupying the position of judge, Mike occupied the position of analyst, encouraging me to talk about things I had never been able, much less encouraged, to talk about before.

Given a little urging and a lot of support from someone who was already well acquainted with both the practice and the value of psychoanalysis, I told Mike about the year I had Miss Labonnia for sixth-grade English. She was just out of college and thus a greenhorn when it came to discipline, quite literally chas-

---

16 Rachel Bowlby, Introduction, viii.

17 To speak of the "owner" of the voice is what might be called a necessary fiction, for as Dolar points out in *A Voice and Nothing More,* "The source of the voice can never be seen, it stems from an undisclosed and structurally concealed interior, it cannot possibly match what we can see. [...] Every emission of the voice is by its very essence *ventriloquism,*" 70, his emphasis.

ing the spirited Eugene F. around the classroom, jostling desks in the process and making papers fly, and instituting policies such as the following: if you throw a balled-up piece of paper at the trashcan and it misses, you get twenty licks with a wooden paddle. This policy was an attempt to keep the boys from treating the trashcan like a basketball hoop, but it backfired when model-student Melanie W. walked directly to the can, dropped her crumpled-up lunch bag in, and, because the can was so full, watched in horror as it bounced out of the can and onto the floor. *That'll never happen to me!* I thought to myself as Melanie received her licks. But it did, albeit over a new policy, and I found myself making an abject trek to the front of the classroom where the punishment was meted out. Miss Labonnia sighed deeply as she prepared to paddle me, feeling genuine regret that she could not bend the rules for a favorite student.

"Are you wearing shorts beneath your skirt?" she asked as she always did of the girls.

"Yes," I whispered, the embarrassment just as great as if she had lifted up my skirt to show everyone.

"Then I'll have to hit you harder," she replied. But the licks did not hurt, and I knew, along with the rest of the class, that she had taken it easy on me. I waited until I got back to my desk to cry, but then the shame overcame me, and I hid my face in my neatly folded arms, soaking them with silent but wet tears.

Sharing this story with Mike, I suddenly realized that although I may have been horrified by the thought of a public paddling, many of the boys appeared to intentionally provoke Miss Labonnia. Perhaps they imagined the paddle as an extension of Miss Labonnia's hand and, because the buttocks are in close proximity to the genitals, the contact between paddle and flesh called up makeshift images of the "hand job." Could they have been getting an erotic charge right under everyone's nose? This question led to another more pertinent one: did watching the boys receive their licks day after day lead to my beating fantasies or shore up already-existing ones? Until sharing my story with Mike, I had not known how common this type of fantasy was and probably still is, for Freud discusses it at length in "A Child Is Being Beaten," an article that first appeared in 1919 as a contribution to the study of the origin of sexual perversions. According to Freud, in the third phase of the beating fantasy, there are a number of children receiving blows. In girls' fantasies, for example, it is usually boys who are being beaten, but, states Freud, "the essential characteristic [...] is this: the phantasy now has strong and unambiguous sexual excitement attached to it, and so provides a means for onanistic gratification."[18] Having been introduced to Freud's

---

18 Freud, "A Child Is Being Beaten," 104.

article, it was beginning to dawn on me that I was not the only one who entertained such images in the private theater of her imagination and that some people, perhaps many, were actually bringing such images to life.

"Do you want to try it?" asked Mike, fingering a thin leather cord that looked as if it were capable of creating welts or drawing blood.

Because I have been through childbirth, it would not be true to say that getting whipped with that cord was the worst pain I have ever endured, but it was right up there with the pain I experienced when I spilled a pot of hot coffee on my socked foot. The burn was severe enough that the college nurse gave me a shot of morphine to ease the pain. Although I was determined for both Mike's sake and my own to be a good sport in the realm of sexual experimentation and erotic possibility, I had to admit a few whippings later that the beating fantasy was far better in theory than in practice. Having searing pain applied to one's buttocks obviously turns some people on, but not me. And yet it was both liberating and instructive to be able to test this fantasy out with someone I trusted.

Also liberating and instructive was the quintessential question of the 1990s posed by social anthropologist Ted Polhemus in *Rituals of Love:* "What is sex?" Before beginning to study psychoanalysis, I would have had no difficulty answering this question, nor would I have derived any particular pleasure from trying to do so. But once I began reading Freud and Lacan alongside books such as *Rituals of Love* and *Susie Bright's Sexual Reality*, both published in the early nineties and given to me by Mike, the question suddenly seemed a lot more complicated and the potential answers more interesting and varied. In attempting to tackle the question, Polhemus contrasts the 1960s to the 1990s, arguing that back "in the sixties when [he] was a teenager, such a question would have seemed absurd—you either did *it* or you didn't."[19] When he was writing *Rituals of Love*, however, the very "*meaning* of sex itself [was] changing—broadening, expanding and becoming less distinct."[20] One of the ways that Polhemus characterizes the change that took place in the lapse of thirty years is through the concepts of modern and postmodern sex:

> modern sex, like modern design is *functional*. In contrast, *post*-modern sexuality, like post-modern design, takes functionalism with a pinch of salt. [...] If the modern sex of Michael Leigh's swingers [...] saw its objective as drawing the shortest possible line between arousal

19 Ted Polhemus, *Rituals of Love*, 3, his emphasis.
20 Polhemus, *Rituals*, 3, his emphasis.

and release, the post-modern sex of the Scene delights in placing impediments in the path of this "functional" and "practical" imperative.[21]

Given these characterizations, the impediment my hysteria placed in the path of functional sex could be viewed as a form of postmodern sexuality rather than as a form of dysfunction. Instead of seeing myself as broken, crippled, or sick, the concept of postmodern sexuality allowed me to see myself as part of the Scene.

In drawing a parallel between postmodernism and "the Fetish Scene," "the S/M Scene," or simply "the Scene," Polhemus argues that

> both respect history—looking backward in order to look forward, mocking the sixties' idea that the future must be "liberated" from the past. Both dwell in a world of symbolism—endeavoring to be thought-provoking, conceptual as well as sensual. Both are unrepentantly eclectic—sampling from sources as diverse as possible, refusing to accept traditional distinctions between "good" and "bad" taste, high and low culture. Getting off on the mix. Both recognize the value of imagination and fantasy—rejecting the modern notion that reason and logic alone are sufficient.[22]

Much of what Polhemus says about postmodernism and the Scene can be said about psychoanalysis itself and the use Mike made of it in his sexual *Weltanschauung*, one he invited me to adopt. While some critics of psychoanalysis accuse it of being ahistorical, it is anything but that. In fact, it would be impossible to undergo analysis without looking back at one's personal history, a history always embedded in cultural and social histories that must be taken into account as well. And more than any other theoretical discourse, psychoanalysis is conceptual as well as sensual. Mike, too. Not only did he endeavor to be thought-provoking in bed, but also he recognized the value of imagination and fantasy, encouraging me to incorporate my imaginings and fantasies into our sex life. Although my bouts of aphasia made this difficult, I enjoyed storytelling, and as long as I cleaved to the notion of the self as other, I could avoid the silence brought on by shame. Like Freud and Lacan, Mike was unrepentantly eclectic, getting off on a mixture of high and low culture. On his bookshelves, for instance, one could find Emmanuel Levinas's *Ethics and Infinity* rubbing shoulders with Guido Crepax's cartoon version of *The Story of O*. The eclectic couplings present on Mike's bookshelves were not unlike those of my childhood bookshelf, and we both delighted in having "rangy" literary tastes.

---

21 Polhemus, *Rituals*, 26, his emphasis.
22 Polhemus, *Rituals*, 26–27.

If this sounds like a story bound for a happy ending, however, it is not. Mike and I divorced after six years of marriage, just before our young son turned three. The demise of our relationship can perhaps best be explained by Dolar when he argues that because the "voice is elusive, always changing, becoming, elapsing, with unclear contours," it "deprives us of distance and autonomy."[23] While I felt deprived of desire in my relationship with Philip, I only occasionally felt deprived of distance and autonomy. But, of course, Philip's voice had never acted on me like the voice of a Siren, a voice that can make one forget reason and rush headlong into disaster. And so what had been a seduction of the ear became an assault upon it, the cause of desire morphing into demand. Instead of sounding like the aural equivalent of a powdered baby's bottom, Mike's voice now struck my ears like the howl of an importunate toddler.[24] But my voice changed, too, for the more demands Mike made of me, the more mute I grew. And while it may be frustrating to have demands made on one, it is equally frustrating to be stonewalled. Several years after we divorced, Mike made a seven-minute film entitled *What Talking Means*. It is one of the most poignant films I have ever seen, and I am what might be called its leading lady. But there is no acting in the film, just pure neurotic dumbness as I struggle ineffectually to say something to Mike. The film begins with Jean-Luc Godard uttering the word "silence," and, like our marriage, it ends in silence as thick as fog.[25]

---

23 Dolar, *A Voice*, 79

24 I have made this claim regarding Mike's voice in slightly different form in "Desperately Seeking Wilco," 34.

25 *What Talking Means* can be found at the following website: https://vimeo.com/152004006.

Chapter 7
The Reeve's Paranoid Eye, or The Dramatics of "Bleared" Sight*

> If you don't go away, I shall punch you in the hurt.
> —Jacques Lacan, *Book III: The Psychoses*

> Two is a crowd.
> —Pete Yorn, "Black"

Persecution

Because paranoia is a form of psychosis that is often referred to as "a drama of seeing," the eye grossly deceived and looming large, it seems appropriate to begin discussion of the Reeve's paranoid eye with a reference to anamorphosis, an eighteenth-century coinage defined by Lacan as "any kind of construction that is made in such a way that by means of an optical transposition a certain form that wasn't visible at first sight transforms itself into a readable image."[1] Lacan gives a number of examples of anamorphosis, one of which is Holbein's painting *The Ambassadors* and another of which is a seventeenth-century chapel wall eighteen meters long that depicts a scene from the life of the saints or a nativity scene. In the case of Holbein's painting, there is at the feet of one of the two men an indecipherable blot that looks "roughly like fried eggs,"[2] a blot that only becomes decipherable as a human skull when the viewer occupies a particular vantage point vis-à-vis the painting. In the case of the chapel wall, the scene is completely unreadable from any point in the room itself, but if the viewer approaches by means of a certain corridor, the dispersed lines come together and, for a brief moment, allow the viewer to perceive the depicted scene.

If my starting point for discussion of the Reeve looks curiously like an indecipherable blot on the canvas or wall of Chaucerian scholarship, there is good reason, for what I introduce my students to when I teach *The Canterbury Tales* is a pedagogical form of optical anamorphosis, which requires them to approach the *Reeve's Tale* from aslant rather than head on. Taking a detour through the

---

* An early version of this chapter, now substantially revised and expanded, appeared with the same title in *ANaMORPHOSIS* 5 (2002): 91–129. I wish to thank editorial board member Martine Aniel for permission to reprint.

1 Jacques Lacan, *The Seminar of Jacques Lacan, Book VII*, 135.
2 Lacan, *The Seminar of Jacques Lacan, Book VII*, 135.

https://doi.org/10.1515/9781501514104-009

tales of the Knight and the Miller, my students and I approach the Reeve from an oblique angle, bringing something that is not visible at first glance into focus. Approaching the detour by way of Alfred Hitchcock and Franz Kafka, two latter-day masters of the paranoid scene, what looks like an indecipherable blot of anger created by the Reeve's choleric temperament gets transformed into a readable image: that of the Reeve's paranoid drama and his occulted object of desire.

Drawing upon Lacan's discussion of anamorphosis in relation to illusion, Slavoj Žižek makes use of the concept to talk about the way Hitchcock creates suspense in his films, a suspense that cannot help but give rise to paranoia. According to Žižek, what Hitchcock understood about filmmaking was that "the menacing horror should not be placed outside, next to the idyllic interior, but well within it, more precisely: under it, as its 'repressed' underside."[3] If, for example, a character in the film notices the out-of-place detail, suddenly sees too much, or gets access to surplus information, this has the disconcerting effect of rendering everything—even the most commonplace gestures—suspicious: "the 'true' action is repressed, internalized, subjectivized, i.e., presented in the form of the subject's desires, hallucinations, suspicions, obsessions, feelings of guilt."[4] The out-of-place detail that creates this paranoid perception is what Žižek refers to as the point of anamorphosis, "the element that, when viewed straightforwardly, remains a meaningless stain, but which, as soon as one looks […] from a precisely determined lateral perspective, all of a sudden acquires well-known contours."[5] Because this "meaningless stain" has the power to make everything appear suspicious, it propels one into the search for a meaning—"nothing is what it seems to be, everything is to be interpreted, everything is supposed to possess some supplementary meaning"[6]—in a now hostile world.

We see this phenomenon vividly illustrated in Kafka's very brief "My Neighbor," a story told through the voice of a paranoid narrator who looks at his circumstances awry, thus seeing a thinly veiled threat in everything his new neighbor does. In words that betray both his narcissistic *Weltanschauung* and his feelings of persecution, Kafka's narrator begins his two-page story thus: "My business rests entirely on my own shoulders. Two girl clerks with typewriters and ledgers in the anteroom, my own room with writing desk, safe, consulting table, easy chair, and telephone: such is my entire working apparatus. So simple

---

3 Slavoj Žižek, *Looking Awry*, 89.
4 Žižek, *Looking Awry*, 90.
5 Žižek, *Looking Awry*, 90.
6 Žižek, *Looking Awry*, 91.

to control, so easy to direct. I'm quite young, and lots of business comes my way. I don't complain, I don't complain."[7] With the first line, the narrator suggests that he is a one-man business, but he immediately undercuts this with the line that follows. For in describing his office space, he admits to having not just one but two clerks in the anteroom. What results from the juxtaposition of these two connotatively disparate statements is a split between the narrator's perception of reality and the reader's. Do the girls not count? Are they considered by the narrator to be mere pieces of office furniture, simply cogs in the wheel of the machinery that he operates? This split is further widened when the narrator indicates that his business is simple and successful and then assures the reader, not once but twice, that he has no reason to complain. Although this repetition is meant to reassure the reader (and perhaps the narrator himself) that what he says is true, it fails to do so. In fact, it creates the opposite effect. It makes us uneasy. We begin to doubt our narrator and to wonder whether he is as successful as he claims. Perhaps we even find ourselves asking, "Is his business on the verge of collapse?"

If the doubling of the girls and the narrator's obvious lack of interest in them does not prepare us for a tale of paranoia, then the narrator's use of the phrase "working apparatus" should, for with it comes an image of what Victor Tausk has called the "influencing machine" or a "suggestion apparatus," the appearance of which represents one stage in the development of a paranoid delusion. Following Freud, who believed that when a complicated machine appears in one's dream, it represents the dreamer's genitalia, Tausk hypothesized that this delusional machine or apparatus is a projection of the patient's body, which has become one big genital zone. In an effort to escape the feelings of isolation that result from the paranoiac's narcissistic regression, his body is projected outward.[8] It is, then, narcissistic regression that explains why Kafka's narrator is capable of blithely overlooking the importance of the girls, and it is the mechanism of projection that makes it possible for the narrator to view his office (that is, his body) as a working apparatus so "simple to control, so easy to direct." Although the narrator is already suffering the psychical decomposition characteristic of paranoia, something happens that disturbs the simplicity of his machine, forcing him to create complications where none need or do exist.

As the narrator tells us, a young man has moved into the office next door, a space that the narrator had long planned to rent but for which he had failed to make a bid. This office, he explains, is just like his own, except for the existence

---

7 Franz Kafka, "My Neighbor," 424.
8 See Victor Tausk, "On the Origin of the Influencing Machine in Schizophrenia."

of a kitchen. The reason for his foolish hesitation, then, was that he could not figure out what use might be made of the supplementary space, the surplus room. Given the similarity of the two spaces, it is clear that the narrator's office functions as the subject, while the neighbor's office functions as the subject's double, his mirror image plus what is "in him more than him." When the office next door—an office that in the narrator's imaginary world already belongs to him—is suddenly occupied or invaded by an/other, the narrator feels threatened, crowded out. Appropriately, the name that appears on the neighbor's door is "Harras Bureau," or at least that is the name the paranoid narrator sees. As the story draws to a close, we become less and less convinced that Harras is the one doing the harassing. In fact, we begin to wonder whether Harras even knows of the narrator's existence and, if so, whether he concerns himself about it one way or the other. The narrator, on the other hand, states with complete conviction that Harras is stealing his business, spying on him, and generally working against him: "I might assert that Harras does not require a telephone, he uses mine, he pushes his sofa against the wall and listens; while I at the other side must fly to the telephone, listen to all the requests of my customers, come to difficult and grave decisions, carry out long calculations—but worst of all, during all this time, involuntarily give Harras valuable information through the wall."[9]

Obviously, the narrator's simple, easy-to-direct machine has become hopelessly complicated, but such is the nature of paranoia. As Joan Copjec points out, because the subject is constructed in language, it is necessarily predisposed to paranoia, for in learning to speak, the child obtains its language and its thoughts from others. Hence, the paranoid notion that others can read one's mind actually has some grounding in reality. In the case of Kafka's narrator, however, paranoia is not simply a fleeting feeling but his general mode of operation, his machine or working apparatus becoming complicated because he has added parts "in an attempt to strengthen the inhibition of a repudiated wish for libidinal discharge."[10] As the machine grows more complex, intellectual interest increases and libidinal interest weakens. Given the narrator's apparently unprovoked fear of and hostility toward Harras, the direction in which his libidinal discharge would be aimed, were it not repudiated, is clear. If Kafka's narrator desires his neighbor, if the neighbor is the object of his affections, can we not think of his complex machine as a defense against this desire, a means of erect-

9 Kafka, "My Neighbor," 425.
10 Joan Copjec, "The Anxiety of the Influencing Machine," 55.

ing barriers when the only thing separating the two men is a "wretchedly thin" wall?

In connection with this ambivalent relation to the object of affection, it is fruitful to note again Lacan's discussion of courtly love, which appears at dead center of his *Ethics* seminar, the "empty" core or vacuole around which his commentary circulates. He speaks of courtly love poetry as having posited an object that he "can only describe as terrifying, an inhuman partner," arbitrary and cruel, separated "from him who longs to reach it by all kinds of evil powers, one of the names for which, in the charming Provençal language, is *lauzengiers*. The latter are jealous rivals, but also the slanderers."[11] He then mentions a medieval poet by the name of Guillaume de Poitiers who referred to the object of his affections as *Bon vezi* or "Good neighbor."[12] This same Guillaume was the first recorded troubadour, and, according to George Kane, in some of his more obscene poetry he registered the ambivalence with which the courtly lover, or "servant," viewed his "domna," or the lady who dominates. Kane suggests that if it was the "calculatedly obscene verse of Guillaume" that prompted Giraut de Bornelh to ask, nearly a century later, "[w]here the crime of speaking ill of ladies has come from [...]. From whom, themselves or the lovers?" it also supplied the answer.[13] Although Kane's suggestive remark does not supply an explicit answer, Lacan does so when he makes mention of the famous troubadour Arnaud Daniel, who wrote a poem in support of Lord Bernart's refusal to honor his lady's request for anilingus. According to Daniel, there are some things a man should never be asked to do, one of which is to put his mouth to his lady's "stinking trumpet," the implication being that if asked to do such a thing, a man is within his rights to speak ill of his lady love. Whether Chaucer had Daniel's poem in mind as he was writing the *Miller's Tale* I cannot say, but when Alisoun thrusts her "hole" out of the bedroom window and offers it to Absolon to kiss, she is making the same request as Lord Bernart's lady. And, like Lord Bernart, Absolon would prefer not to have (had) his desire tested in this manner. And yet his hysterical disgust at having kissed Alisoun's "nether ye" is an ambivalent affect, for disgust is a reaction formation signaling our ability to be simultaneously aroused by unconscious desire and repelled by shame and morality. As William Ian Miller so plainly and usefully puts it, "Disgust makes the genitals of the other smell bad and look ugly and one's own appear as a source of shame."[14] Its linguistic

---

11 Lacan, *The Seminar of Jacques Lacan, Book VII*, 150–51.
12 Lacan, *The Seminar of Jacques Lacan, Book VII*, 151.
13 George Kane, "Chaucer, Love Poetry, and Romantic Love," 240–41.
14 William Ian Miller, *The Anatomy of Disgust*, 109.

analogue is the word "perfume," inside of which is nestled the word for "shit,"[15] and it comes into play when one has encountered the terrible enjoyment of *jouissance* and/or been confronted with the *extimité*, a dimension located in neither the interior nor the exterior but "where the most intimate interiority coincides with the exterior and becomes threatening, provoking horror and anxiety."[16] An example of the *extimité* is the rim-structure of the anus, a rim-structure that plays a central role in both Miller's and Reeve's tales.

Here, then, is where we see come together the dispersed lines of the Knight, who tells a tale of courtly love introduced by a drama of seeing, the eye a rim-structure not unlike that of the anus; the Miller, who mocks courtly love by "bler-yng" its eye; and of the Reeve, who, because of his own repudiated desire, blears the Miller's eye. The Reeve and the Miller appear to already know each other, perhaps the only true neighbors among the group of pilgrims headed for Canterbury, and so the back story that emerges through their interaction could easily be titled "My Neighbor," for the Miller is both the Reeve's "Harras Bureau," or *lauzengier*, and his *Bon vezi*, the object of desire. Like the fear and hostility that cloak the desire of Kafka's narrator, the Reeve's choleric attitude toward the Miller masks another, much less choleric attitude. We know that when someone protests too much, the protest comes to be registered by the acute observer not as a negation but as an admission. A good example of this can be found in Tim Dean's discussion of the aggressive homophobia that catches many ostensible heterosexuals in its grip: "Lacan makes clear that evil obscenity from which we shrink in our neighbor is in fact the expression of our own jouissance. As cultural subjects, our desire is produced as the desire not to enjoy, thereby rendering jouissance Other."[17] Before the Miller even begins his tale, the Reeve is already cringing at the "evil obscenity" he assumes his neighbor will offer up. As is soon made clear by the audience's response, however, it is not the Miller

---

15 Valerie Allen, *On Farting*, 51. According to Allen, the "Middle English *fume* is a hunting term meaning 'deer turd.' The word entered English from French, *le fumier* [manure]. So, *pare-fumier* is so named as an antidote to dung."

16 Mladen Dolar, "'I Shall Be with You On Your Wedding Night,'" 6. Although Erin Labbie uses slightly different terms, she supports this reading when she argues that the "terrifying proximity of the very real flesh and mucous of the woman in Arnaut's text serves as a close-up that is too close," and thus this "'too much' of the closeness of reality must be resisted and so ambivalence, the hatred of the desire within the self, enters the scene as a form of negativity." See Labbie's *Lacan's Medievalism*, 98. Valerie Allen says something similar about the fart in *On Farting*: "An intimacy one hesitates to share with just anyone, the fart brings the other near at hand, into a state of 'intimate exteriority or "extimacy"' in which one is neither fully subject nor fully object, neither pure identity nor pure difference," 45.

17 Tim Dean, "The Psychoanalysis of AIDS," 112.

but the Reeve himself who presents his audience with the evil obscenity from which they shrink. The adulterous act, the fart, and the subsequent branding that occur in the Miller's narrative seem almost decorous when juxtaposed to the contents of the Reeve's, a revolting blend of sexual violation and what Bruce W. Holsinger expressively refers to as "the musical perversion of the family, an incestuous and sodomitical intermingling of the mouths and anuses of father, mother, and daughter."[18] In short, what the Reeve sees in the Miller actually resides within himself.

Let us begin, then, with the tale told by the Knight, which at first glance appears to be innocent enough but which, when examined more thoroughly, exposes the horror that lurks behind it. Following Statius's *Thebaid*, Chaucer sets the story in ancient Greece just after Theseus has killed Creon, king of Thebes, in battle, and so we are immediately reminded of an earlier story majestically articulated by Sophocles in *Oedipus the King*. This is the story of an eye tragically caught between seeing too little and seeing too much, a story that ends with Oedipus wounding himself in the eye, both as punishment for a look gone awry and as a means of escaping his own gaze and the gaze of others. As the servant who witnesses Jocasta's suicide and Oedipus's self-immolation reports,

> He tore the brooches—
> the gold chased brooches fastening her robe—
> away from her and lifting them up high
> dashed them on his own eyeballs, shrieking out
> such things as: they will never see the crime
> I have committed or had done upon me!
> Dark eyes, now in the days to come look on
> forbidden faces, do not recognize
> those whom you long for—with such imprecations
> he struck his eyes again and yet again
> with the brooches.[19]

The story that the Knight tells is thus set against a backdrop of incest and Oedipal conflict, in which a man kills his father, gains access to the forbidden maternal object, and mutilates himself in what Freud will later call a gesture of castration, the eye standing in for the male member.

Although the Knight's tale suppresses Oedipus's cries of grief and outrage, they are given voice to by and echoed in the cries of the women who waylay Theseus as he approaches the outskirts of Thebes, en route to Athens after having

---

18 Bruce W. Holsinger, *Music, Body, and Desire in Medieval Culture*, 186.
19 Sophocles, *Oedipus the King*, lines 1268–78.

been at war with, and having conquered, the Amazons. While he has obviously turned a deaf ear to the cries of the defeated Amazons, bringing back as part of his war booty two beautiful captives, Theseus hears and is sympathetic to the grieving Theban women whose men have been slain, their dead bodies left unburied because of Creon's edict. According to the story-telling Knight, Theseus immediately takes pity on the women, promises to help them, and does so by attacking the city and killing Creon. After the victory, Theseus's men are pillaging and looting when they stumble upon two young Theban knights who have been wounded and who are thus neither "fully quyke, ne fully dede" (I (A), 1015). Because they are said to be the sons of two sisters from the royal House of Thebes, it seems clear that Chaucer is encouraging us to think of them as the sons of Oedipus's daughters, Antigone and Ismene, and thus as the nephews of Oedipus's sons, Eteocles and Polyneices.[20] Because the two young knights are of royal blood, Theseus does not have them killed but locks them in a tower "thikke and stoong," where they are to remain perpetual prisoners.

It is from within the confines of this tower that both knights, Palamon and Arcite, are again wounded, this time in the eye through the sight of the beautiful Emelye. Palamon is the first to see her: "[...] thurgh a wyndow, thikke of many a barre / Of iren greet and square as any sparre, / He cast his eye upon Emelya, / And therwithal he bleynte and cride, 'A!' / As though he stongen were unto the herte" (I (A), 1075–79). When Arcite asks what ails him, Palamon replies, "This prison caused me nat for to crye, / But I was hurt right now thurghout myn ye / Into myne herte, that wol my bane be" (I (A), 1095–97). As Palamon is praying to Venus to have compassion on his lineage that "is so lowe ybroght by tirannye" (I (A), 1111), Arcite "gan espye / Wher as this lady romed to and fro, / And with that sighte hir beautee hurte hym so, / That, if that Palamon was wounded sore, / Arcite is hurt as muche as he, or moore" (I (A), 1112–16). When they recognize that they have fallen in love with the same woman, a fight ensues during which each argues that he saw her first. Seeing, then, is both cause of pain and proof of ownership.

Set in motion by the eye, the drama that follows is, in many respects, the same drama of fraternal strife that played itself out in Thebes when Polyneices

---

20 David Anderson further underlines the theme of incest when he argues that "Theseus's exclamation that Palamon is 'a kynges brother sone, pardee' can suggest only one person, and that is Polynices," thus drawing upon the *Thebaid*'s "tradition that Polynices had an incestuous affair with his sister Antigone." See "Theban Genealogy in the 'Knight's Tale,'" 314. The only problem with Anderson's argument is that both Eteocles and Polyneices are the brothers of a king, i.e., they are both brothers and sons of Oedipus because of his incestuous relationship with Jocasta.

and Eteocles fought over possession of the throne. In fact, argues David Anderson, "'fraternal strife' is the single most prominent motif in the legendary history of Thebes as it appears in the works of Statius, Ovid, Seneca, and the medieval posterity of these works, such as the *Roman de Thèbes*."[21] What this motif of fraternal strife suggests is the presence of psychosis, in which hostile imaginary relations dominate. One of the surest ways to distinguish a psychotic from a neurotic is by determining his or her conflictual realm. For the neurotic, conflict will always be expressed through complaints about the symbolic Other such as a parent or an authority figure from whom the neurotic wishes to gain approval. For the psychotic, on the other hand, conflict will be expressed through complaints about an imaginary other such as a rival or a competitor by whom the psychotic is being persecuted. The belief that one is being persecuted is a belief that arises out of imaginary relations, and persecution is, as Bruce Fink argues, the central feature in paranoid psychosis.[22] "If there is love and war," states Sarah Kay, "it is thanks to the imaginary," the realm of the ego and the "régime of the brother."[23]

What the rivalrous relations of the two sets of men (Palamon/Arcite and Eteocles/ Polyneices) suggest, then, is the aggressivity associated with the narcissistic ego. This aggressivity finds its root in "the alienation via an image specific to the mirror phase which constitutes itself as 'a primary identification that structures the subject as a rival with himself.'"[24] Although Lacan does not adhere to the idea of developmental stages, we can nevertheless speak of the "fiction" of our development as a kind of narrative: when a child lies in its mother's arms with its mouth firmly attached to her breast, or when her voice envelops it in sound, or when her gaze rests upon it, the child experiences itself as part of the mother or the mother as part of itself. In other words, the relation between mother and child is experienced as a non-relation, as a form of "oneness." You might say all is well, all is one, until weaning occurs, at which point the child must give up the breast and the intimate bodily contact that it has regularly enjoyed. Perhaps no child is happy at the loss of this important object, but how it learns to cope with the loss depends a good deal upon the intervention of the father, or the paternal metaphor.

In the usual course of development, the loss of the breast and the disconcerting split that the child experiences between itself and its mirror image is inscri-

21 Anderson, "Theban Genealogy in the 'Knight's Tale,'" 315.
22 Bruce Fink, *A Clinical Introduction to Lacanian Psychoanalysis*, 96.
23 Sarah Kay, "The Contradictions of Courtly Love and the Origins of Courtly Poetry," 231. See Juliet Flower MacCannell's *The Régime of the Brother: After the Patriarchy* in which she discusses modern social life as brother-dominated and thus psychotic.
24 Mary Ann Doane, *The Desire to Desire*, 128.

bed into the register of the symbolic. It is the father who takes responsibility for the loss because it is his law that denies the child continued access to the mother: "The Law offers words instead of things (instead of the Thing); it guarantees the objective world instead of the object."[25] If, on the other hand, the father fails to intervene as representative of the law, as guarantor of the objective world, the loss or lack (of the Thing) is not registered. It situates itself outside the law as an outlaw of sorts, and when this loss or lack remains at large, it is experienced as a lack of lack rather than as a lack in ourselves that causes us to seek out others who might fill that lack. The missing part is experienced as a surplus, something that crowds us out, something that occupies too much space. In other words, when the father's "no" is inoperative, everything is positivized. What this means is that the mirror image is not seen as part of oneself but as a hostile other: "The double is that mirror image in which the *objet a* is included. So the imaginary starts to coincide with the real, provoking a shattering anxiety. The double is the same as me plus the *objet a*, that invisible part of being added to my image."[26] The imaginary is the arena of the dyad and/or the double, and thus the subject is always in conflict in this register, for it believes that it must win its place at the expense of the other; it must annihilate or be annihilated.

This, then, is the position the Reeve finds himself in as the storytelling contest begins: stuck in the conflictual register of the imaginary. When the Knight finishes speaking, his tale ending with the blissful marriage of Emelye and Palamon—"And Emelye hym loveth so tendrely, / And he hire serveth so gentilly, / That nevere was ther no word hem bitwene / Of jalousie or any oother teene" (I (A), 3103–6)—Harry Bailly begins casting about for a proper follow-up tale, thus hitting on the Monk, who represents the Knight's counterpart on the social ladder. But perhaps because the drunken Miller knows more about Greek tragedy than anyone is prepared to give him credit for, he cannot let the Knight's tale go unrequited or—more accurately—uncorrected. Like moviemakers who change the endings of books to please their movie-going audiences, the Knight has taken it upon himself to lift the curse that plagued the House of Thebes and to give a happy ending to a story that should have ended tragically. He has also elided the effective position of women in feudal society, passing over the fact that Emelye, like her older sister, Ypolita, is powerless to determine her own fate or the direction of her desire. She is, as Lacan says, "essentially identified with a social func-

---

25 Dolar, "'I Shall Be with You On Your Wedding Night,'" 15.
26 Dolar, "'I Shall Be with You On Your Wedding Night,'" 13.

tion that leaves no room for her person or her own liberty."[27] The Miller may be a churl and a thief, but, in his desire to "correct" the Knight's romanticism with realism, he is also a bit of a feminist.[28] For, unlike Emelye and Ypolita, Alisoun is a woman with a "likerous ye" who actively takes charge of satisfying her own sexual desires. Thus, argues Glenn Burger, the tale the Miller tells "challenges its audience to 'see' via the nether eye; that is, to learn through a feminine, queer touch as much as a masculinist, dominating gaze."[29]

Before the Monk has time to consent, decline, or reply to Harry's request in any fashion, the Miller, who is half on and half off his horse, pipes up in a loud voice, swearing, "By armes, and by blood and / bones, / I kan a noble tale for the nones, / With which I wol now quite the Knyghtes / tale" (I (A), 3125–27). The fact that he can barely stay in the saddle and that he is in a drunken condition to boot suggests already the sort of tale he will tell: one in which all of the repressed violence and sex of the courtly romance return fully exposed in the earthly fabliau. Harry knows this and, acting in much the same way the censoring agent does toward desires that try to worm their way out of the unconscious, attempts to derail the Miller by evoking societal values such as propriety and forbearance: "Abyd, Robyn, my leeve brother; / Som bettre man shal telle us first another. / Abyd, and lat us werken thriftily" (I (A), 3129–31). The brutish Miller, however, is not to be derailed. As he makes abundantly clear, he will tell his tale or he will go his own way.

In order to keep the peace and the group intact, Harry allows the Miller to tell his tale, but when the Miller introduces its subject matter—"For I wol telle a legende and a lyf / Both of a carpenter and of his wyf, / How that a clerk hath set the wrightes cappe" (I (A), 3141–43)—he is suddenly interrupted by the Reeve, who tells the Miller to shut his trap, that it is a sin and a great folly "[t]o apeyren any man, or hym defame, / And eek to bryngen wyves in swich fame" (I (A), 3147–48). As we learn in the *General Prologue*, there are among the ranks of the pilgrims a carpenter and his wife, but the one identified as carpenter is not the one who objects to the subject matter of the Miller's tale. It is instead the Reeve, whose main employment is that of farm manager, description of his keen managerial skills taking up most of the lines of his portrait. Only in an aside do we find that he had, as a youth, learned the skills of carpentry.

---

27 Lacan, *The Seminar of Jacques Lacan, Book VII*, 137.

28 Glenn Burger seconds this when he states that however churlish the Miller might be, he "offers a breath of fresh air by providing a moment of fictional verisimilitude more directly mirroring the present of the Canterbury pilgrims." See his "Erotic Discipline ... or 'Tee Hee, I Like My Boys to Be Girls,'" 246.

29 Burger, "Erotic Discipline," 255.

Obviously, then, the Miller has hit a nerve, touched an open wound, as he unwittingly prepares to expose a truth about the Reeve that the Reeve wishes to keep suppressed. Despite the fact that the Miller is drunk and admits as much before beginning his tale, he responds to the Reeve's angry outburst quite reasonably, saying, in effect, "Why be upset? We both have wives, but that does not make us cuckolds. For every bad wife, there are plenty of good wives around. You'd be mad not to recognize that. And, anyway, why assume yourself to be a cuckold if you have no proof? It's best not to inquire too deeply into the affairs of one's wife." Nothing in the Miller's response suggests hostility toward the Reeve, nor does Chaucer-the-pilgrim say anything to indicate that the Miller has malicious intentions. In fact, the worst he has to say of the Miller is that his tale is one of "harlotrie": "What sholde I moore seyn, but this / Millere / He nolde his words for no man forbere, / But tolde his cherles tale in his manere" (I (A) 3167– 69).

As the Miller begins to speak, it becomes clear that offense could be taken by a number of pilgrims. The Monk, for example, could see the brash Miller's insistence on being next in line as an affront to the rule of "right order" or to the church in general. The Knight, too, has reason to take offense, for the Miller is fairly champing at the bit to requite his tale with one that makes an utter mockery of the chivalric code and courtly love, replacing the noble Palamon and Arcite with the "hande" Nicholas and the "joly" Absolon, and the virtuous Emelye with the lascivious Alisoun. The Wife of Bath, or Dame Alys, could also feel insulted if she chose, since much of what the Miller says of "his" Alisoun is true of the Wife of Bath. (In fact, the Miller's tale could be a chapter straight out of the Wife of Bath's life.) The lean and threadbare Clerk could feel hot under the collar —or elsewhere—if he were to identify too closely with the lustful Nicholas, who gets stung on the "toute" by a hot coulter. Even the Pardoner, who has the long, blond locks that Absolon is said to sport, and the Squire, who sings and dances just as Absolon does, could feel impugned by the Miller's characterization of the silly and vain parish clerk who serves the church where Alisoun goes to worship. The point is that the Miller, acting like the unconscious turned inside out, lays everyone low with his tale. It is a virtual wrecking ball, and yet the only one to take offense at it is the Reeve, for as the narrator tells us, "When folk hadde laughen at this nyce cas / Of Absolon and hende Nicholas, / Diverse folk diversly they seyde, / But for the moore part they loughe and pleyde. / Ne at this tale I saugh no man hym greve, / But it were oonly Osewold the Reve" (I (A), 3855– 60). Why, then, is the Reeve so aggrieved?

Given that jealousy plays such a central role in both the Miller's tale and the Reeve's payback, we can attempt to answer this question by looking at an essay Freud wrote on the relationship between jealousy, paranoia, and homosexuality.

He begins his discussion by distinguishing between three types of jealousy: 1) competitive or normal, 2) projected, and 3) delusional. Competitive jealousy is constituted by grief over the thought of losing the beloved object, hostility toward the successful rival, and criticism leveled at the self for its inadequacies. Projected jealousy, on the other hand, arises when one has actually been unfaithful or when the desire to be so has succumbed to repression. In this case, the partner is accused of infidelity in an attempt to ease one's own conscience. As Freud argues, "[T]he person can justify himself with the reflection that the other is probably not much better than he is himself."[30] Delusional jealousy, which Freud refers to as the worst type, also has its origin in a repressed desire to be unfaithful. The object of this desire, however, is of the same sex as the subject: "As an attempt at defense against an unduly strong homosexual impulse it may, in a man, be described in the formula: 'Indeed I do not love him, she loves him!'"[31] It seems, then, that Freud discovered the part homosexuality plays in paranoia through an analysis of delusional jealousy, for here the subject's repressed homosexual desires are projected onto the spouse. The formula for delusional jealousy is simple enough: "Indeed I do not love him, she loves him!" And although the formula for persecutory paranoia follows the same rules, it goes through a number of permutations before it emerges as a conscious thought. It begins with the statement, "I do not love him—I hate him." But because this proposition is unacceptable in its present form, it gets converted into yet another one: "He hates (persecutes) me, which will justify me hating him." What finally emerges from the original wishful fantasy of loving a man appears as if it were the result of an external perception: "I do not love him—I hate him because he persecutes me."

The Reeve's discomfort, like that of the jealous husband or the persecuted paranoiac, ultimately reduces itself to this: he watches his neighbor's unconscious mind much more closely and regards it as far more important than anyone else would think of doing. Only he perceives the Miller's words to be aimed in a specific direction; only he regards the Miller's words as laden with significance. Clearly, something in what the Miller says functions for the Reeve as the "meaningless stain" that renders the constituents of the Miller's tale suspicious. Although the rest of the pilgrims see the tale as nothing more than the drunken ribaldry of a pilgrim who can barely stay in his saddle, the Reeve sees it otherwise. But, as Freud points out, these manifestations of persecutory

---

30 Sigmund Freud, "Certain Neurotic Mechanisms in Jealousy, Paranoia, and Homosexuality," 161.
31 Freud, "Certain Neurotic Mechanisms," 162.

paranoia do not come out of the blue. Paranoiacs "let themselves be guided by their knowledge of the unconscious, and displace to the unconscious minds of others the attention which they have withdrawn from their own."[32] In other words, the hostility that the Reeve sees in the Miller is a reflection of his own hostile impulses toward the Miller, all of which arise as a defense against his desire for the Miller.

Obviously, the word "reflection" will play an important role in any discussion of paranoia, for, as has already been stated, it is out of the mirror stage that the aggressivity which characterizes paranoia arises. And the Reeve's response to the Miller's story is certainly an act of aggression, for instead of laughing at the hilarity of his neighbor's tale as the other pilgrims do, or simply "quiting" the Miller's story with one of his own, he says, "I pray to God his nekke mote to-breke [...]" (I (A), 3918). Even those who hold to the doctrines of the Old Testament cannot fail to note the difference between "an eye for an eye" and a broken neck for a broken arm. That is to say, the Reeve's revenge far outweighs the supposed insult, for while it is more or less the gullible carpenter's own fault that, having violated Cato's rule about marrying one's "simylitude," he falls and breaks his arm in the Miller's tale, the miller in the Reeve's tale is bloodied up and beaten senseless not only by the two clerks but by his own wife: "And with the staf she drow ay neer and neer, / And wende han hit this Aleyn at the fulle, / And smoot the millere on the pyled skulle, / That doun he gooth, and cride, 'Harrow! / I dye!' / Thise clerkes beete hym weel and lete hym / lye [...]" (I (A), 4304–8). If the Reeve cannot literally break the Miller's neck, he does so metaphorically at the conclusion of his tale.[33]

What the reader may fail to see is just why the neighbor poses such a threat to men such as the narrator of Kafka's story and the Reeve. But if we understand the threat as somehow connected to a manifestation of the double, then perhaps the anxiety created becomes less puzzling. As Dolar says of the double,

> [O]nly the subject can see his own double, who takes care to appear only in private, or for the subject alone. The double [...] arranges things so that they turn out badly for the subject, he turns up at the most inappropriate moments, he dooms him to failure [...]. In the end, the relation gets so unbearable that the subject, in a final showdown, kills his double, unaware that his only substance and his very being were concentrated in his double.[34]

---

32 Freud, "Certain Neurotic Mechanisms," 164.

33 A much later story from the other side of the Atlantic readily comes to mind, here, and that is Edgar Allan Poe's "The Cask of Amontillado," in which Montresor kills Fortunato for some unnamed insult received at the hands of his fellow wine-expert.

34 Dolar, "'I Shall Be with You On Your Wedding Night,'" 11.

I am not suggesting that the Miller is an apparition appearing only to the Reeve but that, unlike the way he appears to the other pilgrims, he appears to the Reeve in the form of the double, his mirror image plus what is "in him more than him"—that excess "sprout of enjoyment" which he must renounce in order to function as a member of the social community.

It is easy to see how the Miller could take on the exaggerated dimensions of the Reeve's anxiety-producing double, his surplus, for everything about the Miller is big, loud, and imposing. Recall, for example, how his body is described in the *General Prologue:* "The MILLERE was a stout carl for the nones; / Ful byg he was of brawn, and eek of bones" (I (A), 545–46). The Reeve's body, on the other hand, is described as slender and choleric. Further description of the two men calls up the image of Jack Sprat's fat wife and the skinny Jack Sprat himself, for as the narrating pilgrim says of the Miller, "At wrastlyng he wolde have alwey the ram. / He was short-sholdred, brood, a thikke knarre [...]" (I (A), 548–49) and of the Reeve, "Ful longe were his legges and ful lene, / Ylyk a staf; ther was no calf ysene" (I (A), 591–92). While the Miller's body is stout and fleshy—the image used is that of a thick knot—the Reeve's body is thin and unmuscled, the contours that give shape to the leg, non-existent. Chaucer-the-pilgrim's use of the image of the knot suggests what Lacan would call the kernel of the real, that empty core around which the subject constructs itself. This mention of the knot also calls to mind Lacan's three-link "Borromean knot," which shows the way in which the symbolic, the imaginary, and the real are imbricated. Operant in each of the three registers, the Miller functions as the core or knot around which the Reeve constructs himself.

If the Miller's body is more imposing, more *there*, than the Reeve's, so, too, is his virility.[35] Perhaps because he has the story of Samson in mind, Chaucer-the-pilgrim uses hair to suggest strength, vigor, and sexual potency. In describing the Miller's hirsute features, he has this to say: "His berd as any sowe or fox was reed, / And therto brood, as though it were a spade" (I (A), 552–53). Even the wart on the Miller's nose is decorated with (in the sense of decorated with a medal) "a toft of herys, / Reed as the brustles of a sowes erys [...]" (I (A), 555–56). His body provides fertile soil in which to grow hair, and just as the

---

35 Walter Clyde Curry argues in "Chaucer's Reeve and Miller" that Chaucer was almost certainly familiar with the Middle English *Secreta Secretorum*, which would say of the Miller's big facial features, "Tho that haue grete visachys and fleschy bene dysposyd to concupyscence of fleschy lustes," 200.

nose is often seen as a phallic protuberance, so, too, is the wart.[36] The Miller, then, is trebly endowed, fairly bursting at the seams with vitality and life. As for the Reeve, his lack of virility is suggested by his lack of hair: "His berd was shave as ny as ever he kan; / His heer was by his erys ful round yshorn; / His top was dokked lyk a preest biforn" (I (A), 588–90). The words used to "shape" the hair are given significance as well. The image of the spade, for example, is used to describe the Miller's beard. With its narrow handle and broad head, the spade suggests the phallic contours of the male "tool." In opposition to the spade is the "dokked" top of the Reeve, a phallic protuberance minus its crowning glory, the tip.

Chaucer-the-pilgrim also uses the sword to suggest virility, remarking that the Miller carries a sword and shield and that the Reeve's blade is rusty. Whatever the action, whether it be military or sexual, the Miller is prepared for it. The Reeve's rusty blade, on the other hand, suggests a man whose sword has not seen much use, a sex life that has dwindled off to nothing and become little but a dripping tap. Chaucer-the-pilgrim is not the only one to mention the Miller's weaponry, however. The Reeve himself draws considerable attention to it in his tale, bestowing upon his fictitious miller not just one sword but four: "Ay by his belt he baar a long panade, / And of a swerd ful trenchant was the blade. / A joly poppere baar he in his pouche; / Ther was no man, for peril, dorste hym touche. / A Sheffeld thwitel baar he in his hose" (I (A), 3929–33). This description implies two things: that the Reeve, as "open-ers," is acutely aware of the Miller's virility (his sword's blade is sharp), and that the Reeve fears castration by the Miller (Symkyn's multiple blades jut from belt, pouch, and hose).

In addition to the overly present body and magnified virility of the Miller are his cavernous, black nostrils and his big, furnace-like mouth, all of which suggest the devouring aspects of the big bad wolf with his larger-than-life features, an image that plagued the dreams of Freud's patient the "Wolf Man," whose obsessional neurosis was connected to the trauma of the primal scene. The image of the wolf turns up in the Reeve's tale when Symkyn determines to get the better of the two young clerks who have come to the mill to have their corn ground. As the crafty miller says to himself, "The moore queynte crekes that they make, / The moore wol I stele whan I take. / In stide of flour yet wol I yeve hem bren. / 'The gretteste clerks been noght wisest men,' / As whilom to the wolf thus spak the mare" (I (A), 4051–55). Although Symkyn compares himself to

---

36 Curry supports this take on the Miller's wart when he states that "Melampus renders his judgment, that if a Mole appear on the Nose or near the eye, that person is beyond measure Venereal," 206.

the mare that gets the best of the wolf, the clerks are the ones who ultimately wind up in the position of the mare, for, in the end, they beat the miller at his own game. The Reeve is also suggesting a parallel between the Miller (whose character he draws upon for the miller in his tale) and the wolf, for the Reeve believes himself to have gotten the better of his neighbor through his tale of revenge.[37]

Even more powerful than the big bad wolf, who is able to blow a house down, the Miller is able, using brute strength, to tear any door off its hinges or, using his head as a battering ram, simply to break it down. No carpenter's skills or building materials can stand up to the force that the Miller brings to bear on them, for if the Reeve is good at making doors, the Miller is better still at knocking them down. The Miller's attack on doors and his ability to destroy them also suggest the force of the unconscious. The censoring agent is, in some sense, the equivalent of a closed door or a barrier, but even unconscious desires that remain repressed get through this closed door or barrier in the form of symptoms and parapraxes. As for the Miller's lusty piping, it calls to mind his instrument's single drone and large, round bladder—an image of the male penis and testicles—as well as its loud and mournful wail, used in battle as a means of creating dread and terror in the enemy. Perhaps this is why, as the Miller leads the procession of Canterbury-bound pilgrims out of town with his piping, the Reeve chooses to stay as far away from the Miller as possible, silently bringing up the rear. Not only do the Miller's imposing bodily proportions and physical exertions take up space, but also his piping and dirty stories fill the air with sound. He is, after all, referred to by the narrator as a "janglere and a goliardeys": he both blows on a windbag and acts as one. Thus, for the Reeve, it will be impossible not to feel invaded, through eye, ear, and "openers," by the Miller's all-encompassing presence.

In "Grimaces of the Real," Žižek links the anxiety-producing double who embodies the subject's surplus, or that "Thing" that is "in the subject more than the subject itself," to the figure of the debauched anal father. This father, as I have pointed out, is the reverse of the Oedipal father whose law actually allows the subject to become a member of the community. What Žižek calls the anal father is often referred to as the primal father, but, as Žižek points out, the concept of "anal father" is meant to emphasize "the obscene nature of the father qua pre-

---

37 As John H. Fisher notes, this reference to the wolf comes from one of the Reynard stories: "The mare told the fox who wanted to buy her colt that the price was written on its back hoof. When he went to read it, the colt kicked him, whereupon the mare made the observation about 'greatest clerks,' etc." See Fisher's *The Complete Poetry and Prose of Geoffrey Chaucer*, 72n.

symbolic 'partial object.'"[38] It is appropriate that the Reeve's double be identified with this anal father, for the paranoid subject is always in search of the missing father, and his or her delusion is, as Mary Ann Doane puts it, "a desperate attempt on the part of the paranoiac to compensate for the absence of the paternal signifier."[39] Because the law, or the paternal signifier, does not operate for the paranoiac, he or she constructs a simulacrum of the law through the paranoid delusion. Although Doane is discussing the paranoid delusion in relation to gothic film, what she says about it applies to the Reeve's narrative as well, for he creates a simulacrum of the law through his hyperbolic "image of the aggressive, punishing, castrating Father [...]."[40] From the Miller's ability to wrestle any man to the ground and any door off its hinges to his possession of multiple blades, he is the image of the aggressive, punishing, castrating father writ large. No courtly love poetry could have posited an object more terrifying and inhuman for the Reeve than Chaucer's Miller.

Unfortunately for the Reeve and other paranoiacs, the paranoid delusion gives rise to a catch-22 situation: although the delusion is an attempt to create an object relation, the Other who gets created is so menacing that there arises on the heels of this construction a need to destroy it. Without the presence of the benign law-giving father, who creates a mediating distance between objects, the world is always claustrophobically close, its features threatening and monstrous in their proportions. As we know from Edgar Allan Poe's story "William Wilson," the destruction of his threatening Other makes Wilson more an outcast of society than ever, for he begins his story with the following complaint: "Oh, outcast of all outcasts most abandoned!—to the earth art thou not forever dead? to its honours, to its flowers, to its golden aspirations?"[41] Because the appearance of his double causes him social embarrassment on numerous occasions, Wilson blames his troubles at school and with society at large on his double, not realizing that his tie to the community will exist only as long as his double does. Once he has killed his double, Wilson is no longer stitched into the social fabric. He exists in the all-or-nothing of foreclosure. Thus, to murder one's double is not the proper response when confronted with its uncanny presence.

It would seem, then, that the cards are stacked against the Reeve, given the strength of his opponent, but he fights against his double through the mechanism of projection. (If killing it is not the proper response, neither is merging with it as we know from David Cronenberg's *Dead Ringers*, a film about twin gy-

---

38 Slavoj Žižek, "Grimaces of the Real, or When the Phallus Appears," 54.
39 Doane, *The Desire to Desire*, 133.
40 Doane, *The Desire to Desire*, 145.
41 Edgar Allan Poe, "William Wilson," 1.

necologists who are so attached to each other that if one dies, so, too, must the other.) Projection is the Reeve's protection against psychosis, but it also signals his troubled relationship to the symbolic community. Like the paradoxical nature of the homeopathic remedy, the symptom that shows the subject's attempt to cure itself is the same symptom that points to its illness, the symptom being part and parcel of the disease.[42] Because paranoia is constituted by a disturbance in the relation between subject and object or the internal and the external, projection is used as a means of correcting this disturbance, reasserting the oppositional relation when it appears to have collapsed. This collapse is well illustrated by the transitivism that can be observed in very young children: the child who hits will say that he or she has been hit, and the child who sees another fall will cry. What is at play, here, is the merging of self and other characteristic of the imaginary, the register in which there exists no clear division between subject and object. The problem with projection as a corrective, argues Doane, is that when one transforms an internal representation into an exterior perception— and this is the defensive mechanism of projection—one destabilizes the opposition between internal and external, subject and object. Thus, argues Doane, "the boundary between the two is constantly in flux."[43] It is because of this fluctuating boundary that Freud describes the paranoiac as seeming "almost normal" and, at times, even refers to paranoia as a neurosis. He did, after all, title his essay on paranoia "Certain *Neurotic* Mechanisms" rather than "Certain *Psychotic* Mechanisms in Jealousy, Paranoia, and Homosexuality."

Ultimately, the appropriate response to the double is to situate oneself at a proper distance from it. It does not work to kill it as we know from a story such as "William Wilson," nor does it work to merge with it as we know from *Dead Ringers*. Just as one must situate oneself properly in order to see—to be too close creates myopia and to be too far away, blindness—one must situate oneself properly in order to live peacefully with one's double. In the imaginary, however, it is impossible to achieve the proper distance, for one is always either too close

---

42 It is interesting to note that the pervert's fetish functions in much the same way that the paranoiac's delusion does. Because both perversion and paranoia upset defining limits and thus destabilize boundaries, both the fetish and the delusion are defenses against psychosis. The pervert's fetish is the means by which he reestablishes fantasy and the field of illusion, both of which involve an opposition between absence and presence, surface and depth, the veiled and the unveiled. Similarly, it is through the paranoiac's delusion that the opposition between internal and external is reconstructed. Both perverse and paranoid subjects attempt to repair broken boundaries by finding a substitute for the missing paternal signifier.

43 Doane, *The Desire to Desire*, 130.

(rejoining with the double) or too far away (fighting it to the point of annihilation).

Primal Scene

For the Reeve, the Miller's function is polyvalent. To cover the fact that the Miller is his "Good neighbor," the Reeve turns him into his "Harras Bureau," but the Miller also operates as the unconscious of his fellow pilgrims. In discussing the primal scene, however, I shall argue that the Miller functions most acutely as the Reeve's unconscious while Harry Bailly functions as his failed censoring agent. The fact that the Reeve tries to prevent the Miller from speaking, once Harry has failed to stop him, suggests that the tale the Miller is about to tell is one that the Reeve already unconsciously "knows," one that he wishes to keep repressed. In other words, the bawdy tale the Miller tells to the delight of his fellow pilgrims points toward the Reeve's psychic disorder and reconstructs its originating moment, the primal scene. The fact that the Miller tells the tale of a carpenter is important, not because it is an attack on the Reeve but because the Reeve's carpentry is a thing of the past, a skill he learned in his youth. Because the central character in the Miller's tale is a carpenter, a link is thus established between a bit of the Reeve's youthful history and the primal scene. As Doane points out, in paranoia's repudiation of the father, its regressive character allies itself with the dyadic structure of narcissism, the imaginary, and the pre-Oedipal, thus evincing "strong links between paranoia and the primal scene."[44]

From the very outset of the Miller's tale, then, we have the Oedipal threesome required for the trauma of the primal scene: the carpenter, his wife, and their lodger, Nicholas. (Like the kitchen in Kafka's "My Neighbor," Absolon functions as a kind of surplus in the Reeve's primal scene.) We know, too, from the Miller's description of the three characters that Nicholas is lecherous and sly, the carpenter's wife young and wild, and the carpenter old and jealous—two characteristics of importance, for the infirmity that accompanies old age is often equated with the awkwardness and lack of coordination that is manifested in infancy, and jealousy is almost always associated with the workings of the paranoid mind. Although the carpenter has taken young Alisoun as his wife, the true love alliance, if any alliance in the tale can be referred to as such, is that of Alisoun and Nicholas. In fact, the first instance of dialogue occurs between these two when Nicholas tells Alisoun of his desire and convinces her to participate

---

44 Doane, *The Desire to Desire*, 131.

in a secret tryst with him: "This Nicholas gan mercy for to crye, / And spak so faire, and profred him so faste, / That she hir love hym graunted atte laste, / And swoor hir ooth, by Seint Thomas of Kent, / That she wol been at his comandement, / Whan that she may hir leyser wel espie" (I (A), 3288–93). If the carpenter's own eye is responsible for the situation he finds himself in, that is, married to a woman far too young and attractive for him, then it is Alisoun's eye that will betray him, for it is her eye that will "espie" a "leyser" moment in which to make her husband a cuckold. Right from the start, then, the carpenter is positioned as the outsider, the one who does not know the woman's desire, the one whose look is impotent except in its ability to wound the carpenter himself.[45]

Nicholas puts his plan for bedding Alisoun into action at the first opportunity, disappearing into his room for a day or two—just long enough to arouse the carpenter's concern. When the carpenter's servant-boy is sent upstairs to look in on the lodger and returns to tell his master that "[t]his Nicholas sat evere capyng upright, / As he had kiked on the newe moone" (I (A), 3444–45), the carpenter grows still more concerned and decides to pay Nicholas a visit himself. What he finds out during his visit is that Nicholas has determined through his study of astrology that a flood twice as bad as Noah's is about to hit and that the only ones who can be spared are the carpenter, his wife, and Nicholas: "But Robyn may nat wite of this, thy knave, / Ne eek thy mayde Gille I may nat save; / Axe nat why, for though thou aske me, / I wol nat tellen Goddes pryvetee" (I (A), 3555–58). In one fast move, Nicholas has placed himself in the position of God or father, for he is the one who knows when the rains will begin, who may or may not be saved, and how to construct a makeshift ark.

Both God-like and father-like, the sly lodger is now *de facto* head of the household, issuing orders to the carpenter who acts as an obedient son: "Anon go gete us faste into this in / A knedyng trogh, or ellis a kymelyn, / For ech of us, but looke that they be large, / In which we mowe swymme as in a barge, / And han therinne vitaille suffisant / But for a day—fy on the remenant!" (I (A), 3547–52). Not only does Nicholas instruct the carpenter to purchase tubs and fill them with the necessary food supplies, but also he commands him to hang the tubs from the rafters: "But whan thou hast, for hire and thee and / me, / Ygeten us thise knedyng tubbes thre, / Thanne shaltow hange hem in the roof ful hye, / That no man of oure purveiaunce espye" (I (A), 3563–66). Espe-

---

45 The same can be said of Absolon, for, like John, he does not know what Alisoun desires. And it is his eye's inability to discern what it sees that leads Absolon to kiss Alisoun's "nether ye" and wound his dignity thereby.

cially ironic is the reward Nicholas says the carpenter will reap when he has accomplished these tasks:

> And whan thou thus hast doon as I have seyd,
> And hast oure vitaille faire in hem yleyd,
> And eek an ax to smyte the corde atwo,
> [...]
> Thanne shaltou swymme as myrie, I undertake,
> As dooth the white doke after hire drake. (I (A), 3567–69, 3575–76)

What Nicholas's words imply is that once the carpenter has done as he has been told, he will be emasculated, a duck rather than a drake. The carpenter's impending emasculation is further implied when Nicholas says that after the flood, he and the carpenter will "be lordes al oure lyf / Of al the world, as Noe and his wyf" (I (A), 3581–82).[46] These statements are, perhaps, the only moment of fair play in the sly clerk's deception of the carpenter. He does, after all, warn him of the consequences of following these orders, but the simple carpenter misses the danger signs because all he can see is the vision of the world's end. In this respect, the carpenter is not unlike Daniel Paul Schreber, the psychotic judge who, as Freud tells us, "became convinced of the imminence of a great catastrophe, of the end of the world."[47] Voices told him that the earth's allotted span was nearly over and that he was "the only real man left alive," the same ideas that the voice of Nicholas whispers into the ear of the carpenter.

As the Miller rightly states, "Men may dyen of ymaginacioun, / So depe may impressioun be take" (I (A), 3612–13). Allowing himself to be duped by the voice of Nicholas, who supposedly gets his information straight from God, the gullible carpenter actually begins to hallucinate: "This sely carpenter bigynneth quake; / Hym thynketh verraily that he may see / Noees flood come walwynge as the see / To drenchen Alisoun, his hony deere" (I (A), 3614–17). As Doane points out, "At the extreme end of paranoia as psychosis, we witness the annihilation of both the object of desire and subjectivity itself, manifested most explicitly in the paranoiac's delusion of the 'end of the world.' Here, the mechanism of projection breaks down altogether."[48] Amidst a deluge of hallucinations, tears, and grief, the carpenter sets to work, however; and on the appointed day, the three climb into their suspended tubs to await the flood. Nicholas has, of course,

---

46 Nida Surber sees these statements rather differently, arguing that the "deerne love" of which Nicholas knows is non-heterosexual and that the real triangle of desire is that of John, Nicholas, and Absolon. See *The Fierce Parade*, 48–49.
47 Sigmund Freud, *Case Histories II*, 207
48 Doane, *The Desire to Desire*, 130–31.

told the carpenter that he must hang well apart from his wife during the flood and that there must be no sin between them—"Namoore in lookyng than ther shal in deede" (I (A), 3591). Here, Nicholas seems to function as the Oedipal father, the one who denies the child incestuous access to the mother, and yet in this case he also denies the child that important moment in which the discovery of sexual difference occurs, that is, the moment of looking.

In fact, nearly everything about the carpenter's primal scene is problematic. Although the setting is right—he sleeps in the security of his suspended crib, while his "parents" engage in sexual intercourse in the bed below—the genders of the central players are confused. For example, Nicholas is described as "lyk a mayden meke for to see" (I (A), 3202). Even the way in which he decorates his chamber and perfumes himself sounds curiously feminine: "Ful fetisly ydight with herbes swoote; / And he hymself as sweete as is the roote / Of lycorys or any cetewale" (I (A), 3205–7). If Nicholas is as maidenly and sweet-smelling as any girl, his rival, the unexpected interloper who stands at the window serenading Alisoun, is described in equally effeminate terms: "Crul was his heer, and as the gold it shoon, / And strouted as a fanne large and brode; / Ful streight and evene lay his joly shode. / His rode was reed, his eyen greye as goos. / With Poules wyndow corven on his shoos, / In hoses rede he wente fetisly" (I (A), 3314–19). Everything about Absolon suggests the ambiguous sexuality of the fop, from his dainty demeanor and his fine clothes to his high treble singing, his fastidious speech, and his squeamish dislike of flatulence.[49] As Dolores Warwick Frese points out, "By scrupulously adhering to the canons and categories of idealized feminine beauty as they were prescribed by the medieval rhetorical handbooks, Chaucer deliberately constructed a suitor more 'ladylike' than the country-bred girl whose favor he seeks."[50]

Not only is the sexual identity of the male characters ambiguous but also that of Alisoun. By the light of day, there is no question that Alisoun is a woman, but when the lights go out, confusion reigns. As the Miller tells it, Absolon makes it a point to keep tabs on Alisoun, and when he hears that her husband is out of town, he immediately makes a beeline for her darkened bedroom window. Not knowing that someone else has already beaten him into the desired bed, he makes his lovelorn plea and is soundly rebuffed. Unwilling to take "no" for an answer, he enters into a deal with her, promising that if she will give him

---

49 John H. Fisher notes that "Absalom, who was killed because his long hair caught in an oak as he rode under (II Samuel, 18:9 ff.), was regarded as a type of effeminate beauty and vanity." See Fisher's *The Complete Poetry and Prose of Geoffrey Chaucer*, 60n.

50 Dolores Warwick Frese, "The Homoerotic Underside in Chaucer's *Miller's Tale* and *Reeve's Tale*," 145.

one kiss, he will go away and leave her in peace. As Absolon waits for Alisoun to approach the window, he thinks to himself that once he has gotten the first kiss, perhaps something more will follow. What Alisoun offers him in the darkness is "hir naked ers," however, which he kisses with a great deal of savor before the "bare" facts have time to register. Once they do, "Abak he stirte, and thoughte it was amys, / For wel he wiste a womman hath no berd. / He felte a thyng al rough and long yherd, / And seyde, 'Fy! allas! what have I do?'" (I (A), 3736–39). What Absolon has kissed is not the luscious lips of his lady but a bearded "face." As Peter Beidler has pointed out, Chaucer is unique in having Alisoun thrust her buttocks out of the window, for in all of the tale's European analogues, it is the male lover who does so.[51] What Chaucer's deviation from his analogues does, as Burger argues, is blur the difference between Nicholas and Alisoun, suggesting "that both sex and gender are slippery and sliding signifiers, as much multiply contested sites of meaning as regulatory fictions."[52] Further complicating Alisoun's gender identity is the fact that the narrating Miller compares her to a "wether" or a castrated male sheep when he says that she is "softer than the wolle is of a wether" (I (A), 3249). The thing to notice, as Mark Miller points out, is that Alisoun "is being imagined as a castrated male, and a sexy one at that."[53]

If gender identity is confused in this bedroom scene, so, too, is sexual desire. When Absolon realizes what has happened, he is furious. Instead of enjoying the fact that he has been allowed intimate contact with his beloved's private parts, he bites his lips in anger, wiping at them and rubbing them with dust, sand, straw, and cloth. His is hardly the behavior one expects of a courtly lover, unless that lover be Lord Bernart. In fact, his behavior suggests a certain aversion to the earthy aspects of sexuality, to its real face rather than its imaginary. He does not simply go away mad, however. He vows revenge. To punish his lady for what he may perceive to be an unreasonable test, Absolon returns with a red-hot coulter, borrowed from the blacksmith down the street, and calls Alisoun to the window again.[54] This time Nicholas answers the amorous call, apparently hoping to have

---

51 Peter Beidler, "Art and Scatology in the *Miller's Tale*," 92.
52 Glenn Burger, "Erotic Discipline," 252.
53 Mark Miller, "Naturalism and Its Discontents in the 'Miller's Tale,'" 27–28.
54 As James H. Morey states, "Ploughshares and coulters were used in trials by ordeal to determine the guilt or innocence of women accused of adultery. [...] Two types of ordeal involving parts of the plow should be distinguished: treading barefoot on nine hot plowshares, and carrying a hot coulter in the hands for a certain distance (usually three paces or, sometimes, the length of the church nave). Simply accomplishing the ordeal was not enough; the real test was whether the wound scabbed cleanly or putrefied. Such trials were always supervised by clergy and were most common from the ninth to the twelfth centuries in cases without witnesses or

his naked "ers" kissed as well. When Absolon says, "Spek, sweete bryd, I noot nat where thou / art" (I (A), 3805), Nicholas "leet fle a fart / As greet as it had been a thonder-dent" (I (A), 3806–7) and is rewarded for this trumpet blast with a "hoote kultour" on the "toute." Despite the humor, vulgarity, and the fart that veil the erotics of the scene, the image that springs to mind is, as many have noted, one of two men engaged in sodomy.

In the carpenter's primal scene, then, the men look, smell, and act like women, while the woman sports a beard. And instead of delighting in his opportunity to kiss Alisoun's hinder-parts, Absolon goes away in disgust. His more successful rival appears to desire the attentions of Absolon, which do not manifest themselves as a kiss but as a prod on his rump with a hot rod. As James H. Morey points out, "[T]he first syllable of 'cultour' ['cul' is French for 'buttocks'] more than hints at the coulter's destination. The second syllable, in its Middle English sense of 'turn,' or 'taking one's turn,' also foreshadows what Alisoun and Nicholas do with their 'culs.'"[55] The homoerotics of the scene are further supported by Frese's reminder that the "almost surely homosexual" English king Edward II was murdered in a fashion not unlike the "poetic execution" of Nicholas: "Edward somme tyme kynge was brought from Kenelworthe [prison] to the castelle of Berkeley, where he was sleyne with a hoote broche putte thro the secret place posterialle."[56] What I am suggesting, in short, is that any child looking in on this scene would be hard pressed to make sense of gender identity and sexual desire. And for the carpenter, confusion will be coupled with physical pain and linguistic impotence.

"Water" is the word that brings the two triangulated narratives together— that of the carpenter, his wife, and Nicholas, and that of Alisoun, Nicholas, and Absolon. As Nicholas cries out for water to cool his burning flesh, and this is the ejaculatory cry that brings the scene to its climax, the carpenter awakens from his slumber and cuts the rope that keeps his tub suspended. This sudden cry can be read as the sound a child hears in the night, that mysterious sound which betrays the parents' lovemaking activity. Doane explains the relationship between the paranoiac's primal scene and his particular delusions in this way:

> The fixation to the primal scene elucidates the paranoiac's activation of sound and image as the material supports of the symptom (the obsession with "hearing voices" and "being

---

physical evidence. The body served as the 'text' of last resort upon which guilt or innocence would be written." See Morey's "The 'Cultour' in the *Miller's Tale*," 374.

55 Morey, "The 'Cultour' in the *Miller's Tale*," 373.
56 Frese, "The Homoerotic Underside," 147.

watched"). For the young child watching and listening to its parents in the primal scene must itself remain unseen, unheard. As [Guy] Rosolato points out, sound has a double polarity at the level of this originary fantasy. For it can potentially "betray" not only the parents but the little voyeur as well: sound would expose the parents for their act and the child for its desire to see that act. Sound exists, in this context, as a betrayal of the desire to see.[57]

Like any curious child, the carpenter responds to this cry by "dropping in" to the scene of coitus. Knocked out of the security of his crib and into the adult world, the carpenter swoons, waking up moments later to a broken arm and accusations of madness. If the father's gift of language allows the child to be sutured into the signifying chain and positioned securely within the symbolic community, then Nicholas refuses his "son" this gift, for he (along with Alisoun) refutes everything the carpenter says: "For whan he spak, he was anon bore doun / With hende Nicholas and Alisoun. / They tolden every man that he was wood" (I (A), 3831–33). Because language is a vehicle of exchange between speaking subjects and because it is the glue that keeps society from falling apart or unraveling into fragmented pieces, it is no small thing to be denied access to language. But that is precisely what Nicholas and Alisoun do to their "child" by telling the community that he is crazy and that his words mean nothing. Instead of paving his way into the community as good parents are supposed to do, Nicholas and Alisoun alienate him from it: "For what so that this carpenter answerde, / It was for noght; no man his reson herde" (I (A), 3843–44).[58]

---

57 Doane, *The Desire to Desire*, 132.

58 Of interest, here, is Mark Miller's argument that it is not John's reason that is repudiated but his reasons for desiring intimacy: "John's punishment, then, is less a denial of the rationality of intimacy than an attempt to destroy the possibility that the desire for intimacy might have reasons for it, born of the fearful fact that the reasons you have might be ones that no one else is willing or able to hear." See Miller's "Naturalism and Its Discontents in the 'Miller's Tale,'" 34. The fact that the person with whom John wants intimacy—that is, Alisoun—does not want intimacy with him is an illustration of Lacan's bombshell statement, "[I]l n'y a pas de rapport sexuel," or "[T]here's no such thing as a sexual relationship." Although the French wording "rapport sexuel" is ambiguous in that it can be translated as "sexual intercourse," Lacan was not asserting that people are not having sex. He was asserting that there is no immediate or direct relationship between men and women, that something always stands between them, mediating, blocking, and thus skewing their interactions. For example, when a man and a woman are in bed together, both function under the illusion that they are coupling with each other although they are actually coupling with something else entirely: an/Other partner. For the man, this Other partner is *objet a*, and for the woman, it is the phallus—both of which represent imaginary objects. In other words, men and women do not couple with each other but with their unconscious fantasies about each other.

The fact that Nicholas and Alisoun operate as one negates the reality of difference; and, as Ellie Ragland points out, the suffering the psychotic is subject to "comes precisely from not having been signified in identification by a 'law' of difference powerful enough to separate him or her from the excesses of the mother's jouissance."[59] What this means is that in psychosis, difference is not acknowledged; the psychotic subject clings to its primordial identifications with the mother, rendering its ego rigid and non-dialectical. And if we look at the Reeve's position with respect to his fellow pilgrims, we see the effects of this non-dialectical ego. As Chaucer-the-pilgrim describes each pilgrim in turn, he also recounts who rides in company with whom and who rides where. Of the Reeve, he says, "And evere he rood the hyndreste of oure route" (I (A), 622). The Reeve never changes position, never gallops to the head of the procession, never rides abreast of another pilgrim. His position at the rear remains rigid. What this petrified position at the rear also suggests is the Reeve's identification with the mother and/or woman, for in the tale he tells, he says that when Symkyn and his wife appear in public, the miller struts in front while his wife follows behind: "On halydayes biforn hire wolde he go / With his typet wounde aboute his heed, / And she cam after in a gyte of reed [...]" (I (A), 3952–54).[60] As we know from the description of the Miller given in the *General Prologue*, he leads the procession out of town, playing his bagpipes at full tilt. This positioning, the Miller in front with his bagpipes and the Reeve at the rear, parallels the position of husband and wife on holidays as the Reeve describes it in his tale. And thus it points toward the conflict that lies at the heart of paranoia—the defense against a homosexual wish. Just as Judge Schreber's defense against his homosexual desire for his doctor manifested itself in a sexual delusion of persecution and later converted itself into the grandiose notion that he was to be transformed into a woman for the purpose of coupling with God, the Reeve's unconscious desire for the Miller manifests itself in both his delusions of persecution and his identification with the woman's position.

Like the riddle of the Sphinx ("What goes on four legs in the morning, two at midday, and three in the evening?"), answered correctly by Oedipus when he says, "Man: in infancy he crawls; in maturity he walks on two feet; and in his dotage he uses the support of a cane," the Miller's tale is a riddle that only the Reeve can answer. For the tale is a screen on which is projected the Reeve's nightmarish primal scene, a scene that operates oddly in the temporal world, si-

59 Ellie Ragland, *Essays on the Pleasures of Death*, 45.
60 In order to avoid confusion, I distinguish between the Miller as pilgrim and the miller who appears in the Reeve's tale by using an uppercase "M" for the former and a lowercase "m" for the latter.

multaneously showing the Reeve as child, the Reeve as youth, and the Reeve as dotard. As a child, the Reeve had access to the mother and the marital bed because the father was inoperative, suspended in a tub, waiting for the end of the world. As a youth, the Reeve's sexual relation with a woman was interrupted by the call of another youth whose "hoote kultour" pressed against his "toute" produced the ejaculatory cry of climax. As a dotard, the Reeve has become the originary object of contempt, the inoperative father suspended in a tub, waiting for the end of the world. What is hinted at but perhaps elided is the stage between youth and dotard in which the Reeve behaves as Absolon does, fooling himself into believing that he desires a woman but when confronted with the real thing, her "real thing," he not only turns away in disgust but also wishes to destroy it.

Corps Morcelé

The "Evil Eye"

As if thoroughly to impress upon his audience the high points of his story, the Miller ends his tale by briefly summarizing the events he has just narrated. In his summary, he says, "And Absolon hath kist hir nether ye" (I (A), 3852). His use of the word "nether" is interesting because it suggests something that lies beneath, as in the nether world, a region thought to lie below the earth's surface, a region in which we find ourselves bumping into ghosts and shades, or remainders, shadows, and traces. Acting as a kind of pseudo-analyst, the Miller is offering the Reeve an opportunity to kiss his own nether eye, that is, to confront his own unconscious desires. But, unlike Oedipus, who seeks out the truth and finally takes responsibility for the plague that has troubled Thebes, the Reeve refuses the truth, turning a willfully blind eye toward it. Instead of taking responsibility for his own paranoid relationship to the community, he blames the Miller. Instead of attacking his own eyes, he attacks his neighbor's. Instead of kissing the nether eye, which floats unbidden into his prologue, he turns it into an evil eye and throws it back to the Miller, for the first thing he says is "So theek […] ful wel koude I thee / quite / With bleryng of a proud milleres ye […]" (I (A), 3864–65). Like the paranoid narrator of Poe's "The Tell-Tale Heart," whose sole complaint against the old man he kills is his possession of a vulture-like "pale blue eye, with a film over it," the Reeve focuses his ire (and his eye) on what he perceives to be the Miller's evil eye. Of course, the Reeve does not literally refer to this eye as evil, but the way it functions for the Reeve suggests as much, for not only does he begin but also he ends his prologue with reference to the Miller's eye: "He kan wel in myn eye seen a stalke, / But in his owene he kan nat seen a balke" (I (A), 3919–20).

In *Seminar XI*, Lacan talks at length about the relationship between the eye and the gaze, and so it is useful to note what he has to say about the concept of the evil eye: "It is striking, when one thinks of the universality of the function of the evil eye, that there is no trace anywhere of a good eye, of an eye that blesses. What can this mean, except that the eye carries with it the fatal function of being in itself endowed [...] with a power to separate."[61] Lacan's statement is surely meant to remind us of little Ernst's game of making himself disappear: "He had discovered his reflection in a full-length mirror which did not quite reach to the ground, so that by crouching down he could make his mirror-image 'gone.'"[62] Like little Ernst, very young children seem to believe that by closing their eyes, they can make themselves go away. Thus, the eye is given tremendous power despite the fact that it is easily deceived. But aside from suggesting that it is in the realm of the visual that presence and absence operate, what Lacan is pointing to, here, by attributing to the eye the "fatal function" of the "power to separate" is the traumatic moment in which the child sees its mother naked and discovers that her sexual organs are different from those of the father. This is the moment of seeing that marks sexual difference and institutes the castration complex. From this point on, therefore, the eye will always be associated with castration and/or death.[63]

For the Reeve, the Miller's eye acts as what Lacan refers to as the *fascinum*, or "that which has the effect of arresting movement and, literally, of killing life."[64] Given this, how else can the Reeve view the Miller's storytelling but as an attempt to arrest his movement and pin him to the moment of trauma, a trauma from which he has never managed to recover? In the face of this perceived arrest, the Reeve attempts to counter with a moment of seeing, albeit not one of his own, for if the *fascinum* is anti-movement, then the moment of seeing is its corrective. As Lacan says, it "can intervene here only as a suture [...] and it is taken up again in a dialectic, that sort of temporal progress that is called haste, thrust, forward movement [...]."[65] But let me be more concrete. Recall,

---

61 Jacques Lacan, *The Seminar of Jacques Lacan, Book XI*, 115.
62 Sigmund Freud, *Beyond the Pleasure Principle*, 9
63 The eye's connection to death can be seen more concretely if one calls to mind the Bernardo case in which two young girls were murdered because they saw the faces of their rapist-captors. Knowing the connection between seeing and dying, one of the girls, whose blindfold had become loose, asked that it be retied.
64 Lacan, *The Seminar of Jacques Lacan, Book XI*, 118.
65 Lacan, *The Seminar of Jacques Lacan, Book XI*, 118.

for a moment, the bedroom brawl in the Reeve's tale that ensues when Aleyn mistakenly crawls into bed with a snoring Symkyn, takes him by the neck, and whispers tidings of his sexual prowess in the miller's ear: "Thou John, thou swynes-heed, / awak, / For Cristes saule, and heer a noble game. / For by that lord that called is Seint Jame, / As I have thries in this short nyght / Swyved the milleres doghter bolt upright, / Whil thow hast, as a coward, been agast" (I (A), 4262–67). The miller, in a reciprocal gesture, grabs Aleyn by the "throte-bolle," and the men "walwe as doon two pigges in a poke [...]" (I (A), 4278). Although Aleyn manages to land a hard punch in the miller's face, the darkness of the bedroom inhibits accuracy. The clerks win the fight, however, with the aid of the eye, or a moment of seeing. And this moment of seeing, faulty as it turns out to be, is attributed to the miller's wife, who

> saugh a whit thyng in hir ye.
> And whan she gan this white thyng espye,
> She wende the clerk hadde wered a volupeer,
> And with the staf she drow ay neer and neer,
> And wende han hit this Aleyn at the fulle,
> And smoot the millere on the pyled skulle [...]. (I (A), 4301–6)

The wife's eye, then, is what gives the clerks the upper hand. For once Symkyn's wife has hit him with the staff, he cries out, "Harrow! I dye!" and, having pinpointed his position, the clerks descend on him with all their fury. As the Reeve says, "Thise clerkes beete hym weel and lete hym / lye" (I (A), 4307). Ultimately, then, the Reeve uses a "whit thyng" to get back at the Miller, and what is this white thing if not the white wall or blank tablet mentioned in the *Book of the Duchess*? The grieving knight says that when he was a youth, his mind was "As a whit wal or a table, / For hit ys redy to cacche and take / Al that men wil theryn make [...]" (780–82). As Susan Yager explains, "The 'whit wal' of the young man's mind has not, at this point, been painted with the image of the beloved. In the *Book of the Duchess* the Knight, his mind like a white canvas, waits to see whom to love [...]."[66] If the Miller offers the Reeve repressed material to examine, the Reeve's tale is an attempt to negate the unconscious, to erase the black marks that have been put on the "nether" page. Although the Reeve believes that he has "quit" the Miller with his tale and bleared his eye, what the Reeve fails to recognize is that his own eye is the one that is deceived, for he "sees" in the Miller all the jealousy and aggressivity that is his own.

---

66 Susan Yager, "'A Whit Thyng in Hir Ye': Perception and Error in the Reeve's Tale," 397.

The Fragmented Body

Although the bloody bedroom scene is rife with images that "represent the elective vectors of aggressive intentions,"[67] it is in the Reeve's prologue that he calls attention to his own fragmented body and the aggressivity that accompanies it. During the flow of comments and laughter that follow the Miller's tale, the Reeve begins to "grucche," and although perhaps no one enjoys the rantings of a man full of ire, it is clear from Harry's response to the Reeve's preliminary comments that he recognizes the Reeve as a paranoiac. For, as Lacan has usefully pointed out, "people have always known how to define the paranoiac as a touchy, intolerant, and distrustful gentleman, who is in a state of verbalized conflict with his surroundings."[68] It is clear, too, that Harry has not really been listening to the meaning of the Reeve's words, for he cuts him off rather impatiently, saying, "What amounteth al this wit? / What shul we speke alday of hooly writ? / The devel made a reve for to preche, / Or of a soutere a shipman or a leche" (I (A), 3901–4). The Reeve has not been preaching or speaking of holy writ; he has been talking about his dismembered body and the rage that arises in response to it. In fact, the Reeve's entire prologue is a verbal articulation of the frustration that accompanies the mirror stage. According to Lacan, it is during the mirror stage that the still-dependent toddler recognizes itself in its mirror image. What it sees is a "whole" being, one whose limbs are connected and work in tandem. There is, then, a moment of exultation in which the child thinks that it has regained what it lost when the mother's breast was withdrawn. But directly on the heels of this exultation comes the disappointing realization that its lived experience of the body is quite different from its specular image. What this disappointment gives rise to are frustration and aggressivity because the image in the mirror is seen as far superior to, and thus more "together" than, the child itself. This explains why the imaginary is always a conflictual register. What the child fails to understand, however, is that the image it sees in the mirror is not whole either. In fact, the eye is not only the great deceiver, but also it is radically limited in its capabilities, for we cannot see ourselves from the point at which we look at ourselves. The thing that escapes our view is our coincidence with ourselves. In other words, there is always something missing, and the part that is missing is the unspecularizable *objet a*, a part of us (such as the

---

67 Jacques Lacan, *Écrits: A Selection*, 11.
68 Jacques Lacan, *The Seminar of Jacques Lacan: Book III*, 92.

mother's breast) that was never ours to begin with but that we continue to long for nevertheless.[69]

The Reeve's first complaint—"Til we be roten, kan we nat by rype [...]" (I (A), 3875)—articulates the vel of lack or division in which the subject is constituted.[70] What the Reeve is complaining about in this line is his lack of coincidence with himself, a state that Lacan calls *manque-à-être* or want-in-being. This want-in-being is connected to *aphanisis*, the temporary eclipse, or the fading, of the subject. As Lacan explains it, "[W]hen the subject appears somewhere as meaning, he is manifested elsewhere as 'fading,' as disappearance."[71] Thus, the Reeve cannot be ripe (have meaning) without being rotten (disappearing). This sleight-of-hand is further clarified by Lacan's discussion of the imaginary:

> [E]very imaginary relation comes about via a kind of *you or me* between the subject and the object. That is to say—*If it's you, I'm not. If it's me, it's you who isn't.* That's where the symbolic element comes into play. On the imaginary level, the objects only ever appear to man within relations which fade. He recognises his unity in them, but uniquely from without. And in as much as he recognises his unity in an object, he feels himself to be in disarray in relation to the latter.[72]

And what does the Reeve say about this want-in-being, about the frustrating discrepancy between a "hoor heed" and "grene tayl"? He says that all he is left with in the face of this vel are four live coals: "Avauntyng, liyng, anger, coveitise" (I (A), 3884). Like the child discovering its want-in-being or division in its mirror image, the Reeve is enraged by the impossibility of closing up the gap. And although he denies or negates (in other words, lies about) his desire to pay the Miller back—saying, in essence, "I could pay the Miller back if I liked to speak of ribaldry, but I'm too old for that"—what is his tale but an angry act of vengeance against his rival mirror image? Thus, the Reeve's four live coals burn his tale into existence; they are the hot coltour applied to the Miller's (that is, the bad father's) "toute." The Reeve's glowing coals—boasting, lying, anger, and covetousness—are akin to the aggressive intention "organized in those reactions of opposition, negation, ostentation, and lying" that Lacan's clinical experience has shown to be characteristic of the exercise of the ego in dialogue.[73] The

---

69 This explanation of the mirror stage can be found in a slightly different form in my essay "Pounding the 'Amy' Out of Imagism, or 'Jouiring' Like an 'Idiot' Carrying a Big Stick," 29.

70 When Lacan uses the Latin word *vel*, he is referring to a forced choice such as "your money or your life."

71 Lacan, *The Seminar of Jacques Lacan, Book XI*, 218.

72 Jacques Lacan, *The Seminar of Jacques Lacan, Book II*, 169, his emphasis.

73 Lacan, *Écrits: A Selection*, 15.

mote in the Reeve's eye, then, is his own over-sized ego, which makes him boast, lie, rage, and covet.

Appropriately, Freud uses the image of the patch (in other words, a piece of material that covers the blind or bleared eye) to explain the origin of the psychotic delusion: "the delusion is found applied like a patch over the place where originally a rent had appeared in the ego's relation to the external world."[74] Perhaps the best way to think about Freud's statement is in relation to the concept of suture. We can understand this rent as castration, the mark of the divided subject, a rent that we all suffer and that is made up for through suture into the symbolic network. Because the psychotic is not sutured, however, he or she uses the delusion as a kind of "substitute" suture. But it is a substitute that does not work very well, for what it gives rise to is the aggressivity that accompanies "captation by the imago of the human form," a form that Lacan argues is "invested with all the original distress resulting from the child's intra-organic and relational discordance during the first six months, when he bears the signs [...] of a physiological natal prematuration."[75] In analysis, images of the fragmented body often arise when the progress of the analytic work has brought about in the analysand a certain level of aggressive disintegration—that is, perhaps, when the delusion ceases to work as a patch and the fabric falls apart. This level of aggressive disintegration seems to be at play when the Reeve says of himself, "Oure olde lemes mowe wel been unweelde, / But wyl ne shal nat faillen, that is sooth" (I (A), 3886–87), for he exposes a perception of his body as unwelded limbs. What this image suggests is stagnation or petrification at an archaic stage of development. Although the passage of years has reduced his "streem of lyf" to mere drops upon the "chymbe," the Reeve is still functioning as if he has encountered his mirror image for the first time.

The Murder Weapon

The Reeve may occupy a similar "outcast" position and exhibit the same murderous impulses toward his double that Poe's characters do, but there is one significant difference between Chaucer's paranoiac and Poe's. The Reeve sublimates, while the narrators of "The Cask of Amontillado," "William Wilson," and "The Tell-Tale Heart" do not. Instead of walling up his opponent in a wine cellar, run-

---

74 Sigmund Freud, "Neurosis and Psychosis," 215.
75 Lacan, *Écrits: A Selection*, 19.

ning him through with a rapier, or murdering him in his bed, the Reeve tells him a story.[76] As the Reeve says in his prologue, "For whan we may nat doon, than wol we speke [...]" (I (A), 3881). His "murder weapon," then, is metaphor, and if he commits a crime, it is that of injuring the ears of his audience with a story they do not like, the result of which is his further alienation from the community.

The question that arises is this: if both the Miller and the Reeve are "cherls" who tell tales of "harlotrie," why do the pilgrims respond positively to the drunken Miller's tale but ignore and/or meet the Reeve's tale with silent disapproval?[77] One answer has to do with the obscurity of the Miller's supposed crime. In other words, it is probably not clear to the group of pilgrims precisely why the Reeve is so infuriated by the Miller's tale, but it is certainly clear to them that the Reeve intends the Miller harm with his story. Perhaps the fact that the punishment meted out by the Reeve does not seem to fit the crime explains in part why the Reeve's tale does not get the applause the Miller's does. Another answer has to do with numbers. The Miller's tale revolves around the number three (the love triangles of Nicholas, Alisoun, and John and that of Nicholas, Alisoun, and Absolon), while the Reeve's tale revolves around the number two (two clerks, two parents, and two children). Without consciously noting it, perhaps the pilgrims are vaguely aware that the doubling in the Reeve's tale is somehow connected to his troubled relationship with the community. For what the mirroring two rather than the triadic three evoke is the claustrophobia that a narcissistic over-identification with the mother gives rise to. It is only through the introduction of the third term, or the father, that (a) space is opened up, thereby allowing a subject to emerge. As Julia Kristeva articulates this spatial relation, "[T]he paternal agency alone, to the extent that it introduces the symbolic dimension between 'subject' (child) and 'object' (mother), can generate [...] a strict object relation. Otherwise, what is called 'narcissism' [...] becomes the unleashing of drive as such, without object, threatening all identity, including that of the subject itself. We are then in the presence of psychosis."[78] In short, the pilgrims

---

76 Sublimation is, as Lacan defines it, satisfaction of the drive without repression. Although I am not comparing the Reeve to James Joyce, it is interesting to note that Lacan believed Joyce's writing was the only thing that prevented his collapse into psychosis.

77 It is not completely accurate to say that no one responds to the Reeve's tale with approval. As the Reeve has been telling his tale, the drunken Cook has been enjoying himself in the same way that one enjoys having an itch scratched: "The Cook of Londoun, while the Reve spak, / For joye him thoughte he clawed him on the / bak" (I (A), 4325 – 26).

78 Julia Kristeva, *Powers of Horror: An Essay on Abjection*, 44.

respond positively to "normal" object relations and negatively to the narcissism of psychosis.

As we see from the Miller's response to the Reeve when asked to "stynt" his "clappe," the Miller is quite secure in his identity, but he is not so puffed up that he cannot imagine his wife cheating on him. He has simply found a way to cope with the possible disappointments and unpleasure that life affords. And thus while the Miller begins his tale with the Oedipal triad of the carpenter, Alisoun, and Nicholas, the Reeve begins his tale with a description of the swaggering Symkyn, attributing to him the same jealous impulses that the Miller has attributed to the old carpenter in his story: "Was noon so hardy that wente by the weye / That with hire dorste rage or ones pleye, / But if he wolde be slayn of Symkyn / With panade, or with knyf, or boidekyn. / For jalous folk ben perilous everemo—" (I (A), 3957–61). There is nothing to suggest that the Miller suffers from jealousy, but there is every indication that the Reeve does, and so from the very start, we see the mechanism of projection at work in the Reeve's tale. Everywhere he looks, the Reeve sees only himself, but it is a self that he refuses to recognize.

Once the Reeve has described each of Symkyn's family members, of which there are four—two parents and two children—he begins a narrative in which there are two clerks, John and Aleyn, both of whom are from the same village in the north and both of whom are Bible students at Solar Hall in Cambridge. The kind of binarism that Lacan argued against with the triangulation of the symbolic, the imaginary, and the real is suggested, too, by the Reeve's north/south opposition.[79] The only discernable difference between the two clerks is that one "swyves" the miller's daughter and the other, his wife. On the heels of this double coupling comes the bloody fight, which leaves Symkyn lying in a pool of blood with broken nose, mouth, and pate. What this final scene suggests is the rejection of the nay-saying Oedipal father. In other words, the "twins" win out and, with them, all of the aggressivity and conflict of the imaginary.

Chaucer's pilgrims would have been aware of the regularity with which murderous battles took place between town and gown or between students of different nationalities. As John Gardner reports, Chaucer himself "may well have taken part himself in such battles, tip-toeing down alleyways, pressed close against the walls, making use, perhaps, of old war skills."[80] And in his *Medieval Panorama,*

---

79 Lacan argued that no two agents can be coupled or contrasted without the mediating third.
80 John Gardner, *The Life and Times of Chaucer*, 150–51.

G. G. Coulton describes a jury report narrating an armed confrontation between Scottish students and southern and western students who met at Grope Lane:

> [...] and there the said Robert de Bridlington with a small arrow, smote [...] Henry of Holy Isle and wounded him hard by the throat, on the left side in front; and the wound was of the breadth of one inch, and in depth even to the heart; and thus he slew him [...]. And in the same conflict John de Benton came with a falchion into Grope Lane and gave David de Kirkby a blow on the back of the head, six inches in length, and in depth even unto the brain. At which same time came William de la Hyde and smote the aforesaid David with a sword across the right knee and leg; and at the same time came William de Astley and smote the said David under the left arm with a misericorde, and thus slew him [...].[81]

Whatever the cause of this armed confrontation, one can only agree when Gardner argues that "the numerous records of beatings and street wars give a slightly chilling dimension to Chaucer's merry fabliaux of rough-and-ready Oxford and Cambridge students."[82] As we have seen from the Reeve's delusions of persecution, the reconstruction of his primal scene, and his aggressive response to the Miller's tale, he has not been properly sutured into the symbolic network, for the lack that castration implies has not been registered. Thus, this lack appears as a presence, one that threatens him with destruction. Because his understanding of boundaries—interiority and exteriority, subject and object—is confused, he thinks only in terms of annihilating or being annihilated. In short, there is not enough room in his world for both Miller and Reeve. Two is a crowd.

---

81 G. G. Coulton, *Medieval Panorama*, 402.
82 Gardner, *The Life and Times of Chaucer*, 151.

Chapter 8
Farting and Its (Dis)contents, or Call Me Absolon

> But sooth to seyn, he was somdeel squaymous /
> Of fartyng, and of speche daungerous.
> —Geoffrey Chaucer, *The Miller's Tale*

The Haves and Have-Nots

Becoming a single mother just two years after beginning a tenure-track job as an assistant professor of English was an interesting challenge. At the same time I was charting my son's traversal through what Freud identified as the oral, anal, and phallic stages of psychosexual development, I was teaching a course on Chaucer's *Canterbury Tales* organized very much like this book. We began, just as this book does, with the concept of neurosis and made our way through the perversions of fetishism, masochism, and sadism, ending with paranoia and psychosis. It was probably one of the most enjoyable courses I have ever taught but also one of the most difficult.

Since my arrival here in Mobile, Alabama, I have taught courses in critical theory, film, gender, and literature at a university not far from where Hurricane Katrina wreaked unspeakable havoc on Gulf Coast life and property while also exposing the very wide gap between the haves and the have-nots. Many of my students fall into the category of the have-nots, coming as they do from the working-class poor, households ravaged by desertion or drugs, and environments deeply hostile to and suspicious of the clerisy, and thus I find myself constantly laboring to make what I teach relevant to their everyday lives—and, for that matter, to my own. Because of the circumstances under which many of my students both live and have been educated, the desire to learn often seems to have been drummed out of them, the "instinct for knowledge" having been replaced with "a will not to know (a *ne rien vouloir savoir*)."[1] This "will not to know" is, I believe, a reaction to and defense against having one's desire to know suppressed, and when one's desire to know has been suppressed, ignorance emerges as a "passion greater than love or hate[,]"[2] a passion that can only be overcome through the teacher's desire. Although many American therapists believe that only those who truly want help can engage in successful therapy, Bruce Fink begs to differ.

---

1 Bruce Fink, *A Clinical Introduction*, 7

2 Fink, *A Clinical Introduction*, 7.

https://doi.org/10.1515/9781501514104-010

What brings people into analysis is precisely a crisis of desire, he argues, and thus it is not the analysand's *flagging* desire that fuels analysis but the analyst's *unflagging* one. The same can be said of the classroom.

Getting an education is not the same thing as undergoing psychoanalysis, and yet education can have salubrious effects just as psychoanalysis can have pedagogical. In fact, I would argue that there are a number of striking parallels between the classroom and the couch, teacher and analyst, student and analysand. For example, the teacher's desire is (or should be) not unlike the analyst's "purified desire," which is, as Lacan describes it, an "enigmatic desire" that makes it impossible for the analysand to determine what the analyst wants him or her to say or do,[3] for one is not really engaged in analysis when one attempts to gratify or rebel against the analyst's desire. This is true for students as well. If they are simply attempting to gratify or rebel against the teacher's desire, as I was in the years following Mrs. Gorham's reprimand, they are not engaged in true learning. Although many teachers are required to state course directives and objectives on their syllabi, this is probably one of the most effective ways to sabotage a student's desire to learn. As teachers, we should take a lesson from John Cage and make getting lost a way of life in the classroom. In writing about her friend and fellow artist, Joan Retallack says of Cage that he was at his happiest when he "genuinely [did] not know where the processes he had set in motion would lead. This was not in order to produce the market value of an 'original' commodity, but to move into a zone of unintelligibility, the only place where the possibility of discovery lies, where the future is not at the outset already a thing of the past."[4] Rather than stating a desire for this or that outcome, which makes the future already a thing of the past, the analyst's job is to get the analysand to engage in the work of analysis: "to come to therapy, to put his or her experience, thoughts, fantasies, and dreams into words, and to associate to them."[5] Something very similar can be said of the English teacher's job, which is to get her students to engage in the work of (textual) analysis: to come to class, to put their experiences, opinions, and thoughts into words and to draw them into association with the texts being studied. Instead of depositing information, "banking" style, into the students' empty educational accounts, the teacher must encourage her students to move into a "zone of unintelligibility" where the work of analysis can most fruitfully take place.

---

3 Fink, *A Clinical Introduction*, 6.
4 Joan Retallack, *Musicage*, xxvi.
5 Fink, *A Clinical Introduction*, 7.

Believing as I do that some of my students come to me with a full-blown crisis of desire and that this may account for their apparent reluctance to learn, I have had to find new ways to engage them. The first thing that I must address, however, is the fear they feel when they encounter a discourse such as psychoanalysis, a discourse as unfamiliar and thus as disagreeable to them (at least, initially) as the language of Middle English. One of the ways I begin to attenuate this fear is to point out that, according to Lacan, the human subject is characterized by ambivalence, and thus it is not only okay but also quite normal to feel both resistant to and intrigued by the material. I also point out that in the analytic setting, ego discourse (or speech associated with a denial of the unconscious) is actively discouraged, and thus psychoanalysis has created a space in which *not* knowing is not merely acceptable but necessary. When my students complain after a first reading that they just do not "get" it, I remind them of what the nineteenth-century German theologian Friedrich Schleiermacher argues: the normal situation for a reader is rarely one of immediate and unimpeded understanding of a text's subject matter. Sounding very Lacanian indeed, he states that the "more lax practice of the art of understanding [...] proceeds on the assumption that understanding arises naturally. [...] The more rigorous practice proceeds on the assumption that misunderstanding arises naturally, and that understanding must be intended and sought at each point."[6] Encouraging my students to reread, I admit that even though I have been lucky enough to study with some of the best Lacanians in academia—Joan Copjec and Slavoj Žižek, to name but two—I continue to struggle to understand the body of work produced by and continuing to be produced by psychoanalytic thinkers. Understanding is an ongoing process, not a terminal condition, I say.

As I persist in trying to reduce my students' anxiety, I also begin casting about for ways to help them make sense of the unfamiliar (psychoanalysis) by way of the familiar (everyday life), and that is where a combination of auto and anecdotal theory comes in handy. Using my own experiences as anecdotes, I theorize in a way that I hope "honors the uncanny detail of lived experience," as Jane Gallop puts it.[7] In order to explain how the unconscious makes itself known through avenues such as the dream, the slip of the tongue, and/or the bungled action, I tell my students about something that happened when Mike and I were dating. Although the word "dating" strikes them as quaint, they enjoy hearing about my love life. *That* they can relate to, especially when I say that this something happened in the aftermath of a bad fight, one bad

---

6 Schleiermacher quoted in Hans-Georg Gadamer, *Philosophical Hermeneutics*, xiii.
7 Jane Gallop, *Anecdotal Theory*, 2.

enough that I packed up my station wagon and drove to my parents' house seventeen hours away. I did not tell Mike that I was leaving town; I simply left. Within the first day or two of my departure, however, I began to realize that behaving so precipitously had been a childish mistake. ("How did you *know?*" they ask, their eyes as round as saucers.) The first indication came as I was making a pitcher of iced tea and nearly set the kitchen on fire. Now, making iced tea is a simple business—all one has to do is to bring a small pot of water to boil, toss several teabags in to steep, pour the well-steeped tea into a pitcher, add sugar and water, and then serve with a glass full of ice cubes and a slice of lemon—and yet I managed to bungle it. As I tossed the teabags into the boiling water, one of the strings fell into the flame beneath the pot, setting itself and its little cardboard tag on fire. Once I had put out the miniature conflagration, I poured the requisite amount of sugar into a measuring cup, spilling it all over the kitchen counter and onto the floor in the process. The burning of the teabag string and tag and the spilling of the sugar occurred not once but three times during the week I stayed with my parents. I am not generally a clumsy person, and so I was forced to ask myself why these particular bungled actions were repeating themselves. The answer to this question came when I was standing on a friend's front porch. As I leaned against the railing, it suddenly broke, and I fell backwards into the yard.

"What was the answer to this question?" I ask my students. "And why did falling off the porch help me to figure it out?"

Once they get the hang of it, they enjoy free association like the kind I ask them to engage in. It is a hermeneutical process that makes sense to them. "Does the teabag represent home?" asks one student. Snapping her fingers as if a light bulb has just gone off, another student answers for me, saying, "Yeah, and the string could be your mama's apron strings!"

"But," says a third student, "that would make Dr. McLaughlin the little cardboard tag." Everyone laughs at that, including me.

"How does the porch fit in?" asks the first student.

"What is a porch?" I ask in return.

"A covered shelter," says another student. "And the railing is what keeps you from falling."

"But it also makes the porch an enclosed space, doesn't it?" asks yet another.

"So it's kind of like parents," says the first.

"Or training wheels," says another.

"Yeah, they protect you, but they can also limit you," says the first.

The fact that they are beginning to understand not only how free association works but also extended metaphor makes it possible for me to tackle three important Lacanian concepts through use of the fart, a force of nature that every-one is acquainted with for better or worse. One cannot get much more down-to-earth(y) than with a reference to flatulence. And while making use of the fart in the classroom may seem like a crude thing to do, I am not in bad company. Lacan makes reference in his *Ethics* seminar to a troubadour named Arnaud Daniel, who ungallantly speaks of a woman's "stinking trumpet" in his love po-etry, and the greatest poet of the English language allowed a fart as "greet" as a "thonder-dent" to occupy center stage in his most famous of tales. As everyone knows who has had even the most cursory relationship to *The Canterbury Tales*, the fart plays a central role in the tale the Miller tells, and yet it has gotten short shrift in my discussion of the Miller and Reeve's interaction. Given my family's attitude toward farting, perhaps one could argue that repression was at work when I was writing about the Reeve's paranoid eye. If so, what follows in this shadow chapter is the return of the repressed in the form of what might be thought of as the "satyr play" of the shadow chapters.

Things That Go "Toot!" in the Night

As children we all go through potty training, learning to "pee" and "poop" in the "pot" rather than in our pants. But when and how we are taught not to fart (at least, within ear- or nose-shot of others) is far less clear. Perhaps because the fart is neither liquid nor solid, it has a marginal status that blurs the protocol sur-rounding its emission. Its marginal status is also registered in language, for the word "smell" can be used to refer to the passive act of perceiving a smell or the more dynamic act of emitting one.[8] No wonder there is, frequently enough, ambiguity regarding the identity of the fart producer, for, as Valerie Allen argues in *On Farting*, "[s]mell, somewhere in between the aloofness of vision and the immediacy of touch, throws into question the ontological and epistemological relation between ipseity and alterity."[9] The fact that the fart breaches the boun-dary between self and other may explain why there was no clear consensus on the dynamics of farting when the question of whether women laugh when they fart was posed on the Straight Dope Message Board in 2001. The only "fart fact" that nearly everyone seemed to agree upon was that mothers do not fart. Ever. The person who initiated the question, CnoteChris, surmised that farting is "a strictly male thing" since no woman he has ever dated "has been amused by

---

8 Valerie Allen, *On Farting*, 45.
9 Allen, *On Farting*, 47–48.

farts the way that [he's] been."[10] Using anecdotal evidence to support his conjecture, he states, "I've never run across a woman who's been proud that they could out-fart one of their friends, let alone take credit for passing a gas so noxious it cleared out a room. But many a guy, including myself, have done so."[11] It may be the case that for men such as CnoteChris, a fart functions very much like a joke, for, as Freud has pointed out, "no one can be content with having made a joke for himself alone. An urge to tell the joke to someone is inextricably bound up with the joke-work."[12] As for the joke's success, it can only be evaluated by the listener, not by the teller, and Freud quotes lines from Shakespeare's *Love's Labour's Lost* to remind us of this fact: "A jest's prosperity lies in the ear / Of him that hears it, never in the tongue / Of him that makes it ...."[13] The same is true of the fart. Its prosperity lies in the ear and/or the nose of him who hears and/or smells it, not in the bowels of him who produces it.

In his research on laughter, Robert Provine and his assistants engaged in 1,200 case studies, finding that "while both sexes laugh a lot, females laugh more. In cross-gender conversations, females laughed 126% more than their male counterparts, meaning that women tend to do the most laughing while males tend to do the most joking. Men seem to be the main instigators of humor across cultures."[14] Given this difference between men and women, Provine sought to determine whether laughter played a role in romance, and he found his answer in personal ads. According to Provine, "[F]emales were 62% more likely to mention laughter in their ads, and women were more likely to seek out a 'sense of humor' while men were more likely to offer it. Clearly, women seek men who make them laugh, and men are eager to comply with this request."[15] If Provine's findings are an accurate representation of men's and women's patterns of laughter, then perhaps this would explain why CnoteChris is under the impression that farting, like joking, is generally male, not female, territory.

Begging to differ, a number of women posted responses to CnoteChris's question, some of whom appeared to take great pleasure in refuting his suppositions about fart culture and gender. A respondent named Gundy writes, "I don't fart a lot (no, really, I don't) but when I do I giggle. And when my boyfriend or son farts, I giggle. And when someone says 'fart' or 'poot,' I giggle. [...] Farts are

---

10 See boards.straightdope.com.

11 See boards.straightdope.com, ¶ 7–8.

12 Sigmund Freud, *Jokes and Their Relation to the Unconscious*, 194–95.

13 Freud, *Jokes*, 196.

14 Robert Provine, "The Science of Laughter," ¶ 8.

15 Provine, "The Science," ¶ 9.

funny. However, I am not competitive about farting, and don't know anyone who is, not even guys."[16] A much more productive and proactive farter is Diane, who writes the following: "If I feel a really big bufford coming on, I will run and call my best friend on the phone and blast a fart in the receiver as soon as she answers. We always get a huge laugh over this no matter how many times we do it to each other."[17] And while Diane is "a firm believer that an ability to fart at will is second only to the ability to fly[,]" she advises her fellow women farters to "[n]ever admit that you know how to fart when you meet a new guy. Never, ever."[18] According to Diane, gender does play a role in fart culture because women are to behave like perfect ladies around their boyfriends while they may treat girl friends and family members as fair game for "gas warfare."

Engaging in what might be called a comparative analysis, CrankyAsAnOldMan writes, "I fart more quietly than my husband, but more often and more noxiously. So generally I cut one, start to smell it, know it's going to be bad for him, and start to giggle. Within moments he knows why. I've nearly died laughing over this type of thing."[19] There is a puzzling sense of aggression suggested by Cranky's laughter at her husband's outrage, for she continues her commentary, saying, "[L]ast month I farted in the middle of the night and it was so awful that I woke us both up. My husband was outraged, but I must have laughed off 1000 calories. I couldn't get back to sleep because I [kept] having uncontrollable giggles."[20] Perhaps Cranky's giggles arise in part because of her knowledge of a late-fifteenth-century play entitled *The Farce of the Fart* in which a man named Hubert unsuccessfully attempts to sue his wife for farting in his presence. The judge rules in the wife's favor, arguing that through marriage the two are made one, and thus his wife's ass is his own and one cannot sue one's own ass.[21] As for Cranky's aggression, if we make use of the word "sadism" in its popular sense—that is, as the tendency to derive pleasure from inflicting pain, suffering, or humiliation on others—then it does seem to be the case that farting is often used sadistically to assert power or dominance.[22] In fact, many of the re-

---

16 See boards.straightdope.com, ¶ 11–12.
17 See boards.straightdope.com, ¶ 77.
18 See boards.straightdope.com, ¶ 83.
19 See boards.straightdope.com, ¶ 86.
20 See boards.straightdope.com, ¶ 87.
21 See Valerie Allen's *On Farting*, 53–55.
22 As Valerie Allen points out, "The lesson from the vocabulary of medieval faculty psychology [regarding the connection between the words 'passion,' 'passive,' and 'patient'], now erased by Modern English, is that the 'I' who senses, the subject of the act of inhaling, is in that moment also the object of the act. To sense is to suffer, to undergo," 45–46.

sponses to CnoteChris's question contain stories about having been held captive by a farter, either in a moving car, under the bed covers, or in a tight space such as a bathroom or a closet. According to Medstar, for example, her brothers "thought it was extremely funny to cut 'wolf-ass,' noxious, tear-inducing farts in the basement bathroom, lie in wait for me or one of my sisters, throw us in the bathroom and lock the door. They would laugh maniacally when we would pound on the door, screaming to be set free."[23]

Perhaps the theory suggested by Colibri's mammalogist friend helps explain the power dynamics of farting, for she "theorized that farting among human males was a form of assessing dominance and marking territory[,]" and while Colibri himself has doubts about the validity of his friend's theory, arguing that "the usual response is laughter, not submission[,]" he does acknowledge that "the guy who can fart loudest often attains a sort of legendary status among a group of males."[24] And while a woman such as Diane engages in competitive farting with her best friend, she does seem to be an anomaly. Gala Matrix Fire lends support to the anomalous nature of the female fart enthusiast when she asserts that she has "almost never heard a woman fart, even in Basic Training."[25] Although a male respondent named Revtim makes reference to a female coworker who "very obviously cut one in front of [him] as a joke[, lifting] her leg and everything[,]" he admits that "she's a rare gal."[26] CnoteChris voices his surprise at the responses posted by women farters, saying, "Call me male chauvinist, but I honestly thought it was limited to being a guy thing. Not that I'm upset about it, no. I'm surprised, to say the least."[27] However, his surprise morphs into skepticism when he adds, "But come on, women folk, you can't tell me this is the norm, can you? [...] Is it me, or are you gals an odd bunch?" to which Diane responds, "Well, yeah. You just noticed?"[28]

On the other end of the spectrum are what CnoteChris calls "flatuphobians" or what Romansperson refers to as the "fart-repressed." (As an aside, I must say I find it striking that the language of psychoanalysis turns up in a non-academic venue such as a popular message board, but given Freud's description of repression, it is little wonder that the concept would find its way into a thread on an object of disgust such as the fart: "To put it crudely," says Freud, "the current memory stinks just as an actual object may stink and just as we turn away

---

23 See boards.straightdope.com, ¶ 48.
24 See boards.straightdope.com, ¶ 51–52.
25 See boards.straightdope.com, ¶ 124.
26 See boards.straightdope.com, ¶15.
27 See boards.straightdope.com, ¶ 108–9.
28 See boards.straightdope.com, ¶ 111, 113, 134.

our sense organ (the head and nose) in disgust, so do the preconscious and our conscious apprehension turn away from the memory. This is *repression*."[29]) Growing up in "a fart-repressed family," Romansperson declares, "I have NEVER heard my father fart. Ever. And he's 74 now. If you never hear farts, it's hard to laugh at them!"[30] And then there's Persephone, who denies having farted even once in her entire life. The most poignant post comes from Pepsigirl, however, whose level of fart suppression is so high that it sometimes causes her physical pain:

> I have never farted on purpose in front of anyone except for my daughter. This includes my husband of over 16 years. I don't know why but I would rather die than fart in front of him. I was raised in Texas and girls did not do it, talk about it or laugh about it. My father was very strict and we could not even say the word fart when I was little. Sounds dumb now but it is still a hard habit to break. I have had times where I have been literally doubled over in pain but would not pass gas until I could get to a bathroom by myself.[31]

Perhaps part of the reason I find Pepsigirl's post so poignant is because it reminds me of myself. I grew up in the Arkansas Delta, where girls did not laugh at or talk about farts either. A Diane delivering "big buffords" over the telephone would have been unimaginable. And while I would never describe my parents as strict, I suppose my family was among the fart-repressed, for no one in my family, including my father and younger brother, ever used the word "fart." In fact, they still do not. It is hard to say why or how this linguistic interdiction came to exist, for I do not remember ever being directly forbidden to use the word, but it was considered to be just as much of a "dirty" word as "piss," "shit," or "fuck," three other words that were never uttered in the household of my youth. When I was growing up, it was more acceptable to fart (at least, in private) than to say the word, which was not acceptable at all. Perhaps my parents felt that while one cannot control the body's internal workings, one can control what one says. And, thus, if we had to speak of farting, we referred to it as "tooting." Why one word would have been more acceptable than the other is rather hard to understand unless one delves into the realm of phonetics with its plosives and fricatives. Plosives, also known as stops, are consonant sounds made by blocking the vocal track so that all airflow ceases. The letter "t" is an example of a plosive. Fricatives, on the other hand, are consonant sounds made by forcing air through a narrow constriction. This causes the air

---

29 Sigmund Freud, *The Origins of Psychoanalysis*, 232.
30 See boards.straightdope.com, ¶ 161.
31 See boards.straightdope.com, ¶ 58.

to flow turbulently, creating a noisy sound, not unlike that of flatulence. The letter "f" is an example of a fricative. In these definitions, then, we might find an explanation for why the word "tooting" would have been found more acceptable than the word "farting."

Although my mother and two younger sisters never farted in my presence, and presumably never in the presence of anyone else, I was occasionally guilty of farting in order to get a rise out of my siblings and to rebel against having to act like a lady. In fact, the two motivations for farting were probably linked, for my sisters toed the line as far as ladylike behavior was concerned, while I did not. My farts were not just an opportunity to harass my sisters but an attempt to get them to rebel with me against the oppression entailed in growing up female, especially in what I considered at that time to be the hypocritical and regressive "Bible Belt." Like Peter Travis, who believes that, in Chaucer's poetry, "sound carries a discursive, and indeed political, charge[,]"[32] I believe that, in the sonic space of my childhood home, my farts had a political dimension although they were not necessarily as complex as the fart in the *Summoner's Tale*. While it would be many years before I would read Simone de Beauvoir's *The Second Sex*, Betty Friedan's *The Feminine Mystique*, Kate Millett's *Sexual Politics*, and Marilyn French's *The Women's Room*, the second wave of the feminist movement was in full swing as I was growing up in the 1960s and seventies. And thus what Freud says about tendentious jokes seems applicable to my tendentious farts: "tendentious jokes are especially favoured in order to make aggressiveness or criticism possible against persons in exalted positions who claim to exercise authority. The joke then represents a rebellion against that authority, a liberation from its pressure."[33] Like the joke, the fart represented liberation from the pressure to be a lady. During my adolescence, I was anything but ladylike, a little stinker blowing hard from both ends. Like the "silent but deadly" fart, however, there were silent but deadly forces at work that would bring a halt to my liberation, and thus if I began adolescence as the loud and boisterous Miller, I brought it to a close by becoming the squeamish parish clerk, Absolon.

Classroom Gas

When I was a sophomore in college, I lived off campus with three other young women. At that time, there was a long list of words that I could not utter,

---

32 Peter Travis, "Thirteen Ways of Listening to a Fart," 325.
33 Freud, *Jokes*, 149.

words that my mouth simply could not form—"fart," for example. I could fart in private, but to *say* the word was impossible. In fact, saying it would have held far more shame for me than doing it. I had never even written the word. When my pragmatic, midwestern housemates got wind of this linguistic difficulty, they immediately set out to cure me by a tactic we might call desublimation. One night I returned home from class to find that the entire house had been decorated with the word, and the *pièce de résistance*, drawn on the bathroom mirror using a bar of soap, was a visual image of a woman's buttocks expelling a thundercloud of flatulence. While laughter may be the best medicine for whatever ails you, it did not cure me. But the ease with which my housemates, who were no more or less ladylike than I, handled the word "fart" suggested that my problem could no longer be written off as mere southern gentility. It was, in fact, part of my hysterical complex, a nexus of aphasia, disgust, prudery, and shame.

If we fast-forward forty years, we find that I have (mostly) overcome my hysterical symptoms, particularly those of aphasia and the affect of disgust. But my fall into hysteria and recovery from it are the events of another story, and so I pass over them here and say only this: if my old college housemates could see me now, they would be both shocked and pleased by my newly found linguistic freedom regarding the word "fart." They would be both shocked and pleased to hear how easily it rolls off my tongue with no apparent trace of embarrassment or disgust. That said, I nevertheless do feel a slight sense of trepidation just before I introduce the word "fart" into the classroom. How will my students react? I wonder. Perhaps as long as I utter the word matter-of-factly, I say to myself, it will be received matter-of-factly. And then the word is said, and there is no taking it back. It startles my students, some of whom laugh appreciatively and some of whom blush in embarrassment. But whatever their reaction is, I press forward because I am determined not to let the squeamish and fastidious Absolon in me (or in my students) get the upper hand. I also want, like Gallop, to introduce a sense of humor into theory, and so I say to my students that I intend to use the fart to explain the operation of and the relationship among Lacan's three registers: the real, the imaginary, and the symbolic.

Because some of my students continue to express ambivalence about homosexuality, I avoid using this situation to challenge their sexual politics, but I do apologize for asking them to imagine a hetero-normative scene in which the central subject is a woman, for I realize that not everyone will be able to personally identify with the scene I intend to lay out before them. Fortunately, most of the students in this upper-level class are English majors, and so they have had a good deal of practice at reading novels and short stories with narrators and/or characters whose desiring structures are different from their own.

"Imagine that there's a guy you've had your eye on for a while," I say to my students. "You don't know him well, but you've seen him around and perhaps even had a few brief but casual conversations with him. You think he's awfully good-looking, and he seems nice." Of course, in describing this imaginary guy, I have to admit that my own desires come into play, for not everyone requires good looks in a sexual partner, nor does everyone want a nice guy (or girl). This admission made, I continue, saying, "You're not particularly aggressive when it comes to guys, and so you moon around, hoping he'll call and ask you out." Here, again, I have to admit that the scene I am describing is probably a bit outmoded since few college-age students date anymore. Hook-up culture has, it would seem, rendered "the date" obsolete. It is probably also the case that college-age girls no longer wait to be wooed but take matters into their own hands. On the other hand, change occurs slowly in the Deep South, and so perhaps contemporary mating rituals do not differ from those of the past as much as might be supposed.

"Finally," I say, "the glorious day comes when he calls and asks you out. You're overjoyed because you're sure, absolutely sure, that he is your knight in shining armor, your handsome prince, the one you've been waiting for all of your life. Perhaps you even begin imagining a future together. Perhaps you imagine the enormous size of the engagement ring he'll buy you and the beautiful white dress you'll wear on your wedding day." While these imaginings may seem rather far-fetched, they are not. I have encountered many a female student who has no boyfriend but who has already planned her wedding down to the smallest detail. "I know exactly the kind of ring I want," says one student. "It's a princess-cut with a floating halo." I have no idea what she is talking about, never having had or wanted an engagement ring in my entire life. And when another student begins discussing the "4Cs: color, cut, clarity, and carat weight," I am seriously out of my depth. Although I know something about the cut of clothing, I am astounded by the specificity with which my students speak of the bridesmaid gown. One student says she plans to have eight bridesmaids, each of whom will be dressed in a "mint-green, sleeveless 'Cinderella' gown with an asymmetric neckline and a court train," while yet another says she wants something a little simpler, for example, "a raspberry chiffon gown with an A-line, racer neckline, natural waist, and gathered skirt." Nothing sounds simple about either of these gowns, and nothing will be simple about paying for a wedding that includes eight bridesmaids, but none of that occurs to these students. They are too swept up in their fantasies to think very realistically about finances. But that is all to the good, as far as explaining Lacan's register of the imaginary goes, for, like fantasy, the "self" or the ego is a construct built upon ideal images. Clearly, when one can plan one's wedding without a groom, one is under the sway of the narcissistic and self-deluded ego, which is chock-full of false images.

Returning to the imagined scenario, I say, "The night of the date arrives, and the guy—let's call him Mr. Perfect—comes to pick you up in his little red Corvette. Unlike Shania Twain, the fact that he obviously likes to 'shine his machine' does indeed impress you. He's the total package: a good-looking guy who seems nice and who drives a cool car. 'Yay, me!' you think to yourself as you and Mr. Perfect speed away. And when he punches in a CD of your favorite band, you enter serious identification mode. 'I love that song,' you say, and he affirms your musical taste when he says he saw the band in concert and they were awesome. 'We like the same music,' you say to yourself, and that's important because you've known guys who are into death metal, and that is totally not your thing. So as far as you're concerned, this date is off to a great start, and you are really grooving on it until, suddenly, you smell something foul, rank, and thoroughly offensive. Disconcerted, you look out the tinted window of Mr. Perfect's car to locate the source. There are no cows grazing in a pasture to account for your unpleasure. There are no low-lying chicken coops. You are nowhere close to the local paper company, nor is the wind blowing in your direction. What, then, could account for the "'wolf-ass,' noxious, tear-inducing" smell that is now invading your nostrils? You look over at Mr. Perfect to see whether he's registering the same unpleasure you are, and you observe a funny, little smirk on his face. And then it dawns on you: he has farted. If you are not a flatuphobic or one of the fart-repressed, you ask Mr. Perfect, 'Did you fart?' But you already know the answer. Mr. Perfect's funny, little smirk says it all."

At this point, I bring the scenario to a close, for we have all of the ingredients necessary for explaining how Lacan's registers of the real, the imaginary, and the symbolic operate: "The real is represented, here, by the moment of unpleasure in which you smell something offensive but cannot locate its source and thus its name. You feel the effect of something that is yet unsymbolized," I say and then point them in the direction of Bruce Fink, whose lucid explanations of Lacan's registers are quite useful. According to Fink, "The real is perhaps best understood as that which has not yet been symbolized, remains to be symbolized, or even resists symbolization."[34] I then continue, saying, "Once you've put your finger on the source of the smell (metaphorically, of course) and had it confirmed —that is, once you name the smell as 'fart'—you are operating within the register of the symbolic, of language. This recognition, in turn, has an effect on the imaginary, for it alters the image that you have of Mr. Perfect for better or worse. If

---

34 Bruce Fink, *The Lacanian Subject*, 25.

you're a flatuphobic or one of the fart-repressed, it probably changes your image of Mr. Perfect for the worse, and you say to yourself that you'll never go out with this disgusting caveman again. If, however, you're like my old high school chum Emma B., you might have a different reaction. At lunch one day during our senior year, she told me that her boyfriend enjoyed holding her down, squatting over her, and farting in her face. Much to my surprise and disgust, this was a great source of delight for both of them, a sort of mating ritual *par excellence*. Those of you in Emma's camp might feel a sudden sense of relief. You might say to yourself, 'Ah, he's comfortable enough with me to fart, which means that I can be comfortable enough with him to do the same. Good! We've recognized each other; we identify; we're alike.' Either way, you're functioning in the register of the imaginary when you identify with someone or when identification reverses itself and becomes hostility."

For those who have been puzzled by Absolon's violently negative reaction to kissing Alisoun's "nether eye," the fart scenario that I have sketched goes a long way toward explaining it: Absolon's fantasy of Alisoun turns sour when the real, that is, the anal rim structure, intrudes upon the imaginary: "To looke on hire hym thoughte a myrie lyf, / She was so proper and sweete and likerous" (I (A), 3344–45). Although I have devoted most of the previous chapter to discussion of the relationship between Miller and Reeve, the character of Absolon is not without interest, for he represents the rather unusual figure of the male hysteric. I have never liked the squeamish and fastidious parish clerk, preferring instead the sly and "hande" Nicholas, but perhaps this dislike is telling, an apparent lack of affinity on my part masking identification. In other words, what I dislike in Absolon, I also dislike in myself.

Chapter 9
Retractor

Retractor
/re·trac·tor/ (-trak′ter)
1. an instrument for holding open the lips of a wound.
2. a muscle that retracts.
—*Dorland's Medical Dictionary for Health Consumers*

The Sleep of Dialectic

The Book of the Duchess is the first of Chaucer's major poems and *The Canterbury Tales* his last, and thus these texts function as the bookends for Chaucer's body of work. If a reader were to make his or her way through Chaucer's texts in chronological order, these are the texts that would be encountered first and last, and in them the reader would find Chaucer struggling with what it means to be a poet, betraying tremendous anxiety vis-à-vis his relation to writing and, by extension, to reading. It is fitting that Chaucer chose the dream motif for *The Book of the Duchess* and used the pilgrimage as a framing device for the short tales that make up his final work, for what is a writer if not one who travels in a foreign land, a wayfarer? And nothing could be more foreign than the landscapes of dream and language itself as the big Other with its twin chains of discourse: unconscious, unintentional, "other" discourse always interfering with conscious, intentional, ego discourse, an interference that, more often than not, makes language opaque, duplicitous, strange, and *radically* other. As Cixous says, "So perhaps dreaming and writing do have to do with traversing the forest, journeying through the world, using all the available means of transport, using your own body as a form of transport."[1] And this is why Chaucer's texts are, of necessity, enigmatic dreams or pilgrimages into the unconscious and thus a traversal of the forest for both writer and reader, a journey through the world that uses all available means of transport, including a descent or plunge into the symptom and beyond. These texts represent Chaucer's movement from desire to drive, from the flow of words set in motion in *The Book of the Duchess* to the sudden onset of silence in *The Canterbury Tales*. One might say that in *The Book of the Duchess*, we see a writer pulling himself together through the act of reading, while in *The Canterbury Tales*, we see him falling apart, just as the

---

1 Hélène Cixous, *Three Steps on the Ladder of Writing*, 64.

https://doi.org/10.1515/9781501514104-011

word "book" suggests a text with a central and coherent idea or subject while the word "tales" suggests the book shattered into fragments. These are Chaucer's first and last "cuts" and, like mine, one could be styled "reading as salvation" and the other "writing as damnation."

The Book of the Duchess is about a loss suffered, a limit imposed, *jouissance* sacrificed—all of which are central to the concept of castration as Lacan articulates it—and about the narrator's initial inability to register this loss, limit, or sacrifice. He knows that something is wrong with him, but he cannot say what that something is, only that it has plagued him for eight years.[2] Whatever it is, however, has created a fixation or blockage that must be overcome through symbolization, for language is the very antithesis of fixation, language being the mechanism that allows for substitution and displacement. We know from the way psychoanalysis defines it that trauma is a remainder or scrap of the real, a residual experience that has become a stumbling block for the subject. As Bruce Fink explains, "When, as is the case in melancholia, no such substitution or displacement is possible, fixation is at work, and some part of the real remains to be symbolized."[3] And, thus, by "getting an analysand to dream, daydream, and talk, however incoherently, about a traumatic 'event,' we make him or her connect it up with words, bring it into relation with ever more signifiers."[4]

This dialectizing of the traumatic kernel is precisely what the narrator of *The Book of the Duchess* achieves through his account of the dream. But what makes it possible for the narrator to sleep, to dream, and finally to write is his ability to identify with the characters in the story he reads, for in its best guise, identification is a metaphorical gesture. Even in his paralysis, he recognizes that reading a book is "better play" than chess or backgammon, "play" suggesting movement or unimpeded motion. The narrator's ability to identify with these characters makes further metaphorical moves possible. And so we have, between the covers of the original book over which the narrator falls asleep, the narrator's dream, that is, his own creative project superimposed on that of another. Because the narrator is unable to name what he has lost and to properly mourn it—Freud defined melancholia as a failure to mourn—he dreams up someone who can (the black knight), and thus we have the story of a movement from melancholia to desire via mourning.

---

2 In Peter Travis's exquisite essay on *The Book of the Duchess*, elegantly entitled "White," he argues that the poem's "first mater" is the narrator's inability to understand himself as well as to cope with "his own sense of fragmentation and self-alienation," 39.

3 Bruce Fink, *The Lacanian Subject*, 26.

4 Fink, *The Lacanian Subject*, 26.

What we see happening to the narrator of *The Book of the Duchess* sounds eerily like Nancy Miller's experience of reading memoirs during the 1990s. As she says in her preface to *But Enough About Me: Why We Read Other People's Lives:* "I came to see my life as an unwitting but irresistible collaboration between other texts and other lives. Sometimes my identifications with the stories not about me (not even remotely) came to feel like a rediscovery of my own life and memories, like a haunting."[5] If it sounds a bit farfetched to suggest that Chaucer and Miller have anything in common, McGerr makes it sound less so in her discussion of Chaucer's open poetics:

> Chaucer's poetry reflects the belief that the art of literature imitates the art of memory. In *The Legend of Good Women*, for example, books become the "key of remembrance." As the prologue to this work explains, it is impossible for people to rely totally on their own experience for knowledge. First, they would lose the theological truths that they hold by faith; second, they would lose information about the past experience of others, which is preserved in books.[6]

McGerr continues this line of thinking, arguing that because *The Canterbury Tales* is structured around a narrator recounting his own experience through the stories of others involved in that experience, "the recreation of the narrator's past experience in the realm of his memory becomes, for readers, the creation of an ongoing experience in the realm of imagination. In other words, the poem posits a parallel between the functions of memory and literature."[7]

With Freud, the same seems to be true, for in his 1908 preface to the second edition of *The Interpretation of Dreams*, he says that writing the book was part of his own self-analysis, an attempt to work through his father's death, which had occurred in 1896. And in a letter to Wilhelm Fliess in 1901, he called the case history of Dora a continuation of the dream book, and thus it can be considered a continuation of his own self-analysis. Beneath discussion of Dora's hysteria lies discussion of his own: Dora as text, Freud as sub-text. (Beneath discussion of the Prioress's hysteria lies discussion of my own: Prioress as text, *moi* as sub-text.) He may have treated his analysands with the "talking cure" (a function of memory), but he treated himself with the "writing cure" (a function of literature). Several years before Freud published his self-analysis, however, Charlotte Perkins Gilman had written and published "The Yellow Wallpaper." As I mentioned earlier, Gilman claimed to have written the story in order "to save people from

---

5 Nancy Miller, *But Enough About Me*, xiii.
6 Rosemarie McGerr, *Chaucer's Open Books*, 140.
7 McGerr, *Chaucer's Open Books*, 141.

being driven crazy." But she also wrote it in order to save herself. Having been treated by S. Weir Mitchell with the "rest cure" and instructed "never [to] touch pen, brush, or pencil again[,]" Gilman suffered a nervous breakdown. "Only by disobeying his orders, by starting to work, to write, was Gilman able to cure herself of her hysteria."[8] What Chaucer, Miller, Freud, and Gilman all seem to suggest—and what I downright declare—is that a dialectical exchange that takes place between reader and writer through storytelling is a necessity if we are to avoid and/or recover from paralysis, melancholia, and, finally, madness.

Upon Waking, Shipwreck

It is striking that Chaucer begins *The Book of the Duchess* by narrating a story of shipwreck, for *The Canterbury Tales* is what might be called a shipwrecked text, and the tale that is responsible for this shipwreck, the tale on which the collection founders, is precisely a story of shipwreck. I am referring, of course, to the *Man of Law's Tale*, in which is told the story of Custance. If in *The Book of the Duchess* identification functions as metaphor and thus creates movement, then in *The Canterbury Tales* the fantasy of difference—twenty-nine pilgrims of various estates—collapses. That is to say, each story that gets told is the same traumatic story, each pilgrim telling the tale of the "cut." As Harry Bailly says in the *General Prologue*, "Now draweth cut, er that we ferrer twynne (I (A), 835). This draw of the cut (or the straw) initiates a string of cuts or tales that are precisely about the subject's castration, which both wounds and defines.[9] For example, the *Miller's Tale* illustrates how the primal scene cuts us, for the carpenter awakens in the night to noises down below and then drops into the scene of coitus, where he suffers a broken arm, heartache, and humiliation. The Prioress tells a tale about a child's cut throat and a life short-circuited, a reference finally to her own plight, her own "song" cut off in mid-stream. Harry directs a castrating gesture at Chaucer-the-pilgrim when he cuts off his *Tale of Thopas*, saying, "Thy drasty rymyng is nat worth a toord!" (VII, 930). And in his prologue, the Man of Law speaks of the way in which he has been cut, or made to lack, by Chaucer as the father of all tales. In his view, Chaucer has drained the barrel dry and left him with nothing.

---

8 Diane Herndl, "The Writing Cure," 52.
9 This commentary on the collapse of the fantasy of difference appears in my "Chaucer's Cut" in slightly different form, the two examples used those of the Miller's tale and the Wife of Bath's prologue.

In other words, when Chaucer-the-pilgrim says in the *General Prologue*, we were "as one" in fellowship, he speaks a truth of the band of Canterbury pilgrims that will only be recognized later when, like a character in a David Lynch film, Chaucer himself falls into the narrative frame as the one who "hath al," the one who has told all the stories, all the stories being the same story of psychical trauma and its defining and wounding properties. It is at the site of shipwreck, then, at the site of the *Man of Law's Tale* that Chaucer bumps into the Thing that is in him more than him, for this is the site at which Chaucer is doubled and redoubled: we have all in one locale the fictive narrator we know as Chaucer-the-pilgrim, who recounts what the Man of Law says; the fictive Man of Law himself; the fictive merchant who has supplied the Man of Law with the tale he tells; and Chaucer the writer, who functions as both a diegetic and an extra-diegetic "fiction." If this pile-up of fictive Chaucers creates a moment of vertigo for the anonymous reader, what does it do to Chaucer as he reads what he has written? *It scares him.*

It is impossible to locate a Chaucer that is not a fiction, and yet one of these Chaucers is responsible for the fiction that exists. As if in an oneiric fugue, Chaucer downshifts from a poetry with velocity to the plodding prose of the Parson and finally comes to a halt in the Retraction. Perhaps in the movement from high speed to stasis, he was asking himself the same question Edmond Jabès poses in "The Book or the Four Phases of a Birth": "Could it be that man is a book which he can only read in the book he will write?"[10] At death's threshold maybe Chaucer knew, as Jabès knows, that "[w]riting means making an opening"—a cut?—"in our life through which life becomes text."[11] Chaucer was, then, or had become, all the stories that words presented to him, the daring of the stories that recited him.[12]

The Master in Pieces

Referring to the Retraction as a "split lens," Peter Travis argues that Chaucer's readers "find themselves trapped willy-nilly in the middle of Chaucer's final, paradoxical assessment of his art": approbation on the one hand and disapprobation on the other.[13] While humanist scholars have struggled hard to come up

---

10 Edmond Jabès, "The Book or the Four Phases of a Birth," 123.

11 Jabès, "The Book," 123.

12 Here, I am echoing Jabès when he says, "We are forever the story which recites us and the daring of this story," 125.

13 Peter Travis, "Deconstructing Chaucer's Retraction," 147.

with reasons not to take too seriously Chaucer's last words including, notes Travis, one scholar who "has suggested that it is really a wry joke, at the expense of the reader or perhaps of God himself, who must determine which of the Canterbury tales do, and do not, 'sownen into sinne,'"[14] I would argue that not only is it *not* a joke but also it is meant to be taken quite seriously. The Retraction, like the *Pardoner's Tale*, is a parable that points to another, the Parable of the Tares, and like the field of wheat into which tares have been sown, Chaucer's body of work might be said to contain both wheat and tares. While he seems prepared to say which of his works he thinks are the wheat and which the tares, he is strangely reticent regarding *The Canterbury Tales*, saying only that he begs forgiveness for the tales that "sownen into synne." But how are we to determine which ones those are? And what if, in trying to gather up and destroy the "tares," we root up also the "wheat"? To prevent a reader's temptation to choose, to divide, and thus to cast out, Chaucer has intentionally created ambiguity, and he has done so in a number of ways.

First, in choosing to refer to his last words as his "retracciouns," he might have been using the word in the same way that we use it today—that is, as a "taking back" or "rescinding"—but, according to Terry Jones, it is unlikely, for there is no written record of this particular use until the mid-sixteenth century. What is more likely, argues Jones, is that Chaucer was using the word in the same way Saint Augustine used the Latin "retractatio," which had a number of meanings including "reconsideration" and "remembrance."[15] Second, in using the word "revoke," Chaucer is making use of the word's polyvalence, for although it did have our current meaning of "retract" or "disown," it also had another: "to recall to mind," "to rescue," or "to bring back, revive."[16] In fact, Jones points out that "the only other time Chaucer uses the word, he uses it in this latter sense."[17] And, third, Chaucer states quite clearly, "[a]ll that is written is written for oure doctrine," and, in so doing, he echoes Jerome and Pseudo-Augustine when they argue that Jesus commands us to allow the tares to grow along with the wheat because "evil contributes to good."[18]

Despite the Retraction's split lens, however, it has a "ring of finality."[19] What it does not have is the ring of closure. And yet in courses such as World Masterpieces, where one expects to find texts that "have it all together," one always

---

14 Travis, "Deconstructing," 138

15 Terry Jones, *Who Murdered Chaucer?*, 328–29.

16 Jones, *Who Murdered Chaucer?*, 328.

17 Jones, *Who Murdered Chaucer?*, 328. See Chaucer's *Troilus and Criseyde*, III, lines 1117–20.

18 Stephen Wailes, *Medieval Allegories*, 106.

19 Jones, *Who Murdered Chaucer?*, 336.

finds Chaucer's *Canterbury Tales* on the list of required reading. But what is a "masterpiece," and does Chaucer's "roadside drama" qualify? If we understand a masterpiece to be the culmination of an artist's talent, a textual product in which the artist has mastered (that is, gained dominion over, controlled, over-powered, subdued) language and/or a particular subject matter, then I would argue that Chaucer's *Canterbury Tales* does not qualify as one, nor does any great work of art. However, if we define masterpiece differently—as something that cannot be mastered, as something that forces us to return to it again and again without ever achieving the sense of having "cracked its code," as some-thing that keeps desire in play (as Lacan says, "desire is interpretation")—and if we place the emphasis on the word "piece" rather than on the word "master," then Chaucer's *Canterbury Tales* certainly qualifies. For what is his Retraction if not a means of holding open the edges of a wound, of making the flesh of the text gape? Chaucer has intentionally thrown a monkey wrench—or, in this case, a surgical retractor—into the works. If *The Canterbury Tales* is a wound, it is one that will never heal, for Chaucer's cut, that is, his work, is a wound that cannot be sutured. The Retraction, although it comes at the end of *The Can-terbury Tales*, does not create closure. It is not a moment of serene conclusion but of disavowal, a holding of two opposing ideas at once, and like the "greyn" laid upon the tongue of the little clergeon, which allows his two lips to remain open in song, Chaucer's Retraction will allow him to continue singing for centuries to come.

Bibliography

Adams, Parveen. "Of Female Bondage." In *Between Feminism and Psychoanalysis*, edited by Teresa Brennan, 247–65. New York: Routledge, 1989.

Albin, Andrew. "The *Prioress's Tale*, Sonorous and Silent," *The Chaucer Review* 48.1 (2013): 91–112.

Allen, Valerie. *On Farting: Language and Laughter in the Middle Ages*. New York: Palgrave Macmillan, 2007.

Allman, W. W. and D. Thomas Hanks, Jr. "Rough Love: Notes Toward an Erotics of the 'Canterbury Tales.'" *The Chaucer Review* 38.1 (2003): 36–65.

Althusser, Louis. *Lenin and Philosophy and Other Essays*. New York: Monthly Review Press, 2001.

Anderson, David. "Theban Genealogy in the 'Knight's Tale.'" *The Chaucer Review* 21.3 (Winter 1987): 311–20.

Archibald, Elizabeth. *Incest and the Medieval Imagination*. Oxford: Oxford University Press, 2001.

Bale, Anthony. *Feeling Persecuted: Christians, Jews and Images of Violence in the Middle Ages*. London: Reaktion Books, 2010.

Barnett, Allen. *The Body and Its Dangers*. New York: St. Martin's Press, 1990.

Barthes, Roland. "An Almost Obsessive Relation to Writing Instruments." In *The Grain of the Voice: Interviews 1962–1980*, translated by Linda Coverdale, 177–82. New York: Hill and Wang, 1985.

——. *Image—Music—Text*. Translated by Stephen Heath. New York: Hill and Wang, 1977.

——. *The Pleasure of the Text*. Translated by Richard Miller. New York: Hill and Wang, 1975.

——. *Sade / Fourier / Loyola*. Translated by Richard Miller. New York: Hill and Wang, 1976.

Bataille, Georges. *Erotism: Death and Sensuality*. Translated by Mary Dalwood. San Francisco: City Lights Publishers, 1986.

——. *Literature and Evil*. Translated by Alastair Hamilton. London: Calder & Boyers, 1973.

——. *Oeuvres completes*. Paris: Gallimard, 1976.

Beidler, Peter. "Art and Scatology in the *Miller's Tale*." *The Chaucer Review* 12 (1977): 90–102.

Bell, Rudolph. *Holy Anorexia*. Chicago: University of Chicago Press, 1985.

Benamou, Michel. "Presence and Play." In *Performance in Postmodern Culture*, edited by Michel Benamou and Charles Caramello, 3–7. Madison, WI: Coda Press, Inc., 1977.

Benson, C. David. "Chaucer's Pardoner: His Sexuality and Modern Critics." *Mediaevalia* 8 (1985, for 1982): 337–49.

Bentley, Joseph. "Satire and the Rhetoric of Sadism." *The Centennial Review* 11.3 (Summer 1967): 387–404.

Berger, John. "Ways of Seeing." In *Ways of Reading: An Anthology for Writers*, edited by David Bartholomae and Anthony Petrosky, 49–72. 4th ed. Boston: Bedford Books, 1996.

Bernheimer, Charles. Introduction: Part One to *In Dora's Case: Freud—Hysteria—Feminism*, edited by Charles Bernheimer and Claire Kahane, 1–18. 2nd ed. New York: Columbia University Press, 1990.

Berry, Wendell. *Standing by Words: Essays by Wendell Berry*. San Francisco: North Point Press, 1983.

https://doi.org/10.1515/9781501514104-012

Besley, Tina. "Foucault, Truth-Telling and Technologies of the Self: Confessional Practices of the Self and Schools." In *Why Foucault? New Directions in Educational Research*, edited by Michael Peters and Tina Besley, 55–69. Bern, Switzerland: Peter Lang Publishing, 2007.

Besserman, Lawrence. "Ideology, Antisemitism, and Chaucer's 'Prioress's Tale.'" *The Chaucer Review* 36.1 (2001): 48–72.

Bloch, R. Howard. "Chaucer's Maiden's Head: *The Physician's Tale* and the Poetics of Virginity." *Qui Parle* 2.2 (Fall 1988): 22–45.

Bloomfield, Morton. "The Man of Law's Tale: A Tragedy of Victimization and a Christian Comedy." *PMLA* 87.3 (May 1972): 384–90.

Boenig, Robert. *Chaucer and the Mystics: The Canterbury Tales and the Genre of Devotional Prose*. Lewisburg, PA: Bucknell University Press, 1995.

Boler, Megan. *Feeling Power: Emotions and Education*. New York: Routledge, 1999.

Boswell, John. *Christianity, Social Tolerance, and Homosexuality: Gay People in Western Europe from the Beginning of the Christian Era to the Fourteenth Century*. Chicago: University of Chicago Press, 1980.

Bowlby, Rachel. Introduction to *Studies in Hysteria*, by Sigmund Freud and Joseph Breuer, translated by Nicola Luckhurst, vii–xxxiii. New York: Penguin, 2004.

Boylorn, Robin and Mark Orbe. *Critical Autoethnography: Intersecting Cultural Identities in Everyday Life*. Walnut Creek, CA: Left Coast Press, 2014.

Brewer, Derek. *Chaucer in His Time*. London: Thomas Nelson and Sons Ltd, 1963.

Bright, Susie. *Susie Bright's Sexual Reality: A Virtual Sex World Reader*. Pittsburgh, PA: Cleis Press, 1992.

Brooks, Peter. *Reading for the Plot: Design and Intention in Narrative*. New York: Alfred A. Knopf, 1984.

Brown, Emerson, Jr. "What Is Chaucer Doing with the Physician and His Tale?" *Philological Quarterly* (Spring 1981): 129–49.

Bullard, Rebecca. Introduction to *The Secret History in Literature, 1660–1820*, edited by Rebecca Bullard and Rachel Carnell, 1–16. Cambridge: Cambridge University Press, 2017.

Burger, Glenn. "Erotic Discipline ... Or 'Tee Hee, I Like My Boys to Be Girls': Inventing with the Body in Chaucer's *Miller's Tale*." In *Becoming Male in the Middle Ages*, edited by Jeffrey Jerome Cohen and Bonnie Wheeler, 245–60. New York: Garland Publishing, 2000.

Bynum, Caroline Walker. *Fragmentation and Redemption: Essays on Gender and the Human Body in Medieval Religion*. New York: Zone Book, 1991.

—. *Holy Feast and Holy Fast: The Religious Significance of Food to Medieval Women*. Berkeley: University of California Press, 1987.

Campbell, Alan D. "The Monetary System, Taxation, and Publicans in the Time of Christ." *The Accounting Historians Journal* 13.2 (Fall 1986): 133–34.

Chaucer, Geoffrey. *The Canterbury Tales*. Translated by Nevill Coghill. London: Penguin Books, 1977.

—. *The Complete Poetry and Prose of Geoffrey Chaucer*. Edited by John H. Fisher. New York: Holt, Rinehart and Winston, 1977.

—. *The Riverside Chaucer*. Edited by Larry D. Benson. 3rd ed. Boston: Houghton Mifflin, 1987.

Cixous, Hélène. *Three Steps on the Ladder of Writing.* Translated by Susan Sellers and Sarah Cornell. New York: Columbia University Press, 1994.

Cixous, Hélène and Catherine Clément. *The Newly Born Woman.* Translated by Betsy Wing. Minneapolis: University of Minnesota Press, 1991.

Clavreul, Jean. "The Perverse Couple." In *Returning to Freud: Clinical Psychoanalysis in the School of Lacan,* edited and translated by Stuart Schneiderman, 215–33. New Haven: Yale University Press, 1980.

Coghill, Nevill. *The Poet Chaucer.* Oxford: Oxford University Press, 1949.

Cohen, Maurice. "Chaucer's Prioress and Her Tale: A Study of Anal Character and Anti-Semitism," *Psychoanalytic Quarterly* 31 (1962): 232–49.

Collette, Carolyn P. "Sense and Sensibility in the 'Prioress's Tale,'" *The Chaucer Review* 15.2 (Fall 1980): 138–50.

Condren, Edward. "The Prioress: A Legend of Spirit, a Life of Flesh." *The Chaucer Review* 23.3 (Winter 1989): 192–218.

Cooper-Rompato, Christine F. *The Gift of Tongues: Women's Xenoglossia in the Later Middle Ages.* University Park: The Pennsylvania State University Press, 2010.

Copjec, Joan. "The Anxiety of the Influencing Machine." *October* 23 (1982): 43–59.

——. "Cutting Up." In *Between Feminism and Psychoanalysis,* edited by Teresa Brennan, 227–46. London: Routledge, 1989.

——. "Flavit et Dissipati Sunt." *October* 18 (1981): 20–40.

——. "Montage of the Drives." *Umbr(a): A Journal of the Unconscious* 1 (1997): 11–13.

——. "The Sartorial Superego." *October* 50 (Autumn 1989): 56–95.

Coulton, G. G. *Medieval Panorama: The English Scene from Conquest to Reformation.* Cambridge: Cambridge University Press, 1949.

Cramer, Patricia. "Lordship, Bondage, and the Erotic: The Psychological Bases of Chaucer's 'Clerk's Tale.'" *Journal of English and Germanic Philology* 89.4 (October 1990): 491–511.

Curry, Walter Clyde. "Chaucer's Reeve and Miller." *PMLA* 35.2 (1920): 189–209.

Daichman, Graciela S. *Wayward Nuns in Medieval Literature.* Syracuse, NY: Syracuse University Press, 1986.

Davis, R. H. C. *A Medieval History of Europe.* New York: David McKay, 1970.

Dawson, Robert B. "Custance in Context: Rethinking the Protagonist in the 'Man of Law's Tale.'" *The Chaucer Review* 26.3 (Winter 1992): 293–308.

Dean, Carolyn. *The Self and Its Pleasures: Bataille, Lacan, and the History of the Decentered Subject.* Ithaca: Cornell University Press, 1992.

Dean, Tim. "The Psychoanalysis of AIDS." *October* 63 (Winter 1993): 83–116.

Delany, Sheila. "Womanliness in the 'Man of Law's Tale.'" *The Chaucer Review* (1974): 63–72.

Deleuze, Gilles. *Coldness and Cruelty.* New York: Zone Books, 1991.

Denzin, Norman K. *Interpretive Ethnography.* Thousand Oaks, CA: Sage, 1997.

Derrida, Jacques. "Force of Law: The 'Mystical Foundation of Authority.'" *Deconstruction and the Possibility of Justice,* edited by Drucilla Cornell et al., 3–67. New York: Routledge, 1992.

Diderot, Denis. *The Nun.* London: Penguin Books, 1974.

Dinshaw, Carolyn. *Chaucer's Sexual Poetics.* Madison: University of Wisconsin Press, 1989.

Doane, Mary Ann. *The Desire to Desire: The Woman's Film of the 1940s.* Bloomington: Indiana University Press, 1987.

Dolar, Mladen. "'I Shall Be with You on Your Wedding-Night': Lacan and the Uncanny." *October* 58 (1991): 5–23.

——. "The Legacy of the Enlightenment: Foucault and Lacan." *New Formations* 14 (Summer 1991): 43–56.

——. *A Voice and Nothing More.* Cambridge: MIT Press, 2006.

Dollimore, Jonathan. "The Cultural Politics of Perversion: Augustine, Shakespeare, Freud, Foucault." *Genders* 8 (1990): 1–16.

Donaldson, E. Talbot. *Chaucer's Poetry: An Anthology for the Modern Reader.* New York: Scott Foresman & Co., 1975.

——. *Speaking of Chaucer.* New York: W. W. Norton, 1970.

"Do Women Laugh When They Fart?" *Straight Dope Message Board.* boards.straightdope.com/sdms/archive/index.php/t-90868.html.

Durand, Régis. "The Disposition of the Voice." In *Performance in Postmodern Culture*, edited by Michel Benamou and Charles Caramello, 3–7. Madison, WI: Coda Press, 1977.

Dworkin, Andrea. *Pornography: Men Possessing Women.* New York: Putnam, 1981.

Eberle, Patricia J. "Crime and Justice in the Middle Ages: Cases from the *Canterbury Tales* of Geoffrey Chaucer." In *Rough Justice: Essays on Crime in Literature*, edited by M. L. Friedland, 19–51. Toronto: University of Toronto Press, 1991.

Edwards, Jonathan. "Sinners in the Hands of an Angry God." In *The Norton Anthology of American Literature: Literature to 1820*, edited by Nina Baym, 498–509. 6th ed. New York: W. W. Norton, 2003.

Ellis, Carolyn, et al. "Autoethnography: An Overview." *Forum: Qualitative Social Research* 12.1 (2011): Art. 10, http://nbn-resolving.de/urn:nbn:de:0114–fqs1101108.

"Encounter Groups." *Exploring Psychology.* http://www.mhhe.com/cls/psy/ch14/encount.mhtml.

Felman, Shoshana. *Writing and Madness: (Literature/Philosophy/Psychoanalysis).* Translated by Martha Noel Evans and the author with the assistance of Brian Massumi. Ithaca, NY: Cornell University Press, 1985.

Ferster, Judith. "'Your Praise Is Performed by Men and Children': Language and Gender in the Prioress's Prologue and Tale." *Exemplaria* 2.1 (1990): 149–68.

Fineman, Joel. "The History of the Anecdote: Fiction and Fiction." In *The New Historicism*, edited by H. Aram Veeser, 49–76. New York: Routledge, 1989.

Finger, Roland. "Cracking the Whip: Sadomasochistic Heroics in 'The Wife of Bath's Prologue.'" *Exit 9: The Rutgers Journal of Comparative Literature* 5 (2003): 65–74.

Fink, Bruce. *A Clinical Introduction to Lacanian Psychoanalysis: Theory and Technique.* Cambridge: Harvard University Press, 1997.

——. *The Lacanian Subject: Between Language and Jouissance.* Princeton: Princeton University Press, 1995.

Fitz, Donald. "Reflections in a Golden Florin: Chaucer's Narcissistic Pardoner." *The Chaucer Review* 21.3 (Winter 1987): 338–59.

Flannery, Mary C. "A Bloody Shame: Chaucer's Honorable Women." *The Review of English Studies* 62.255 (June 2011): 337–57.

Fletcher, Alan J. "The Topical Hypocrisy of Chaucer's Pardoner." *The Chaucer Review* 25 (1990): 110–26.

Foucault, Michel. *The History of Sexuality; Volume I: An Introduction.* Translated by Robert Hurley. New York: Vintage Books, 1990.

Fowler, Albert. "Sensibility Since Sade." *Southwest Review* 45.3 (Summer 1960): 240–50.

Fradenburg, Louise O. "Criticism, Anti-Semitism, and the *Prioress's Tale*." *Exemplaria* 1.1 (1989): 193–231.

Frank, Hardy Long. "Seeing the Prioress Whole." *The Chaucer Review* 25.3 (1991): 229–37.

Freire, Paulo. *Pedagogy of the Oppressed*. Translated by Myra Bergman Ramos. New York: Herder and Herder, 1970.

Frese, Dolores Warwick. "The Homoerotic Underside in Chaucer's *Miller's Tale* and *Reeve's Tale*." *Michigan Academician: Papers of the Michigan Academy of Science, Arts, and Letters* 10 (1977): 143–50.

Freud, Sigmund. *Beyond the Pleasure Principle*. Edited and translated by James Strachey. New York: W. W. Norton, 1961.

——. *Case Histories*. Vol 2: *The "Rat Man," Schreber, The "Wolf Man," A Case of Female Homosexuality*. Edited by Angela Richards and translated by James Strachey. Middlesex, England: Penguin Books, 1979.

——. "Certain Neurotic Mechanisms in Jealousy, Paranoia, and Homosexuality." In *Sexuality and the Psychology of Love*, edited by Philip Rieff, 160–70. New York: Collier Books, 1963.

——. "A Child Is Being Beaten." In *Sexuality and the Psychology of Love*, edited by Philip Rieff, 97–122. New York: Simon & Schuster, 1963.

——. "'Civilized' Sexual Morality and Modern Nervousness." In *Sexuality and the Psychology of Love*, edited by Philip Rieff, 10–30. New York: Simon & Schuster, 1963.

——. *Dora: An Analysis of a Case of Hysteria*. New York: Collier Books, 1963.

——. *Jokes and Their Relation to the Unconscious*. Edited by Angela Richards and translated by James Strachey. Middlesex, England: Penguin Books, 1976.

——. "Neurosis and Psychosis." In *On Psychopathology*, translated by James Strachey, 209–18. New York: Penguin Books, 1979.

——. *The Origins of Psychoanalysis: Letters to Wilhelm Fliess, Drafts and Notes: 1887–1902*. Edited by Marie Bonaparte et al. and translated by Eric Mosbacher and James Strachey. New York: Basic Books, 1954.

——. "The 'Uncanny.'" In *The Standard Edition of the Complete Psychological Works of Sigmund Freud*, vol. 17. Gen. ed. James Strachey. London: Hogarth Press, 1955.

Friedman, Albert B. "The 'Prioress's Tale' and Chaucer's Anti-Semitism." *The Chaucer Review* 9.2 (Fall 1974): 118–29.

Gadamer, Hans-Georg. *Philosophical Hermeneutics*. Translated and edited by David E. Linge. Berkeley: University of California Press, 1976.

Gallop, Jane. *Anecdotal Theory*. Durham, NC: Duke University Press, 2002.

——. *Intersections: A Reading of Sade with Bataille, Blanchot, and Klossowski*. Lincoln: University of Nebraska Press, 1981.

Gammel, Irene. Introduction to *Confessional Politics: Women's Sexual Self-Representations in Life Writing and Popular Media*, edited by Irene Gammel, 1–10. Carbondale, IL: Southern Illinois University Press, 1999.

Gardner, John. *The Life and Times of Chaucer*. New York: Alfred A. Knopf, 1977.

Gaynor, Stephanie. "He Says, She Says: Subjectivity and the Discourse of the Other in the Prioress's Portrait and Tale." *Medieval Encounters: Jewish, Christian, and Muslim Culture in Confluence and Dialogue* 5.3 (1999): 375–90.

Gilmartin, Kristine. "Array in the 'Clerk's Tale.'" *The Chaucer Review* 13.3 (Winter 1979): 234–46.

Green, Richard. "The Sexual Normality of Chaucer." *Mediaevalia* 8 (1985, for 1982): 351–59.

Hampl, Patricia. "Memory and Imagination." In *The Dolphin Reader*, edited by Douglas Hunt, 93–104. 2nd ed. Boston: Houghton Mifflin, 1990.

Hanson, Thomas B. "Chaucer's Physician as Storyteller and Moralizer." *The Chaucer Review* 7.2 (Fall 1972): 132–39.

Hausrath, Adolph. *A History of the New Testament Times: The Time of Jesus*, vol. 1. Edinburgh: Williams and Nargate, 1878.

Hawkins, Harriet. "The Victim's Side: Chaucer's *Clerk's Tale* and Webster's *Duchess of Malfi*." *Signs: Journal of Women in Culture and Society* 1 (1975): 339–61.

Hawthorne, Nathaniel. *Selected Tales and Sketches*. New York: Penguin Books, 1987.

Henryson, Robert. "Orpheus and Eurydice." In *The Complete Works*, edited by David J. Parkinson. TEAMS Middle English Texts Series. Kalamazoo: Medieval Institute Publications, 2011. https://d.lib.rochester.edu/teams/text/parkinson-henryson-complete-works-orpheus-and-eurydice.

Herndl, Diane. "The Writing Cure: Charlotte Perkins Gilman, Anna O., and 'Hysterical' Writing." *NWSA Journal* 1.1 (Autumn 1988): 52–74.

Hesiod. *Theogony and Works and Days*. Translated by M. L. West. London: Oxford University Press, 1999.

Hobbs, Kathleen M. "Blood and Rosaries: Virginity, Violence, and Desire in Chaucer's 'Prioress's Tale.'" In *Constructions of Widowhood and Virginity in the Middle Ages*, edited by Cindy L. Carlson and Angela Jane Weisl, 181–98. New York: Palgrave Macmillan, 1999.

Hodges, Laura F. "Reading Griselda's Smocks in the *Clerk's Tale*." *The Chaucer Review* 44.1 (2009): 84–109.

Hoffman, Arthur W. "Chaucer's Prologue to Pilgrimage: The Two Voices." *ELH* 21.1 (1954): 1–16.

Holloway, Julia Bolton. "Convents, Courts and Colleges: The Prioress and the Second Nun." In *Equally in God's Image: Women in the Middle Ages*, edited by Julia Bolton Holloway et al., 198–216. New York: Peter Lang, 1990.

Holsinger, Bruce W. *Music, Body, and Desire in Medieval Culture*. Stanford, CA: Stanford University Press, 2001.

Horney, Karen. "The Problem of Feminine Masochism." *The Psychoanalytic Review* 22.3 (1935): 241–57.

Hoyt, Sarah F. "The Etymology of Religion." *Journal of the American Oriental Society* 32.2 (1912): 126–29.

Iser, Wolfgang. "The Reading Process: A Phenomenological Approach." In *The Critical Tradition: Classic Texts and Contemporary Trends*, edited by David Richter, 102–14. Boston: Bedford/St. Martin's, 2007.

Jabès, Edmond. "The Book or the Four Phases of a Birth." In *Performance in Postmodern Culture*, edited by Michel Benamou and Charles Caramello, 123–36. Madison, WI: Coda Press, Inc., 1977.

Jacobus, Mary. *Reading Woman: Essays in Feminist Criticism*. New York: Columbia University Press, 1986.

Jones, Terry, et al. *Who Murdered Chaucer? A Medieval Mystery*. New York: St. Martin's Press, 2003.

Kafka, Franz. "My Neighbor." In *Franz Kafka: The Complete Stories*, edited by Nahum N. Glatzer, 424–25. New York: Schocken Books, 1971.

Kahane, Claire. Introduction: Part Two to *In Dora's Case: Freud—Hysteria—Feminism*, edited by Charles Bernheimer and Claire Kahane, 19–32. 2nd ed. New York: Columbia University Press, 1990.

——. *Passions of the Voice: Hysteria, Narrative, and the Figure of the Speaking Woman, 1850–1915*. Baltimore: Johns Hopkins University Press, 1995.

Kane, George. "Chaucer, Love Poetry, and Romantic Love." In *Acts of Interpretation: The Text in Its Contexts, 700–1600*, edited by Mary J. Carruthers and Elizabeth D. Kirk, 237–55. Norman, OK: Pilgrim Books, 1982.

Kant, Immanuel. *Anthropology From a Pragmatic Point of View*. Edited by Robert B. Louden. Cambridge: Cambridge University Press, 2006.

Kay, Sarah. "The Contradictions of Courtly Love and the Origins of Courtly Poetry: The Evidence of the *Lauzengiers*." *The Journal of Medieval and Early Modern Studies* 26.2 (1996): 209–53.

Kelly, Henry Ansgar. "A Neo-Revisionist Look at Chaucer's Nuns." *The Chaucer Review* 31.2 (1996): 115–32.

Kendrick, Laura. *Chaucerian Play: Comedy and Control in the "Canterbury Tales."* Berkeley: University of California Press, 1988.

Kittredge, George Lyman. *Chaucer and His Poetry*. Cambridge: Harvard University Press, 1915.

Kline, Daniel T. "Jephthah's Daughter and Chaucer's Virginia: The Critique of Sacrifice in the Physician's Tale." *Journal of English and Germanic Philology* 107.1 (January 2008): 77–103.

König, René. *A La Mode*. New York: The Seabury Press, 1973.

Koretsky, Allen C. "Dangerous Innocence: Chaucer's Prioress and Her Tale." In *Jewish Presences in English Literature*, edited by Derek Cohen and Deborah Heller, 10–24. Montreal and Frankfurt: McGill-Queen's University Press, 1990.

Kotzé, Annemaré. "The Puzzle of the Last Four Books of Augustine's *Confessions*: An Illegitimate Issue?" *Vigiliae Christianae* 60.1 (2006): 65–79.

Kristeva, Julia. *Powers of Horror: An Essay on Abjection*. Translated by Leon S. Roudiez. New York: Columbia University Press, 1982.

Kruger, Steven F. "Claiming the Pardoner: Toward a Gay Reading of Chaucer's Pardoner's Tale." *Exemplaria* 6.1 (1994): 115–39.

Labbie, Erin Felicia. *Lacan's Medievalism*. Minneapolis: University of Minnesota Press, 2006.

Lacan, Jacques. *Écrits: A Selection*. Translated by Alan Sheridan. New York: W. W. Norton, 1977.

——. *The Seminar of Jacques Lacan, Book II*. Edited by Jacques-Alain Miller. Translated by Sylvana Tomaselli. New York: W. W. Norton, 1988.

——. *The Seminar of Jacques Lacan, Book III*. Edited by Jacques-Alain Miller. Translated by Russell Grigg. New York: W. W. Norton, 1993.

——. *The Seminar of Jacques Lacan, Book VII*. Edited by Jacques-Alain Miller. Translated by Dennis Porter. New York: W. W. Norton, 1992.

——. *The Seminar of Jacques Lacan, Book XI*. Edited by Jacques-Alain Miller. Translated by Alan Sheridan. New York: W. W. Norton, 1977.

——. *The Seminar of Jacques Lacan, Book XX*. Edited by Jacques-Alain Miller. Translated by Bruce Fink. New York: W. W. Norton, 1998.

Lee, Jonathan Scott. *Jacques Lacan*. Amherst, MA: University of Massachusetts Press, 1990.

Leicester, H. Marshall. *The Disenchanted Self: Representing the Subject in the* Canterbury Tales. Berkeley: University of California Press, 1990.

Levi-Strauss, Claude. *The Raw and the Cooked: Introduction to a Science of Mythology*, vol. 1. Translated by John and Doreen Weightman. New York: Harper Colophon Books, 1975.

Lispector, Clarice. *The Hour of the Star*. Translated by Giovanni Pontiero. New York: New Directions, 1986.

Little, Lester. *Religious Poverty and the Profit Economy in Medieval Europe*. Ithaca, NY: Cornell University Press, 1978.

Lomperis, Linda and Sarah Stanbury. Introduction to *Feminist Approaches to the Body in Medieval Literature*, edited by Linda Lomperis and Sarah Stanbury, vii–xiv. Philadelphia: University of Pennsylvania Press, 1993.

London, April. "Secret History and Anecdote." In *The Secret History in Literature, 1660–1820*, edited by Rebecca Bullard and Rachel Carnell, 174–187. Cambridge: Cambridge University Press, 2017.

Lukacher, Ned. Foreword to *Hysteria from Freud to Lacan: Body and Language in Psychoanalysis*, by Monique David-Ménard, translated by Catherine Porter, vii–xxi. Ithaca, NY: Cornell University Press, 1989.

MacCannell, Juliet Flower. *The Régime of the Brother: After the Patriarchy*. London: Routledge, 1991.

Makowski, Elizabeth M. "The Conjugal Debt and Medieval Canon Law." *Journal of Medieval History* 3 (1977): 99–114.

Malo, Robyn. "The Pardoner's Relics (And Why They Matter the Most)." *The Chaucer Review* 43.1 (2008): 82–102.

Manly, John M. *Some New Light on Chaucer*. New York: Henry Holt, 1926.

Martin, Priscilla. *Chaucer's Women: Nuns, Wives and Amazons*. London: Macmillan Press, 1990.

Marvin, Corey J. "'I Will Not Thee Forsake': The Kristevan Maternal Space in Chaucer's *Prioress's Tale* and John Garland's *Stella Maris*." *Exemplaria* 8.1 (1996): 35–58.

McAlpine, Monica E. "The Pardoner's Homosexuality and How It Matters." *PMLA* 95.1 (January 1980): 8–22.

McCullers, Carson. *The Ballad of the Sad Café and Other Stories*. New York: Mariner Books, 1979.

McDougall, Joyce. *A Plea for a Measure of Abnormality*. New York: International Universities Press, 1980.

McGerr, Rosemarie. *Chaucer's Open Books: Resistance to Closure in Medieval Discourse*. Gainesville, FL: University Press of Florida, 1998.

McLaughlin, Becky. "Big Sex: The Story of the Silver Nail and Other Objects of (Mass) Construction." *Writing From Below* 1.2 (2013): 19–30.

——. "Chaucer's Cut." In *Approaches to Teaching Chaucer's Canterbury Tales*, edited by Peter W. Travis and Frank Grady, 156–59. 2nd ed. New York: Modern Language Association, 2014.

——. "Desperately Seeking Wilco." *Rock Music Studies* 5.1 (2018): 29–45.

——. "Gothicizing Apotemnophilia: Live Burial, Secret Desire, and the Uncanny Body of the Amputee Wannabe." *Word and Text: A Journal of Literary Studies and Linguistics* 3.2 (December 2013): 133–47.

——. "Literature, Theory, and the Beatific Effects of Reading." In *Literature and Ethics: From the Green Knight to the Dark Knight*, edited by Steve Brie and William T. Rossiter, 159–74. Newcastle upon Tyne: Cambridge Scholars Publishing, 2010.

——. "Pounding the 'Amy' Out of Imagism, or 'Jouiring' Like an 'Idiot' Carrying a Big Stick." *The Journal of Imagism* (Fall 2000): 23–33.

——. "The Reeve's Paranoid Eye, or The Dramatics of 'Bleared' Sight." *ANaMORPHOSIS: A Journal of the Lacanian School of Psychoanalysis and the San Francisco Society for Lacanian Studies* 5 (2002): 91–129.

——. "Sex Cuts." In *Jane Sexes It Up: True Confessions of Feminist Desire*, edited by Merri Lisa Johnson, 65–90. New York: Four Walls Eight Windows, 2002.

——. "Staging Perversion: The Restoration's Sexual Allegory of (Un)civil War." In *Sexual Perversions, 1670–1890*, edited by Julie Peakman, 51–71. New York: Palgrave Macmillan, 2009.

——. "The Very Small Things That Fall." *Westview: A Journal of Western Oklahoma* 20.2 (Spring/Summer 2001): 15–27.

——. "The Wounded Student and the Crisis of Desire in the College Classroom." In *Putting Theory into Practice in the Contemporary Classroom: Theory Lessons*, edited by Becky McLaughlin, 1–32. Newcastle upon Tyne: Cambridge Scholars Publishing, 2017.

Milgram, Stanley. "The Perils of Obedience." In *The Dolphin Reader*, edited by Douglas Hunt, 431–44. 2nd ed. Boston: Houghton Mifflin, 1990.

Miller, Clarence H. and Roberta Bux Bosse. "Chaucer's Pardoner and the Mass." *The Chaucer Review* 6.3 (Winter 1972): 171–84.

Miller, Jacques-Alain. "On Perversion." In *Reading Seminars I and II: Lacan's Return to Freud*, edited by Richard Feldstein et al., 306–20. Albany: SUNY Press, 1996.

Miller, Mark. "Naturalism and Its Discontents in the 'Miller's Tale.'" *ELH* 67.1 (Spring 2000): 1–44.

Miller, Nancy K. *But Enough About Me: Why We Read Other People's Lives*. New York: Columbia University Press, 2002.

Miller, Richard. *Writing at the End of the World*. Pittsburgh, PA: University of Pittsburgh Press, 2005.

Miller, William Ian. *The Anatomy of Disgust*. Cambridge, MA: Harvard University Press, 1997.

Minnis, Alistair J. *Fallible Authors: Chaucer's Pardoner and the Wife of Bath*. Philadelphia: University of Pennsylvania Press, 2008.

Mitchell, Charles. "The Moral Superiority of Chaucer's Pardoner." *College English* 27.6 (March 1966): 437–44.

Mitchell, J. Allan. "Chaucer's 'Clerk's Tale' and the Question of Ethical Monstrosity." *Studies in Philology* 102.1 (Winter 2005): 1–26.

Mitchell, J. Allan and Will Stockton. "Time Change/Mode Change." In *Burn After Reading*, vol. 2: *The Future We Want*, edited by Jeffrey Jerome Cohen, 157–63. Brooklyn, NY: punctum books; Washington, DC: Oliphaunt Books, 2014.

Mitchell, Juliet. *Psychoanalysis and Feminism*. New York: Penguin Books, 1976.

Montaigne, Michel. *Essays*. Translated by J. M. Cohen. London: Penguin Books, 1958.

Morey, James H. "The 'Cultour' in the *Miller's Tale:* Alison as Iseult." *The Chaucer Review* 29.4 (1995): 373–81.

Morrison, Susan Signe. *Excrement in the Late Middle Ages: Sacred Filth and Chaucer's Fecopoetics.* New York: Palgrave Macmillan, 2008.

Mulvey, Laura. "Visual Pleasure and Narrative Cinema." *Screen* 16.3 (August 1975): 6–18.

Myers, A. R. *England in the Late Middle Ages.* London: Penguin Books, 1953.

O'Connor, Flannery. "Good Country People." In *The Complete Stories of Flannery O'Connor,* edited by Robert Giroux, 271–91. New York: Farrar, Straus, and Giroux, 1971.

Olson, Clair C. "Chaucer and the Music of the Fourteenth Century," *Speculum* 16.1 (January 1941): 64–91.

Orwell, George. "Shooting an Elephant." In *The Dolphin Reader,* edited by Douglas Hunt, 906–17. 2nd ed. Boston: Houghton Mifflin, 1990.

Paffenroth, Kim. "Bad Habits and Bad Company: Education and Evil in the *Confessions.*" In *Augustine and Liberal Education,* edited by Kim Paffenroth and Kevin L. Hughes, 3–14. Lanham, MD: Lexington Books, 2008.

Percy, Walker. *The Message in The Bottle: How Queer Man Is, How Queer Language Is, and What One Has to Do with the Other.* New York: Farrar, Straus and Giroux, 1975.

Poe, Edgar Allan. "The Philosophy of Composition." In *The Norton Anthology of American Literature Vol. 1,* edited by Robert S. Levine, 790–98. New York: W. W. Norton, 2017.

⸺. "William Wilson." In *Tales of Mystery and Imagination,* 1–20. London: J. M. Dent & Sons, 1984.

Polhemus, Ted and Housk Randall. *Rituals of Love: Sexual Experiments, Erotic Possibilities.* London: Picador, 1994.

Price, Merrall Llewelyn. "Sadism and Sentimentality: Absorbing Antisemitism in Chaucer's Prioress." *The Chaucer Review* 43.2 (2008): 197–214.

Provine, Robert. "The Science of Laughter." *Psychology Today.* Psychology Today, 1 Nov. 2000. https://www.psychologytoday.com/us/articles/200011/the-science-laughter.

Quinn, William A. "The Shadow of Chaucer's Jews." *Exemplaria* 18.2 (Fall 2006): 299–325.

Ragland, Ellie. *Essays on the Pleasures of Death.* New York: Routledge, 1995.

Ragland-Sullivan, Ellie and Mark Bracher, eds. *Lacan and the Subject of Language.* New York: Routledge, 1991.

Reik, Theodor. *Masochism in Sex and Society.* Translated by Margaret H. Beigel and Gertrude M. Kurth. New York: Grove Press, 1941.

Reiss, Edmund. "The Final Irony of the Pardoner's Tale." *College English* 25.4 (January 1964): 260–66.

Retallack, Joan. *Musicage: Cage Muses on Art Music Words.* Hanover, CT: Wesleyan University Press, 1996.

Rex, Richard. *"The Sins of Madame Eglantine" and Other Essays on Chaucer.* Newark, DE: University of Delaware Press, 1995.

Ricoeur, Paul. "Life: A Story in Search of a Narrator." In *Facts and Values: Philosophical Reflections from Western and Non-Western Perspectives,* edited by M. C. Doeser and J. N. Kraay, 121–32. Dordrecht, The Netherlands: Martinus Nijhoff Publishers, 1986.

Ridley, Florence. *The Prioress and the Critics.* Berkeley: University of California Press, 1965.

Riviere, Joan. "Womanliness as a Masquerade." In *Formations of Fantasy,* edited by Victor Burgin et al., 35–61. New York: Routledge, 1989.

Robertson, D. W., Jr. "The Doctrine of Charity in Mediaeval Literary Gardens: A Topical Approach Through Symbolism and Allegory." *Speculum* 26 (1951): 24–49.

——. *A Preface to Chaucer*. Princeton: Princeton University Press, 1967.

Rorty, Richard. *Philosophy as Poetry*. Charlottesville: University of Virginia Press, 2016.

Roth, Michael S. *Beyond the University: Why Liberal Education Matters*. New Haven: Yale University Press, 2014.

Rowland, Beryl. "Animal Imagery and the Pardoner's Abnormalities." *Neophilologus* 48 (1964): 56–60.

Rudat, Wolfgang E. H. "Gender-Crossing in the *Prioress' Tale*: Chaucer's Satire on Theological Anti-Semitism?" *Cithara* 33.2 (1994): 11–17.

Russell, Jeffrey Burton. *Dissent and Order in the Middle Ages: The Search for Legitimate Authority*. New York: Twayne Publishers, 1992.

Russell, J. Stephen. "Song and the Ineffable in the 'Prioress's Tale.'" *The Chaucer Review* 33.2 (1998): 176–89.

Salecl, Renata. "The Satisfaction of Drives." *Umbr(a)* 1 (1997): 105–9.

Sartre, Jean-Paul. *What Is Literature?* Translated by Bernard Frechtman. New York: Harper Colophon Books, 1965.

——. "Why Write?" In *Everyday Theory: A Contemporary Reader*, edited by Becky McLaughlin and Bob Coleman, 20–33. New York: Pearson Education, Inc., 2005.

Scarry, Elaine. *The Body in Pain: The Making and Unmaking of the World*. Oxford: Oxford University Press, 1985.

Schlauch, Margaret. *Chaucer's Constance and Accused Queens*. New York: New York University Press, 1927.

Schneiderman, Stuart. *Jacques Lacan: The Death of an Intellectual Hero*. Cambridge: Harvard University Press, 1983.

Scudder, Samuel. "Learning to See." In *The Dolphin Reader*, edited by Douglas Hunt, 661–64. 6th ed. Boston: Houghton Mifflin, 2002.

Sedgwick, Eve Kosofsky. *Between Men: English Literature and Male Homosocial Desire*. New York: Columbia University Press, 1985.

Severs, J. Burke. *The Literary Relationships of Chaucer's "Clerkes Tale."* New Haven, CT: Yale University Press, 1942.

Shiach, Morag. *Hélène Cixous: A Politics of Writing*. London: Routledge, 1991.

Sigler, David. "The Rhetoric of Anti-Pedagogical Sadism in Jacques Lacan's 'Seminar VII.'" *Interdisciplinary Literary Studies* 9.2 (Spring 2008): 71–86.

Silverman, Kaja. *The Acoustic Mirror: The Female Voice in Psychoanalysis and Cinema*. Bloomington: Indiana University Press, 1988.

——. *Male Subjectivity at the Margins*, New York: Routledge, 1992.

Smith-Rosenberg, Carroll. *Disorderly Conduct: Visions of Gender in Victorian America*. New York: Alfred A. Knopf, 1985.

Sophocles. *Oedipus the King*. Edited by David Grene and Richmond Lattimore. Translated by David Grene. Chicago: University of Chicago Press, 1991.

Stevens, Martin and Kathleen Falvey. "Substance, Accident, and Transformations: A Reading of the 'Pardoner's Tale.'" *The Chaucer Review* 17.2 (Fall 1982): 142–58.

Stockton, Eric W. "The Deadliest Sin in *The Pardoner's Tale*." *Tennessee Studies in Literature* 6 (1961): 47–59.

Straus, Barrie Ruth. "Reframing the Violence of the Father: Reverse Oedipal Fantasies in Chaucer's Clerk's, Man of Law's, and Prioress's Tales." In *Domestic Violence in Medieval Texts*, edited by Eve Salisbury et al., 122–38. Gainesville: University Press of Florida, 2002.

Sturges, Robert. *Chaucer's Pardoner and Gender Theory: Bodies of Discourse*. New York: St. Martin's Press, 2000.

——. *Dialogue and Deviance: Male-Male Desire in the Dialogue Genre (Plato to Aelred, Plato to Sade, Plato to the Postmodern)*. New York: Palgrave Macmillan, 2005.

Surber, Nida. *The Fierce Parade: Chaucer and the Encryption of Homosexuality in the Canterbury Tales*. Genève: Éditions Slatkine, 2010.

Tabor, James M. *Blind Descent: The Quest to Discover the Deepest Place on Earth*. New York: Random House, 2010.

Tausk, Victor. "On the Origin of the Influencing Machine in Schizophrenia." *The Journal of Psychotherapy Practice and Research* 1.2 (Spring 1992): 185–206.

Tenney, Merrill C., ed. *The Zondervan Pictorial Bible Dictionary*. Grand Rapids, MI: Zondervan Publishing House, 1967.

Tertullian, Quintus. "On the Veiling of Virgins." In *The Ante-Nicene Fathers*, vol. 4, edited by Alexander Roberts and James Donaldson. Buffalo, NY: Christian Literature Publishing, 1885.

Travis, Peter. "Deconstructing Chaucer's Retraction." *Exemplaria* 3.1 (1991): 135–58.

——. "Thirteen Ways of Listening to a Fart: Noise in Chaucer's *Summoner's Tale*." *Exemplaria* 16.2 (2004): 323–48.

——. "White." *Studies in the Age of Chaucer* 22 (2000): 1–66.

"Trombone." *Wikipedia: The Free Encyclopedia*. Wikimedia Foundation, Inc. http://en.wikipedia.org/wiki/Trombone.

Twitchell, James. *Dreadful Pleasures: An Anatomy of Modern Horror*. Oxford: Oxford University Press, 1995.

Van, Thomas A. "Walter at the Stake: A Reading of Chaucer's *Clerk's Tale*." *The Chaucer Review* 22.3 (Winter 1988): 214–24.

Vickers, Nancy. "'The blazon of sweet beauty's best': Shakespeare's *Lucrece*." In *Shakespeare and the Question of Theory*, edited by Geoffrey H. Hartman and Patricia Parker, 95–116. New York and London: Methuen, 1985.

Wailes, Stephen L. *Medieval Allegories of Jesus' Parables*. Berkeley: University of California Press, 1987.

Warner, Michael. "Uncritical Reading." In *Polemic: Critical or Uncritical*, edited by Jane Gallop, 1–24. New York: Routledge, 2004.

Welch, Bronwen. "'Gydeth My Song': Penetration and Possession in Chaucer's *Prioress's Tale*." In *The Canterbury Tales Revisited: Twenty-First Century Interpretations*, edited by Kathleen A. Bishop, 127–50. Newcastle upon Tyne: Cambridge Scholars Publishing, 2008.

Williams, Linda. "When the Woman Looks." In *Re-Vision*, edited by Mary Ann Doane, Patricia Mellencamp, and Linda Williams, 83–99. Los Angeles: The American Film Institute, 1984.

Woolf, Virginia. *Orlando: A Biography*. London: Harcourt, 1956.

Yager, Susan. "'A Whit Thyng in Hir Ye': Perception and Error in the *Reeve's Tale*." *The Chaucer Review* 28.4 (1994): 391–404.

Žižek, Slavoj. *Enjoy Your Symptom! Jacques Lacan in Hollywood and Out.* New York: Routledge, 1992.

——. "Grimaces of the Real, or When the Phallus Appears." *October* 58 (1991): 44–68.

——. *Looking Awry: An Introduction to Jacques Lacan through Popular Culture.* Cambridge: MIT Press, 1991.

——. "Rossellini: Woman as Symptom of Man." *October* 54 (1990): 18–44.

——. *The Ticklish Subject: The Absent Centre of Political Ontology,* 2nd ed. London: Verso, 2009.

Index

https://doi.org/10.1515/9781501514104-013